Free Bonus from Captivating History (Available for a Limited time)

Hi History Lovers!

Now you have a chance to join our exclusive history list so you can get your first history ebook for free as well as discounts and a potential to get more history books for free! Simply visit the link below to join.

Captivatinghistory.com/ebook

Also, make sure to follow us on Facebook, Twitter and Youtube by searching for Captivating History.

Contents

Part 1: Celts

A Captivating Guide to Ancient Celtic History and Mythology, Including Their Battles Against the Roman Republic in the Gallic Wars

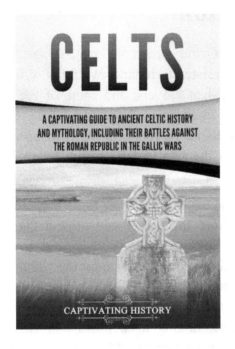

Introduction

Today, the word Celtic means so many things. To most of us, it means something related to Ireland. We think of intricately designed Irish crosses, four-leaf clovers, and some of the more well-known stories of Celtic mythology. However, while Celtic culture has stayed alive in Ireland, its roots run much deeper, and they extend much farther than the small island nation off the coast of modern-day Great Britain.

The Celts could actually trace their roots back to the Bronze Age. The Hallstatt culture that developed around the Danube River in Austria gave way to the La Tène culture, and, over time, the Celtic language emerged. This set the stage for the Great Celtic Migrations, which started in roughly 500 BCE and ended in c. 100 BCE. During these 400 years, the Celts, in seemingly endless waves, spread out throughout Europe, raiding local tribes and claiming territory for their own, so much so that by 200 BCE, the Celtic language was being spoken in the modern-day nations of Britain, France, Spain, Portugal, Germany, Austria, Switzerland, the Czech Republic, Poland, Slovakia, Bulgaria, Croatia, Italy, and, to a lesser extent, Turkey.

However, while it's easy for us to see that the Celts had a profound impact on the rise of European civilization, it's difficult for us to see pretty much anything else. The Celts wrote nothing down—there's even evidence to suggest they scorned the activity—but it's more likely they simply didn't have a written language. This means that our knowledge of these ancient peoples is limited to what the archaeological evidence tells us. There are considerable references to Celtic people in Greek and Roman texts, but these are difficult to take as fact given that the Greeks and Romans did not speak Celtic and therefore would have been limited in their ability to communicate.

Because of this lack of sources, modern-day perceptions of Celtic culture are typically exaggerated or just plain wrong. Most of us think of the Celts as being a barbarous, warring people with little or no social structure or value for human life. But this image comes straight from Greek and Roman interpretations of the culture and does not accurately reflect what the ancient Celts were really like.

Of course, war was an important aspect of Celtic life, but the ancient Celts were also devoutly religious—they practiced an elaborate pagan religion we still do not fully understand today—and they were skilled artisans who had a profound impact on the development of European art and culture.

However, despite all of these redeeming qualities, the Celts were also hopelessly disorganized. Hundreds, if not thousands, of different tribes existed throughout Europe that all spoke some version of the Celtic language, but they rarely, if ever, came together to form a unified culture. In fact, it was much more frequent for them to fight amongst one another and rely on a third party, such as the Romans, to help them solve their conflicts.

All of this means that when Julius Caesar first set his eyes on two important Celtic cultural centers of the time, Hispania (modern-day Spain and Portugal) and Gaul (the region that roughly coincides with the modern-day nation of France), Celtic culture was doomed. Caesar was able to march through Celtic territory and conquer it in less than a decade, and the Celts of Central Europe were slowly conquered by the Romans and made into provinces of the Roman Empire. As this happened, their language and cultural norms slowly disappeared.

However, this did not completely wipe Celtic culture off the face of the Earth. It remained in Britain, and although the Romans were able to conquer most of the island, they were not able to conquer all of it. As a result, Celtic culture continued to exist in parts of western England, Ireland, and Scotland, and after the Anglo-Saxon invasion of Britain, the Celts crossed the English Channel once again and settled in the modern French region of Brittany. Because of this, the remnants of Celtic culture still exist today. More than one million people in northwestern Europe are native speakers of a Celtic language, including 562,000 people in Wales, which is nineteen percent of its population.

Overall, though, the story of the Celts is one of a rapid rise to prominence followed by a slow decline due to the influence of the Romans. But even so, Celtic culture has remained strong in Europe and has been able to persist to this day. So, even though the Celts represent just a small part of today's modern world, they are a massive part of its history, which means that studying the ancient Celts today is a great way to unlock some of the secrets buried in the depths of ancient history.

Chapter 1 – Who Were the Celts?

When most of us think of the Celts, our minds tend to go directly to modern-day Ireland, Scotland, and England. However, this association propagates falsehoods about the origins of the Celts and their culture and language. In fact, we know very little about the true origin of the Celts, largely because of a lack of coherent sources. But one thing we do know for sure is that the regions of the world that are considered Celtic today represent just a small portion of the territory that was once occupied by this large and diverse ethnolinguistic group. Instead, the Celts were spread out across most of Europe, and they made contact with some of the premier civilizations of the ancient world, such as the Greeks and the Romans, leaving their mark on not only the history of these cultures but on all of humanity.

Origin

As a defined people and culture, the Celts first entered our collective history with the Greeks and the Romans. References from texts written in the 5th and 6th centuries BCE mention a group of people living in Northern Europe. The Greeks called them the *Keltoi*, and the Romans referred to them as Gauls. However, it is believed that Celtic culture dates back much further than that, to around 1200 BCE, to a culture known as the Hallstatt culture.

The Hallstatts were relatives of the Urnfield culture (c. 1300 BCE–750 BCE) of Central Europe that developed along the banks of the Danube River starting over 3,000 years ago. The Urnfields themselves were descendants of the Unetice (c. 2300–1600 BCE) and Tumulus cultures (1600 BCE–1200 BCE), meaning the origins of Celtic history can be traced all the way back to c. 2300 BCE, although a distinct Celtic culture would not emerge until the final millennium BCE.

These prehistoric cultures were mainly warrior societies known for burning their dead and burying them in urns in open fields. Archaeological sites, typically identified by these urns, have been found all over Central Europe in modern-day countries such as Poland, the Czech Republic, Austria, Hungary, Germany, and Russia. Many scholars place the origin of these cultures in the Czech Republic, claiming that they expanded outward following the Danube and Rhine and settling the fertile land throughout the rest of Bohemia, but there is no evidence to definitively prove this theory.

The Hallstatts are believed to have emerged as a distinct culture starting around 1200 BCE, and they were a preeminent society in the region until around 450 BCE. They were primarily a farming society, but by this time in history, ironworking had become considerably advanced, and it's believed the Hallstatts were exceptionally proficient in this trade. They established large trade networks throughout Central Europe, and they made contact with several Mediterranean civilizations, including Greece. Furthermore, the Hallstatts established salt mines near their settlements, which quickly became the most significant source of the commodity in the ancient world. The wealth that came from the abundance of this resource allowed for the development of chieftain and warrior classes, which would have been considered more elite, and it also allowed for some degree of specialization, meaning the Hallstatts would have been considerably advanced for the period in which they lived.

Generally speaking, this is the explanation of the origin of the Celts accepted by most who study this ancient culture. But because of the ambiguity of the archaeological evidence and the lack of written primary sources, it's difficult to say for sure if this is the exact nature of how the Celts came into existence. Another theory places the origin of the Celts much farther west. Part of this is because one of the earliest mentions of the Celts in written history is from the Greek historian Herodotus, who mentions the Celts as being close to the Danube, which, according to the rest of his writings, he believed to be located near the Pyrenees, giving rise to the idea that the Celts were primarily based in Gaul and the Iberian Peninsula.

Furthermore, another theory has emerged as a result of some of the genetic evidence collected over the past few decades. This information suggests that many of the tribes scattered around Europe that we identify as Celtic largely because of their language as well as their art and culture are actually not related to one another. In fact, the "ethnic" group with which most Europeans share a common ancestry is Basque, which was a non-Indo-European ethnolinguistic group that settled in northern Spain and southern France. This complicates the picture considerably because it goes against the idea that the Celts originated in one place and then spread throughout Europe.

Instead, it seems to suggest a process of "Celtization" wherein many distinct cultures slowly adopted the Celtic language and culture as it spread from the Hallstatt zone. Yet while this could explain some of the genetic differences amongst the various Celtic tribes in Europe, it doesn't account for the fact that Celtic cultures seemed to appear in different parts of Europe seemingly at the same time. Because of this, it's difficult to say for sure where the first Celtic settlements emerged, and because of the lack of written texts, we may never know.

However, what we do know is that the culture that developed in the Hallstatt zone eventually spoke a language we would identify as Celtic, and that by c. 400–300 BCE, the Celtic culture and language were present in many different forms in many different parts of Europe. As a result, it might not matter too much that we can't firmly identify the origin of the Celts, yet being able to determine this with certainty would allow us to considerably clarify our understanding of the Celts as they relate to the overall course of human history.

Geography

One of the more interesting aspects of Celtic history is just how widespread it was. However, despite the presence of many different Celtic cultures throughout all of Europe, there was never one "unified" Celtic culture, which could perhaps explain why many of the Celtic societies throughout Europe eventually disappeared or were absorbed into other cultures. Still, the scope of Celtic society in Europe is quite impressive.

Some of the most prominent Celtic settlements were located near the Hallstatt zone in what is now Germany and the Czech Republic. But we know the Celts were numerous and powerful in France from the writings of the Romans, who referred to the Celts as the Gauls. The Celts also had a considerable presence on the Iberian Peninsula, mainly along the northern coast in the modern-day regions of Galicia, Asturias, and Cantabria. Celtic civilizations were also found in the Alps of northern Italy, as well as in the modern-day nations of Serbia, Ukraine, Bulgaria, and Turkey. There is some evidence to suggest that the Celts made it as far as Egypt; however, they never established a settlement there.

Lastly, the Celts established a considerable presence on the lands we now call the British Isles. This particular branch of Celtic culture is referred to as the Insular Celts. They spoke their own version of the Celtic language, known as Insular Celtic, and it's believed they settled the region during the Iron Age expansion of Celtic culture. All of the remnants of Celtic culture and language that still exist today can be traced back to the Insular Celts, which is why most people today associate Celtic culture with England, Ireland,

Scotland, and Wales. But, as we can see, Celtic culture was prevalent in many more places throughout Europe and beyond. Below is a map of the areas in which Celtic culture was prevalent in the third century BCE.

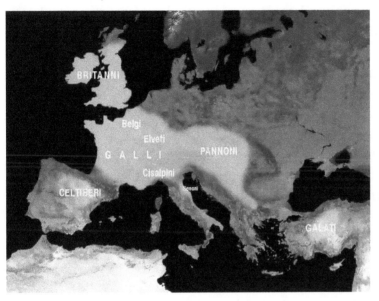

Source:
https://commons.wikimedia.org/w/index.php?curid=3545841

Language

Despite the lack of political unification amongst Celtic cultures, these many different civilizations are connected and identified with one another mainly because of their linguistic similarities. The Celtic languages descended from Proto-Celtic, which is believed to have developed during the Hallstatt period (c. 1200 BCE–450 BCE). It is a branch of the Indo-European linguistic group, meaning it belongs to the same family of languages which has produced modern-day tongues such as English, Spanish, French, German, Hindi, Punjab, Persian, Italian, and Portuguese.

Within the Celtic linguistic group, there are two main branches: Continental and Insular. Insular Celtic refers to the version of the language spoken in what is now England, Scotland, Ireland, Wales, and Brittany, and Continental Celtic refers to the version spoken throughout the rest of Europe. Continental Celtic is extinct, whereas Insular Celtic still exists, although it is spoken as the distinct languages of Gaelic, Welsh, Scottish Gaelic, Breton (spoken in Brittany, France), and, to a lesser extent, Manx (spoken on the Isle of Man) and Cornish (spoken in Cornwall). The various Celtic languages still spoken today are typically divided into either Brittonic or Goidelic, also known as Gaelic. Celtic is still spoken in some regions of continental Europe, but these linguistic groups speak a variation of Breton, which was brought to the region by British settlers. Other Celtic languages, such as Celtiberian, Galatian, and Gaulish, are no longer spoken in modern times. There are other regional languages, such as Lusitanian (spoken in parts of the Iberian Peninsula), Rhaetian (spoken in parts of Switzerland and Austria), and Pictish (now extinct but once an important language on the British Isles) that may have originated from the Celtic language but whose true origins remain a mystery.

Examples of written Celtic first emerged in the 6th century BCE, but many examples of written Celtic still remain due to the rich literary tradition that developed in many different parts of the Celtic world, specifically Ireland. This tradition helped the Celtics establish and spread their culture, and it also led to the spread of their religion and mythology but only in post-Roman times. Before the Romans, writing was discouraged and even forbidden, which has left modern scholars in the dark when it comes to deciphering information about the ancient Celts.

Conclusion

The lack of a unified political structure and primary sources before the middle of the last millennium BCE makes it difficult to pinpoint the true origins of Celtic culture. However, the emergence of the Celtic language between 1200 and 800 BCE, plus references made to the Celts by the Greeks and the Romans, helps us gain a good understanding of where this culture came from and how it spread and developed to be one of the largest and most influential in ancient Europe.

Chapter 2 – The Celtic Migrations

While Celtic culture can trace its roots back to the end of the second millennium BCE, its impact on European culture became even more significant after c. 500 BCE. It was around this time that the Celts began to expand out of their homeland near the Hallstatt zone throughout the rest of Europe. This period, which lasted some 300 years, is typically referred to as the "Celtic Migration," and it is believed to be the result of overpopulation in the Celtic homeland. However, Celtic culture, which had developed into a stratified and highly unequal society by the middle of the first millennium BCE, also put an emphasis on raids and required a constant supply of luxury resources to maintain itself.

During this period, the Celts began to make contact with the cultures of Southern Europe, most specifically the Romans and, to a lesser extent, the Greeks. The Celts that left the Hallstatt region for other lands began settling wherever possible, bringing with them their unique culture and language and increasing the scale of Celtic influence in Europe. However, the expansion of Celtic culture, as is often the case, eventually led to its downfall, largely because as the Celts made contact with other cultures, they also made enemies, most specifically with the Romans, who, by the 3rd century BCE, were growing ever more powerful and looking to expand their sphere of influence in Europe, Africa, and Asia. Nevertheless, this period of expansion known as the Celtic Migration is an important part of Celtic history and is one of the main reasons why the Celts managed to have such a large impact on European and world culture.

Hallstatt and La Tène Social Structures

As mentioned, the predecessor to the Celts was the Hallstatt culture, which developed in the regions surrounding the southern Danube. After the Hallstatts, there was the La Tène culture, which formed to the north of the Hallstatt zone. These cultures were similar in that they were largely chiefdom societies where the warriors were considered to be the elite class, and the leader of the group, the chief, was chosen from this higher segment of society.

This type of social structure was held together by what is called a "prestige goods" system, which means that the elite class maintained their position by possessing unique and luxurious items that were out of reach to lower members of society. They traded items of lesser value, often food and other staples grown on the land they owned, to the rest of the society in exchange for the other goods and services they needed to live and so that they could hold onto their powerful position.

The prominence of this type of social structure is significant for a few reasons. First, it gave these cultures motivation to establish trade routes with other societies in Europe, mainly the Greeks. They sent metals and salt down to the Mediterranean in exchange for wines, olives, gold, and other luxury items. However, it also meant that these cultures were rather unstable, and whenever there was a shortage of luxury goods for the elite class or tradeable resources to acquire them, one of the only methods of acquiring them was to raid a nearby settlement. This meant the early Celtic cultures were frequently fighting amongst one another, something that shouldn't come as much of a surprise to students of ancient history. This concept of raiding became an integral part of the Celtic culture that would develop over the latter part of the first millennium BCE.

Many Tribes as One

Before going into further detail about the Celtic Migration, it's important to point out one other aspect of Celtic culture, which is the diversity that existed within it. More specifically, we must understand that the group of people we refer to today as "Celts" was made up of many different distinct tribes who shared the same culture and language. However, they all spoke different dialects of Celtic, and they also had different cultural practices, although they were similar. The word Celt comes from the Greek word *Keltoi*, which means barbarian, and it is a reflection of how the Greeks saw their neighbors to the north: a dangerous nuisance to their peace and prosperity.

This means that as the Celts moved to other parts of Europe, they developed their own cultural identity. In the modern-day nation of France, for example, there were several Celtic tribes that once lived there, but Caesar and the Romans referred to all of them as Gauls since they referred to the territory occupied by the Celts as Gaul or Gallia. However, within Gaul were many different tribes living there, many of whom were Celtic but many who were not. Elsewhere, the Celts took on different names. In modern-day Turkey, they were known as Galatians, and in modern-day England and Ireland, they were referred to as Britons and Gaels respectively. In modern-day Spain, they were called Celtiberian.

The main reason there are so many names for the Celts is due to the lack of unity among the original Celtic people. Many different tribes existed throughout Central Europe that we now identify as Celtic, but at the time, their only connection was language and culture. They had no political affiliation whatsoever. So, when one tribe decided it was time to leave their homeland in search of new territory to raid, they would rarely be followed by another. This meant that Europe quickly became populated with many different Celtic tribes who all had their own unique version of Celtic culture and language. For those of us studying the history of the Celts, all this does is make things rather confusing since it's common to see Celtic tribes referred to by their specific identity, meaning the average student of history might not immediately recognize the connection between the many different tribes occupying Europe before the Romans began to expand their influence across the continent.

The Celts Expand in Central Europe

Although various theories exist about the origins of the Celts, there is little debate that they had become centralized in the region of the Danube River by the 5th century BCE. However, with the problems of overpopulation and the need to find new lands and cultures to raid, the Celts began expanding to other regions in Europe, spreading their cultural influence and making their mark on this chapter of European history.

Generally speaking, the Celts began moving east and west along the Danube River, finding new areas to settle. It is believed that during this period they made it as far west as the Marne region of France, which is just to the southeast of modern-day Paris. There is also evidence of Celtic populations in Germany, most specifically near the Rhine River in western Germany.

During this migration, the Celts also settled in Bohemia and Bavaria, as well as Switzerland. These tribes, while also speaking their own unique versions of the Celtic language, eventually became some of the most populous and wealthiest settlements in the entire Celtic world. They developed strong trade relations with the Romans, which helped them prosper, and the Gallic tribes, those living in modern-day France and Switzerland, are thought to have been responsible for disseminating the subdivision of the Celtic language known as Continental Celtic.

In the east, the Celts moved across the Great Hungarian Plain, settling it as they did and reaching all the way to what is now the modern-day nation of Romania. Some archaeological sites that can be connected to the Celts can be found as far east as central

Romania, specifically the region of Transylvania. However, different from the Celts who would settle in other parts of Europe, such as Italy and Greece, the Celts that spread out along the Danube and into France, Germany, the Czech Republic, and Romania maintained a significant level of cultural homogeneity. Trade was frequent and steady within the region, and this made it easier for the free exchange of both people and ideas.

Moving South

By c. 400 BCE, the Celts had become the dominant culture in what had previously been the Hallstatt zone, and despite having their own language, they assumed many of the cultural traditions of their predecessors, such as the prestige goods social structure and their emphasis on raids. However, by this time, the Celts populating the region near the Danube and beyond were beginning to face a considerable threat: overpopulation. This would have created significant instability within the region because it made it considerably more difficult for the ruling classes to find enough resources needed to trade with the working classes in exchange for their labor and fealty.

As a result, the Celts began to look south, the region where they got their luxury goods from and an area that they perceived as being rich and bountiful. This led to a rather rapid migration of Celtic populations from the basins of the Danube River south into the region known as the Po Valley, which is the large geographical area surrounding the Po River in northern Italy.

These migrations also helped to spread out power within the Celtic community. This was because when populations in one community swelled, one or more elites would break off in search of a new territory. If they found something suitable, they would establish a new settlement and put themselves atop the social structure. However, at times, these warrior leaders could not find a suitable location, and this often pushed them to move south toward Italy. When they did this, they would often announce to local tribes and communities of their march south, and because overpopulation was such a widespread problem, considerable numbers of Celts would flee their hometown or village to join the warlord moving south, giving the migrating Celts a considerable force should they find resistance to their movement into better, more fertile lands.

The March on Rome

Anyone with even a slight understanding of the map of Europe will know that if you head south from the Danube valley in Austria and into Italy, and you keep going, you will eventually find the city of Rome. And while Rome at the beginning of the 4th century BCE was not yet the power that it would become in the final centuries of the millennium, it was still a strong city with considerable control over the territory in central Italy, and it was also a kingdom that had ambitions of expanding.

But when the Celts first started moving south, they did not appear to have ambitions of marching on Rome. However, a group of Roman ambassadors appeared in the region of Marne sometime around 395 BCE to negotiate trade; these talks disintegrated, and the Roman ambassadors, along with their forces, engaged in a battle with the Celts in which a member of the Roman embassy killed the Celtic warlord. This represented a massive affront to the Celts in the region, and it inspired them to march south toward Rome to exact revenge.

It is believed the Celts made it as far south as Rome in 390 BCE, and they engaged with the Roman army at Allia, a tributary of the Tiber River. The Celts dealt the Romans a crushing blow by destroying their army and sacking the city. However, lacking any real political organization, the Celts did not move in and take control of the city. Instead, they camped on its outskirts as the elites worked out a deal. Records indicate the warriors began to die of disease, and the Celts and Romans eventually came to an agreement that led to the Celtic departure from the region.

At this point, the Celts continued to make waves in northern Italy, raiding nearby populations and establishing their own settlements. But they also played an important role in the region by serving as mercenaries for local lords and kings seeking men to help them expand their power. In these arrangements, many of the Celts living in the region actually fought on behalf of the Romans, but there is also evidence of additional attacks by the Celts on Rome in 367 BCE, and there may have been additional confrontations throughout the following centuries.

This division amongst the Celts in Italy helps point to the lack of unity that existed in this ancient culture. Their common language was not enough to bind them together politically, and this helped contribute to the fact that they never built up an empire the size of those seen around this time in the ancient world, despite having the population and the resources to do so.

The Celts in the Balkans and Greece

The first recorded contact between the Greeks and the Celts took place in 335 BCE when Celtic emissaries traveled to Macedon to present themselves to the court of Alexander the Great and negotiate a treaty of friendship. However, it's believed the Celts had been in the region for the better part of the century, with evidence, mainly in the form of battle artifacts, suggesting that the Celts made it into Greece around the same time they moved into northern Italy: c. 390 BCE.

This initial contact did not have much of an impact on either culture, but when Alexander the Great died in 323 BCE, and his empire was broken up and distributed to those who had served under him, the Celtic groups in the region must have seen this as an opportunity for them to expand further in the area.

The Celtic leader Cambaules led the first Celtic expedition into Greece, specifically the region of Thrace, in 298 BCE, but he was pushed back by those occupying the region. Eighteen years later, in 280 BCE, another group of Celts, led by a war leader named

Bolgius, attacked the Greek region of Heraclea, but they, too, were pushed back and unable to secure a victory. However, after this, the two armies combined forces and began advancing quickly to the south, destroying Greek cities and farmlands along the way and treating the local population extremely harshly. Eventually, they reached the sacred Greek city of Delphi in 279 BCE and launched a considerable attack, but they were defeated, and the story recorded by the literate Greeks paints the Celts as barbaric and uncivilized and the Greeks as heroic defenders of their territory, images of both cultures that still remain to this day.

After being defeated at Delphi, the Celts began to retreat out of Greece to the north, but others moved east into Thrace and formed a settlement at Tyle. From there, the Celts were able to demand tribute from the city of Byzantium for a considerable period of time, but the Thracians eventually destroyed the settlement at Tyle in c. 212 BCE. However, another group of Celts was hired by the leader of Bithynia, a region in northwest Asia Minor which included Byzantium (later Constantinople, now Istanbul) as mercenaries, which brought the Celts across the Hellespont and into Asia Minor.

The Britons and Gaels

Today, the countries we most closely associate with Celtic culture are Ireland, Wales, Scotland, and, to a lesser extent, England. However, as we now know, the Celts did not originate here, and their primary sphere of influence was actually in Central Europe. But archaeological evidence suggests that Celtic people were living in what is now England and Ireland starting as early as the 5th or 6th century BCE, which would mean that the Celts settled this part of the world as part of the overall Celtic Migration that took place in the first half of the first millennium BCE.

Over time, the Celts in modern-day England, Wales, Scotland, and Ireland developed their own version of the Celtic language which we now refer to as Insular Celtic. It is similar to Continental Celtic in many ways, but it was distinct enough to earn its own designation.

The only versions of Celtic that are still spoken today are subdivisions of Insular Celtic.

The Celts in Galatia

While most of the Celts that had attacked Greek cities throughout Thrace and Macedon and that had been invited to cross the Hellespont to fight for Bithynia were soldiers, there is evidence to suggest that a large portion of the group was not. These soldiers, which all came from similar tribes, traveled with women and children, which suggests that at least part of this expeditionary force left the Celtic homeland to try and find new lands to settle. The failed invasions of Greece limited their options, and so, they crossed into Asia Minor.

In the early years of their presence in Asia Minor, the Celts formed a part of the Bithynian army, but in 275–4 BCE, the Bithynians suffered a catastrophic defeat at the "Elephant Battle," and the Celts found themselves on the wrong side of history. The Seleucid king who then took control of Bithynia, Antiochus I, banished the Celts to a barren region in central Anatolia. The people in Asia Minor at the time referred to these Celtic tribes as Galatians, so the area they eventually occupied was known as Galatia.

For the next few centuries, these Galatians ran frequent raids against the various cities in Asia Minor. Each of the three different tribes that had banded together to settle in Asia Minor had its own region to raid, and this practice was rather lucrative against the relatively wealthy city-states in the area which had benefited from Greek trade and cultural influence. This made it possible for the Celts to maintain their traditional way of life, i.e., their prestige goods society. In addition, the Celts also frequently served as mercenaries in the Seleucid armies, and their strong warrior culture made them a powerful addition to this kingdom's military.

However, by the 2nd century BCE, the Romans had become the most powerful empire in Europe, and they had begun to flex their muscles in Asia Minor. Specifically, in 191 BCE, the Romans offered support to the Pergamenes in a campaign against the Seleucids and their Galatian mercenaries, and they won a resounding victory. During the peace talks, the Celts (Galatians) agreed to stop all raids into the surrounding territories, and in exchange, the Romans agreed to help the Galatians remain free from Pergamene control. However, this peace treaty only lasted two years as the Celts began raiding once again. Yet the Romans interfered and defeated them soundly and negotiated a new peace treaty again.

Stripped of their ability to raid surrounding settlements for resources, the Galatian social structure began to weaken. They no longer had the resources needed to support their prestige goods economy, and this caused them to gradually integrate into the local culture. Celtic tribes arrived from Europe from time to time, and raiding would ensue, but by the first century CE, the Galatians had been almost entirely absorbed into the culture of Asia Minor. However, they maintained their language and strong ethnic identity, mainly by continuing to identify themselves as Galatians. They did this so well that when Roman apostles traveled to Galatia in the 4th century CE, they were able to recognize the similarities between the language spoken in Galatia and those spoken in lands throughout the rest of Europe that still identified as Celtic.

The Celts in the Pontic-Caspian Region

Somewhat surprisingly, a significant quantity of Celtic artifacts has also been found in the Pontic-Caspian Steppe, which is the territory stretching from the mouth of the Danube River in the Black Sea all the way east to the Caspian Sea. However, historians and archaeologists have been unable to identify exactly why these artifacts are there. The two prevailing theories are: 1) the area was settled as part of the overall Celtic Migration that began in the Hallstatt zone and spread throughout the rest of Europe; and 2) the Galatians, after having their right to raid in Asia Minor revoked by the Romans, moved north into the Pontic-Caspian region. However, there is no evidence to prove either theory, and because of a lack of written records, little is known about the Celtic cultures living in this part of Europe and Asia during and after the Celtic Migration.

The Celtiberians

While most of the Celts living in the Hallstatt zone and the Danube River valley began migrating throughout Europe starting in roughly 500 BCE, the Celts who lived on the Iberian Peninsula, which today houses the modern-day nations of Spain and Portugal, most likely arrived sometime around 1000 BCE. They mostly settled in the northwestern part of the peninsula, primarily in the modern-day region of Galicia, and they coexisted with many other different cultures.

That there is evidence of Celtic culture on the Iberian Peninsula dating back to 1000 BCE is curious because at this point in time, the Celts were just beginning to differentiate themselves from the other cultures in the Hallstatt zone, and also, there is no evidence of a larger scale migration of Celts during this time period. The lack of written records from this time means we may never know what drove the Celts to this part of the world at this moment in history.

Some argue that the presence of the Celts in Western Europe at the end of the first century BCE is evidence that the Celtic culture did not emerge in the Hallstatt zone and that their origin is really from the western coasts of Europe. However, there is no evidence to suggest this is, in fact, the case, and since we do know the Celtic Migration that took place starting in the 5th century started in the Hallstatt zone, it's difficult to use this early appearance of the Celtiberians as evidence of a different origin. However, no matter which theory you use to describe the origin of Celtic culture, Celtic influence on the Iberian Peninsula became much more pronounced in the second half of the first millennium BCE when the Celts were expanding out of the Hallstatt zone to the rest of Europe.

Conclusion

The Celtic Migration is one of the most significant examples of human movement in history, both in terms of the number of people as well as area. The Celts, which we believe formed into a distinct culture toward the beginning of the first millennium BCE, went from occupying a relatively small territory near the Danube River to occupying the modern-day nations of Spain, France, Germany, Italy, the Czech Republic, Poland, Russia, Slovakia, Bulgaria, Greece, England, Scotland, Wales, Ireland, and Turkey, among others.

This extensive migration was partly the result of the need for land, as this growing population needed to expand out of the Danube River valley. But it also came from the Celts' unique way of life, specifically raids. Raids were established early on in Celtic history as an important aspect of society, and Celtic men wishing to increase their social status often engaged in raids largely because the bounty they acquired could be distributed to win the loyalty of those in their tribe or settlement. This enhanced prestige also made it easier for the same leader to recruit more men for the next raid, which would make the campaign more successful and increase his status even more. This type of social structure provided a great incentive for more and more raids, and this eventually became an integral part of the Celtic way of life. Because of this, the Celts were especially motivated to continuously expand, meaning Celtic culture and their way of life quickly spread around Europe and beyond.

However, perhaps even more surprising is the way in which Celtic culture was maintained throughout this diaspora. As mentioned, there was no unified political structure that united the various Celtic cultures. Instead, it was their way of life, i.e., raids, religion, and art, as well as their language, that bound them together. Furthermore, because of the strength of their culture, Celtic tribes who settled in other regions of Europe were able to maintain their cultural identity despite being surrounded by a number of distinct cultures. As a result, Celtic culture remained strong as Europe changed considerably under the influence of the Romans, and it also had a considerable impact on the other cultures developing in the region, an impact that can still be felt today.

Chapter 3 – The Many Celtic Tribes of Europe

Whether or not Celtic culture originated with the Hallstatt culture and expanded out to the rest of Europe, or whether distinct ethnicities "Celtized" over time, one thing is for sure: by c. 200 BCE, most of Europe was settled by people speaking some version of the Celtic language. Yet while it would be nice to think of these different cultures that all shared the same language as homogeneous, mainly because it would make it easier to study them, this simply isn't the reality. Instead, there existed a great diversity within the Celtic culture, ranging from how people lived to the version of the Celtic language they spoke.

There are a few different reasons for this. The most obvious is that there was no unified Celtic political structure that was able to impose a dominant culture and therefore bring the many different subdivisions closer together. But another reason was that the Celts who migrated throughout Europe started off as different cultures. Tribes that moved from the Hallstatt zone into the Po Valley may have been completely different from those that moved into the Rhineland, Marne, southern France, Britain, and the Iberian Peninsula. Instead, we see various tribes of different backgrounds, all speaking the same language, taking very different paths to establish themselves in different places in Europe.

So, in order to properly study the Celts, it's important to learn more about the different subdivisions that exist within the Celtic culture. The best way to do this is to break the Celts up by region, and even though there are many different ways to do this, one of the easiest, at least for those familiar with modern geography, is to divide the Celts into the Celtiberians, the Gauls, and the Britons. Within these groups, there are many more subdivisions, and knowing their names, as well as some background information about them, can make it easier to piece together the rest of ancient Celtic history.

Celtiberians

As the name suggests, the Celtiberians are actually a mixture of Celtic and Iberian peoples, the Iberians being the natives of the Iberian Peninsula who spoke their native Iberian language. Generally speaking, the Celtiberians occupied the northern parts of the Iberian Peninsula, whereas the Iberians occupied the south. Both groups caused the Romans considerable trouble when they first landed on the peninsula and tried to conquer it. But within the subdivision of the Celtiberians, there are several other groups that are important to understanding the Celtic presence on the Iberian Peninsula.

Lusitanians

The Lusitanians were a major tribal group that occupied the region between the Tagus and Douro Rivers in what is now Portugal and the Spanish region of Extremadura. However, the Lusitanians are best understood as more of a tribal confederation that was made up of several similar tribes that also called the region home. They spoke a language that is believed to have been linked to Celtic, and they also practiced a similar religion, although there is evidence that they also borrowed some of these practices from the nearby Basque culture. During the Roman conquest of Iberia, the Lusitanians were one of the principal leaders of the Celtiberian resistance to Roman rule, although they were eventually defeated and over time became Romanized.

Astures

Located on the northern coast of Spain in the modern-day autonomous regions of Asturias and Leon, the Astures were a culture based around horse riding and cattle raising. It is possible, according to archaeological evidence, that the Astures migrated to the Iberian Peninsula as a part of the Celtic Migration that originated in the Hallstatt zone which resulted in the Celtization of most of the European continent.

As compared to other Celtic cultures at the time, the Astures were rather centralized. They had a confederation of tribes, and they built a citadel that was used as a capital. They also appear to have worshiped some of the gods we now associate as being characteristically Celtic, such as Taranis and Lugh. Evidence of this comes from the fact that many towns in the region are named after these gods and have been since Roman times.

Cantabri

The Cantabri made their home to the east of the Astures near the modern-day region of Cantabria. Over time, they appear to have adopted some version of a Celtic language, although there is evidence of considerable mixing with nearby tribes, including the non-Celtic Basques. This makes the Cantabri a perfect example of how difficult it can be to discern a clear connection between one Celtic tribe and another.

The Cantabri were major antagonists to the Romans as they attempted to conquer the Iberian Peninsula on their way to imperial glory. In fact, the Cantabrian Wars were the final part of the Romans' two-century-long conquest of Hispania. After this war, the Cantabri were incorporated into Latin culture and lost much of their Celtic heritage.

Gallacei

The Gallacei were a tribal confederation made up mostly of Celtic tribes but likely included tribes of several distinct ethnicities. They existed in the northwestern region of Spain and the northern region of Portugal. They joined the Lusitanians in the fight against Rome, and there is evidence they served as mercenaries in Hannibal's armies during Carthage's wars with Rome. Known for being fierce fighters, the Gallacei caused the Romans considerable trouble throughout their conquest. Today, Celtic culture remains alive in these regions of Spain and Portugal, although the Gallacei were largely Romanized after their conquest.

Gauls

The Romans called all the Celtic peoples living in the modern-day nations of France, Belgium, Luxembourg, and parts of Switzerland, northern Italy, the Netherlands, and Germany, Gauls. The region of Gaul was divided into several provinces, all of which were eventually annexed by the Romans. This conquest led to the eventual Romanization of the Celtic peoples living there, and over time, Latin became the dominant language, which mixed with Anglo-Saxon, German, Norse, and many other languages to produce the diverse set of languages we see today in this part of Europe.

However, while the Romans' classification of the region simply as "Gaul" made it easier for them to understand it, this greatly oversimplified the diversity that existed there at the time. In fact, listing all of the tribes that we can identify as Celtic, or Gallic, would be an impossible task, but to understand the history of the Gauls, especially as it relates to that of the Romans, it's important to know the distinctions between the many different Celtic groups that called the region home.

Ligures

The Ligures lived on the northern Mediterranean coast in the southern part of what is now northwestern Italy and southeastern France. They developed their own language, Ligurian, which probably developed on its own accord before taking on Celtic undertones after the Celtic migrations of the first millennium BCE. It's possible the Ligures were a mixture of Hallstatt and La Tène cultures (which were decidedly Celtic) but also of cultures from Northern Europe, which helped them develop a unique identity.

Greek historians write of the Ligures as being particularly fearsome mercenaries, and the Ligures fought long, hard battles with the Romans throughout their conquest; however, they were one of the first regions of Gaul to be annexed as part of the Roman Empire. Liguria is significant in the Gallic Wars because when the Ligures offered to allow the Helvetii free passage, they defied Roman rule and essentially forced Caesar to march into Gaul and conquer it. As punishment for their repeated defiance of Roman rule, many Ligures were deported to other parts of the Roman Empire, which led to their rapid Romanization and the disappearance of their culture.

Helvetii

The Helvetii was one of the most significant tribes of ancient Gaul in terms of both population and controlled territory. They populated the area which is the modern-day nation of Switzerland, and Caesar wrote that there were some 400 villages scattered around the region. He counted some 263,000 people, although most modern scholars believe this is too high. Still, that there were several hundred thousand people of one culture in this part of the world at this time is a sign that the Helvetii were a flourishing and prospering culture.

The Helvetii are also significant because they were the first tribe to confront Caesar as he marched north. But they had no kings and therefore had no organization, and their most famous leader,

Orgetorix, was executed when he tried to name himself king to fight the Romans. After Caesar's victory, the Helvetii were incorporated into Roman culture and lost all distinction in the first few hundred years of Roman rule.

Belgae

The Belgae was a confederation of Celtic-Germanic people in Northern Europe, near the modern-day nation of Belgium. Because of their proximity to the Germanic tribes to the east, it's difficult to know for sure if the Belgae were more Celtic or Germanic, but judging by the makeup of the confederation, most historians today believe they were, in fact, Celtic. They were fierce fighters, particularly those who belonged to the Nervii subdivision, who probably came closer than any other tribe in Gaul to resisting Roman advances and remaining independent. However, like their counterparts in the rest of Gaul, they eventually fell, and the land of the Belgae was annexed as a Roman province.

Boii

The Boii made their home in northern Italy, Hungary, and the Czech Republic,, and they are significant to Celtic culture because they were one of the first tribes to march south into Italy and attack the Romans. They held close ties with the Helvetii and actually joined them in their fight against the Romans, but they were defeated. The Boii could also be found in other parts of Europe, such as in the Danube valley and in Eastern Europe. It's believed these people are both a distinct branch of the Boii that moved during the Celtic migrations but who were later fortified by those who fled Italy after the Romans defeated them and annexed northern Italy to their imperial realm.

Lingones

The Lingones are significant because they were one of the wealthier Celtic tribes in the region. They made their home in the region between the Seine and Marne Rivers. Due to their strategic location in central Gaul, they became wealthy by establishing trade networks between the many different Celtic and Germanic tribes that lived in the region. After Romanization, the Lingones were responsible for minting coins in the Roman Empire, which helped keep their capital, Andematunnum, which was renamed Langres over time, an important economic hub of the Roman Empire. However, the Lingones ceased to be a distinct Celtic culture by the end of the 1st century BCE.

Aedui

The Aedui were another important tribe in central Gaul, and their role in the lead-up to the Gallic Wars helps show why the Celts were so vulnerable to conquest at the time Julius Caesar marched north. Specifically, when the Aedui were invaded by another Celtic tribe, the Sequani, they appealed to Rome for help, which they got. This further entrenched the Romans in intra-Gallic affairs. However, the Aedui ended up joining the Gallic alliance against the Romans, and when they were defeated, they were assimilated into Roman culture.

Britons

The Celtic culture that remains in the modern day is at least somewhat related to that of the Britons. They first appeared on the British Isles in the first millennium BCE, but their exact origins remain unknown. Perhaps they migrated along with the rest of the Celts, or perhaps they adopted Celtic languages and cultural norms over time. But no matter their origins, the Britons proved to be the most resilient.

More specifically, they resisted the Romans for many years, and the northern inhabitants of the island, the Picts, who may or may not have been Celtic, managed to remain independent from the Romans after the conquest. This made it possible for the Celtic culture to exist throughout Roman times and remain until the present day. Together with the Gaels, the Britons make up the division of Celts known as Insular Celts, which is in contrast to the Continental Celts.

Catuvellauni

The Catuvellauni was one of the most powerful of all the Insular Celtic tribes. They were believed to be quite wealthy and may have been minting coins before the Romans invaded in the first century CE. They managed to expand outward from their capital, Camulodunum (modern-day Colchester), and received tribute from several other Celtic tribes in the region, making them one of the best examples of a Celtic kingdom that we have.

When the Romans invaded in 43 CE, the Catuvellauni led the resistance and continued to be a nuisance to Roman governors for at least a century. They were Romanized, but their distinct culture remained and led to the formation of a Romano-British culture, which reflected both Roman and pre-Roman cultures.

Iceni

The northern neighbors of the Catuvellauni, the Iceni were another strong Celtic tribe in eastern Britain that played a key role in resisting Roman rule. The uprising led by their queen, Boudica, nearly drove the Romans from the island for good. However, they were eventually beaten and forced to integrate into Roman culture. There is also evidence of coin minting from the Iceni tribe in the years before the Roman invasion, suggesting they shared a similar level of wealth as their neighbors, the Catuvellauni.

Trinovantes

The Trinovantes were probably the most powerful kingdom in Britain at the time the Romans invaded. They were neighbors to both the Catuvellauni and the Iceni, and they likely shared their wealth. In the early years of Roman intervention in Britain, the Romans attempted to maintain a balance of power between the Trinovantes and the Catuvellauni, but when this failed, the Romans were left with no choice other than to invade, which led to the annexation of Britain to the Roman Empire.

Ordovices

The Ordovices occupied the territory on the western coast of Britain which is now Wales. Like most Celtic tribes of the time, they made their living farming and keeping sheep, but this suggests they were probably less wealthy than their neighbors to the east. Nevertheless, the Ordovices were one of the tribes that resisted Roman rule, and they led a rebellion that temporarily pushed the Romans out of western Britain.

Gaels-Scotti

The Gaels are a separate subdivision of the Celtic culture that shared Britain with the various Briton tribes in the centuries following the Roman withdrawal from Britain. Scotti is the Latin name for Gaels, whereas the word Gael is what these people called themselves in their native language. The Gaels eventually became a Celtic culture, but DNA evidence suggests their origins may actually be from somewhere in Central Asia.

After the Roman invasions of southern Gaul, the Gaels, a local tribe, fled the area to the modern island of Ireland. The Gaels expanded their dominance in Ireland throughout the succeeding centuries, spanning the entirety of Roman rule in Britain. Following the Roman withdrawal from Britain in the early 5th century, the Gaels began to expand across the Irish Sea to modern southwestern Scotland. Thus began the Gaelic culture in Britain itself.

Conclusion

Naming and describing all the different tribes that can be identified as Celtic is a near impossible task. However, by looking at just a few, we can see how Celtic culture is both so prevalent in Europe—it's hard to find a group not influenced by the Celts—but also so diverse, which is probably why the Celts were never able to organize politically and bring more uniformity to their culture and way of life. As a result, it should come as no surprise that they were in significant danger of being conquered when the Romans set out to conquer Celtic-controlled territory, starting with the conquest of the Celtic territories in northern Italy in 224 BCE, just prior to the outbreak of the Second Punic War.

Chapter 4 – The Celtiberians

While most people don't associate the modern-day nations of Spain and Portugal with Celtic culture, various Celtic cultures had been living on the Iberian Peninsula since the early years of the Celtic Migration. However, it's possible that Celtic peoples were living on the Iberian Peninsula as early as 1000 BCE. Once again, this raises questions about the origins of the Celts. Did they migrate slowly from the Hallstatt zone? Or did their culture spread to already existing peoples until most of Europe was Celtized?

Of course, we may never know the answer. But what we do know about the Celts on the Iberian Peninsula is that they often mixed with the native Iberian tribes to form a unique form of Celtic culture known as Celtiberian. They flourished in the northwestern half of the peninsula and were major opponents of the Romans as they attempted to conquer the land they called Hispania.

However, eventually, the Celt, Iberian, and Celtiberian cultures of the Iberian Peninsula fell to Rome, which was one of the first provinces outside of Italy that the Romans conquered, meaning the Celtiberians were Romanized early on in Roman history and soon became integrated into their culture. However, by looking at the way the Celtiberians resisted the Romans, we can understand a little bit more about the extent of their civilization before the Roman conquest.

Early Trouble with the Mediterranean Civilizations

The tribes on the Iberian Peninsula had longstanding trade relations with the rest of the ancient world starting with the Phoenicians who established contacts and set up colonies on the peninsula starting in about 1200 BCE in what is now Lisbon and in about 1100 BCE in what is now Cadiz. However, when Carthage lost a significant portion of the Mediterranean islands they ruled over after the First Punic War from 264 to 241 BCE, the Carthaginians decided to invade southern Iberia as a way of maintaining the size of their empire as well as their power.

At the time, Rome had also established some contacts on the peninsula and had shown interest in expanding its influence, but both sides agreed to not extend their dominion beyond the Ebro River, which runs through northeastern Spain. However, when Hannibal Barca attacked the pro-Roman Iberian city of Sagnutum, the Romans intervened. This sparked the Second Punic War (218–201 BCE), which resulted in the Roman conquest of Iberia. This gave the Romans a stronghold on the Iberian Peninsula, an excellent jumping-off point for conquering the rest of the territory. However, the territory that exchanged hands between Rome and Carthage during this period had been previously occupied mostly by Iberians and not Celts, which should have kept the Celts out of the conflict. However, many of the Celtic tribes on the peninsula, such as the Lusitanians and the Gallaeci, fought for Hannibal and Carthage, which was a sign of things to come for Rome.

Resistance to Roman Rule

Shortly after the Romans took control of Carthaginian Iberia, they began making alliances with local Celtiberian tribes to try and ensure peace in the coming years. But they knew these treaties probably wouldn't last the test of time, so the Romans began establishing permanent settlements along the Iberian coast. Furthermore, over the next decade or so, the Romans began importing people and technology, which began the process of Romanization in southern Iberian. Roman generals forced local tribes to provide them with set amounts of agricultural goods, a move which most likely disrupted the pastoral, semi-nomadic lifestyles of these tribes. All of this made the locals rather hostile to the Romans, and the Iberians, often with the support of Celtiberian mercenaries, proved rather difficult to rule.

However, over time, the Romans succeeded in subjugating the Iberian tribes of the south, but this put them in closer contact with the Celtiberians of northern Iberian. Fearing the Romans were going to continue their advance northward (which they were planning to do), the Celtiberians began attacking the Romans on their own, increasing hostilities and forcing the Romans to dedicate more and more resources to the pacification of the peninsula, which eventually led to an all-out war between the Romans and the Celtiberians.

The Celtiberians managed to build up coalitions with other Celtic tribes on the peninsula, such as the Vaccei and the Vettones, to attack the Romans. They did so in 197, 195, 193, and 185, and they achieved considerable success, putting the Romans under pressure and threatening their ability to continue their wars of conquest in Iberia. However, with the threat of losing territory looming ever larger, the Romans doubled down and managed to push the Celtiberian tribes back but not after having to fight a series of hard-fought wars.

The First Celtiberian War

Although the Celtiberian tribes had been fighting Rome in one way or another since the end of the Second Punic War, it wasn't until 182 BCE, when the Roman general Quintus Fulvius Flaccus increased Roman military movements and conquered the city of Urbicua that all-out war broke out. In response to this, the Celtiberian tribes gathered an army of 35,000 men, which would have been one of the largest armies ever assembled in Celtiberian history, a fact we can determine simply by looking at the population numbers of Celtiberian tribes at the time.

However, Quintus Fulvius Flaccus recognized the threat and also increased the size of his army, which allowed him to defeat the Celtiberians at Aebura, a Celtiberian site in central Spain. Once he had achieved this victory, he moved on to Contrebia, a city thought to be located near the modern-day city of Cuenca, where he forced the Celtiberian army to surrender. Quintus Fulvius Flaccus then turned his army over to another general, Tiberius Sempornius Gracchus, and he returned to Rome.

Gracchus then conducted several campaigns throughout 179 BCE, defeating the Celtiberians at Munda, Certima, and Alce, all of which are in southern Spain. At this point, many of the other Celtiberian tribes on the peninsula began surrendering to Rome since they could see that they were no match for the Roman armies and that resisting would lead to death or, even worse, slavery. As a result, Gracchus met with the various tribal leaders of Celtiberia to negotiate peace terms.

In general, the terms of this treaty were favorable to the Celtiberians, most likely because Gracchus was trying to prevent future wars and therefore wanted to make friends with the local tribes. To do this, he resettled some of the more impoverished people living in Celtiberia, and he imposed a grain tax that was considerably less demanding than many of the taxes the Romans imposed on the tribes they conquered elsewhere in Europe.

However, the Romans imposed a law that forbade the natives from forming new cities, although they were allowed to fortify existing ones. This stipulation would later cause problems and lead to new conflicts between the Romans and the Celtiberians. But in general, this approach seems to have been rather successful since Iberia entered a period of relative stability for the next twenty years.

This period also marks the beginning of Celtiberian Romanization. The Romans established administrative institutions and began importing their people so as to spread their language and customs. However, it would take several more rounds of fighting for the Celtiberians to finally give in to Roman rule and become a part of the Roman Empire.

The Second Celtiberian War

As mentioned, the peace terms negotiated by Gracchus helped establish peace in Celtiberia for the better part of a quarter century. However, fighting would resume in 154 BCE when the Celtiberian tribe, the Belli, opened the doors of their capital to surrounding towns and allowed them to settle there. At the same time, they began construction on a new city wall.

The Romans interpreted this as an attempt to build a new city, which would have been a violation of the peace treaty negotiated by Gracchus. In response, the Romans made tribute demands on the Belli and sent a group of Roman soldiers to the city to collect it. The Belli people approached the Romans and claimed that they were not building a new city and that they also had been granted an exemption from tribute. However, the Roman Senate ignored these claims and prepared for war, perhaps because it was worried that the Belli were becoming too powerful and would therefore become a problem moving forward.

In 153 BCE, when the Belli found out the Romans were marching toward them to make war, they fled to a territory occupied by another Celtic tribe, the Arevaci, who were located in the northeastern portion of the peninsula. This Celtiberian coalition attacked the Romans by surprise, and although the Romans technically won, they suffered heavy losses. Shortly thereafter, the Celtiberians engaged the Romans at Numantia, a small but important town in northern Spain. Once again, the Celtiberian coalition was able to inflict heavy losses on the Romans, but this time, they emerged victorious. This victory on its own would have put Roman Celtiberia in jeopardy, but shortly afterward, the Belli and the Arevaci were joined by additional Celtiberian tribes who were eager to free themselves from Roman rule and saw this as the opportunity to do so.

After these defeats, the command of the Roman army changed hands, and in 152 BCE, they attacked the city of Ocilis, in north-central Spain, and managed to take it and capture hostages. When this happened, the people of Ocilis asked for peace, but the Romans would not accept it until the Belli and the Arevaci also agreed to peace. These tribes ended up sending envoys to Rome to ask for peace, which they were granted, and by 151 BCE, the Second Celtiberian War came to an end.

However, the fighting was not yet over. In 151 BCE, Lucius Licinius Lucullus, the new consul, took control of the Roman legions in Hispania, and he began attacking the Vaccaei, another Celtic tribe in northern Spain. These actions never led to an all-out war, although the Celtiberians made pleas to Rome to punish their official for his actions. It's possible this request was ignored because the Roman Senate could see that they were getting close to fully pacifying the peninsula and therefore deemed it unnecessary to continue pandering to Celtiberian claims. However, it's also possible the Roman Senate was simply not interested in helping them because the Lusitanians were revolting in the western part of the peninsula, which would have proved to be a big distraction from the plight of the Celtiberians.

The Numantine War and Romanization

After the end of the Second Celtiberian War, Rome was closer than it had ever been before to fully pacifying Hispania and completing its annexation to their empire. In addition to fighting back most of the peninsula's Celtiberian tribes, the Romans had also managed to subdue the rebelling Lusitanians. However, after the end of the Lusitanian War, their leader, Viriathus, fled to Arevaci territory to join up with the Celtiberians for one last stand against the Romans.

At first, things looked good for this Celtiberian-Lusitanian coalition. They were able to win several victories in the early years of the war

(143–138 BCE), and the Roman commander at the time actually negotiated peace with the tribes.

The fighting continued throughout the next several years until the two sides met at Numantia in 134 BCE. Here, the Romans managed to win a decisive victory that ended the Numantine War. The peace that was negotiated after this battle marked the end of the conflicts between the Romans and the Celtiberians, and while Iberian tribes would continue to give the Romans trouble over the next century, it marked the official beginning of Romanization and the end of autonomous Celtic cultures on the Iberian Peninsula.

Conclusion

The story of the Celts in Iberia is very similar to that of the Celts in Gaul. The fact that the Celtiberian tribes were only unified by language and that they lacked political organization made them an easy target for the invading Romans. So, although their legendary warrior culture made it possible for them to inflict heavy losses on the Roman armies and resist their rule for some time, it was ultimately impossible for them to avoid conquest and the process of Romanization. As a result, while some of the people currently living in Spain recognize their Celtic heritage, there are few tangible traces of the culture left on the peninsula.

Chapter 5 – The Gallic Wars

By 200 BCE, the Celts had gone from being a small yet distinct culture that made their home in the Hallstatt zone surrounding the Danube River to being a significant cultural force throughout all of Europe. However, the differences that existed among the different tribes we now refer to as the Celts, combined with their lack of political unity and reliance on raiding, limited the influence the Celts could have had on the overall development of Europe.

It's impossible to know if these circumstances would have changed had the various Celtic tribes living across Europe been given more time to come together as one. They possessed a significant advantage in that they shared a common language and culture, and many of the tribes operating in Gaul (France), as well as Switzerland, Germany, and Belgium, had managed to establish strong trade links with both the Greeks and the Romans, which helped make them considerably wealthy. However, competition amongst the different tribes, exacerbated by their dependence on raids as well as their illiteracy, meant that the Celts were also ripe for conquest. And Rome was growing in power around this time and would soon become the dominant empire in the region, reshaping society and instilling Roman values and culture on the many different cultures who fell under the jurisdiction of Rome.

Because of this, the history of the Celts after the Celtic Migration is closely tied to the history of Rome, largely because Roman expansion in Western Europe came at the expense of the Celts. Even though Celtic culture remains to this day, it would never be as prominent as it was before the Romans marched their legions into the territory they called Gaul.

Gallic Confederations

To understand the Gallic Wars between Caesar's armies and the people of Gaul, it's important to understand how Gaul was organized at the time. We've mentioned before that there was no uniform political structure, but by the time the Romans rose to power, the various tribes living in Gaul, especially the Celtic ones who shared a common language and common ancestry, often worked together to facilitate trade and provide for the common defense. Their main enemies were the Germanic peoples who lived in much of what is the modern-day nation of Germany and who, like the Celts in the first millennium BCE, were undergoing their own migration and expansion. However, in some instances, as in the case with the Belgae, Celtic and Germanic tribes came together and formed trade networks, leading to a peaceful coexistence between the two different ethnic groups.

However, these confederations were not organized political structures but were rather loose agreements between many different tribes. It was forbidden for any one person to become king of the confederation, and the penalty for trying to do so was death. However, the need for continuous raids in order to maintain the Celtic social structure meant that the tribes who were allied with one another were also frequently at war with one another, coming together only when there was a threat from abroad, specifically from the Germanic tribes.

To the Romans, all Gauls, or Celts, were the same. They spoke the same language and had a similar culture, and this is why the Romans referred to the territory occupied by these people simply as Gaul. However, to assume this meant there was an effective and uniform political or social structure in Gaul is incorrect. Conflicts frequently arose amongst members of the same confederation, and there were few systems in place to help the tribes involved deal with these conflicts in a peaceful way.

As a result, they often had to look to outside help, particularly to the Romans, to work through their difficulties. Managing these conflicts and maintaining peaceful relations with the Celts of Gaul was in the Romans' best interest because these tribes provided a nice buffer between Roman territory and Germanic lands, and the Germanic tribes had proven to be much more aggressive and dangerous to Rome than Gallic ones. However, when Julius Caesar entered the scene in the first century BCE, his own political ambitions provided him with the incentive for becoming more involved in intra-Gallic politics and expanding Rome's influence in the region.

The Romans and the Celts

As mentioned earlier, the Romans and the Celts came into contact with one another during the Celtic Migration when the Celts marched into and past the Po Valley and sacked Rome in 390 BCE. However, the Romans did not take this defeat lightly, and by 283 BCE, they had recovered enough to begin marching against the Celtic tribes in Italy that they felt posed a risk to the safety of Rome. The Romans defeated the most powerful Celtic tribe in Italy, the Senones, and expelled them from Italy. Finally, the Celts were restricted to the Po Valley.

But the Romans were not free from the Celts just yet. The First Punic War (fought between Rome and Carthage) began in 264 BCE and lasted until 241 BCE, and this meant the Romans were not paying close attention to northern Italy. So, the Celtic tribes, who were still migrating from the other side of the Alps, began taking control over more and more territory. Specifically, the Boii teamed up with other Celtic tribes, such as the Gaesatae, the Insubres, and the Taurisci, and began marching south into Italy. They were stopped, however, in 225 BCE at Telamon, and the Romans followed up with campaigns that allowed them to win back territory the Boii had conquered.

A brief period of peace came afterward, but then Hannibal employed Celtic mercenaries in the Second Punic War (218–201 BCE) as he marched into Rome, but the Celts were once again unable to beat the Romans in battle. The Roman victory over Carthage in the Second Punic War eliminated the danger to the south, and this allowed the Romans to turn their attention back to the Celtic-controlled parts of northern Italy.

The results of this effort were a peace treaty with the Cenomani tribe in 225 BCE, the conquest of Como in 196 BCE, and the establishment of a colony in Bologna in 196 BCE. These successes successfully pacified the northern part of Italy. However, this did not stop Celtic tribes from crossing over the Alps and entering the Po Valley, and because these tribes would have had no affiliation or connection to those already in Italy, they raided Roman settlements as they saw fit, creating problems for the Romans for the next decade.

Typically, the Roman army, which was much stronger and more organized than the Celts, was almost always able to drive the Celts back and retake territory, but this constant warfare drained Roman resources and made it difficult for them to focus their attention elsewhere. This is why the conquest and pacification of all of Gaul became a primary goal for the Romans in the first century BCE, especially with the rise of Julius Caesar and the founding of the Roman Empire.

The Rise of Caesar

Although Julius Caesar rose to power in southern Spain, which was rather far from the nearest Celtic tribes who were in the north of

Spain, his ascension in Roman politics is significant to the history of the Celts in that it led to their eventual conquest. Caesar was elected to the Roman consulship—the highest political position in the Roman Republic —in 59 BCE, but to do so, he needed to go into political debt with a man named Crassus, another considerably powerful Roman citizen who played a significant role in determining the public affairs of Rome. This is because Caesar had incurred a good deal of financial debt during his time as governor in Spain, and Crassus covered his debt in exchange for political support.

However, after Caesar's tenure as consul ended at the end of 59 BCE, he was granted control over Cisalpine Gaul (northern Italy), Illyricum (the modern-day nation of Croatia), and later, Transalpine Gaul (southern France). This left him with a considerable amount of power, and because he still had several legions under his command, it also meant he had the means to go out on military campaigns, something which would have provided him with the spoils needed to pay his debt.

Caesar would eventually move on the tribes throughout Gaul, which were nearly all Celtic, but this was actually not his initial intention. As mentioned, the Romans had established good relations with the different Celtic tribes in Gaul, and this had made these cultures wealthy and powerful. Instead, Caesar planned to march on the Germanic tribes to the north of Gaul, largely because they themselves had been advancing south into Gaul, a move Caesar interpreted as a threat. However, when the Celts learned of Caesar's intentions to move north, they interpreted this as a declaration of war against them, and they, too, began to prepare for battle. Caesar took this as an act of aggression, so he changed his target and began marching into Gaul to conquer the various tribes that had been occupying the territory.

All of this means that Caesar's decision to launch the Gallic Wars against the various Celtic tribes in Gaul was really the result of a series of miscommunications and misinterpretations. However, no matter the reason why, Caesar was marching north, and this would have a profound impact on Celtic culture and history.

The Gallic Wars Begin: Caesar Invades the Helvetii – 58 BCE

The Helvetii were a combination of tribes living in the territory between the Rhone and Rhine Rivers. According to Roman records, there were four different tribes that made up the Helvetii and that cooperated with one another. However, as was the case in much of the Celtic world, the Helvetii do not appear to have had any kings. Instead, they were governed by a class of elites, or nobles, all of whom were responsible for maintaining control over the population through the use of the "prestige goods" social structure.

According to Caesar's supposed census numbers, the Helvetii suggest there were some 263,000 Helvetii living on the Swiss Plateau, but modern scholars doubt this number is accurate and believe it was much lower. Nevertheless, the Helvetii were far and away the most dominant culture in the region before Julius Caesar marched his armies north in search of conquest.

Later on in life, Caesar wrote about his conquests in Gallic territory and talked about what he considered to be a massive migration of the Helvetii from the Swiss Plateau into southwestern Gaul. And while we do know that the Helvetii soon began marching out of their homeland toward Gaul, it's impossible to know if this migration was really a desire to conquer the Roman-controlled territory, if it was merely an attempt to escape the Romans as they marched north, or if it was to move away from the Germanic tribes that were beginning to move south and encroach on Helvetii territory.

But no matter the motive, we know that in 58 BCE, after the famed Helvetii leader Orgetorix died, possibly by his own hand or possibly by that of those who thought he was conspiring with other Celtic leaders to become king, the Helvetii in Switzerland began moving west into Gaul. Caesar wrote that they burned their homes before leaving so as to convince undecided members of the tribe to join them in their migration, but this has been difficult to prove with archaeological evidence.

However, the Helvetii were successful in convincing several other Celtic tribes, such as the Latobrigi, the Tulingi, the Rauraci, and the Boii, to join them on their journey. And no matter the reason for their movement, it's clear that it did happen, and it's believed these tribes were heading toward the western coast of France, the modern-day region of Saintonge. This would have meant that they would need to pass directly through the Roman-controlled Rhone valley, setting the stage for a confrontation with Caesar.

Caesar Responds

When Caesar heard of the Helvetii movements, he was south of the Alps, and he had only left one legion of soldiers in Transalpine Gaul, the region that was being threatened by the Celts' westward movements. He quickly left for Geneva to begin to prepare his defense, and in the meantime, he ordered the destruction of the Rhone bridge. The Celts attempted to negotiate for a peaceful passage over the river, but Caesar refused, and while negotiations were taking place, Caesar built a 19-mile (30.4 km) trench near the river in preparation for a battle with the migrating Helvetii.

Realizing they would not be able to pass through Transalpine Gaul because Caesar would not let them, the Helvetii began negotiating with other Celtic tribes in the area to secure free passage across Gaul to their destination on the western coast of modern-day France, which they managed to secure. This put the Helvetii on the western side of the Rhone River in the territory of the Sequani, where they began to raid the tribes calling this region home as they continued to move west.

Unable to stop the Helvetii from destroying their land, stealing their goods, and killing their people, the Roman-allied Gallic tribes asked Caesar to help them defend themselves, and Caesar agreed. He took four legions with him and attempted to ambush the Helvetii at the Arar River, a river in eastern France that is also a tributary of the

Rhone. However, when he and his armies got there, most of the Helvetii had already crossed, yet one-quarter of them remained on the eastern side of the river. The battle that ensued, the Battle of the Arar, also known as the Battle of the Saône, resulted in the total destruction of this part of the Helvetii army.

The Battle of Bibracte

What remained of the Helvetii army continued west on their journey toward their new homeland, but Caesar and his armies followed in pursuit. The Helvetii were able to win victories over the Aedui, a Celtic tribe that had allied with Caesar, but the Romans were eventually able to catch up with the Helvetii near Bibracte, the main hill fort in the Aedui territory which served as the tribe's *de facto* capital. Once there, the two sides engaged in the hotly contested Battle of Bibracte, which lasted a full day and resulted in a Roman victory.

After the battle, the future looked grim for the Helvetii, and those who had survived left everything they had behind them and continued west. Moving quickly, the Helvetii covered around sixty kilometers of territory in just four days, reaching the lands of the Lingones, another Celtic tribe located in central Gaul. But when they arrived, they were refused the support they asked for because Caesar had sent messengers ahead warning the Lingones of the potential consequences for providing support to the Helvetii. This left the Helvetii with no other choice than to surrender, which they did, although some 6,000 men fled and tried to escape. Caesar told his troops to follow and capture them, and we can assume those who were not killed were most likely sold into slavery.

Incorporating the Helvetii

Once captured, Caesar had a census conducted on the remaining Celts, and this study shows that only about thirty percent of the Helvetii and their allies that left their homes in 58 BCE survived. However, there is reason to suspect that these numbers are exaggerated, both because of Caesar's political motives (he was trying to gain more power in Rome and achieving a significant military victory against the Gauls would have done this) and also because of the way Caesar treated the Helvetii who survived, as he allowed them to return to their homeland to rebuild it and live peacefully. He also made arrangements to ensure they had all the supplies they needed to survive and prosper, and the Helvetii were also named as one of the few tribes who formed into a *foederati*, which was a tribe who was allowed to settle in Roman territory and live relatively freely in exchange for providing military support to the Romans when the need arose.

Granting this prestigious status to the Helvetii suggests that they may have been a more difficult opponent than Caesar made them out to be, but there were also strategic reasons for allowing the Helvetii to return to their homeland, mainly that they served as a nice buffer between Roman-controlled lands and the Germanic tribes to the north of the Rhine River. But no matter the motive, one thing is for sure: after Caesar's campaigns against the Helvetii, this particular Celtic tribe ceased to cause the Romans problems, and they soon became absorbed into the Roman Empire and their way of life.

The Suebi and Belgae Campaigns

After Caesar defeated the Helvetii, many of the other Celtic tribes congratulated him for restoring peace and order to the region, a prime example of how the Romans had become arbiters of intra-Gallic affairs. However, this relationship would end up serving as a justification for Caesar's desire to move against some of the Germanic tribes in the north. Remember, Caesar was campaigning at this time partly to defend Rome and secure more territory for the Roman Republic but also to earn money to pay back his debts and to build his prestige and political power back in Rome.

Caesar was able to use his good relations with the Celts when a Germanic tribe, the Suebi, began organizing an offensive against some of the Celts living in the Rhine River region. The leader of the Suebi, Ariovistus, had been declared a friend of Rome, meaning

Caesar could not attack him without significantly damaging his political capital back in Rome. But Ariovistus continued to march west into territories controlled by Celtic tribes that were loyal to Rome, and while Caesar could not set his armies in motion, he told Ariovistus that he could not cross the Rhine into Gaul and that he must treat the Gauls he conquered kindly.

Ariovistus agreed to these terms in principle, but he quickly broke them when he crossed the Rhine in 58 BCE, entering Gaul and threatening the autonomy of the Celtic tribes living there. Caesar sent his troops to Vesontio, a city located on the French-Swiss border, thinking this was Ariovistus' target. While Ariovistus was headed in this direction, it's difficult to know for sure if this was the purpose of his advance into Gaul.

When Ariovistus learned of Caesar's movements, he sent several emissaries to negotiate, and they agreed to a truce, but this truce was broken by Ariovistus when his men attacked some of Caesar's men on their own accord. However, Caesar, still trying to avoid going against the wishes of the Senate, did not want to attack Ariovistus but rather lure him into battle, which he finally managed to do through the use of skirmishes. Caesar then unleashed the full might of his army and defeated that of Ariovistus', forcing them back across the Rhine and ending the threat of Germanic invasion. This victory again helped Caesar strengthen relations with the Celtic tribes in the region for it showed that he was willing to stand up to powerful enemies and protect them even when it might not be in his best political interest to do so.

A similar story played out in the northern regions of Gaul, in modern-day Belgium, between the Belgae tribes and the Celts. The Belgae were a powerful tribe in Gaul that some believe may have been Celtic-speaking and others believe may have spoken a Germanic language. But no matter what their exact origin was, they were a warrior culture, and in 57 BCE, they attacked a Celtic tribe that had allied itself with Rome, pushing Caesar into action. However, before Caesar could attack, his armies were ambushed by the Nervii, one of the most powerful Belgae tribes at the time. But Caesar regrouped and marched on the Belgae, defeating them soundly and giving him control over the region we now refer to as Belgium.

Securing the Rest of Gaul

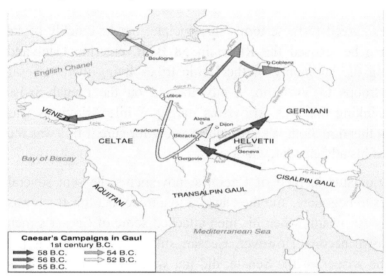

Source:
https://commons.wikimedia.org/w/index.php?curid=18316812

After defeating the Nervii and bringing the Belgae under Roman control, Caesar's ambitions changed considerably. More specifically, instead of serving as an intermediary between various Celtic and Germanic tribes, Caesar began seeking the conquest of these territories so that he could add them to the Roman Republic and expand his political prestige. For example, after his victories in Belgium in 57 BCE, Caesar moved west and subjugated the Veneti, a Celtic tribe living on the northwestern coast of France in the modern-day region of Brittany. He won swift victories, and by 56 BCE, this tribe had been incorporated into the Roman world.

Shortly thereafter, almost at the same time as he was engaging with Germanic tribes east of the Rhine, Caesar launched a series of invasions against the Britons, the Celtic tribe that lived in modern-day Britain. But bad weather and an underestimation of the size and strength of the Britons weakened the Romans and almost led to their defeat. However, Caesar was able to regroup, and he returned to Britain in 54 BCE with a much larger army, conquering the Britons and the Catuvellauni, another powerful Celtic tribe in Britain. However, he was unable to hold onto these territories for very long, largely because the Roman political institutions were not strong enough to consolidate power this far from the center. These victories did help him stay at the center of public discussions in Rome, although many saw these campaigns as costly and essentially useless.

After his campaigns in Britain in 55 and 54 BCE, Caesar had gained control over much of Gaul, but in 53 BCE, a rebellion broke out amongst the Eburones tribe in northeastern Gaul. Caesar marched his armies into the territory and all but exterminated the tribe, securing the area for the Romans. However, rebellion was not over in Gaul. To the south, the Arverni tribe, another group of Celts and one of the most powerful in all of Gaul, launched an uprising against Rome in 52 BCE. When they did this, they brought many Celtic tribes together to join their cause, turning this into a full-scale Gallic rebellion. Not wanting to lose the gains he had made over the previous years, Caesar chose to respond with force.

The Battle of Alesia

United under the king and chieftain of the Arverni tribe, Vercingetorix, the Celts who had chosen to rebel against Caesar while he was campaigning in northern Gaul and Britain were in significant danger by 52 BCE, as the rebellious Gauls were running out of places to go. Vercingetorix, in lieu of surrendering or trying to engage Caesar in battle, chose to retreat to Alesia, an important population center for the Mandubii, which was a confederation of Celtic tribes who occupied much of what is now central France.

Seeing this as an opportunity to squash the Gallic rebellion once and for all, Caesar marched his armies to Alesia and decided to besiege the city, intending to cut it off from all supplies until the Celtic armies inside died of starvation or surrendered. Estimates indicate there were around 80,000 people inside the walls of Alesia, and to cut them off, Caesar built a set of fortifications around the city ten miles (sixteen km) long. Fighting took place during construction, but the Romans were able to fight them off. However, because Vercingetorix was able to sneak some of his troops out and send them to other parts of Gaul to rally support for the defense of Alesia, Caesar had to embark on even more ambitious constructions projects.

For example, he built trenches some 2,000 ft (500 m) behind the Roman lines and also constructed parapets and fences to make it easier for his soldiers to defend themselves against an attack from the city or from behind.

However, while Caesar's military fortifications were elaborate and effective, what really helped him win this battle was Alesia's dwindling food supply and his ruthless treatment of the rebels. For example, facing a rapidly dwindling food supply, Vercingetorix sent the city's women and children out of the city, hoping Caesar would take them as hostages and feed them, but he refused, so the Gauls had no choice but to try and attack.

When the armies from elsewhere in Gaul arrived, Vercingetorix ordered a dual attack in which those inside the city attacked the inner parts of the Roman line and those outside attacked the back end. However, this was unsuccessful. After several more days of similar attempts, Vercingetorix and his other commanders realized they would not be able to defeat the Romans, and so, they chose to surrender, ending the Gallic rebellion and placing all of Gaul firmly under Roman control. This battle was the last time the Gauls were ever able to seriously resist Roman rule, and it marked the effective end of the Gallic Wars. Caesar was honored by the Roman Senate for his victory, and Gaul was made a province of Rome.

Over time, the people living in Gaul, especially the Celts, became incorporated into the Roman Empire and adopted the Roman way of life, eventually achieving the status of citizen. However, during the early years of Romanization, some aspects of Celtic culture still remained, mainly their language. But over time, Roman influence became so strong that Continental Celtic disappeared and was replaced by Vulgar Latin.

Conclusion

Caesar's Gallic Wars were significant in that they officially made Gaul a Roman territory. Furthermore, his victory won him considerable prestige in Rome, and he used this power to start the civil war that eventually resulted in him being named the supreme military dictator of Rome. When this happened in 45 BCE, it paved the way for the Roman Empire to be formed. Gaul was divided into several provinces and ruled according to Roman custom. The formation of the empire after the conquest of Gaul launched a new era in Roman history and changed the course of human history forever.

However, when looking at this moment in history from the perspective of the Celts, it's difficult to say what the impact was. Some argue that being conquered by the Romans and being incorporated into the Roman Empire was a good thing. It brought stability to the region, bringing an end to the constant infighting that defined much of Celtic history up until this point in time. But, on the other hand, it halted a period of growth in Celtic history. Who knows what would have become of Celtic culture had it been given the chance to develop further after the Celtic Migration.

Another important thing to come out of the Gallic Wars is that the center of Celtic culture shifted from continental to insular Europe. Caesar managed to briefly conquer some of the tribes in Britain, but these gains did not last, and many of these tribes remained free and independent. And with the rest of the territories controlled by the continental Celts incorporated in the Roman Empire, the British Isles became the center of Celtic cultural and linguistic development, and the remnants of Celtic culture that still exist today come from these Celts who managed to stay relatively free from Roman control.

Chapter 6 – The Insular Celts

Archaeological evidence suggests the Celts began settling the area now known as Britain during the first millennium BCE, making this movement part of the overall Celtic Migration from the Hallstatt zone. However, it remains unclear whether or not this cultural transformation was the result of an invasion of Celtic culture similar to what we saw in Central Europe or if it was more gradual.

Today, the leading theories suggest that Celtic peoples made it across the English Channel sometime around 500 BCE and began mixing with the local populations, creating a unique ethnic identity. However, regardless of how this happened, we know that by the first century BCE, Celtic was the dominant language on the island, and while the rest of the Celtic world was being absorbed into Roman culture, the Celts in Britain managed to maintain a strong cultural identity that has helped keep Celtic culture alive until this day.

However, much like their cultural counterparts in Gaul, the Insular Celts would eventually become a part of the Roman Empire, which helped reduce Celtic cultural influence in the region. But unlike in Gaul, the Celts in Britain resisted complete conquest, helping keep the culture alive. Yet after the Roman Empire fell, the island was eventually invaded by the Anglo-Saxons, a Germanic tribe, and when this happened, the Celts were relegated to the outskirts of society, pushing Celtic culture even deeper into our collective cultural identity.

Initial Contact with the Romans

As mentioned, the Insular Celtic culture developed gradually over the course of the first millennium BCE. Similar to what happened in Gaul, the Insular Celts managed to establish peaceful trade relations with the Romans. Their main natural resource, tin, had been a commodity desired by ancient civilizations, such as the Greeks, Phoenicians, and Carthaginians, since the middle of the first millennium BCE, and as Rome grew more powerful, it, too, established economic ties that helped create further prosperity in pre-Roman Britain.

However, unlike in Gaul where the Romans frequently interfered with political conflicts to maintain peace and keep the Celtic culture intact as a way of building a buffer between Rome and the Germanic tribes, the Romans had little influence on the tribal relations of Britain. Yet they did have ambitions of bringing Britain more firmly under their control, and this would be a primary concern of the Romans during the first 100 years of the empire.

The first person to try to conquer Rome was, as mentioned, Julius Caesar. He crossed the English Channel in 55 BCE, but bad weather made him turn around. However, when he returned to the island in 54 BCE, he successfully conquered large portions of southern Britain for the Roman Republic, and he was able to establish a Roman-friendly king, Mandubracius, as the leader of the Trinovantes, helping to sway the balance of power in Britain toward the Romans. With the support of Rome, the Trinovantes were able to collect tribute from many of the other Celtic tribes in the region. However, when Caesar left, most historians agree that these tribute payments stopped, which was a sign that Roman influence in the region was not as strong as Caesar and the Romans thought it was when they first established settlements in the region.

For the next 100 years, the Romans did not make another attempt at conquering Britain. Instead, they seemed content to allow and support a balance of power between the island's two most powerful tribes, the Trinovantes and the Catuvellauni, both Celtic. This seemed to be the best way to maintain peace in the region and maintain stable trade relations between the people of the Roman Empire.

However, after the civil war led to the fall of the Roman Republic in 27 BCE and the beginning of the Roman Empire, the Romans began consolidating their power in conquered lands, establishing provinces and exporting their language and cultural norms. In the early years of the Roman Empire, sometime in the 40s CE, this balance of power began to break down. The Catuvellauni had managed to win several victories over the Trinovantes, and they showed ambitions of spreading their power in Britain. Specifically, they began to threaten the Atrebates, a Belgic tribe that had an alliance with the Romans dating back to the times of Julius Caesar. This change in the political situation in Britain inspired the Roman emperor, Caligula, to gather a force and launch an invasion of Britain.

Rome Invades Britain

In 40 CE, Caligula was the first Roman since Caesar to try and invade Britain, but for reasons unknown due to a lack of written sources, Caligula failed to make it across the English Channel and carry out his invasion. However, when he realized he would not be able to invade, he instructed his troops to build huts along the Gallic coast, making things easier for the next emperor, Claudius, to launch a full-scale attack on the Celtic tribes living in Britain.

Claudius appointed Aulus Plautius, an esteemed Roman politician and general, to lead the invasion, and he put together an army of about 40,000 troops. The focus of the invasion was southeastern Britain as this was the richest and most economically important part of the island.

As the Romans prepared and launched their invasion, the various British tribes (all Celtic in some form or another) began to come together to fight as one and protect their homeland. Their leaders were Togodumnus, the king of the Catuvellauni tribe, and his brother, Caratacus. However, before the fighting began, the Dobunni tribe, which was not Celtic but which had been paying tribute to the Catuvellauni, surrendered to the Romans, weakening the ability of the Catuvellauni to summon people to join their army and fight against Rome.

Unfortunately, due to conflicting information in the sources available to us, we cannot say for certain where the Romans departed for their invasion nor where they landed, and there is much debate amongst historians about this topic. But what we do know is that the first confrontation between the Romans and British Celts took place at the River Medway, which is near the modern-day city of Rochester, and the subsequent battle, the Battle of the Medway, marks the official beginning of the Roman conquest of Britain.

The Battle of the Medway

At the time of the Roman invasion of Britain, the Roman legionaries were, by far, the most powerful military unit in Western Europe. However, by putting the Medway River between them and the Romans, the Celts thought they had enough of a defensive advantage to keep the Romans at bay and protect their homeland. However, they were wrong. The Romans, using specially trained soldiers, swam across the river and began attacking the Celtic force on the other side. Then, while the main Celtic force was occupied, the rest of the Roman army swam across and engaged with the rest of the Celtic warriors in the area.

The historical records we have indicate the battle lasted for two days, suggesting the Celts managed to put up considerable resistance to the Roman army, but they were eventually overrun, and the various Celts fighting against the Romans were forced to retreat back to the

Thames River, where they would have a similar but perhaps better defensive advantage given the size and depth of the Thames.

Unfortunately, we do not know much about how the Battle of the Thames was fought, but we do know that it was a Roman victory and that the British Celtic leader, Togodumnus, was killed, leaving the door open for the Romans to march into the Catuvellauni capital, Camulodunum (modern-day Colchester), with little resistance. Once there, the Romans established a colony, and they made treaties with many of the surrounding tribes, eleven to be exact, helping to entrench Roman control in southeastern Britain. These victories also made Britain an official province of the Roman Empire known as Britannia, which is where the modern name for the island originated. But the Celts on the island were not finished fighting and would continue to do so for many years.

Caratacus Continues the Resistance

After the initial victories of Claudius and Aulus Plautius, Celtic autonomy in Britain was officially threatened, but there were still many tribes living throughout the island that had no intention of submitting to Roman rule. Between the years 44 to 50, the Romans slowly pushed their way west and south, toward modern-day Wales, and in 47, the Romans invaded Wales. Caratacus, the brother of Togodumnus, had fled to the western part of the island, near modern-day Wales, and had managed to gather supporters to stand in resistance to the Romans, but he was ultimately unsuccessful and was killed at the Battle of Caer Caradoc in 50 CE, giving the Romans control over most of southern Britain.

However, during this time, several Celtic tribes throughout Britain began to rebel against Roman rule, something that would happen with considerable frequency during the early years of Roman Britain. This led the Romans to embark on a campaign of disarming all the Celtic tribes in Britain, as they felt this was the only way to ensure their rule would be respected and to achieve peace and stability in the region. However, it would be many years before the

Romans would be able to fully subjugate the Celts in Britain, and some tribes would prove to be unconquerable.

The Romans also undertook a policy of trying to destroy the pillars of Celtic society. Specifically, they sought to destroy Druidism. The Druids were elite members of Celtic society who were religious leaders as well as important members of the ruling class. The Romans, whenever they invaded an important city in Celtic Britain, would often destroy important Druid centers, such as temples or courts, as a way of establishing their supremacy and discouraging the Celts from rebelling against Roman rule. However, even this did not have the effect it was immediately intended to have, and the British Celts proved to continue to be difficult to rule.

The Battle of Watling Street

One of the best-known examples of Celtic resistance to Roman rule came in 60 CE from the Iceni tribe, a group of Celts who occupied the territory located to the northeast of modern-day London. Led by their queen, Boudica, the Iceni launched an uprising against the Romans while the Roman governor at the time, Gaius Suetonius Paulinus, was waging war in the western part of Britain. Specifically, they were attempting to conquer the modern-day island of Anglesey, which at the time was a stronghold for the Druids.

Recognizing that the Roman army was far away and therefore distracted, Boudica gathered supporters not only from her own tribe but also from the Trinovantes, one of the more powerful tribes on the island in pre-Roman Britain. Together they marched on Camulodunum, the colony established by Claudius that had been serving as the center of Roman rule in Britain since the early years of the invasion. This force managed to enter the colony and sack it, putting Roman rule in Britain at significant risk. Boudica then led her force out of Camulodunum and then continued west to take back territory controlled by the Romans.

Gaius Suetonius Paulinus heard of the uprising and immediately abandoned his campaign on Anglesey to return to eastern Britain and quell the rebellion. He set out on Watling Street, a road or a series of roads that connected southeastern Britain to the northern part of Wales that had been used by the Celts for centuries and that the Romans paved to facilitate trade. He made it all the way to Londinium, a relatively new city that had been founded in 43 and was the first site of the modern-day city of London. However, by this point, the city was in the hands of the rebels, so he departed, and Boudica and her forces burnt it to the ground. The rebels continued fighting, and as they did, they gained more and more supporters. Contemporary estimates suggest there were some 300,000 men fighting alongside Boudica, but it's likely this number is an exaggeration.

However, when Gaius Suetonius Paulinus finally gathered his army and managed to confront Boudica, he was greatly outnumbered. Nevertheless, he managed to defeat Boudica at what is now known as the Battle of Watling Street, for it is believed to have taken place along this important road in southern Britain that was first laid out by the ancient British before it was paved by the Romans. However, historians have been unable to determine the exact location of this battle.

At this point, the emperor of Rome at the time, Nero, considered withdrawing Roman forces from Britain and abandoning attempts to control it out of fear that it would require too much time and energy to control. However, he ultimately chose not to do this, and the uprising launched by Boudica proved to be the most effective example of Celtic resistance to Roman rule in Britain. However, the Celts would not stop fighting the Romans as they worked their way north to try and subjugate the entire island.

Northern Celts Resist the Roman Advance

With Boudica defeated, the Romans, just a little less than twenty years after Claudius landed on Britain, had managed to secure most of the southern part of the island. Below is a map of the various

Roman movements in Britain during these seventeen years to show the extent of Celtic subjugation in Britain:

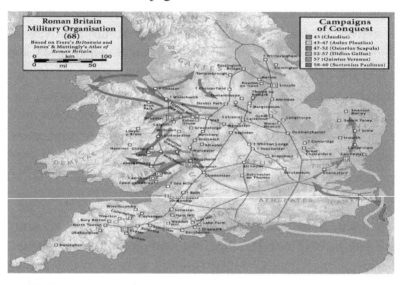

Source:
https://commons.wikimedia.org/w/index.php?curid=11357177

However, as was the case with nearly every ancient civilization, the Romans were not about to stop their advance. They continued to move north throughout the 60s and 70s CE, and, under the command of Agricola, conquered the Ordovices, a Celtic tribe located in northern Wales, in 78. Over the next six years, Agricola would continue to advance north into Scotland, reaching the Caledonians and defeating them in 84. However, the Romans would not be able to advance any farther into Scotland, and turmoil in Rome forced Agricola to return to the capital. During the years that followed this victory, not much is known, except that the Celtic tribes, as well as related groups such as the Picts, managed to win territory back from the Romans, pushing them farther and farther south.

To keep insubordinate tribes at bay, various walls were constructed at different moments in history, the most famous being Hadrian's Wall, with construction beginning in 122 and the wall being completed in 128 CE. However, there is evidence of defensive fortifications in northern Britain dating back to 70 BCE, and Antonine's Wall, which was finished in 154 CE, briefly extended the borders of the Roman Empire farther into northern Britain, deep into the territory we now know as Scotland. It's believed that this proved too difficult to hold, and Hadrian's Wall became the *de facto* border between Roman Britain and the territory controlled by unconquered tribes, many of whom were Celtic.

The Anglo-Saxon Invasion

That the Celtic tribes in Britain put up such resistance to Roman rule is important because it allowed for Celtic culture to remain even as Romanization sped up in the rest of Britain. Some Celtic tribes, particularly those in northern Scotland, remained autonomous throughout the Roman era, and those who did become part of the empire managed to maintain a strong identity. For example, unlike in Gaul where Vulgar Latin went on to completely replace Celtic, the Britons in Roman Britain continued to speak their version of Celtic, and the tribes who lived outside of Roman influence also maintained their Celtic identity, although there was considerable mixing with some of the non-Celtic tribes in the region, most notably the Picts.

The Britons remained prominent in Roman Britain until approximately the fifth century when the Romans were no longer able to maintain control over Britain, which was one of its most remote provinces. During this period, the Anglo-Saxons, a Germanic-speaking people, began moving into Britain, establishing their own social order and intermarrying with the locals. Ethnic Britons who resisted this change were pushed to the west, settling on the western coast of Wales and also crossing the Irish Sea to settle Ireland. Other Britons crossed the English Channel and settled in Armorica, the region of France we now call Brittany.

Over time, Anglo-Saxon became the dominant ethnicity on the island, and the Celts who had called Britain home since the first millennium BCE were forced to find a home elsewhere. However, somewhat astonishingly, these Celts were able to maintain their cultural identity despite being so dramatically outnumbered. To demonstrate just how resilient they were, one only needs to look at where Celtic languages are still spoken today: western Britain (Wales), Ireland, and the Brittany region of France.

Conclusion

As was the case in Gaul, the Roman invasion of Britain played a significant role in the reduction of Celtic influence in Europe. However, while both Gallic Celts and British Celts fought hard against Rome's attempt to conquer them, the British Celts, perhaps because they were on an island and perhaps because they did not have to deal with additional enemies like the Gauls did (specifically the Germanic tribes), were able to maintain some degree of cultural identity throughout the roughly 400 years of Roman rule. Furthermore, even though they were eventually pushed off their land by the Anglo-Saxons, the resilience of the British Celts is one of if not the reason why Celtic culture and language still exists in the modern day.

Chapter 7 – Celtic Warriors

The Celts enter our collective history with the Greeks and the Romans who spoke of the Celts as "barbarians," or fierce warriors, who dominated the territory in Northern Europe that the Greeks and Romans had barely been able to explore in the early years of their history. However, the term "barbarian" in today's language implies that the Celts were wild, unorganized fighters who, despite their strength, may not have been capable of posing a significant threat to a large, well-trained army. But this was simply not the case. The Romans lived in perpetual fear that the Celts who lived on the Iberian Peninsula or who roamed throughout Gaul could and would march into Rome and wipe them off the face of the earth, something that almost happened in 390 BCE.

This fear the Greeks and the Romans propagated has helped exaggerate the image we have of Celtic warriors today. It's true they were effective on the battlefield, but many modern conceptions of Celtic warfare are the product of fantasy video games and embellished literature. These images show Celts wearing armor or behaving in a way that is simply not supported by the evidence available to us in the modern day. Of course, anything is possible, but it's important to reconstruct the Celtic warrior using what we know, not what we wish was true.

One thing we do know, however, was that war was an integral part of Celtic society, and this meant the Celtic warrior was held in high regard. Status and prestige were closely associated with one's ability to fight in war, and nobles won and earned loyal subjects based on their ability to raid and conquer surrounding territories. But because of the rich diversity that existed amongst the various Celtic cultures spread out across Europe, the Celts developed many different ways of fighting. However, due to their cultural similarities, we can find some parallels across different Celtic cultures when it comes to the ways in which they waged war.

War in Celtic Society

As mentioned, there was no uniform political structure in ancient Celtic culture. Instead, loyalty was given to a chieftain or noble in exchange for security. But to get this security, one needed to be ready and willing to offer labor and other goods in exchange, a system not too different from feudalism. However, in this system, the nobles were dependent on these laborers for production, so they needed to do something to prove they were deserving of that loyalty, and the easiest way to do this was to be successful when raiding nearby tribes, even if those tribes were also Celtic.

Warfare and raiding were also some of the principal ways of acquiring wealth in ancient Celtic society. Raids would allow a chieftain or warlord to not only acquire the resources of a nearby tribe which he could trade to other cultures in exchange for goods, but it also allowed him to gather people together to be sold into slavery in Greece and Rome, a lucrative business that became an important part of Celtic culture.

However, beyond the importance of war amongst the Celtic nobility, it was also significant to the "free men," the class of people who were situated just below the elite classes in Celtic society. Success in battle was a chance for an average Celtic man to prove his worth in society, and because of this, it was often easy for a noble to gather men to fight in a raid against a nearby tribe. Furthermore, Celtic men often lent their services as mercenaries, as this gave them an opportunity to show off their skills as a warrior and earn status in Celtic society. The most famous example of this comes from the Second Punic War. The leader of Carthage at the time, Hannibal, hired thousands of Celts to help him invade Italy and defeat Rome. And while this proved to be unsuccessful, this experience instilled in the Romans a fear toward the Celts that lasted all the way until the Romans managed to conquer both Gaul and Britain. The Roman historian Polybius wrote about how the Romans saw their Celtic enemies, saying they were

terrified by the fine order of the Celtic host, and the dreadful din, for there were innumerable horn-blowers and trumpeters, and…the whole army were shouting their war-cries…Very terrifying too were the appearance and the gestures of the naked warriors in front, all in the prime of life and finely built men, and all in the leading companies richly adorned with gold torcs and armlets.

It's believed the Celtic tradition of trying to scare their opponents by blowing horns, shouting, taunting, and making lots of noise was closely linked to the Celtic understanding that war was a chance for someone to prove their worth to society. The idea was that being more fearsome earned one more respect within society but only if one could support this posturing with good fighting skills. However, this quote mentions Celtic warriors fighting naked as a way of trying to intimidate their opponents, and while this may have happened from time to time or within a certain tribe or mercenary group, it's difficult to say if this was a typical Celtic custom.

Training for War

Because of the lack of formal political and social institutions in Celtic society, there were no formal methods of training soldiers for war. Instead, a young man who wanted to advance his fighting skills to be able to one day join in a raid or an invasion had to find other ways of training so that he could live up to the reputation Celtic soldiers had throughout most of the ancient period.

Some of these activities included hunting, cattle rustling, slave raiding, and engaging in smaller skirmishes with local tribes that were led by nobles who were feuding amongst themselves. These fights were considered to be less aggressive than all-out wars against the Romans or another powerful Celtic tribe, but they gave a young Celtic warrior the opportunity to practice his weapon-handling skills and also mentally prepare for a life at war.

Another way to train was to join a mercenary group. These bands of soldiers often formed close unions, and they had systems in place to train younger soldiers to be able to fight with the same intensity as the group. However, entry into these elite mercenary groups was restricted to only the most skilled warriors, meaning a fighter would need to spend considerable time honing his skills elsewhere before he could hope to be granted a place among the ranks of the mercenaries.

This lack of political structure, combined with the connection between one's self-worth and fighting, meant that Celtic warriors often entered the battlefield primarily for themselves. There is little evidence of a Celtic warrior feeling exceptional loyalty toward a king, although there are examples of Celtic warlords gaining considerable popularity while leading raids against invaders. One of the best examples of this is the uprising led by Boudica in Britain during the first century CE.

Celtic Weapons

Because Celtic culture was spread out across such a wide territory, Celtic warriors used many different weapons. Different Celtic tribes fashioned different weapons, and these often became models for the Romans as their military grew and eventually became the most dominant throughout all of Europe.

The most common types of weapons used by the Celts included spears, two-handed hammers, axes, and, as ironworking became more prominent in Celtic culture, swords. The quality of the swords ranged considerably, with most archaeological evidence suggesting that the common folk had small, thin iron swords. Some sources written by those living at the time report of swords that would bend or break when they first came into contact with another hard object, such as another sword or a shield.

But there are plenty of examples of Celtic tribes carrying well-crafted, high-quality swords, especially in Britain, although there is some speculation these may have been used for rituals rather than fighting. These swords have infiltrated public perception to give the Celts a reputation for wielding high-quality swords when they went into battle, but this was most likely not the case. Instead, most Celtic warriors probably carried a small sword or a dagger and spear.

On the Iberian Peninsula, however, the Celtiberian tribes who fought against the Roman soldiers carried a rather effective double-edged sword that was said to be good for stabbing, and many believe this became the model for the types of swords the Roman legions used throughout Rome's rise to power.

Other weapons the Celts used include long-range fighting tools such as javelins, harpoons, bows, and slings. These weapons would have been used to launch projectiles into oncoming troops so as to inflict damage before the hand-to-hand combat began. There is evidence that some Celtic tribes, especially those located throughout the Alps, put poison on the weapons they would launch into enemy ranks so as to increase their effectiveness, and some tribes may have had an early version of the crossbow. But neither of these cases represent the norm across the various Celtic tribes in Europe.

Although not a weapon, Celtic soldiers also often carried some form of an instrument, such as a horn, to use when entering battle. A great example of this is the *carnyx* (below), which was a bronze trumpet believed to have been used by the Celts who roamed Europe from c. 300 BCE to 200 CE. It was common for Celts to blow this horn repeatedly as they prepared to charge, and it's believed this was another way for a warrior to demonstrate his strength and power while also striking fear into the hearts of enemies.

In terms of armor, the Celts are considered to have been the first people in Europe to wear iron chainmail, although this would not have been standard issue for the average Celtic warrior. Instead, this type of protection was reserved for the nobility or anyone who had the means to craft such armor. The same was the case with iron chest plates; they existed in the Celtic military, but they were hardly the norm. Instead, it was much more common for the average Celtic warrior to wear leather armor or no armor at all. Bronze armor was available, but again, being able to wear it in battle depended considerably on one's means. Some other examples of more elaborate types of armor are often attributed to the Celts, but this is likely more an exaggeration of reality so as to enhance the already glorified image we have of Celtic warriors. Instead, the reality is that while the average Celtic warrior was probably very well trained and capable, he was likely poorly equipped due to the inequality that existed within Celtic society at the time.

However, one interesting thing that we can learn about Celtic warriors from classical texts, and that has been affirmed to one degree or another from archaeological research, is that many Celtic warriors used to wear bright, colorful clothing into battle, presumably as a way of intimidating their enemy or perhaps as a way of demonstrating to their fellow warriors their merit as a soldier. But again, it's hard to know if this was something practiced by all Celtic soldiers or if it was a tradition reserved for those with the means to acquire what would have probably been valuable ancient commodities.

Modern images of Celtic warriors almost always include helmets, and some have gone so far as to say that the Romans copied the Celts when designing and building helmets for their legionaries, but it's difficult to say if this is true or not. It's equally as likely that the Celts copied the Romans after their first contact with them. Another common image of the Celtic warrior is with the horned helmet. Again, this may have existed; there is evidence of horned helmets dating all the way back to the British Iron Age (c. 800–100 CE). However, we do know that the early Celts usually fought without helmets, and it wasn't until the closing century of the Celtic Migration (200s BCE) that helmets started becoming more common atop Celtic heads. These were still relatively rare, though, suggesting that owning this piece of armor was dependent on one's wealth and status.

Organization of the Celtic Armies

Because there are no texts written by the Celts themselves, we cannot know for sure how their armies were organized. However, it is clear that they did not have an organized military as we understand it today, or as the Greeks or Romans understood it. Instead, Celtic armies were organized around warlords or chieftains. At times, various warlords would band together to fight against a common enemy, but these collaborations were usually brief. The Celts did not need to worry about requiring men from conquered territories to join the army because fighting was expected. Those who resisted fighting were often killed, sold to the Greeks or Romans as slaves, or banished from society.

However, there were various types of Celtic soldiers, and when they fought together, they were often organized into different groups. For example, some Celtic soldiers fought on horseback, and others used chariots, although by the 3rd century BCE, most Celtic tribes in Europe, with the exception of the Britons, had abandoned chariots in favor of cavalry, helping them be more effective when fighting their enemies. When combined with regular infantry, these mounted warriors would be used as we would expect a cavalry to be used: to scout, skirmish, and charge.

Typically, the Celts fought on land, but there is some evidence to suggest that the Veneti tribe which occupied the northern coast of France, near the modern-day region of Brittany, had a strong seafaring tradition. They were conquered by Caesar in 56 BCE, but his commentaries on the conflict suggest these Celts were a formidable opponent both at land and sea. However, because no Celtic ships have been found and because of the lack of written Celtic sources, little is known about naval traditions elsewhere in the Celtic world.

Conclusion

As we can see, the image we have today of Celtic warriors is not a particularly good reflection of what these warriors were actually like. It's possible some of the myths that exist today are grounded in truth, but the vast majority are just that, myths. However, that these images of fierce, well-armed, and well-armored warriors might not be completely true, we should not take this as proof that the Celts were nothing more than "barbarians" who could fight.

Instead, we should consider the facts. It's likely true that your average Celtic warrior was at least four inches taller than the average Roman or Greek soldier, and there is some evidence to suggest that warriors used to dye their hair bright white using lime, which would have made them look terrifying. Plus, due to their long tradition of hunting, raiding, and waging war, the average Celtic warrior was skilled and brave, and this would have made him a challenging opponent.

Of course, in the end, the Celts proved to be no match for the armies of Rome, but this is probably more due to their lack of organization, both politically and militarily, than it is to their fighting ability. But even without those critical components of a successful military, the Celts still wreaked havoc on the Romans' attempts to control Central, Western, and Northern Europe for the better part of 700 years, and despite the repeated Roman attempts to wipe them off the face of the earth, they remained, and their culture still exists to this day.

Chapter 8 – Celtic Way of Life

Modern depictions of the Celts usually reflect the stories told about them by the Greeks and Romans, meaning they focus on the Celtic obsession with warfare. And since the Celts were nothing more than mysterious and savage barbarians who did nothing but raid their people and cause them trouble to the Greeks and Romans, it's easy to see why this image of the Celts emerged.

However, as is often the case, these depictions are biased and incomplete. It's true that war was an important part of ancient Celtic society, but it was not the only thing that was given significance. No culture could exist for as long as the Celts did if all it did was fight wars. Instead, the Celts who did not go on raids built up a large and thriving civilization that made it possible for them to not only spread throughout all of Europe but also to make a marked impact on surrounding cultures.

Unfortunately, though, because the Celts did not write anything down, we have little written evidence of how they lived. But the plethora of archaeological artifacts they left behind, combined with a careful analysis of the texts left by the Greeks and the Romans, allow us to reconstruct, at least partly, what life might have been like for your average Celt living in ancient times.

Celtic Daily Life

For the most part, the ancient Celts were farmers. They planted fields in square plots, and they stored food in clay pots which they often buried underground. There is also evidence of them raising livestock, mainly pigs and sheep. It's likely the vast majority of the people living in ancient Celtic societies would have spent most of their time working in agriculture, but these would have also been the same people who would join the local chieftain to fight when they were required to do so.

Those who were not farmers but who were not a part of the upper warrior class were skilled craftsman of some sort. Professions included jewelers, blacksmiths, metalworkers, and cobblers. There existed a small intellectual class that was made up of priests, poets, and jurists, which is where the famous Druids would have fallen, but it's likely these individuals represented just a small part of the Celtic social structure. It's likely there was some sort of a merchant class in ancient Celtic society due to the extensive trade networks they established with cultures both near and far, but little is known of these people and how they fit into the rest of Celtic society.

The Celtic people wore long robes or tunics that were made of wool or linen, but there is evidence that the wealthier members of society may have had access to silk, which came from China, an indication of the existence of extensive trade networks. Longer, heavier cloaks made of wool were most likely the garment of choice during colder periods of the year.

There is some evidence to suggest that women held a slightly higher status than they did in other parts of the ancient world, such as in Greece or Rome. For example, some burial evidence suggests that women may have been allowed to fight alongside men in battle, a sign that they were considered equal, but there are not enough of these examples to make any sort of conclusive generalizations about the role of women in Celtic society. However, stories such as that of Boudica in Britain provide us with some examples where women took up leadership roles.

In the early years of Christian Ireland, women had the right to divorce their husbands for no cause, and some historians believe this may have been a vestige of pre-Roman Celtic cultures, although without written records, it's impossible to ever know if this was a common feature of Celtic society or if it was an isolated example. There exists practically no evidence of how families were organized in the ancient Celtic world, which means we are left completely in the dark about this aspect of Celtic society.

However, we do know that the Celtic people were deeply religious and that religious practice probably played an important part in daily life. The Celts most likely practiced in temples and perhaps also in their own homes, but it's difficult to know for sure which was more common. Human sacrifice and ceremonies played an important part in Celtic religious life, and it's believed these rites were carried out by the priestly class, known as the Druids in some parts of the Celtic world.

Celtic Social Structure

Celtic social organization has its roots in the warrior cultures of the Hallstatt and La Tène periods. Warlords and chieftains were at the top, and they maintained their power by providing protection to farmers and other laborers who would also be required to fight for them when the time came. One's status as a warlord or chieftain was determined by two things: wealth and military success. The more luxury goods one had, the more highly regarded one was in society, and the more successful raids one conducted, the more followers one could have. Raids were also a way to acquire more wealth, which is why they formed such an important part of Celtic society.

Below the warlords and chieftains was the intellectual class. This group was made up primarily of priests, but it also included artisans, specifically poets, and legal professionals. Sadly, there is no evidence as to what the Celtic legal system was like, so it's difficult to know exactly what role these legal professionals played in society.

Priests presumably maintained no affiliation to one warlord over another, choosing instead to travel and share their wisdom with different settlements. Some of these groups developed considerable prestige in society, the most classic example being the Druids of Britain, and they may have even been considered as important as the warlords themselves. But again, without written records from the Celts themselves, it's essentially impossible to confirm or deny if this was true. All we have to go on is archaeological evidence and the words written by the Romans, who were almost certainly telling just part of the story.

Below the priestly class came everyone else, the farmers and the laborers. These individuals had to promise their allegiance to a local warlord, and he (or she) would provide them with security as well as the needed means to work the land and survive. In return, they would be expected to fight for their warlord when he (or she) decided to raid or go to war with a neighboring tribe. However, allegiances were likely not strong. If the chieftain lost his or her raid or if another more powerful one came along, these individuals could switch their loyalty and begin fighting for another noble.

There is also evidence that slavery existed in ancient Celtic culture, although it's difficult to know to what extent it impacted the overall social structure. We know that the slave trade was one of the primary reasons for initial contact between the Celts and the Greeks/Romans and that collecting slaves to be shipped to the south was often one of the primary reasons for raiding. It's believed that Celtic slaves were offered opportunities to earn their own freedom, but little is known about how they were treated or how they lived.

Celtic Government

As far as we know, no form of centralized government existed in the Celtic world that connected the many different tribes scattered across Europe. Language and some shared cultural norms were the only things connecting the tribes. However, there are examples of Celtic tribes cooperating with one another to form alliances and provide for the common defense. But we don't know much about these alliances, except that they were loose and often broken. During Roman times, the Romans often served as a mediator of tribal conflicts. Yet there is some evidence that the tribes who lived closer to Rome adopted some form of a centralized government, although it's more likely this was part of the process of Romanization instead of an example of Celtic centralization.

Within tribes, there does appear to be some more centralization that extended beyond the simple chieftain-client arrangement that emerged during the early years of Celtic culture, especially throughout Gaul. Throughout these lands, the Celts established *oppida* (*oppidum*, sing.), which is a Latin term that means "main settlement." An *oppidum* was essentially a large fort, and it served as the central base for one tribe or another. It was where various tribal leaders would meet to discuss the affairs of the tribe and determine matters concerning war. However, we should be wary of calling these cities as they were far from such.

When the Romans conquered Gaul, they often focused their attacks on *oppida* since taking these settlements made it much harder for opposing Celtic tribes to come together as one and resist the Romans. Examples of *oppida* can be found across all of Europe, ranging from Gaul (France) to Germany and Hungary. There are also examples of *oppida* in Britain, but they tend to be smaller and more numerous, suggesting centralization was less intense in these areas. Some of these settlements became the basis for medieval cities, but many of them were destroyed or abandoned during and after the Roman conquest of the Celts in Europe.

Conclusion

For students of history, it's a shame we don't know more about the way in which the Celts lived. They have had such an impact on the development of European culture that knowing more about their lives would help us uncover more information about why the world is the way it is today. But in spite of the lack of written sources coming from the Celts themselves, we are still able to learn a good deal about their culture, and the evidence we do have provides depth to our understanding of these ancient peoples. We no longer consider them to be just savage warriors. Instead, we can now see that there was much more to the ancient Celts, and as we continue to study them and learn new things, we are sure to unlock more secrets about a culture to which many Europeans owe their ancestry.

Chapter 9 - Celtic Religion

One of the most celebrated aspects of Celtic culture today is its religion. There appear to have been a countless number of gods to whom the ancient Celts paid homage, and some of them managed to stay firmly entrenched in the Celtic way of life despite the influence of Roman culture and later Christianity. However, as is the case with most of what we know about Celtic culture, their religion is shrouded in mystery.

The main reason for this is that the Celts did not write anything down, most likely because they were illiterate. Because of this, we have no primary sources that can confirm or deny the stories we now tell about the Celtic gods. Instead, we need to rely on what was left to us by the Romans, which is obviously biased toward a Roman perspective, as well as the stories told by the Irish. This is because Irish mythology draws heavily on its Celtic heritage, and while this helps produce a more coherent picture of some of the basic tenets of Celtic religion, it would not be wise for us to take this as an active representation of the religious beliefs practiced throughout the entire Celtic world.

Nevertheless, by piecing together the sources we do have, we can put together an image of Celtic religion that helps us understand at least a little bit more about what these ancient peoples believed and how they saw the world, though we must accept that whatever we come up with is and always will be incomplete.

Aspects of Celtic Religion

We know that the ancient Celts practiced polytheistic paganism. This means that they worshiped many different gods, and they believed these gods were somehow connected or related to one another. This type of religious belief was common in the ancient world, although by the time the Romans rose to power, this was about to change as Christianity would soon become the dominant religion around most of Europe.

We also know that the Celts practiced their religion in temples and other religious buildings, as well as in natural areas they considered to be sacred, such as groves. The former we know due to archaeological evidence, whereas the latter idea comes from the Roman texts; these ancient groves, for obvious reasons, do not exist today. For some time, historians believed the famous monument of Stonehenge was a place of worship for the ancient Celts, but carbon dating shows that the stones were first placed in their current location some 1,000 years before the Celts occupied Britain, meaning this theory cannot be true and that Stonehenge is not connected to Celtic religion.

Religious practices, according to the Romans, were carried out by a priestly class that we now refer to as the Druids. These individuals are thought to be the only members of ancient Celtic society that were educated in any way, and they were responsible for directing the ancient Celts in their religion. In addition, there are many stories of Druids traveling with Celtic armies to provide spiritual guidance to the warriors and to ward off bad spirits. This ancient Druid class has become the center of much lore, but in reality, due to the fact that the Celts wrote nothing down, we know very little about who these people were and what they did.

Furthermore, we can be fairly confident that the Celts practiced some form of human sacrifice, a rite that would have been carried out by the Druids. According to the records left by the Romans, this was a frequent practice. Another rather gruesome aspect of Celtic religion was the practice of "head hunting." It is thought that the ancient Celts considered the head to be the most important part of the human body and that it was the part that carried the soul. Evidence has been found of sole skulls inside Celtic shelters, which has given rise to the theory that owning the skull of someone important was a way to ensure their soul remained present with that person at all times, although this theory is impossible to verify without more written records from the Celts.

The Celts also made regular votive offerings, which consisted of burying artifacts of importance in the ground to leave for the gods. Most often, the Celts buried items having to do with warfare, which can be taken as a sign that the ancient Celts saw their fate in war as being closely tied to the will of the gods. However, there is also evidence of the Celts leaving other items not related to war, such as jewelry and pottery. Interestingly, the items buried and left for the gods were frequently expensive items, which helps point to the significance the gods most likely had within ancient Celtic culture.

Uniform Religion or Many Different Cults?

One of the things that still remains a mystery to today's Celtic scholars is whether or not Celtic religion was practiced in a uniform manner across the many different tribes that existed throughout Central Europe and Britain. Roman records, as well as archaeological evidence, suggest there were hundreds of gods being worshiped by the Celtic people of Europe. Under normal circumstances, we might take this as a sign that religion was far more cult-based, meaning each tribe or clan worshiped a different deity, but there are some examples of continuity that make this a bit more difficult to determine.

For example, the Matres (Latin for Mothers) are a group of three goddesses who appear to have been worshiped in Britain, Gaul, and northern Italy. The idea was that these goddesses were responsible for determining the destiny of men and women on Earth. This was a popular concept in pre-Christian European religions, and it may have its origins in Norse mythology. However, the votive offerings discovered at different Celtic sites across Europe suggest that the Celts developed their own version of this group of goddesses and continued to worship it even as their culture spread around Europe and changed. It's important to note, however, that there are considerable differences amongst the different depictions of the "matres" in Celtic cultures.

Another example of a common god is the horned god, which is often referred to as Cernunnos. It is believed that this god was responsible for life, fertility, animals, and also the underworld. Of course, many different variations of this god exist depending on which Celtic culture we look at, but he is typically depicted sitting down and surrounded by animals. Examples of this god can be found in cultures across all of Gaul as well as on the Iberian Peninsula and Britain.

The god Lugus, most famously associated with the Irish deity Lugh, or Lug, is also an example of a pan-Celtic god, and his role in history has become even greater largely because of his role in Irish mythology. Generally speaking, Lugus is associated with being the god who grants kings the right to rule. He is most often depicted as a warrior, king, and artist, and he is also said to be the keeper of the truth and the one responsible for executing the law. When the Romans began their conquest of Gaul and Britain, they associated Lugus with their god Mercury, who is one of the most significant gods in Roman mythology.

Taranis is believed to be the Celtic god of thunder, and evidence exists that he was worshiped in parts of Britain, Ireland, Gaul, Gallaecia (modern-day northwestern Spain), and the territories surrounding the Rhine River in Germany. It's believed that Taranis ruled over the human world together with Esus and Toutatis. We do not know for sure the role of Esus, but it's believed that Toutatis was considered to be the protector of tribes. Human sacrifices were often made to this combination of gods. Yet while evidence of Taranis is found in many parts of the Celtic world, his association with the other two gods of this triad is typically only associated with Gaul.

The last significant god that we can confidently say was worshiped by multiple Celtic tribes is Epona. She was almost always depicted riding a horse, and it's believed she was associated with fertility. Some theories also suggest that the ancient Celts believed she was the one responsible for leading souls into the afterlife, although this conjecture has been made mostly by interpreting reliefs. Depictions of Epona are found at Celtic sites in Britain, Rome, and Bulgaria, giving her considerably more geographic reach than many of the other common Celtic gods.

Irish Mythology

When the Romans conquered Gaul and Britain, they came across countless versions of Celtic religion, and as was typical of the time, they associated these gods with their own. This gives the impression that Celtic mythology was a unified religious practice, but this was probably not the case. Instead, it's more likely that religious cults developed in each area the Celts called home, although because of the Celts' shared ancestry and language, some similarities do exist, such as the deities discussed above.

Today, we understand Celtic religion through Irish mythology, and while it's incorrect to assume this is an accurate representation of ancient Celtic religion, it's important to at least look at it because it provides us with some context for what ancient Celtic religion might have been like. The Irish mythologists, who kept their stories alive through an oral tradition, put Irish mythology into writing when Christianity began spreading throughout the island in the 5th and 6th centuries.

This provides us the best possible glimpse we could get into what at least one version of Celtic mythology might have looked like, but many of those who were writing these stories down were, in fact, Christian monks. It's entirely possible they warped these stories to make it easier for them to be synthesized with Christian ideas, which would have made it easier for the monks to convert the non-Christian Irish. However, even knowing that these stories are likely incomplete, it's still important to at least understand them as this gives us the best look into what religion was like in Britain, a largely Celtic territory, before the Romans arrived. And because the Celts in Britain most likely migrated from other parts of Europe, it's possible these religious texts could unlock more secrets of Celtic religion, although we need to be careful about jumping to too many conclusions.

The Irish Gods

Generally speaking, in Irish mythology, the gods and goddesses were seen as the ancestors of the people, and they were connected to the land and the water. Many of deities were female, and it is believed that the ancient Irish (Celts) saw these deities as maternal figures who were responsible for caring for the people on Earth.

The gods and goddesses who were responsible for creating life belonged to the Tuatha Dé Danann, which was a supernatural race that lived in the Otherworld but that could interact with the human world whenever they saw fit. Typically, the Tuatha Dé Danann had to battle the Fomorians, another supernatural race that was considered to be responsible for all the bad things that happened in the world.

In general, the deities of the Tuatha Dé Danann are divided into four main groups. One of these groups is made up of deities often seen in Celtic sites throughout Gaul. Other groups include those who live in the sea, those who live in the Otherworld, and those who make up the vast majority of the stories we now understand as Irish mythology. The two most important gods from the Tuatha Dé Danann were Lugh (who we know to be an important god in other parts of the Celtic world) and Dagda, who is often portrayed as a Druid and a father-figure. Typically, he is depicted as a large, bearded man who holds a club or staff which is supposed to hold magical powers. Danu was considered to be the mother of the Tuatha Dé Danann, making her one of the more important deities in the pantheon. However, little is known about Danu, and there are many different versions of her, making it difficult to know exactly what her role was in Irish mythology.

The existence of a written Irish mythology is exciting because it gives us a glimpse into pre-Roman and pre-Celtic religion. However, it would be incorrect to assume that Irish mythology represents the religious practices of all the Celts. As mentioned, Irish mythology was written down at a time when Christian monks were attempting to convert pagan Britain and Ireland, and there are also considerable similarities between the stories we have in Irish mythology to those that come from Greek mythology, suggesting they may have been simply borrowed and adapted by foreigners so as to make more sense of them. Nevertheless, the little we do know about Irish mythology should remind us just how different the Celts were from the people who came to occupy their land in the centuries after the Celtic migrations.

Conclusion

Much like the rest of what we know about the ancient Celts, Celtic religion is frustrating to understand. The lack of written sources and the fact that the sources we do have were written by foreigners, mainly Romans, leaves us in the dark. Furthermore, because Celtic culture was largely absorbed into that of Rome by the first century, there is little remaining oral tradition, meaning we may never know for sure how the ancient Celts saw and understood the world. Nevertheless, based on the information we do have, we can piece together at least a general understanding of a polytheistic religion that influenced people living as far apart as Britain and Bulgaria, as well as Spain and Turkey.

Chapter 10 – Celtic Art

Although we often associate Celtic culture with its warring and raiding, there are other aspects that are worth mentioning, most specifically its art. And because art does not require writing, we have a considerably larger amount of evidence available to us that allows us to trace the history of Celtic art development from the early Hallstatt culture all the way to the Celtic cultures that remained in Ireland and maintained the tradition throughout the modern ages. Typically, Celtic art is divided into three eras: Hallstatt, La Tène, and Post-Roman Irish.

Art in Celtic Society

Part of the reason art was so important in Celtic society was because of the "prestige goods" system we've discussed. This was essentially a clientelist system, meaning regular people, i.e., laborers, gave their allegiance to a noble in exchange for security. But in order for a person to gain the status of a noble and be able to collect this nobility, he needed to demonstrate his wealth, and one of the ways to do this was to acquire and showcase luxury items.

This practice meant that art was of great value to the Celts right from the very beginning, and the trade networks they established were often designed to help them acquire these artifacts. Some examples include pottery from Greece and Rome, but there is even evidence of silks from China making their way into Central Europe, which serves as evidence as to the importance of these items in ancient Celtic culture. However, this was not the only source of art for the Celts. They also had their own styles, many of which were influenced by the Mediterranean cultures of Greece and Rome.

Furthermore, art was also an integral part of Celtic warrior culture. More specifically, the outfitting of warriors with well-decorated swords, armor, and clothing was an important part of Celtic society. It appears that Celtic warriors were not interested in merely equipping themselves with the gear for war but rather with decorative garments, perhaps as another means of expressing to other warriors and enemies their own self-worth within the fighting unit.

Hallstatt Style

The first culture to emerge that we identify as being Celtic is that which developed in the Hallstatt zone near the Danube River in Austria. During this time, we can see Celtic culture in its early stages. For example, it's believed that a stratified society with nobles and warlords on the top developed during this period, and because of this, significant emphasis was given to art.

The Hallstatt culture developed during the transition from the European Bronze Age to the European Iron Age, which was a period of time in which bronze tools were slowly replaced by stronger, more durable instruments made from iron. As a result, much of the art that remains from this period are decorative iron items, although some of the art from this period was still made from bronze. Generally speaking, these decorations were placed on everyday items, such as swords, knives, spears, and other tools or weapons. Other items made from metal include jewelry, brooches, rings, and ornaments, and they often were made in a geometric style. Spirals and other repeating geometric patterns were very common, and over time, they became a defining characteristic of Celtic art, although it is more than likely that the Celts learned this from other cultures in Europe. These designs can also be found in stone carvings.

However, one rather remarkable example of Hallstatt art are the items known as "cult wagons." These small pieces are tiny replicas of four-wheeled carts or wagons that archaeologists believe may have had some sort of religious significance. They typically depict some sort of scene, such as a sacrifice or offering, and there is a bowl raised above this scene that is supported by several thin pillars. The current theory among archaeologists and art historians is that this was used to place some sort of libation that would be consumed during a ceremony. These small bronze or iron sculptures have almost always been found in graves, which is why they have been attributed religious significance, but a good deal of mystery still remains about their actual purpose and function.

One of the best examples of these cult wagons is the one found at the Strettweg site in Austria. It is made of bronze and depicts a sacrificial scene. It was found near a good deal of other grave goods, which is where the above theory comes from. No matter what its purpose was, the metalworking is intricate and demonstrates that the Celtic people were perhaps gifted artists right from the beginning of their history.

Source:
https://commons.wikimedia.org/w/index.php?curid=26636672

Another popular form of art from this period were carvings, and the most common designs were of humans and animals. Many of these appear to have some sort of religious undertone, meaning they depict a god or some other deity. If we knew more about Celtic mythology from this time period, then perhaps we could connect some of these items to some of the stories the Celts told about themselves, but since this information does not exist, all we can do is speculate.

Another important part of Hallstatt art were human heads. As mentioned, the human head was given considerable importance in Celtic religion, at least based on what we know about it. Heads without bodies have been found in many Celtic sites, including those in the Hallstatt zone but also in those found in other parts of Europe. In instances where the full body is there, the head is usually exceptionally large, offering further evidence of the importance of this body part in Celtic religion.

Stone reliefs can also be found at various Hallstatt sites throughout Europe, although these examples are rare and tend to be centralized around areas where there was a strong Greek presence, suggesting this was not a major part of the Hallstatt artistic culture. Yet despite this, there is a wide range of pieces of Hallstatt art, and this laid the groundwork for a culture of art to flourish in later Celtic societies.

La Tène Style

The La Tène culture emerged after the Hallstatt culture, and as it grew, it slowly developed into our modern understanding of Celtic culture. As a result, much of the art that comes out of this period, from roughly 500 to 50 BCE, can trace its roots to the Hallstatt culture, but there were some considerable advances made during this period that helped make Celtic art stand out as compared to the artistic traditions of nearby cultures.

The best example of this was the introduction of goldsmithing. Celts during the La Tène period got quite skilled at shaping gold, and some of the artifacts to come out of this era include collars, neck chains, clasps, brackets, and, to a much lesser extent, sculptures. One very popular use of gold was the torc, which is essentially a rigid necklace. This is believed to have been worn by those with status, a theory that is in line with the prestige goods social structure mentioned earlier. An example of one of these torcs can be seen here:

Sculpture and engravings also advanced considerably during this time with distinct styles emerging in different parts of Europe. Many of these artifacts are found on weapons, mainly swords, and other tools, showing once again how Celtic military and artistic culture were closely linked. However, during this period, the geometrical shapes found during the Hallstatt era get considerably more elaborate with artisans spending time trying to mimic the patterns and designs seen in nature, especially in vegetation. Again, this emphasis on geometrical symmetry would wind up being an important part of the Celtic artistic traditions that remained after the Roman conquest of most of the Celtic world.

Also during this period, Celtic artists worked to include animal images in their designs. This helped to not only make the designs more aesthetically pleasing and interesting, but it also helped make the artifacts more personal. As they were usually found on swords and other weapons, this suggests these designs may have been a way for the nobility and other elites to distinguish themselves from regular people while on the battlefield.

However, despite all of this attention to detail and emphasis on art, there is still no evidence of painting at this point in Celtic art history. This could have been because they lacked the skills or resources to paint, but it is also equally likely that these artifacts simply do not remain due to their perishable nature, although there is little evidence of painting on other more durable goods, such as pots.

Post-Roman Irish Style

After the Romans invaded and conquered the Iberian Peninsula, Gaul, and Britain, Celtic culture all but disappeared throughout mainland Europe. The Celtic language eventually gave way to Latin, and the Celtic way of life went through a process known as Romanization. However, in Britain, Celtic culture was retained, and seeking a way to preserve their culture, the Celts moved to the western part of Britain (Wales), as well as Ireland.

But there was considerable instability in Ireland during this period, and this hindered the development of a strong pre-Roman Irish Celtic tradition, so the Celtic art styles that remained alive after the rise and fall of Rome are mere shadows of "original" Celtic art, and they also take on a significant Christian undertone. This post-Roman Irish style, sometimes referred to as Irish Celtic, is unique in that it can trace its roots to the first Celtic cultures, but it is also its own style, and we should be wary of making too many connections. Nevertheless, it remained the dominant style on the island until at least the 12th century CE.

Perhaps the best-known examples of this are the Irish Celtic crosses. Featuring intricate designs that include repeating geometric patterns, these crosses are clearly influenced by past Celtic styles, although the Celts themselves probably learned this technique from the Greeks and the Romans. However, the fact these designs show up on Christian crosses shows how pre-Roman Celtic styles managed to survive Roman conquest and influence later versions of Celtic art. Furthermore, since these artifacts are some of the best-preserved and most widely recognized pieces from Celtic traditions, they have helped contribute to the idea that the Celts originated in Britain and Ireland, which we now know to be at least partly false.

Other pieces of art that are characteristic of this period are manuscript illuminations. These were developed by the Irish Celtic missionaries who traveled throughout Ireland and Britain to try and spread Christianity, and they brought these elaborately decorated manuscripts with them that exhibit some Celtic influences. These manuscripts would later influence those made in the Gothic, Romanesque, and Carolingian styles, which were the dominant modes of expression throughout the Middle Ages.

In addition, these missionaries also brought with them metalworking pieces that were made using traditional Celtic styles, meaning they were decorated with intricate geometric patterns. This helped Celtic art to continue to spread throughout the early Middle Ages. However, by the 11th or 12th century, after the Norse invasion of Britain and Ireland, it becomes more and more difficult to distinguish a distinct Celtic style. Today, Celtic art has experienced somewhat of a revival as the Celts still alive today seek to revitalize their culture and keep it alive for future generations, and if we know anything about Celtic culture, it's that it is resilient.

Conclusion

It's somewhat surprising that a culture so focused on raiding and warfare was also capable of creating such distinct pieces of art, but it's perhaps even more surprising that Celtic art was able to maintain its integrity despite its slow disappearance throughout Roman times. This can perhaps be attributed to the resilient nature of Celtic culture, but it's perhaps more accurate to see Celtic art as one piece of the very complex puzzle that is European art. It was originally influenced by the Greeks and Romans, and after it had developed its own character, it, in turn, influenced Christian art, which became the dominant culture in Europe during the times of the Romans until now. This helps us not only understand an important part of our collective history, but it also shows how influential the Celts have been in the development of the world we now live in today.

Conclusion

It's easy to study the history of the ancient Celts and feel frustrated. After all, how could a culture that was so widespread throughout Europe and that used a language spoken in so many places simply disappear with the arrival of the Romans? It seems a shame that these people never took to writing down details about their lives for this would have given us a much more in-depth look into what they were like and how they influenced the world which we call home today.

However, while it's easy to be frustrated, we shouldn't let this diminish what we do know. Archaeological evidence combined with the many texts of the Greeks and Romans have allowed us to piece together the world in which the ancient Celts lived, and thanks to the work of Irish mythologists, who undertook the effort of preserving pre-Roman Celtic religion, some aspects of Celtic culture still exist today.

Hopefully, though, it's now possible to take a wider view of the Celts. We may still associate them with Ireland largely because of the importance the Celts have been given to the rise of Irish culture, but there are actually more speakers of a Celtic language in Wales, and almost everyone in Europe can trace their ancestry back to at least one Celtic tribe. Furthermore, we can now see that the Celts were not just a warrior culture focused on raiding nearby tribes and killing everything they saw. Instead, they were a society based on agriculture that had strong religious values and used raiding as a way to further their way of life. However, Celtic mercenaries may still go down as some of the most fearsome fighters in all of history.

But despite all the mystery, or perhaps because of it, the Celts remain a source of fascination to both serious and casual students of history. As a result, we can expect more time and energy to be spent on trying to unlock their secrets, so we can learn more about one of Europe's most influential ancestors.

Part 2: The Vandals

A Captivating Guide to the Barbarians That Conquered the Roman Empire During the Transitional Period from Late Antiquity to the Early Middle Ages

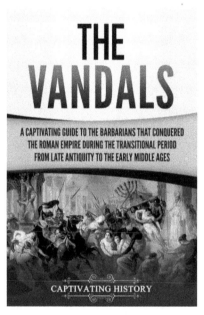

Introduction

In the modern world, when one imagines a vandal, it's often a youth with a covered face drawing graffiti on a wall of a public building. And the act of deliberate defacement, destruction, or damage to public or private property is known as vandalism. This idea became an integral part of world culture with most people using it without knowing that this word is linked to an ancient Germanic tribe called the Vandals. The small number of people that are aware of this link often envision these Vandals as outright barbarians who pillaged and burned, killed and destroyed. They were the antithesis of civilized and cultured life. That image has been engraved in our collective consciousness by centuries of historical propaganda. This was possible because the Vandals didn't leave us any histories written by themselves. Thus, most of the ancient sources on their past were written by their enemies and adversaries, who didn't look too kindly on them. This is especially true for later historians who idealized ancient Rome and blamed the Vandals for its fall. But the question is, how much of it is true?

This book is aimed to answer that question. Were the Vandals really so wild, and were they worse than any other tribe in Europe at that time? It will also present the society and culture of this tribe in an attempt to not only shed light on their reputation in history but to also give their side of the story as the stereotypical bad guys. In essence, this guide will try to give some voice to the voiceless Vandals. Hopefully by the end of this short introduction to the story of the Vandals, you, the reader, will leave with your own picture of who those barbarians were and intrigued to learn more, not only about them but about history in general, as it can teach us a lot about the world we're currently living in.

Chapter 1 – Origins of the Vandals

As with most ancient tribes, especially those who left none of their own histories, the roots of the Vandals are shrouded in the fogs of the past. According to some ancient histories, their origins could be traced to what is today southern Sweden. From there, they migrated together with the Goths, who were another Germanic tribe, to mainland Europe, more precisely to a region which is now known as Silesia in modern Poland, around the Oder River. Modern historians date the end of this early migration to the end of the 2nd and beginning of the 1st century BCE. Once settled there, they became part of the Przeworsk culture, which was located in central and southern Poland. This culture was named after the village where their first artifacts were found. In the past, archeologists argued about this culture, linking it either with the Vandals and other early Germanic tribes or early Slavs. Today, it is mostly considered that this culture was actually a mixture of both Slavic and Germanic tribes that lived in this area.

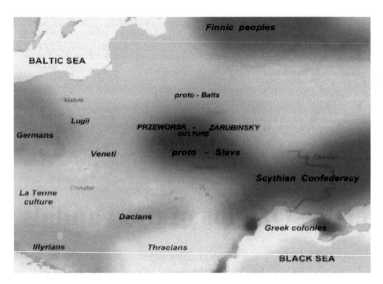

Map of the approximate area of the Przeworsk culture. Source: https://commons.wikimedia.org

The first historical records of the Vandals were written by Roman historians and geographers in the 1st century CE. Usually, this would help to clarify certain aspects of the Vandals' past, but the Romans were rather imprecise when it came to this tribe. Some of them report that people they call Vandilii lived around the Oder River. And in those sources, they mention the Vandals as a broader term which encompasses several tribes that lived in that region. Other Roman writers mention them in a way which is more precisely connected to a single tribe. There are also reports of a Germanic tribe called Lugii living in the same area between the Oder and Vistula Rivers. Modern historians tend to link them with the Vandals, identifying them as the same people under a different name. This only enhances the confusion in the attempt to map the earliest history of the Vandals. Adding to this is the fact that in the early ancient histories, it is difficult to distinguish actual tribes from tribal alliances; also, one's national identity wasn't as firmly structured as it is in modern times, making integrations and changes in the tribes much easier. Not least problematic is the fact that most of the tribes had achieved a similar technological and civilizational level of development with resembling lifestyles and cultures to each other, making even archeological differentiation much harder than in some other cases.

Modern representation of a Vandal couple. Source:
 https://commons.wikimedia.org

One of the best examples of this is burial traditions. Early Vandals have been noted to use mainly cremation; however, the entire Przeworsk culture used it as well, making it harder to distinguish tribes that constituted this group. Other notable examples are the use of iron and pottery, which were created in great variety, as well as the use of well technology, which allowed the Vandals to live farther away from the rivers. Yet, these were also true for many other tribes and ethnic groups, both in the Przeworsk culture and across Central and Northern Europe. There is one slight distinction that separates the Vandals from the majority of other Germanic tribes. Their warriors were usually buried with their war regalia and equipment, and among them were spurs. This suggests that unlike most other Germanic peoples, the Vandals were actually using cavalry as an important part of their warfare. That being said, other non-Germanic tribes were also known for their cavalry, for example, the nomadic

Sarmatians in the east as well as some Celtic tribes in the west. So, in essence, knowing that doesn't help much with determining the earliest Vandal history.

However, things start to become a little bit clearer in the 2nd century CE. During that century, the larger Vandal tribe split into two parts. The first group became known as the Silingi Vandals, who remained on the banks of the Oder River in what is today Silesia. Some historians have even linked the name of this region with the Silingi, though this idea hasn't been widely accepted. The other group, known as the Hasdingi Vandals, moved south toward the borders of the Roman Empire on the Danube. This move was a part of the larger Germanic migration to the south, which created severe pressure on the northern Roman borders, referred to as *limes* by the ancient Romans. Because of that, Roman sources speak more often about them, giving us a bit more information about Vandal history. Around 170 CE, the Hasdingi, under the rule of Kings Raus and Rapt, became the allies of Rome, and they were allowed to settle in the province of Dacia, roughly modern-day Romania. At that period, they were used by the Romans to fight against the Marcomanni tribe and their allies, the Quads and the Iazyges, all located on the Danube border. But it seems they weren't as useful as the Romans had hoped as they soon moved from the Roman lands. From archeological evidence, it seems they decided upon settling in the valley of the Tisza River, which is located in present-day eastern Hungary and northern Serbia.

After that, the Romans continued using the Hasdingi Vandals in their political and diplomatic schemes to relieve the pressure from their own borders, prompting them to fight other tribes around them. Some later histories, most notably by the Gothic historians, tell us about a Vandal kingdom in that period, but modern historians reject these as works of fiction. Since those histories speak of great victories of the Goths over that supposed Vandal kingdom, it is usually seen as mere historical propaganda written several centuries later when actual hostilities between the two Germanic tribes were flaming. Also, there are no archeological signs of political coherence of that sort in the valley of Tisza. Another piece of evidence for this is the fact that the Vandals didn't pose a serious threat to the Roman frontier. Only two or three smaller incursions were noted in the 3rd century, which resulted in Vandal defeats. This is the very reason why Roman sources give us only sporadic and limited information about the Hasdingi. It is possible that they took part in some major invasion led by other tribes, but the fact is that the Romans themselves saw them as a tribe of lesser significance than for example the Goths or the Marcomanni. The Vandals weren't seen as either fierce enemies nor useful allies.

This remained true throughout the 4th century as the Vandals still didn't receive much more attention in the histories. At the beginning of the century, according to the questionable Gothic sources, the Hasdingi yet again got into conflict against the Goths, who lived east of the Vandals. Sources give us a story of their defeat. Despite the unreliability of the sources, there is a good chance that there is some truthfulness to this account as around 330 some of the Hasdingi settled in the Roman province of Pannonia, just west of the Danube River. This could be seen as a sign of them fleeing from the Goths, who were at the time Roman enemies. This time, the Hasdingi stayed as a part of the Roman world for several decades, allowing them to receive parts of the Roman culture. Of course, this cultural trade had been going on since they first arrived at the Roman borders, but now it was intensified. The exact extent of this Romanization is unknown, but archeologists have found that over time, more and more Roman products were buried in the Vandal graves. The Vandals still continued to live primarily as farmers in small circular villages, and they remained famous for their horsemanship skills as well as for their weaponsmithing. But the most important part of this cultural exchange was the fact that during the 4th century the Vandals accepted Christianity.

Normally, this would make the Vandals a more integral part of the Roman world, but the problem was that they accepted the Arian school of Christianity, which was deemed as heresy by the Ecumenical Christian Council of Nicaea in 325. Because of this, the Vandals were still seen as heretics in the eyes of most of the Roman emperors. As for the Silingi Vandals, who remained in Silesia, farther away from the Romans, we have no written accounts. However, it seems that their way of life remained mostly unchanged since the division of the Vandals. But the world around them began to change rapidly in the latter half of the century. At that time, the now famous Huns began appearing in the steppes of the northern shores of the Black Sea. As they moved into Eastern Europe, they began attacking and pushing away other tribes they encountered in that region, who in turn began pressuring the Roman borders once again. Because of that, the Roman army was in need of more troops, so the empire began recruiting from their "barbarian" subjects, among them being the Vandals.

At that point, Vandal soldiers became highly valued because of their riding skills, which allowed some of them to progress rather high in the Roman military hierarchy. The best example of this was Stilicho, who held the highest Roman military rank of *magister militum* and who is today known as one of the last great Roman generals. He was half Vandal, born from a Vandal cavalry officer and a provincial Roman woman. He was in charge of defending the western parts of the empire and fought wars in Britain, Africa, the Balkans, and Italy from 382 to 408 CE. At one point, he was even a regent for the underaged Western Roman emperor Honorius. However, it should be noted that Stilicho most likely saw himself first as a citizen of Rome then as a Vandal. On the other hand, not all Hasdingi Vandals fought for the empire. Some of them were a part of the Gothic forces, which began rebelling against the empire in the last decades of the 4th century. Although we cannot be sure, there is a chance that in some battles Vandal soldiers fought against each other, which is a clear indicator of just how chaotic these times were in Europe.

In the early 5th century, that turmoil worsened. The Huns were moving even closer, prompting more and more Germanic tribes to run away westward, toward the Roman borders. They sought refuge inside this once glorious empire, but not all of them could be allowed in. And those that were allowed were usually mistreated by the local authorities who saw them as uncivilized barbarians compared to their Roman culture and education, despite the fact that Rome, in all aspects, was a mere shell of its former glory. Under such pressure, with the Huns on one side and the Romans on the other, many tribes became restless, rebelling against, attacking, and plundering the empire. The most notable were the Visigoths, or the western Goths, as the Gothic tribe had divided into two distinct groups in the late 4th century. They even created a semi-independent state in the Balkans. The eastern Goths, or the Ostrogoths, became part of the Hunnic realm. The Vandals also felt the same pressure as these other tribes. They began fearing for their survival, mostly from the hands of the Huns but also due to the disarray in the empire itself. Thus, in the first couple of years of the 5th century, they once again began their migration, this time westward toward the Roman province of Gaul, located in present-day France.

Chapter 2 – From the Danube to Africa

At the turn of the 5th century CE, chaos began spreading across Europe. The Roman Empire was crumbling, finally splitting into the Western and Eastern Roman Empires in 395 due to the pressure of the barbarian tribes. Many of those tribes were moving, running away from the Huns, or looking for better fortunes and plunder in the Roman Empire. But none of these tribes moved farther than the Vandals, who began their migration from the Pannonian Plain, which is on the banks of the Tisza and Danube Rivers, and went across Western Europe before finally settling in Northern Africa. What is even more fascinating is that this colossal journey enfolded in less than three decades.

The Vandal expedition began at the very beginning of the 5th century when they first moved to the middle and upper Danube, attacking the Roman province of Raetia, which would have encompassed modern-day eastern Switzerland, parts of southern Germany, and eastern Austria, in 401. They were led by King Godigisel, whose early life remains a mystery. For a few years, the Hasdingi Vandals remained in one place, allowing them to forge a loose alliance with the Germanic Suebi, which consisted of the Marcomanni and Quadi tribes, and the Iranian Alans, who moved from the Pontic steppe due to the pressure from the Huns. Together, they moved toward the Rhine River, which was the eastern border of the Roman province of Gaul, located in modern-day France. On their way there, the Silingi Vandals joined them as well, making the Vandal coalition a more prominent danger to Gaul. However, the Roman *limes* were rather undefended at the time as Stilicho had gathered troops from it to defend Italy from two Gothic invasions during 402 and 405. The only defense of this province were the Franks, another Germanic tribe, who were allowed to settle in Gaul as their allies or *foederati*, as the Romans referred to them. In the last days of December 406, the Vandals decided to cross the Rhine and push into the unprotected Roman lands.

In the past, historians attributed this bold attack not only to the weak state of the Roman defenses in Gaul but also to the fact that the Rhine froze up, making the crossing easier. However, modern historians have begun doubting this as it wasn't mentioned in any ancient sources; it was actually first mentioned by British historian Edward Gibbon in the 18th century. What is known is that the Frankish army put up a fight, managing to kill thousands of Vandals and even their king, Godigisel. According to some sources, the Franks ambushed them, and the total defeat of the Vandals was only avoided because the Alans came to help them. Once this first and only line of defense was broken, the allies began ravaging Gaul. Yet there was no proper response from the Roman imperial government to this threat. For them, the bigger problem was a rebellion and the usurpation of the crown by a Roman general named Constantine in Britain. In the political and ideological consciousness of the Romans, that posed a more dangerous threat than some barbarians plundering Gaul. Thus, while the Vandals continued to harass the local population, the Romans themselves clashed in that very same province in yet another civil war. As such, the Vandals remained in the periphery of the Roman world, leaving them out of the focus of their records, which are, in fact, rather rich and abundant. Because of that, there are little details of what the Vandals and their allies actually did in those years.

From those contemporary sources, historians have concluded that the Vandal coalition was contained in the northern regions of Gaul, sacking cities and the countryside. It seems that the usurper Constantine, who moved from Britain to southern Gaul, managed to contain them a bit; there are even some talks of smaller battles and skirmishes as well as some negotiations, but Constantine's focus remained on fighting the loyalists of the Roman emperor Honorius. With that goal in mind, Constantine invaded the Iberian Peninsula, which was, at the time, still faithful to Honorius, creating a stronghold for himself there. However, his rebel forces began crumbling in early 409 as Constantine was betrayed by the commander of Hispania. Amidst such chaos, the Vandals began moving south, now burning and pillaging in southern France as well. At this point, the entire province of Gaul was plunged into mayhem and destruction as several different forces roamed across it. It is even possible that the Vandals moved south partially because that region was in such a high demand of troops due to their prolonged and complicated civil war. Nevertheless, the Vandals and their allies under King Gunderic, the son and successor of Godigisel, didn't stay long in southern Gaul. In the autumn of 409, they crossed the Pyrenees Mountains into the Roman provinces of Hispania.

Once there, the Vandals realized that the Iberian Peninsula was largely unprotected, which prompted them to once again begin pillaging and looting the Roman citizens. They continued to do so for roughly two more years as the central government of the Western Roman Empire had to also deal with a Gothic invasion of Italy, which culminated in 410 with the Gothic sacking of Rome. The destruction of the Hispanic provinces was worsened by famine and pestilence, making life in those parts of the Roman Empire utterly unbearable. Yet this chaos soon calmed as Rome began recuperating. The Visigoths left Italy and went to Gaul where they soon became allies of the Western Roman emperor Honorius. And the new *magister militum*, Constantius, used them to finally bring the entirety of Gaul under imperial rule, dealing with a rebellion in the northern parts of the province. This show of force intimidated the Vandals and their allies. Thus, they stopped their plundering and sought to be allowed to settle in Hispania peacefully. By 412, they had divided most of the Iberian Peninsula among themselves. The Hasdingi Vandals and the Suebi settled in the northwest of the peninsula in the province of Gallaecia, which was the poorest region of Hispania. The Silingi Vandals got Hispania Baetica in the south, now modern-day Andalusia, while the Alans established themselves in Lusitania, which would now be Portugal and western parts of Spain, as well as in Hispania Carthaginiensis, which was located in southeastern Spain on the Mediterranean coast. The northern and northeastern regions of the Iberian Peninsula remained in Roman hands, at least in theory.

This division of the Iberian Peninsula is also indicative of how the dynamic between the allies themselves had changed. The Hasdingi Vandals, once the leaders of this coalition of tribes, had been given the worst lands to settle on, as they were less fertile and strategically less important than others. Plus, they had to share it with the Suebi. The Silingi Vandals received lands in fertile southern Spain. But it was the Alans who got the biggest, most fertile, and most important parts of the Iberian Peninsula. This suggests that in the six years since the crossing of the Rhine, the Hasdingi lost their leadership, and the Alans became the backbone of the coalition's power. This is corroborated by the fact that this partition of lands was done among the tribes themselves, while the central government only accepted it as factual. However, it proved to be essential for the survival of the Hasdingi Vandals. In the several years after the division of Hispania, there was relative peace and prosperity in these lands. But in 415, the Visigoths crossed the Pyrenees, driven out of Gaul by force and economic pressure. At the time, they were disorganized, and other tribes around them harassed and humiliated them. Yet by 417, they managed to pull themselves together and once again became allies of

Rome. And within a year, they fulfilled their ally duties by attacking other invaders of Hispania.

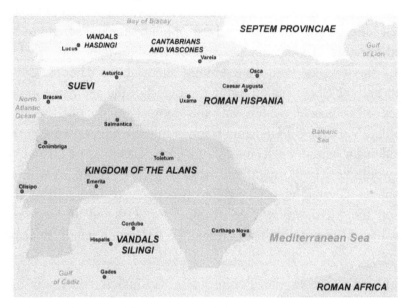

Barbarian division of the Iberian Peninsula. Source:
https://commons.wikimedia.org

Fueled by revenge, the Visigoths were merciless. They massacred both the Alans and the Silingi Vandals, who were seen as the biggest threats to Roman imperial rule. The Hasdingi and the Suebi were spared from this, partially because of their insignificance as well as of the insignificance of the lands they inhabited. And according to the contemporary sources, what remained of the Alans fled to the Hasdingi, while the Silingi were reportedly all killed. The latter is most likely an exaggeration as it is far more likely that they also fled to the Hasdingi. This reinvigorated the Hasdingi Vandals, making them once again a force to be reckoned, and Gunderic became king of both the Vandals and Alans, a title which most later Vandal rulers also used. This prompted the government of the Western Roman Empire to ally with the Suebi to fight against them, as they feared the now powerful group would support one of the imperial usurpers which sought refuge with the Hasdingi several years before. In 419 CE, the Vandals were defeated and the usurper captured, but this

Roman triumph became a Pyrrhic victory. The Vandals were forced out from Gallaecia, which prompted Gunderic to lead his people south, to the more prosperous lands of Baetica.

There the Vandals once again became a problem to Rome, as these rich lands helped them to establish themselves as an important faction on the Iberian Peninsula. In 422, the imperial government launched a joint Roman-Visigothic-Suebi attack on the Vandals, yet those forces were defeated. This unexpected victory helped the Vandals to secure themselves as an important faction in the Mediterranean as the undisputed rulers of southern Spain. They were even reinforced by the surviving Visigoths and the Roman soldiers who joined them after the defeat. As such, not only was this the first known major Vandal victory, but it was also the first step in their consolidation of power. Almost immediately after this victory, the Vandals began sacking and conquering other cities in Hispania. After conquering Carthago Spartaria, modern-day Cartagena in southeastern Spain, they gained control of the maritime routes in the western Mediterranean and also access to some naval power as well. This allowed them to plunder the Balearic Islands and Mauritania Tingitana, which was a Roman province in northern Morocco. Some historians even suggest that through these attacks, the Vandals managed to secure their position in Mauritania Caesariensis as well, though this is highly debated.

Despite these victories, in 428, the Vandals lost their king in the successful siege of Hispalis, which was located in modern-day Seville. Gunderic was succeeded by his half-brother Gaiseric, who was probably Godigisel's illegitimate son from a Roman serf. That fact could have troubled the transition of power, but since there was no reaction from the other Vandals, it seems likely that Gaiseric already commanded enough authority to remain unchallenged on the throne. This is even likelier with the hindsight of a historian as Gaiseric is often seen as the most successful and skilled Germanic ruler of the 5th century. Thus, with a strong base in southern and southeastern Spain, a decent fleet, and an uncommonly talented leader, the Vandals were in a perfect position to finalize their migration from cold Northern Europe to warm Northern Africa.

From the present perspective, this last step seems logical if not inevitable. Yet this most likely wasn't the view of either the Romans or the Vandals. With their series of victories during the 420s, their position on the Iberian Peninsula was unchallenged, and the region of Baetica was rich and plentiful, as it was also a trading hub and a large producer of grain. There was no real incentive for Gaiseric to lead his men any farther south, especially when considering that besides the wealth of his own lands, he could plunder much of the western Mediterranean with little to no resistance or repercussion.

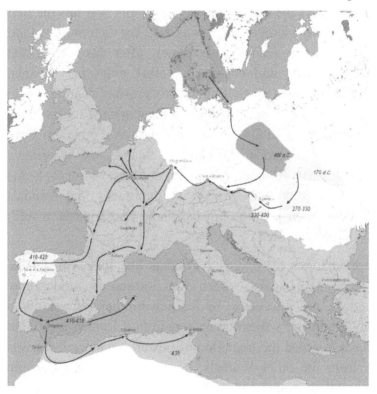

Migrations of the Vandals. Source: https://commons.wikimedia.org

With that in mind, it is likely that the Vandals' crossing into North Africa surprised many, as it was, at the very least, a huge gamble on behalf of the ambitious Gaiseric. He forfeited all their gains from almost a decade of warfare to attempt to gain control of Carthage, which was the most vital city of the Western Roman Empire. According to some later sources, the Vandals were actually invited to cross the Mediterranean Sea by Bonifacius, who was a Roman general in charge of the African provinces. These sources state that due to some intrigues in Italy, Bonifacius was preparing to contest the imperial rule. He even fought off an army of the central government in 427. As such, an alliance with the Vandals did make sense as they were a force to be reckoned with at the time. This scenario remains a possibility, but modern historians haven't found any contemporary evidence to back up or refute this. Because of that, some remain skeptical toward this claim, stating that it is far more likely that a talented king such as Gaiseric simply saw an opportunity to gain better and richer lands. The fact remains that Northern Africa, especially the region around Carthage, was the wealthiest in the western Mediterranean while also virtually undefended. And both the local generals and the imperial government in Italy were more concerned with fighting among each other; dealing with the so-called barbarians was of secondary importance.

In the end, the question of the true motives of Gaiseric's actions isn't that important. What is imperative is the fact that in 429 the entire Vandal force crossed the Straits of Gibraltar into Mauritania Tingitana. Some later sources give us a count of about 80,000 Vandals, including the Alanic and Visigothic followers they had gained in previous years. This number includes both their fighting force as well as the families of the soldiers. Yet some modern historians are hesitant about accepting this number. Their estimates are far lower, with about 20,000 people. However, it would seem that their fighting strength had at least 10,000 seasoned soldiers, making them a fierce enemy as armies at the time rarely numbered more than this. Because of these figures, many historians have assumed that the Vandals' crossing into Africa was done with one huge fleet over the course of several days. One of the reasons for this was the fact that their presence in Mauritania was established several years before; thus, their landing would be pretty much unchallenged. With that in mind, it is also likely that for the Vandals this move wasn't a logistical issue. However, after the crossing was done, there was no way back.

The Vandals abandoned their holdings in Spain, and from Mauritania, their army moved eastward toward Gaiseric's ultimate goal, the city of Carthage. With that, their long journey from the banks of the Danube to the shores of North Africa was in its final stage. Some see this voyage as a result of pure luck and favorable circumstances, others as a hard-fought and well-earned achievement, and some as a mixture of both. Yet no matter how we look at it, their journey was nothing less than amazing.

Chapter 3 – Rise of the Vandal Kingdom

The Vandals' crossing of the Mediterranean Sea is today seen as a turning point in history. It was the first real barbarian invasion of the Roman provinces in Africa, a foundation of the Western Roman Empire and a region that had been untouched for centuries. It was, in a way, a lifeline of Rome. And with the Vandals' invasion, that lifeline was cut, essentially "killing" the Western Roman Empire, which never managed to recuperate from that loss.

The killing blow began in modern-day Morocco, where the Vandal army landed first. But Gaiseric immediately started moving east toward Carthage, which lay in what is today Tunisia. From the get-go, he demonstrated the merciless fury of Vandal attacks, pillaging and slaughtering as he moved along the coast of Northern Africa. Many of the aristocrats and wealthier citizens fled Africa, mostly to Italy, especially as they feared religious persecution. Although both the Vandals and Romans were Christians, the former were Arians and held great contempt toward the Nicene Christians, which had been the formally accepted school of Christianity in Rome since 325. That resentment was partially caused by Roman persecution of the Arians as heretics in their territories, which was fueled by thoughts and works of Saint Augustine of Hippo, a Roman African and an early Christian theologian and philosopher. Thus, the Vandals' attack also showed a sign of being a religious war, though it certainly was only a byproduct of their attack, not its ultimate goal. The Romans, of course, tried to stop their advance through Numidia, which covered the modern-day coast of Algeria. Their army was led by Bonifacius, who had managed to patch his relations with the imperial government as both feared the Vandal invasion.

Bonifacius tried negotiating with Gaiseric, yet those efforts were futile. He then challenged the Vandals to an open battle which the Romans lost. That forced Bonifacius to flee and barricade himself in Hippo, which was a heavily fortified city near the modern border of Algeria and Tunisia and the most important religious center of Roman Africa. Gaiseric besieged it for fourteen long months but failed to capture it. However, during the siege, Saint Augustine died, probably of starvation, which was likely a huge blow to Roman morale. The Vandals continued to move east, but their unsuccessful siege of Hippo allowed Bonifacius to retreat to Carthage and recuperate his forces. At that point, the Western Roman Empire asked their brethren from the Eastern Roman Empire for assistance in Africa. And the eastern empire answered that call, sending an army to help. It joined with Bonifacius' replenished army, but in 432, the combined army of the Western and Eastern Roman Empires suffered a substantial defeat from the Vandals. And prior to that victory, Gaiseric had also managed to conquer Hippo, which was left undefended. Rome had no other choice than to negotiate or, to be more accurate, to accept and affirm the Vandals' possession of Hippo and the lands around it. In return, the Vandals became Roman *foederati*. This peace treaty was signed in 435 after a period of prolonged ceasefire.

At the time, the Western Roman emperor, Valentinian III, probably thought this would satisfy the appetites of the Vandal king. However, Gaiseric had other plans. He restructured his court, expelling all who weren't Arian. He also expelled local Nicene bishops. At the same time, he neglected his ally duties to Rome, as pirates began ravaging the western Mediterranean and he did nothing to stop them. Some historians even suggest that some of those pirates were Vandals themselves and that their king gave them tacit permission to plunder other Roman provinces. By 439, Gaiseric realized that circumstances now allowed him to continue his conquest. In autumn of that year, to the surprise of all the Romans, he broke the treaty and conquered Carthage without any trouble. Contemporary sources tell us of a violent and bloody occupation of this region, yet archeologists haven't found much evidence to prove that. Though most of the portable goods were plundered and some churches gave in to the Arians, it seems that no major destruction occurred. Yet the Roman panic was most likely real. They lost their African jewels, and more frighteningly, the Vandals gained most of the African merchant fleet and its shipyards. The entirety of southern Italy was now open for an invasion.

Archeological site of the ancient city of Carthage. Source:
https://commons.wikimedia.org

As a capable and ambitious king, Gaiseric recognized that opportunity as well and immediately pressed forward, attacking Sicily in 440, but he failed to conquer Palermo, a well-fortified city on the northern coast of the island. That prompted Valentinian III to recall his armies from Gaul, to order the fortification of the coast of southern Italy, and to ask his eastern counterpart to help with the Vandal threat. Eastern Roman Emperor Theodosius II once again gathered some troops and sent them to the west in 441. However, an army of the eastern empire was soon recalled as Theodosius had to fight against the Persians in the east and the Huns in the north. As such, both Valentinian and Gaiseric were forced to resolve the matter through diplomacy. Their negotiations resulted in a new peace treaty signed in 442. According to this agreement, Rome recognized the Vandal control of Proconsularis Africa (a Roman province of Africa), eastern Numidia, Byzacena, and a coastal strip of western Tripolitania. These lands would have been located in modern-day eastern Algeria, most of Tunisia, and a small part of the northwestern coast of Libya. More important than that was the fact that Valentinian III recognized the Vandals as an independent kingdom, meaning that those territories were now no longer part of the empire.

19th-century gravure of King Gaiseric. Source: https://commons.wikimedia.org

In return for that recognition, Gaiseric agreed to send his son Huneric to the imperial court in Ravenna as a hostage and to pay an annual tribute. To secure this deal, the two rulers agreed on the betrothal of Huneric and Eudocia, Valentinian's daughter. Another byproduct of this marriage was a diplomatic realignment of the Vandals because Huneric was already married to a Visigothic princess. Thus, after 442, the Vandals made the Visigoths their enemies, something that was not going to be forgotten easily. However, the treaty proved to be enough to bring a slightly longer lasting peace between the Romans and the Vandals, as for the next dozen years or so there are no clear signs of significant Vandal activities. Some texts do allude to them attacking the Suebi in the old Vandal territory of Gallaecia, possibly to assist imperial campaigns on the Iberian Peninsula. Yet historians aren't certain the attack was actually carried out by the Vandals. But the newfound peacefulness didn't make the Mediterranean world less scared of the Vandals. Many texts from this era show both explicit and implicit fear of possible Vandal attacks on Italy. But this dread spread as far as Alexandria in Egypt and the island of Rhodes, which were still somewhat secure as parts of the stronger Eastern Roman Empire.

The base of this terror was first and foremost the Vandal navy, which Gaiseric used to flex his diplomatic muscle. Despite the real threat that he posed, it was nothing compared to the terror of the Huns, who under Attila came to the Pannonian Plain, the former home of the Vandals. From there, they plundered and pressured the northern borders of both the Eastern and Western Roman Empires. And they did so with the help of many other subdued barbarian tribes, most notably the Ostrogoths, which were the other major Gothic tribe. Compared to that, the Vandals as quasi-allies weren't as terrifying. Thus, once again, the Vandals remained in the backseat of history. But the Hunnic threat was destroyed with the death of Attila the Hun in 453, but his invasions of Gaul and Italy had once again shown how weak the western empire was. And under such tremendous foreign pressure, internal struggles in the imperial court in Ravenna between Emperor Valentinian III and his *magister militum* Aetius further weakened the empire. Valentinian had Aetius murdered, as he began posing a threat to the throne, but within a year, the emperor was assassinated. He was succeeded on the throne by Petronius Maximus, a wealthy senator who married Valentinian's widow and married his own son to the younger daughter of the former emperor.

This foiled Gaiseric's dynastic plans and hopes for his son Huneric. The Vandal king realized he had to act and quickly. At that crucial point, he decided to abandon his previous strategy of diplomatic approach backed with a sword. Instead, he chose to fulfill his threats, and in 455, he finally attacked, with his primary target being the city of Rome itself. Some sources mention that his action was prompted by a letter from Valentinian's widow asking Gaiseric for help against her new tyrannical husband. Yet modern historians are at best skeptical toward this traditional retelling of the event. In any case, by late spring of that year, troops of the Vandal kingdom stood in front of the gates of Rome. The new emperor tried to flee but was killed in the process by his own subordinates. The defense of the city was in the hands of Pope Leo I, who tried to negotiate with Gaiseric. The success of these talks is questionable, but it is possible that he managed to persuade the Vandal king to respect the rights of the sanctuary. Nonetheless, a fortnight of sacking and pillaging befell an unprotected Rome.

19th-century depiction of the sack of Rome in 455. Source: https://commons.wikimedia.org

Today, the Vandals' sacking of Rome is usually represented as mindless destruction and a total massacre with little regard toward culture, making it the root of the term vandalism. However, this is far from the truth; rather, it is a legend propagated centuries after to embellish the fall of the once great empire. The truth is there was no senseless devastation of Rome but a rather well-organized plundering, which especially targeted the valuable cultural monuments and treasures. This was done both to gain wealth but also to demonstrate their power and humiliate Rome. Yet, these material riches weren't the most important Vandal gains. Those were the numerous aristocratic hostages, among which were Valentinian's widow and two daughters. Gaiseric later used them as a diplomatic pressure point with both Roman empires. With that being said, it's important to point out that the Vandals' sacking of Rome wasn't the first nor the last. And actually, it was not much worse, or at least not bloodier, than any other barbarian plundering of any other city. All the bad reputation the Vandals received as a result of this event was more due to historical propaganda than reality. And because so much focus was on the faith of the city of Rome, later events are often overlooked as Gaiseric didn't stop there. He continued raiding the central Mediterranean, mostly southern Italy and the Adriatic Littoral, which were closest to his kingdom. The Vandal kingdom also occupied Sicily, Sardinia, Corsica, and the Balearic Islands, as well as some strategically significant parts of Northern Africa which were previously held by the Romans.

This prolonged conflict was at the time called "the Fourth Punic War," alluding to the ancient wars fought between Rome and Carthage. And for several years, neither the Eastern or Western Roman Empire had a noteworthy response to the Vandal threat, making the fear of Vandal raids even higher. They were so helpless that at the time rumors started spreading that Marcian, the emperor of the Eastern Roman Empire, was a Vandal ally or that he had a personal agreement with Gaiseric not to wage war against him. That deal was supposedly struck when Marcian had to negotiate his release from Vandal captivity which he fell into during the failed Roman campaign against the Vandals in 430. Of course, there is little truth to these claims, as the most likely reason for the eastern empire's inactivity was due to internal political instability.

However, in 457, new rulers stepped forth in both halves of the Roman Empire: Majorian in the west and Leo I in the east. This brought a change to Roman-Vandal relations. Majorian managed to strengthen imperial ties with the Visigoths in Gaul and Spain, giving him enough power and confidence to attempt an attack on the Vandal kingdom. For a couple of years, he had openly bragged about planning such a feat, so when in 460 he finally sent his troops to Africa, Gaiseric was ready. Sources aren't clear what exactly happened, but once again, the Vandal king proved to be the more capable general. The Roman fleet was destroyed, and Majorian fled back to Italy where shortly afterward he was deposed from the throne.

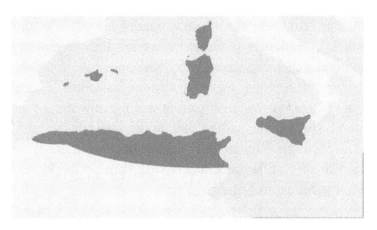

The Vandal kingdom after 455. Source: https://commons.wikimedia.org

This Vandal victory yet again prompted both the Eastern and Western Roman Empires to attempt to deal with Gaiseric via diplomacy. There was some success, as the Vandals returned some of the hostages and Huneric was officially married to Eudocia, Valentinian's daughter. Through this union, Gaiseric continued his efforts to get more involved with imperial policy in the Western Roman Empire. At the same time, the Vandals continued their raids across the central Mediterranean. In the mid-460s, the situation changed. The two Roman empires developed closer ties, pushing Gaiseric out from imperial policy in Italy. As a response, he turned his diplomatic focus to the possible enemies of the western court, talking to the Visigoths in Spain and a disgruntled Roman general in Gaul. The Vandal threat eventually became too irritable to Emperor Leo, who in 468 organized a massive attack on the Vandal kingdom. One fleet was tasked with taking back Sardinia and Sicily, and the other was sent directly to North Africa; another army was also sent from Egypt on foot toward modern-day Tunisia. An exact number of the Roman armies remains a mystery, but some estimates range between 50,000 and 100,000. For a moment, it seemed that the end of the Vandal kingdom was near.

Sardinia and Sicily fell rather easily. The Roman troops from Egypt took the city of Tripoli in modern-day Libya and continued their march toward Carthage, while the large Roman fleet was anchored off the African coast for five days near the Vandal capital. Why this fleet didn't attack immediately is unsure; there are some rumors of bribery or political scheming among the Romans, but it is also possible they waited for the Egyptian troops to come closer. Whatever the actual reason was, that waiting was the downfall of the entire operation. The winds shifted, allowing Gaiseric to send burning ships toward the Roman fleet which decimated it. What survived of the Roman flotilla immediately fled, causing the Roman army from Egypt to retreat to Tripoli.

The Romans soon lost all their territorial gains. The army from Tripoli was recalled within a couple of years as the Balkan provinces of the eastern empire were under attack. And in the early 470s, Sicily and Sardinia were reconquered by the Vandals. And by that time, Vandal authority over the Mediterranean had been regained as they once again started raiding. But more importantly, this defeat lunged the Western Roman Empire into a long civil war and emptied the treasury of the Eastern Roman Empire. Once again, both empires sought to appease the Vandals through diplomacy.

However, by the early 470s, the Mediterranean world began changing rapidly. The Western Roman Empire was slowly disintegrating through both a civil war and foreign invasion. Because of that, Gaiseric quickly lost interest in Italy as a political theater, realizing the meaningless of a western imperial title. This was only confirmed when the Western Roman Empire finally fell in 476 to a barbarian general named Odoacer who created the Kingdom of Italy.

During this year, Gaiseric concentrated on consolidating his control over his overseas lands. He agreed to give back Sicily to Odoacer in exchange for an annual tribute, as he most likely realized that his control over it was slipping. At the same time, probably because of his old age, the Vandal king began negotiating with the Eastern Roman Empire instead of continuing his warmongering politics. This resulted in a treaty of perpetual peace between the Eastern Roman Empire and the Vandal kingdom. It was signed the same year the western empire fell, and it was the first treaty in which the eastern empire, also known as the Byzantine Empire, dealt with the Vandals as a state, making an agreement which lived longer than its signatories. In it, the Byzantine Empire recognized Vandal control over its territories in North Africa and the western Mediterranean islands. In return, Gaiseric stopped the Vandal raids, returned any remaining hostages, and promised to allow Nicene Christians to practice their religion in the Vandal kingdom.

With that treaty, Gaiseric and the Vandals achieved their zenith. He managed to transform them from a small and rather irrelevant tribe to a recognized and well-respected kingdom in about fifty years. On top of that, the old Vandal king also secured peace for his state after decades of continuous wars. Because of these achievements and his long reign, Gaiseric is considered as probably one of the most successful and capable rulers of the 5th century. Unfortunately for the Vandals, he couldn't lead them forever, and in early 477, he passed away from natural causes. His death marked an end of an era and the beginning of the Vandal downfall, as none of his successors were nearly as talented as he was.

Chapter 4 – Downfall of the Vandals

With the strength the Vandals exhibited and Gaiseric's diplomatic skills, their contemporaries likely assumed the newfound North African kingdom was going to last a long time. Even to them, it was evident that a large share of the Vandals' success was owed to the capabilities of their king, but it seemed he had left his kingdom in a strong position and on stable foundations. However, those were times of great change and turbulence. And ever-shifting politics and powers made those foundations more fragile if not taken care of. It was something that Gaiseric was very capable of but a skill his successors lacked.

As a seasoned statesman, Gaiseric knew that after his death there would be a significant chance that his heirs would squabble over the throne. This is why he passed a law which stated that the oldest member of the royal house was to succeed him. At the time, it was his oldest son, Huneric, who was already in his 50s. Thanks to Gaiseric's authority, this transition went through without much commotion. But rather quickly, it became evident that Huneric wasn't even close to holding the abilities of his father. His stance was weaker, less aggressive, and not as responsive. Huneric relied solely on diplomacy, with no military threat to back it up, to help him achieve his goals. This was partially because he simply lacked the warmongering spirit of his father but also because Moorish tribes began pressing on the southern borders of the Vandal kingdom in Africa. These new threats arose because it was only Gaiseric's authority and skillful diplomacy that held them at bay. Of course, not all the tribes were hostile toward the Vandals, as Huneric remained friendly with many of them. But by the end of his reign, the region of the Aurès Mountains in modern-day eastern Algeria broke free from Vandal rule.

Coin of Huneric. Source: https://commons.wikimedia.org

Huneric's rule was also a time of change in domestic politics. As part of his agreements with the Byzantine Empire, the Vandal raiding of the Mediterranean stopped, and Huneric briefly stopped persecuting Nicene Christians despite still being a fervent Arian. On top of that, he even restituted properties taken from Roman merchants in Carthage. For a while, it seemed that the position of the local Romano-African population was getting better, promulgating a more united society in the Vandal kingdom. But later in his reign, Huneric once again began oppressing the Nicene Christians, banishing them, confiscating church estates, and even executing some of the more notable members. This kept the social division within the Vandal state alive and added to the resentment of the non-Vandal population. In 484, Huneric died, and he was succeeded by his nephew Gunthamund. Once again, the change on the throne went without much trouble, as Huneric was unpopular both among the local Roman population and among the Vandals as he had many of his Hasdingi family members killed to prevent them from trying to usurp his throne. The new king quickly eased the pressure on the Nicene Christians, lessening the unrest in the kingdom. This not only brought some peace but also helped stabilize the economy, which was in a crisis after Huneric's rule. And because the Vandals' major enemies were preoccupied with other wars, Gunthamund's reign was peaceful and somewhat successful. But unfortunately for the Vandals, it was cut short in 496 when Gunthamund died in his 40s.

Coin of Thrasamund. Source: https://commons.wikimedia.org

Thrasamund, Gunthamund's younger brother, became the new king of the Vandals. His reign marked another shift in both Vandal diplomacy and the Mediterranean world in general. Most notably, Odoacer's kingdom had fallen in 493 to the Ostrogoths, who were led by Theodoric the Great. As such, the Ostrogoths became a new power in the region, and their king worked on achieving hegemony over all Germanic kingdoms in the west. Very early in his reign, he forced the Vandals to stop raiding Italy. Then, in 500, a diplomatic union through marriage was arranged. Thrasamund married Theodoric's sister, Amalafrida, and was given the westernmost tip of Sicily as a dowry. The new Vandal queen arrived with about 5,000 armed guards, which is why some historians once thought it was a show of force and a sign of Ostrogothic hegemony over the weakening Vandal kingdom. However, it has recently been suggested that this union between the two Germanic kingdoms was between equals, and the troops were to help the Vandals as they were having troubles with the Moors once again. Either way, it seems that Thrasamund was diplomatically shifting away from the Byzantine Empire toward the Ostrogothic kingdom. Yet this alliance proved to be rather flimsy as he didn't help his brother-in-law when the Byzantines attacked southern Italy in 507. And since Thrasamund continued to work in his own interests, the idea of the Vandals being subordinated to the Ostrogoths in some way can be mostly dismissed.

However, the biggest threat to the decaying Vandal kingdom at the time were the Moors, one of the indigenous semi-nomadic Berber tribes who lived south of the Vandal kingdom. They continued to raid the borders and revolt in southern regions of the Vandal state. Most notable were the fights in the Tripolitania region, in modern-day Libya, where the Moors managed to achieve a significant victory over the Vandal cavalry; later, in 523, they even sacked Leptis Magna, an important port city in that region.

In domestic politics, Thrasamund continued his more relaxed stance toward the Nicene Christians. He maintained constant pressure on them in a nonviolent way. As an avid Arian Christian, the Vandal king helped organize the Arian church and went out of his way to persuade the local Roman population to convert to Arianism. He even organized and participated in a public theological debate with Nicene scholars, proving himself to be a well-educated and rather capable orator. This bloodless persecution helped Thrasamund to retain rather friendly relations with the Byzantines, despite still causing many grievances among his Roman subjects. However, by the time of his death in 523, Thrasamund's internal politics hadn't managed to significantly change the religious landscape of the Vandal kingdom. He was succeeded by Hilderic, Huneric's son, who was already in his 50s or 60s.

Hilderic became a very unpopular ruler early on as he was uninterested in warfare due to his old age, leaving the fighting to his younger relatives. Although the Vandals were not nearly as aggressive as in Gaiseric's time, for most of them this was unfitting behavior for a king, especially with the troubles the Moors had been causing for decades. Even worse was the fact that unlike all other Vandal kings, Hilderic issued an edict of tolerance toward the Nicene Christians in 523, ending their persecution and further antagonizing the majority of the Arian Vandals. This unusual turn in religious politics can be explained by the fact that Hilderic's mother was Eudocia, a Roman princess. Hilderic also dramatically changed foreign relations. Due to his new policies toward the Nicene Christians, he became rather close to the Byzantine Empire. And some sources even state that the new Vandal king was a personal friend of Justinian the Great before he became the Byzantine emperor in 527. Also, in 523, Hilderic imprisoned Amalafrida, Thrasamund's widow and Theodoric's sister, where she later died. He escaped Theodoric's punitive expedition only through sheer luck as the Ostrogothic king died in 526.

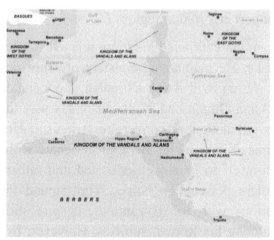

The Vandal kingdom around 526 CE. Source:
https://commons.wikimedia.org.

The culmination of Hilderic's antagonization of his Vandal subjects was his conversion to Nicene Christianity coupled with his nephew's military defeats at the hands of the Moors. For the Vandal nobility, this was too much, and in 530, a coup was staged led by Hilderic's cousin, Gelimer, who was from another branch of the Hasdingi royal family. Hilderic, his nephews, and his closest relatives were imprisoned, and it seems Gelimer had wide support from the Vandal population. However, the Byzantine emperor immediately began applying diplomatic pressure on Gelimer to restore Hilderic to the throne. The new Vandal king refused, prompting Justinian to send another envoy demanding that Hilderic and his entourage be sent to Constantinople for safety. Gelimer once again refused, probably calculating that Justinian's threats were empty words as he was already fighting the Persians in the east. This, as well as the previous disastrous Roman campaigns, would dissuade Justinian from actually attacking. But Gelimer was wrong. Justinian was fueled with a burning desire to rebuild the old Roman Empire and prove himself worthy as a ruler. On top of that, he was driven to retake North Africa because of religious reasons, mainly to save local Nicene Christians from being persecuted once again. It is also possible that his close relations with Hilderic were a motivation for him as well.

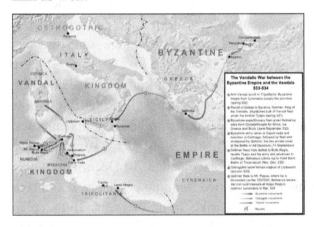

Map of the Vandalic War. Source: https://commons.wikimedia.org

Whatever was the ultimate incentive, Justinian ended the war with Persia in 532 and began gathering troops and resources for an attack. In mid-533, a Byzantine army of 18,000 rather experienced troops, led by the now famous general Belisarius, set sail toward the Vandal kingdom. If that wasn't enough trouble for Gelimer, two rebellions had also broken out in the Vandal state. One was in Tripolitania and led by the local population, which the Vandal king chose to ignore until the threat of the Byzantine Empire boiled over. The other was in Sardinia, where a local governor tried to declare independence and began negotiating with the Byzantines. It seems Gelimer lacked information about the incoming Byzantine army because he sent his brother, Tzazon, with the bulk of his navy and about 5,000 soldiers to put down the Sardinian revolt. Belisarius, on the other hand, had better intel, which he gathered from disgruntled former subjects of the Vandal kingdom who defected to the Byzantine Empire. Thus, he knew that Gelimer left his shores undefended, didn't have an army ready, and faced trouble with the local population. As a seasoned general, Belisarius chose to land immediately before the Vandal navy returned. The Byzantines disembarked on the eastern shore of modern-day Tunisia, about 150 miles (240 kilometers) south of Carthage and immediately began marching toward it.

Gelimer was actually away from his capital, which additionally implies he lacked intel of the Byzantine attack. As soon as he heard of it, he ordered Ammatas, another one of his brothers, who was in Carthage, to gather troops from the city and march south to meet with the Byzantines. He also commanded the execution of Hilderic and his family. At the same time, the Vandal king began shadowing the Byzantine army but decided not to attack it as his most able soldiers were in Sardinia. Instead, he opted to encircle his enemies. Gelimer's plan was to have Ammatas stop them 10 miles (16 kilometers) south of Carthage at a place called Ad Decimum, where he would then divide his troops in two, sending his nephew to attack from the flank while he would strike from the rear. If the plan worked, it would have most likely been a crushing victory for the Vandals. But that wasn't the case. Ammatas arrived too late and was attacked and killed before he could properly arrange his troops. And the Byzantine vanguard caught and decimated the flanking Vandal army. That didn't stop Gelimer as he attacked from the rear, though. He managed to win an astonishing victory, routing the more numerous Byzantine forces. But he found his dead brother, and instead of following up on his initial victory, he paused to bury him. That allowed Belisarius time to reorganize and counterattack, saving himself from a devastating defeat. Gelimer was driven away, and the Byzantine army entered the undefended Carthage.

Coin of Gelimer. Source: https://commons.wikimedia.org

The Vandal king rallied and regrouped his army in the eastern regions of the Vandal state. He recalled Tzazon from Sardinia and mustered as many forces as he could, even gathering some unreliable Moorish troops. With a refreshed army, he marched toward Carthage and laid a siege, cutting off aqueducts and raiding supplies. His intention most likely wasn't to take the city but to force Belisarius to ride out and meet him in battle. He also tried to stir trouble in Carthage itself by sending agents to persuade both the local population as well as Arian soldiers in the Byzantine army to join the Vandal cause. That proved ineffective, and in December of 533, the two armies clashed once again as Belisarius marched out toward the Vandal camp at Tricamarum, 20 miles (32 kilometers) west of Carthage. There, once again, the Vandals proved their mettle, managing to separate the Byzantine army. But during the battle, Tzazon was killed, which broke the fighting will of the Vandal king. In the end, he was beaten and forced to retreat toward Mons Papua in the Numidian highlands. Gelimer was besieged there, slowly starving throughout the winter. With him blocked, Belisarius quickly took over the remaining regions of the Vandal kingdom, including the islands. He gathered the remaining Vandals, promising them fair treatment. On top of that, Gelimer's treasury was captured, meaning that the Vandal king had no way to gather new troops.

By March of 534, Gelimer finally decided to surrender to Belisarius. By that time, he was a mere shadow of his former self, a broken, starved, desperate man who had lost all his riches and family. With that, the Vandal kingdom finally fell, and North Africa once again became part of the Roman Empire. In the summer of that year, Belisarius sent about 2,000 Vandal soldiers and Gelimer to Constantinople, where they were paraded in a triumphant celebration of Byzantine victory. Justinian then spared Gelimer, retiring him to an estate in Galatia, located in modern-day Turkey. The remaining Vandal soldiers, both from Constantinople and Africa, were sent to the eastern frontier to fight the Persians as able cavalrymen. Some of them remained in North Africa while others went back to Spain, where there was a small Vandal community left. But they slowly became assimilated in other societies and nations, and soon after their final defeat, the Vandals lost their ethnic identity. They and their kingdom disappeared from the historical stage, leaving only a faint memory of their former glory.

Chapter 5 – Vandal Society

In modern times, when people think of the barbarian tribes from late antiquity and the early medieval era, they often transcribe our own contemporary ideas of how society and ethnic identity are defined. That would make it easy to assume that the Vandals were a homogenous group of people who lived in a simple tribal society with the same language and ancestors. However, that assumption is both oversimplified and, for the most part, wrong. To be able to fully understand the Vandals' past, one has to begin with understanding their ethnic identity and social structure.

The question of who the Vandals were always begins with their ethnicity. The most common mistake people make with this question is to assume that ancient nationalities were as rigid and defined as they are today. But they weren't. For example, around the 1st century CE, before the great migrations started, the Vandals and the Goths were rather close to each other; in fact, they were almost indistinguishable. They spoke two dialects of the same language rather than two different languages. Their physical appearance was similar, their cultures were similar, and their religions were close to each other. If by chance one member of the Vandal tribe moved to the Goths, he would have no problem fitting in with the new group. Plus, the identities of these groups were usually linked with the ruling family of the tribe, meaning that one would identify as a subject of a Vandal king and not as an ethnic Vandal. This is why historians, to some degree, have trouble identifying and separating early tribal societies of Central and Northern Europe. Of course, these ethnicities began to firm up as time passed, especially when the migrations started and tribes began encountering more and more different groups.

Things become slightly more complicated in situations where several different tribes moved together under one ruler. We can see that the Alans, once a separate tribe, followed the Vandal kings for such a long time that contemporary historians simply counted them as a part of the Vandals, meaning they lost their unique identity, which may be true to some degree. And by the 5th century, when the Vandals under Gaiseric crossed over to Africa and established their own kingdom, the entire army was seen as the Vandals, despite consisting of Goths, Alans, Suebi, and possibly other barbarians as well. To a degree, this was true, as they represented themselves to the Romans as the Vandals. This ethnic unity was especially emphasized in 442 when Gaiseric allotted all his warrior followers hereditary lands through which they could support themselves economically while they fought in his army. By that time, being a Vandal meant that you were a part of the military aristocracy of the Vandal kingdom who lived on the so-called Vandal estates, regardless of one's roots. These people would represent themselves as Vandals to members of other social or ethnic groups. However, it is possible that when these Vandals were interacting among themselves, they recognized their own different roots. Yet there is no sign that this internal differentiation in any way affected the ethnic unity or social organization of the Vandals in general.

This, however, doesn't mean that other factors, besides the ownership of a Vandal estate, didn't bind them in the single ethnic group. There was also religion, as they had adopted Arianism on their way to Northern Africa, and language. All of them spoke dialects of the same Eastern Germanic language, and over time, those dialects became almost indistinguishable. However, not much is known about the Vandalic language itself, apart from their close relation to the Gothic language. It's worth noting, though, that it is likely most of the Vandals were more than proficient in Latin. But language, similar to religion, clearly separated the Vandals from the local Roman and Moorish population. Yet this isn't where the ethnic differences stop. There was also a distinctive masculinity present in the identity of the Vandals, and it was largely restricted to the adult male members of the military aristocracy. This was probably the case because the Vandal group that moved from the Danube to North Africa was more of a wandering warband than a migrating people, even though some of the warriors brought their families with them. Because of that masculine restriction to the Vandal identity, there is an open question of the status that women and children had in their society.

On the one hand, historians are certain women and children were, to a certain extent, a part of Vandal society, but due to the limited exposure in the Roman sources of that time, modern historians can't determine to what degree they could claim Vandal ethnicity. This omission of women could be partially explained by the focus of the sources on political, military, and religious matters, which were at the time almost exclusively male fields, even in the Roman Empire. On top of that, there are no clear mentions of a woman being a Vandal in her own right; rather, she was one only through association. From those sources, we also see that wives and daughters of the Vandals could, to a certain degree, transmit some ethnic rights to her husband and sons, but their own ethnic positions remain unclear. Thus, most modern historians tend to characterize the Vandal identity as being mostly connected with adult males, whereas women and children were only partially acknowledged, although it is possible there were some isolated exceptions to that rule.

Apart from the aforementioned ethnic markers, there is one more mentioned in the sources: their appearance. 6th century Byzantine sources mention the Vandals as being tall, blonde, and pale. That wouldn't separate them much from other Germanic tribes of Northern Europe, but they were quite different from the local Romanized Africans who had darker skin and hair. Besides that, sources imply that long hair, as well as beards and mustaches, were common among the Vandals. There are also mentions of so-called barbarian clothes, which were distinctively different from local attire. But for those we have no description, so we can only guess how they looked. It is likely they had roots in the more traditional clothing of the northerners, like fur and leather; however, this would be mere speculation as they could have also adopted some aspects of local clothing of the former Roman elites. Whatever was the case, clothing and facial hair aren't a clear indicator of one's ethnicity. Many Romanized Africans who served in the Vandal court or who were trying to be close to the elite circles of the kingdom also wore "barbarian clothes" and had longer hair. It is also possible that some of the Vandals chose to shave and wear other attire to emphasize their wealth.

And the majority of the Vandals were rather wealthy, at least since the creation of the Vandal kingdom. It would be easy to assume that most of their treasures came from looting across the Mediterranean, especially during Gaiseric's reign; however, that wasn't the case, even though that surely brought some extra income. The real source of their wealth was their own lands and Vandal estates. The Vandals, as the Roman aristocrats before them, employed workers and land tenants to work their fields, which comprised mostly of wheat, olives, figs, and almonds, and then typically sold the crops to merchants. Luckily for both the Vandals and the local Romanized population, trade didn't die out. After the fall of Rome, trade simply shifted toward Constantinople and the Byzantine Empire as well as Spain, although to a lesser degree. Survival of both trade and local productions, both of food and manufactured products like vases, textiles, oils, etc., meant that the Vandal kingdom was rather prosperous. Of course, the majority of that wealth went into the hands of the Vandals, who were the elite class in the state, but it also overflowed to the local population, which continued to live as decently as it had under Roman rule, at least in economic aspects.

The arrival of the Vandals didn't mean that the local population stopped paying taxes, but there were changes in that system as well. For one, there was no more annual "tribute" in wheat and other food used to feed the city of Rome. That opened new surpluses for the merchants, although they had to work harder to find new markets. Taxes were also lowered for military expenditures, as unlike the imperial army, the Vandals themselves were the core fighting force who lived on the estates given to them. That helped the recuperation of the economy shortly after Gaiseric's conquest. But for most of his reign, the Vandal kingdom didn't mint its own coins. At the time, their need for coins was satisfied through trade and looting; thus, the main money in use was of both the Western and Eastern Roman Empires. Occasionally, they minted some silver and copper coins to satisfy the needs of local use. But in the last two decades of the 5th century, they began minting golden coins and even expanded the production of silver coins. These were still mostly confined to local use and followed the Roman/Byzantine standards in weights and denomination. The Vandals even copied the style of Roman coins both in texts and ruler portraits.

However, looking at the economy of the Vandal kingdom, it is clear that despite the wealth of the country in general, which made most of the Vandals rich, they didn't get too directly involved in it. They left production and trade to the locals while they collected their dues. Their focus was on military issues. The only obligation of every proper member of Vandal society, i.e., adult males, was to fight for his king. And following their older tradition, most of them were a part of the heavy cavalry. They often used lamellar or chainmail armor and metal helmets and fought with lances and swords. Their mounted troops were complemented with infantry corps which used both swords, spears, and shields, as well as bows and arrows. On top of that, there are some indications that unlike most barbarian armies, the Vandals grasped at least the basics of siege warfare as they were rather successful in attacks on fortified cities across the Mediterranean. Lastly, since their arrival in North Africa, the Vandals also became rather able seamen, as their navy was one of the strongest in the region at the time. Of course, not all of the Vandals were necessarily warriors, at least not primarily.

A 5ᵗʰ-century mosaic depicting a Vandal horseman. Source: https://commons.wikimedia.org

A minority of them were first and foremost members of the royal court, which, in essence, was the entourage of the Vandal king. They helped their king rule over the state, advised him, welcomed foreign envoys, and traveled to other courts on diplomatic missions. As such, the royal court wasn't in a fixed location, although most of the time it was located in Carthage. But all of the kings had royal estates farther away from the capital where they also conducted their business, and most of the court followed them there. It is also worth noting that a position in the royal court wasn't exclusively limited to the Vandals. There were some Romano-Africans who managed to "penetrate" the highest circles of the Vandal kingdom. And if we look further away from the court toward local administrative offices, we see that Romano-Africans were the ones who actually held them. However, low-ranking bureaucratic positions weren't of much interest to the Vandals; as such, they were more than willing to leave them in the hands of the local population who was eager to cooperate in exchange for an advance in social status. These administrative workers were also paid from the taxes; thus, there was also an economic incentive as well.

The bureaucratic network was mostly copied from the Romans, as well as education and laws. There were some minor changes, of course, but the Vandal kings generally held up the idea that if something worked, it didn't require change. They were more focused on keeping themselves and their Vandal followers on top of society. With that as their ultimate goal, Gaiseric and his successors created the kingship ideology, which was shaped from Vandal barbarian sentiments and sense of rule combined with the ideals of the Roman imperial power and local political and governmental systems, seasoned with antique Punic traditions and Arian religious justifications. In this system, the Vandal king owned his own royal lands which provided extra income to him, allowing the royal family to remain the center of power and wealth. The king's decisions were the law, and he could take the majority of the plundered wealth. But at the same time, he was responsible for the well-being of his immediate Vandal followers as well as the rest of his subjects. He was the protector and spreader of the "true religion" and the continuation of the old Punic kings of Carthage. And ultimately, he was the supreme military commander who led his men into battle, making military victories necessary for earning respect.

From this mix of ideologies, we can see a pattern which is true of the entire Vandal society. It isn't entirely excluding or limiting, even though it seems so at first glance. The local Roman population could advance despite not being Vandal or Arian, and every Arian Vandal could get ostracized if he disagreed with the king. There was a clear differentiation between the Vandals and Romano-Africans, but there was also a sense of integration, all under the strong rule of a king. This could be explained simply as through what most Vandals wanted to achieve: they wanted to live and be treated as the elite or aristocracy. For that, they needed to amalgamate their society with the rest of the Romano-African population. And in the end, the longer they lived in North Africa, the more and more they indulged in the luxurious lifestyle synonymous with late Roman aristocrats rather than the life of a barbarian warrior. And thanks to Gaiseric's law of succession, most of the kings after him were rather old, lacking the military drive of younger rulers. This combination is often cited as the most important cause of the fall of the Vandal kingdom. Over the decades, the Vandal barbarian society decayed in the same way Roman society did, causing it to crumble from foreign threats.

Chapter 6 – Religion, Culture, and the Vandals

When one thinks of the Vandals, or for that matter any other barbarian tribe, often the first image that comes to mind is a group of rugged ruffians in fur, drinking beer and behaving rather coarsely. And thanks to their legacy, it's even likelier to imagine them burning a book or a painting to roast their meat. Yet this insensitivity to culture wasn't actually a typical characteristic of the Vandals. It was possible this was true of 1st century Vandals, though even then it is highly unlikely. But after they formed their Vandal kingdom in Northern Africa, archeological sources tell us a different story of Vandal behavior and taste.

Despite what most people would expect from a tribe with a reputation like the Vandals, their arrival to North Africa didn't mark a cultural apocalypse of the region. The deterioration actually began before their arrival, as there were many signs of theaters, public baths, and other public structures either becoming rundown or entirely abandoned. The Vandal arrival at best worsened the situation for some of those institutions as chaos and upheaval spread across the lands. But there are no clear signs of them actually targeting cultural centers. And later, during Gaiseric's rule, there are signs of the government repairing some of the public structures. Also, some of the privately owned baths and theaters grew during the late 5th century, something that wouldn't have been possible if the Vandals were opposed to cultivating cultural life. Further evidence to contrast this could be found in works of literature at the time. During the Vandals' rule, North Africa became a rather sprawling hotspot of poets and writers, so much so that some modern historians refer to this period as the Vandal renaissance. They all wrote in Latin and were members of the local Romano-African society, which suggests that the cultural life under the Vandals didn't simply end but dynamically evolved and adapted to their new circumstances.

Many of the critics of that era lamented that the poems' quality was far from the older Roman classics, but looking at other works done in other countries at the time, this isn't something to hold against poets in the Vandal kingdom. But the question remains - why did so many Romano-African writers emerge in a state under the supposedly uncultured barbarian rule? The answer is simple: The Vandals themselves enjoyed their work. Some of them were more than eager to financially support poets who would then in return write poems to embellish the deeds and qualities of their benefactors. These were even done in honor of some of the Vandal kings in the form of panegyric, which is a published poem or text in praise of someone. However, these were lost, as many other works were during this time.

This attitude toward poems is indicative of the entire relationship between the Vandals and culture. They wanted to emulate the Roman elite way of life; thus, they were more than eager to continue to be patrons of the arts as much as the former Roman aristocrats were. This is also why they built Roman-styled villas and adorned them with mosaics and other ornaments, also in the style of the Romans. It also explains why we can't actually talk about Vandal culture but rather about their attitude toward it in this chapter, as almost none of the Vandals actually created works of art—at least, as far as we know. This isn't surprising, considering they were primarily soldiers. But in no sense were they mindless brutes who cared little about the finer features of life.

Mid-5th-century mosaic from Carthage depicting everyday life of a female member of the aristocracy. Source: https://commons.wikimedia.org

This is also evident by the fact that the educational system in the Vandal state remained highly functional, only being matched by the Byzantines and Ostrogoths. Indeed, we once again see them continuing Roman traditions with these schools, offering seven classical subjects: grammar, dialectics, rhetoric, geometry, arithmetic, astronomy, and music. They also read and learned from old Roman writers such as Virgil, Ovid, and Lucan. And many of the educated elites, which also included some of the Vandal kings and aristocracy, held the view that knowledge shouldn't be simply stored by the few but shared and expanded. As such, education and literacy were seen as a prized asset in the Vandal kingdom. These skills were useful for the needs of bureaucracy as well as trade and other business. According to some research, in one remote farming community, basic literacy was at a staggering 15% of the population; this would have definitely been higher in urban centers. If this could be assumed to be the norm, it would prove that the educational system in Vandal Africa was impressive compared to other countries at the time. Another sign of how healthy this system was is the fact that it also produced trained professionals like lawyers and doctors. We hear of them through stories and anecdotes written by poets, but there were also some works written on these topics. Of course, these professions, like education and culture in general, were a continuation of earlier Roman traditions.

There is, however, one substantial distinction between art created in North Africa during the Vandal reign and elsewhere at the time. Unlike pretty much anywhere else in the Mediterranean region and Europe, artists working in the Vandal kingdom created almost exclusively secular works, focusing on profane rather than on religious matters. Once again, this is best seen in poems which focus more on hunting, everyday life and interactions, and court life rather than on the celebration of Christ and God. This is not to say there weren't some texts about religious subjects; after all, there are several concerning the Vandal persecution of the Nicene Christians, but those were in the minority. This secular approach toward culture wasn't a new invention by the Vandal ruling elite as there were signs of it occurring in the decades before their arrival. Yet when the Vandals came, it was a perfect solution for an active peaceful coexistence between the Arian Vandals and the Nicene Romano-Africans. And despite being portrayed as uneducated, vile barbarians, it was their appreciation of art, classical literature, and learning that provided a base for creating common secular relations between the Vandal and Romano-African elites.

Seeing that the Vandals weren't actually unsophisticated wild men, at least not at the level they are usually portrayed as, the question remains why they were represented in such a way. The answer is rather simple. Most of our sources on them were written by either Roman or Byzantine writers or by local Romano-Africans. The former were, for most of the time, open enemies of the Vandals, and they did the best they could to propagate them as vile and menacing to society. This is especially true in the stories about the sack of Rome in 455, which was for centuries represented as the height of barbarianism but was actually plundering by people who knew that the artworks they took were valuable and appreciated. And the latter were often oppressed by their new Arian masters and sought to demonize the Vandals because of it. And that conflict of Arian Vandal invaders and local Nicene Christians seems to be contradictory to the earlier mention of secularity in the culture of the Vandal kingdom. But before that can be explained, the differences between these two schools of Christianity should be explained more clearly.

The main issue in which Nicene and Arian Christians disagree is the nature of the Holy Trinity—God, Jesus, and the Holy Spirit. For the Nicene Christians, and how it is most practiced in Christian churches today, these three are of the same essence and thus equal. On the other hand, Arian Christians, named after the founder of this doctrine Arius, a 3rd-century priest from Alexandria, thought otherwise. For them, Jesus was begotten at a certain point in time as he was the son of God, making him distinctive from God the Father. Because of that, Christ is subordinate to God and thus not his equal. At the same time, the Holy Spirit is only a representation of God the Father's power. Because of that rejection of the conventional Christian doctrine of the Holy Trinity, Arianism has been categorized as a nontrinitarian school of Christianity. The most notable present-day nontrinitarians are Jehovah's Witnesses, who are often called "modern-day Arians," and the Church of Jesus Christ of Latter-day Saints, more widely known as the Mormon Church. At first glance, this dogmatic issue of the nature of the Holy Trinity seems small and rather irrelevant, but for early Christians, it was an important debate whose outcome was a matter of salvation for the believers.

And since North Africa was one of the more important theological centers of the Roman Empire before the arrival of the Vandals, this matter was rather important to the local population, or at least to their bishops and ecumenical leaders. For the Vandals, religion was of secondary importance, especially in the early years of the Vandal kingdom. Gaiseric's attacks on the Nicene churches were guided more by his greediness as those were rather wealthy. This was also an attempt to sever the ties of the local Romano-Africans with the rest of the Roman world so the Vandals could secure their rule. Religious motives were at best of minor importance, if they even existed at all. Some historians even argue that the Vandals converted and stayed Arian only for their own benefit as, at the time of their conversions, some of the Roman emperors were Arian themselves. This could be further attested by Gaiseric's threatening to persecute Nicene Christians as a negotiation tool and then toning down the religious oppression toward them when he secured his alliance with Valentinian III. Later on, there were some religious motives for persecution, most notably under Huneric's rule, but those could have been once again aimed at gathering more lands and wealth from the Nicene Church as well as attempting to secure his rule when it was nearing its end.

Later on, Thrasamund once again put pressure on the Nicene clergy by trying to promote Arianism and form a more concrete and organized Arian Church. His motives behind this were certainly religious to a degree as he honestly felt it was his duty to spread "proper" Christianity. But at the same time, Thrasamund was also guided by pragmatism. He sought to unify the state and the church, emulating the Byzantine model, something that was started during Gaiseric's reign. For the Vandal kings, this was impossible to achieve with the Nicene Christians as they would remain loyal to their religious superiors in Rome and Constantinople and, in extension, to their emperors. The only way for the Vandals to copy this imperial ideology was to bind themselves with the Arian faith, which was still Christianity but not tied with the Roman Empire. Seeing that this was the ultimate goal, Vandal kings, especially Thrasamund, were rather careful not to pressure the common population. Rather, their main targets were parts of the higher clergy. They even tried to make Arianism attractive as much as possible to Romano-Africans, especially to the elites.

Thus, in general, the Vandal religious policy could be classified as "rough tolerance." This type of an approach to religious issues was characterized by longer periods of relative peace which would be intertwined with eruptions of localized and selective oppression and violence toward the native population. And one of the staples of this policy was an avoidance of discussion between the two religious groups, as that would further antagonize them. This was especially true among the common people of the Vandal kingdom; while there were some clerical debates among the clergy, they were done to attract the flock toward one church or the other.

Yet this religious policy shows that for the Vandals, religion was not a matter of primary concern, at least not in the matter of the state. It was only used and abused when needed. This was in striking contrast to most of their contemporaries, especially the Romans. In the end, it seems that the Vandals weren't religious fanatics, as many of the earlier history books and sources represented them to be. They were pragmatics. And when combined with the rectified image of their dealing toward art and culture, we see that most of our misconceptions of them were created through historical propaganda aimed at them. The Vandals weren't behaving like simple-minded barbarians and heathen zealots but rather as unscrupulous businessmen who would do anything to gain more money and power, regardless of the morality of their actions, while at the same time representing themselves as an important part of the elite circles.

Conclusion

Looking at the entire story of the Vandals, it is painfully obvious that this tribe has suffered a bad reputation for centuries without anyone trying to defend their honor. One of the reasons for this is the fact that they themselves remained silent about their actions, as they left us without any sources from their own quills, at least for now. However, their enemies wrote much about them, persuading us that the Vandals were evil and deserved to be destroyed. This also made them the perfect scapegoat for the fall of Rome, which since its disappearance has been romanticized as the pinnacle of civilization and culture. Yet when we look at the Vandals through the eyes of archeology and in a wider historical perspective, we clearly see that this wasn't the reality. This, of course, does not mean that the Vandals were completely innocent. They did pillage, destroy, kill, and torture. But so did pretty much everyone else at the time, even the Romans. The Vandals were no worse or better than others. And yes, they were one of the reasons why the Western Roman Empire fell. But so were the Goths, Franks, Huns, and other tribes, as well as the Roman themselves with their constant civil wars and other internal issues.

And in contrast to the Romans' propaganda, the Vandals were actually patrons of art. They cherished culture, especially poetry. This relation between the Vandals and art goes against the very image of the Vandals propagated by the term "vandalism." They weren't mindless defacers of monuments and artwork. They simply plundered valuables, something conquering armies have done throughout history. Even the term "vandalism" was coined over a millennium after the disappearance of the Vandals during the French Revolution. It was created by a French bishop to describe the devastation of artwork during the revolution, only furthering the perception of the Vandals as wretched barbarians with a thirst for destruction. And the idea of the Vandals being the antithesis of civilized life is the furthest from the truth. Of all the barbarian tribes that formed new states on the ruins of the Western Roman Empire, it was the Vandals who accepted most of the Roman customs, ways of life, and social organization. They were the most Romanized barbarians of them all.

The story of the Vandals teaches us one important life lesson as well. When judging others, don't simply go by the first impression or what others tell you about them. Take a deeper and wider look, take into account all of their circumstances and surroundings, and try to find out their motivations and goals. And then form your own opinion based on facts, not on hearsay. By not doing this, you may end seeing only the worst in some while ignoring the flaws in others, including yourself.

Part 3: The Gallic Wars

A Captivating Guide to the Military Campaigns that Expanded the Roman Republic and Helped Julius Caesar Transform Rome into the Greatest Empire of the Ancient World

Introduction

Rome wasn't built in a day, and neither was the Roman Empire. One of history's most powerful and influential realms established itself as a free and independent republic long before the likes of Julius Caesar and Emperor Marcus Aurelius. Great philosophers and intellectuals like Cicero and Lucretius graced the ancient paved roads of the Roman Republic nearly 2,000 years ago and helped build the reputation of that polity to be as equal to those of the Greeks.

As Rome swelled with tradespeople, artisans, slaves, and wealthy merchant families, its politicians struggled to maintain the fundamental democratic properties of the republican government. Rules were bent and broken, politicians and voters were bribed and lied to, and eventually, the power of Rome fell to the one man who could muster the respect and loyalty of the world-famous Roman army.

That man was Gaius Julius Caesar. A patrician and Populares of the Roman Republic, Caesar used the territorial threat of the Gauls of Western Europe to wage the Gallic Wars and seize ultimate power. His actions eradicated the democratic system, beginning the era of the ruthless tyranny of the Roman Empire in three continents.

Most of the historical record of this series of European wars comes from Julius Caesar himself. Caesar's book, the *Commentāriī dē Bellō Gallicō,* more commonly known in English as *Commentaries on the Gallic War,* is his firsthand account of the wars, although it is written in the third-person narrative. He also made a habit of proudly boasting of his successful military campaigns in letters sent home to Rome.

Chapter 1 – Ancient Gaul

All Gaul is divided into three parts, one of which the Belgae inhabit, the Aquitani another, those who in their own language are called Celts, in our Gauls, the third. All these differ from each other in language, customs and laws.

(Julius Caesar, *Commentaries on the Gallic War*)

Ancient Gauls existed throughout most of Western and Central Europe during the Iron Age, starting in about 500 BCE.[1] More diverse than the writings of Julius Caesar perhaps suggest, the people of Gaul inhabited the lands of modern France, Belgium, and Luxembourg, as well as parts of the Netherlands, Germany, Switzerland, and Northern Italy.[2] The name "Gaul" was given to these people by the Romans, though most of them preferred to call themselves Celts, as did their cousins living on the British Isles.

The Gauls were an agrarian people whose farming societies were divided into classes of laborers and landowners. The ruling class was fierce and expanded their territory at the expense of the neighboring Germanic tribes and the Roman Republic. By 390 BCE, the Gauls had settled along the northern Mediterranean coast, and a group of

---

[1] Hughes, David. *The British Chronicles.* 2007.
[2] "Gaul Definition." *Ancient History Encyclopedia.* Web. 28 April 2011.

them called the Senones boldly moved in to sack Rome.[3] Led by a chieftain named Brennus, the invading tribe burned and plundered the city until both defenders and offenders were exhausted. The remaining Roman soldiers offered the Senones a tidy sum of gold to leave, and the proposal was accepted.

These Celtic tribes were known by several names depending on which region they lived in and who was naming them. The terms "Keltoi," "Celtae," "Celtini," and several others referred to the inhabitants of the different regions of Gaul. The commonalities that bound all the Celtic tribes of these regions together are still not completely known, but their fates would eventually unite them. They and their lands were a target for the Roman Empire and their conquests.

Without written historical information from this era, what is known about the Gauls mostly comes from what has been found in archaeology, some linguistic studies, and, more recently, through genetics. The information that has been gleaned from the remnants of the society shows that the Celtic tribes living in Gaul prior to the Gallic Wars had a successful agricultural society established. Animal husbandry was well developed with these people as well. Trading took place between the tribes in centers that were quite urbanized for the time, and while the tribes kept their own social orders, they traded crafts, agricultural products, and tools consistently. The tribes were still considered to be in the act of expansion, and they were often at odds with each other over territory.

The following map indicates the primary route taken by Gaius Julius Caesar during the Gallic Wars.

---

[3] "Gaul, Ancient Region, Europe." *Encyclopedia Britannica.* Web.

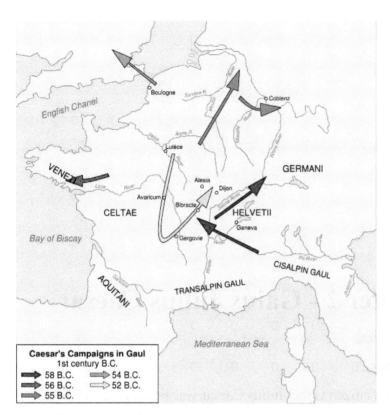

4

Chapter 2 - Gaius Julius Caesar

Veni, vidi, vici.

(Julius Caesar)

The Roman citizen Gaius Julius Caesar was born around 100 BCE to a wealthy and influential family. Part of the aristocratic patrician class, Caesar was born into a society that expected him to serve in the government and the military, as both bodies were considered the pillars of Roman civilization. First, however, as a privileged young boy, Julius Caesar was entitled to the very best education the Western world had to offer.

Young Caesar was tutored by Marcus Antonius Gnipho, a man who had been born free in Gaul before his parents sold him into slavery.[5] Classically educated and eventually freed by his owner, Gnipho set up a school in Rome and became a teacher to many of the Roman Republic's wealthy boys and even some girls. He taught Julius Caesar lessons in literature, rhetoric, oratory, Latin, and Greek, the latter of which was very in fashion among the elite Romans.

---

[5] Toner, Jerry. *How to Manage Your Slaves.* 2014.

During Caesar's childhood and early adulthood, the Roman Republic was engaged in a power struggle with other kingdoms of Italy in what was called the Social War. Lasting from 91 to 88 BCE, the Social War was mostly caused by the refusal of the republic to grant citizenship to its outlying allies throughout Italy.[6] In ancient Rome, citizenship was highly prized and difficult to come by; only men over the age of 18 who had been born free in Rome to parents who were also born there were considered citizens.[7] Citizenship granted one the right to vote and serve in the government, and it was denied to women, children, slaves, and foreigners.

The Roman Republic was victorious in the Social War, but to avoid any such uprising again, it was forced to allow free men of at least 18 years in age who were born within the realm to claim citizenship.[8] The infighting was not finished in the capital city, however, and this time it had a personal impact on the Caesar family. Julius Caesar's uncle, Gaius Marius, and Marius' protégé, Lucius Cornelius Sulla, began a violent feud over their opposing political views. Marius was a Populares: he believed, like many other Romans, that the Senate must work in favor of the working and poor classes. By contrast, Sulla was an Optimate: he and other Optimates believed that the aristocratic and wealthy classes must be upheld, protected, and respected above all.[9]

In 82 BCE, Sulla defeated Gaius Marius the Younger, the son of Gaius Marius (who had died of natural causes in 86 BCE), and established himself as the dictator of Rome.[10] Though by law, Roman leaders—called consuls—were elected and served for only one year, dictatorship was a fail-safe in the republic that could be

---

[6] Dart, Christopher J. *The Social War, 91 to 88 BCE: A History of the Italian Insurgency.* 2016.

[7] Loewenstein, K. *The Governance of ROME.* 1973.

[8] Goldsworthy, Adrian. *Caesar: The Life of a Colossus.* 2013.

[9] Kittridge, Mary and Arthur Meier Schlesinger. *Marc Antony.* 1987.

[10] Ibid.

used in times of military emergencies.[11] As dictator, Sulla punished young Julius Caesar for his connection to Gaius Marius, calling upon him to resign his important position as the high priest of Jupiter and divorce his new wife, Cornelia Cinna. Caesar had no choice but to relinquish his position in the clergy, but he refused to go through with the divorce and instead fled the city with Cornelia. They stayed away, Caesar employed with the military, until Sulla's death in 78 BCE.[12] Since the dictatorial administration had already confiscated his family's wealth, Caesar had little to come back to, but he took on work as a lawyer to earn money and support himself.[13]

Julius Caesar proved to be a popular figure within Rome. He became famous for his public speeches, and within a few years of his return, Caesar was elected military tribune to the Roman Senate. The role involved meeting with government officials, speaking on behalf of the army, and voting on issues that affected the military. Tribunes like Caesar were also responsible for leading cohorts, the ancient Roman equivalent of a modern battalion.[14] The job was considered the first stepping stone into the heart of the Roman government, and that was a direction in which Julius Caesar decided he would like to travel. He made political allies who were also inclined toward the Populares ideology, and by 67 BCE, he had not only worked as quaestor in Hispania but had married, after the death of Cornelia, Pompeia, the granddaughter of Sulla.[15,16]

Seven years later, having served as the governor of a region in Hispaniola and gaining popularity within the political sphere, Caesar formed a pact with two other powerful men to wield the ultimate

---

[11] "Dictator, Roman Official." *Encyclopedia Britannica.* Web.

[12] Mackay, Christopher S. *Ancient Rome.* 2004.

[13] Baker, G. P. *Sulla the Fortunate.* 2001.

[14] Cartwright, Mark. "Tribune." *Ancient History Encyclopedia.* Web. 7 December 2016.

[15] Paterculus. *Historiae Romanae.*

[16] Chrystal, Paul. *Roman Women.* 2017.

power of Rome between them.[17] The group, known as the First Triumvirate, included Gnaeus Pompeius Magnus, more commonly known as Pompey the Great, and Marcus Licinius Crassus. Pompey was a skilled general with experience in Rome's eastern realms, and Crassus was immensely wealthy due to the seizure and sale of lands that belonged to the late Sulla.[18] With their combined experience, the triumvirate had the funds, political knowledge, and social networks necessary to force their way to the top.

In 59 BCE, Caesar instructed his daughter, Julia, to marry Pompey to cement their political alliance.[19] Caesar was elected consul the same year, and to satisfy his allies, he granted free land to army veterans, as was requested from Pompey, and farmers received a tax break, which was requested by Crassus. For himself, the new Consul of Rome took over the governorship of both Cisalpine Gaul and Illyricum, regions he believed put him in a position to become very rich. Soon afterward, he was also granted the governorship of Transalpine Gaul. Both Cisalpine and Transalpine Gaul were in close proximity to Italy, lying on either side of the Alps.

It was the ideal situation for Julius Caesar. Initially, he planned to launch a campaign against Dacia, located in modern-day Romania, for the gold beneath its surface. However, an opportunity in Transalpine Gaul would draw his attention there instead.[20] His time in office was set for five years, and it promised to be full of opportunities for him.

However, this was the worst possible thing for the Celtic tribes of Western Europe.

---

[17] Bunsen, Matthew. *A Dictionary of the Roman Empire.* 1995.

[18] "Marcus Licinius Crassus, Roman Statesman." *Encyclopedia Britannica.* Web.

[19] Bunsen, Matthew. *A Dictionary of the Roman Empire.* 1995.

[20] Waldman, Carl and Catherine Mason. *Encyclopedia of European Peoples.* 2006.

Chapter 3 – The Helvetii Celts

There was no doubt that the Helvetii were the most powerful of the whole of Gaul.

(Julius Caesar)

The Helvetii were one of the Celtic tribes of Gaul. They had come from what is modern-day Southern Germany and were settled in what is current Switzerland up against the Alps. The Germanic tribes to the north and east posed some pressure to this group who had no room for expansion. In fact, their land claims had consistently been reduced by the Germanic tribes bordering them, and both the migrations and expansions were still creating stress between the groups.

Orgetorix, a Helvetii nobleman, persuaded his people around 61 BCE that migrating to the west coast would allow them to expand as needed. This migration would entail crossing the regions populated by other Gallic tribes who saw the migration as an invasion. Further complicating the plan, the coastal region Orgetorix had his eye set on for his people was already inhabited by the Aquitanians. Emissaries were sent to negotiate passage across the lands of neighboring tribes as the Helvetii prepared for the mass migration. Orgetorix's daughter was married to Dumnorix, a neighboring chieftain who aligned with Orgetorix and his ultimate plan for them to become the kings of their respective territories. Casticus, of the neighboring Sequani tribe, was similarly aligned with Orgetorix's plan.

Orgetorix's personal political plans to take over the Helvetii and become their absolute sovereign was discovered and foiled. He took his own life before a trial could take place, and so, when the migration did come to pass, its mastermind was no longer a part of the plan. Caesar notes his adversary's death in *Commentaries on the Gallic War* but gives no specific date as to when it happened. As for the Romans, they did not approve of the Helvetii plan to expand to the coast. The instability of this kind of expansion was thought to be a threat to the Romans who had established routes between the provinces of Italy and Spain. The Romans also disliked the idea of Germanic tribes moving farther into the area the Helvetii left behind them as it would increase their powerful kingdom even further.

Preparations for the big move took about three years, and during that time, crops were maximized in order to bring as much corn and supplies with them when they left. They amassed wagons and animals to pull them, and these supplies were intended to last them throughout the three-month trek. As the migration began, there were other tribes, such as the Rauraci, the Latobrigi, and the Tulingi in Gaul, who decided to join the Helvetii. These groups were not as big as the original migrant group, but with their addition, the migrant group became the largest and most powerful in the whole of Gaul. According to Julius Caesar's account later, there were close to 370,000 people gathered together, including women and children.

The migrants were by no means a peaceful bunch of travelers. They pillaged as they moved across the landscape, consistently burning the villages they encountered, along with any food and valuables they were unable to take with them on their journey. It is believed this was to keep them focused on moving forward; if no villages were left behind, there would be nothing to distract the migrants in terms of potential real estate. It was the Mediterranean coast or nothing at all.

It was a fearful time for other tribes, who worried that their own families, belongings, and lands were at risk from the pillaging migrants. Julius Caesar's own account of these migrants is one of a brave and warlike people. He believed they were unlikely to have an uneventful journey or find peace with inhabitants and neighbors of their new destination—and that included the Roman Republic.

The Helvetii were destined for a major clash with the Romans as they moved toward the west in April of 58 BCE.[21] When Julius Caesar was informed of their approach into Roman territory, he was told the migrants had requested permission to cross it. Here, they faced their biggest obstacle and sent word to the Romans that they would move peacefully across that corner of the empire if they were allowed to pass through.[22] Caesar did not wish to grant such access, nor did he believe that the Helvetii migrants would maintain order if they were permitted to cross. Based on the destruction they left behind them, there was little reason to trust their word.

Caesar responded that their request would be considered. While he awaited a reply back, the governor quickly gathered his armed forces and headed to the place where the Helvetii and their amassed migrant allies wished to cross into Roman territory. Believing the migrants may try to pass without his permission, Caesar set up garrisons and fortifications to stop them from advancing. At the appointed date at which Caesar had promised an answer, the Helvetii were informed that passage would not be given. Furthermore, they were told that if they attempted to force their way across, they would be met with resistance. Caesar's forces were strong and numerous,

---

[21] Rickard, J. "Battle of the Arar, June 58 BC." *History of War.* Web. 17 March 2009.

[22] Yenne, B. *Julius Caesar: Lessons in Leadership from the Great Conqueror.* 2012.

and the travelers had little choice but to change the path of their journey.

With passage through Caesar's province no longer an option, the Helvetii were left with only one option in reaching their destination on the coast: To go through the lands of the Sequani people, along the edge of the Jura Mountains. Thanks to Dumnorix's connection with the people of Sequani, he was able to convince them to allow the Helvetii to pass through their land without obstruction. In return, it was promised that the migrant train would not cause any harm as it passed.[23]

After passing through Sequani lands, the Helvetii arrived in the Aedui territory, where they immediately regressed to pillaging and burning. They plundered and ravaged the fields and towns, taking slaves and any supplies they wanted. The people of Aedui were helpless and had no defenses against this onslaught, and in a panic, they sent ambassadors to seek the help of Caesar and the Romans.

---

[23] Billows, R. *Julius Caesar: The Colossus of Rome.* 2009.

Chapter 4 – The Helvetian War

Delighted at the opportunity to flex his military muscles, Caesar organized his troops. He hadn't managed to invade Dacia as planned, but in answering the plea for help from the Aedui, Caesar had managed to goad the Roman Senate into allowing the ongoing warfare. This was not a decision that the senators took lightly, however. Rome had a policy of participating in defensive wars only, and any expansive warfare could only be allowed after overwhelming senatorial agreement that it was in the best interests of the Roman people themselves. The entire purpose of the electoral process and term limits for government employees was to stop would-be emperors from using Rome's might for his own purposes. Therefore, the senators begrudgingly allowed Caesar to fight the Helvetii in defense of the Aedui, but they tried to keep a very close eye on the proceedings.

Before moving off in pursuit of the migrants, Caesar made his way to Italy to obtain a sizeable, trained army to add to his existing forces. In all, he was given leadership over about 120,000 fighting men. These Roman soldiers were legally forbidden from marrying during their time with the army, and though officially expected to remain celibate over the course of their service, such things were impossible to enforce. Caesar's soldiers were a combination of Roman-born fighters and foreign-born men loyal to the Roman Republic. The latter were called "auxiliaries," and they only earned one-third the wages of the natural Roman citizens they fought beside. While most Roman soldiers spent the majority of their time training and serving as guards, Caesar's army could only find relief during the winter since it was normal to cease warfare during the cold months.

When Caesar and his army of warriors caught up to the Helvetii that June of 58 BCE, the latter were in the middle of a twenty-day expedition to cross the river Saône, near the middle of modern-day France. With a quarter of their numbers still on the eastern bank of the river within reach of the Roman army, Caesar struck in the middle of the night with three of his legions.[24] The migrants were routed, and in Caesar's letters home to the Senate, he claimed his own army put a bridge over the same river and crossed it in one day:

> This battle ended, that he might be able to come up with the remaining forces of the Helvetii, he procures a bridge to be made across the Saone, and thus leads his army over. The Helvetii, confused by his sudden arrival, when they found that he had effected in one day, what they, themselves had with the utmost difficulty accomplished in twenty namely, the crossing of the river, send embassadors [sic] to him.[25]

Politics were always on Caesar's mind, and he wanted to make sure that the people back in Rome had plenty of reasons to admire and support what he was doing in the northern territories. Fully aware that the senators would try to put an end to the military campaign as soon as the Helvetii threat had been dealt with, Caesar had to find a reason to continue moving forward with his army. His new goal was

---

[24] Rickard, J. "Battle of the Arar, June 58 BC." *History of War.* Web. 17 March 2009.
[25] Caesar, Julius. *Commentaries on the Gallic War.*

exactly what the traditional senators were afraid of: no less than the annexation of the rest of Gaul under Roman rule. To facilitate that goal, the governor decided to keep the senators—and the electorate, who hailed him as a hero—updated on all the complex reasons he must do battle outside Roman borders.

By Caesar's own account—although written in the third person—the Roman legions pursued the Helvetii quickly and effectively. Negotiations were attempted on the part of the migrants, but neither could agree on peaceful terms, so both parties rushed onward, moving westward. Low on supplies, Caesar ordered his army to stop at the allied city of Bibracte in June. The Helvetii used this pause as a chance to attack their pursuers from the rear, and as the Romans marched toward the city, the migrant forces followed them stealthily.

The Helvetii, however, were unable to pull off a surprise attack. Caesar's scouts saw them approaching, and once warned about his pursuers, Caesar ordered his cavalry unit to halt and form a wall. Farther beyond the mounted soldiers, the legions were dispersed. The legions with the most experience were placed strategically in a defensive line, while the two newer legions were ordered to flank their superiors upon a hilltop.[26]

The enemy broke through the cavalry line and moved in toward the Roman lines in a classic phalanx structure.[27] The phalanx, commonly used by the ancient Greeks, consisted of a densely packed rectangular arrangement of warriors.[28] Though the battle had been incited by the Helvetii, it was the Romans who threw the first javelins and began breaking up the enemy formation. The Helvetii were no strangers to warfare, and for a time, they managed to gain the upper hand by surrounding the Roman army. Caesar was forced to order a line of his men to about-face and deal with the onslaught

---

[26] Rickard, J. "Battle of Bibracte, June 58 B.C." *History of War.* 18 March 2009.
[27] Ibid.
[28] Time-Life Books. *What Life Was Like at the Dawn of Democracy.* 1997.

from the flank while the remainder continued to battle the bulk of the enemy army.

They fought bitterly throughout the afternoon and into the night until the Romans finally broke through the Helvetii camp and forced them to retreat. The surviving Helvetii moved on, while Caesar's legions stayed behind to rest for a full three days. They were by no means short of supplies since the retreating Helvetii had left most of their possessions behind.[29] A search of the goods revealed a document that tallied all the people involved in the mass migration. In total, Caesar wrote, there were 368,000 marked on the document. After a sufficient recuperation time, the Romans were up and marching once more in pursuit of the Helvetii. The next time they met, the latter surrendered.

Caesar was in charge of what would happen to the defeated migrants, along with the help of members of the Aedui tribe, and together, they decided that some members of the migrant group should be allowed to settle among the Aedui. These were the Boii, a people for whom the Aedui felt a certain kinship.[30] As for Caesar, he was happy to oblige since he did not feel comfortable leaving the uninhabited lands of the Aedui empty; once villages and farms were established, the new inhabitants could better defend it and keep out unwanted tribes.

As for the Helvetii, Tulingi, and Latobrigi, Caesar ordered them to return from whence they came. He wrote that of the reported 368,000 migrants who had tried to reach the western coast of Europe, only 110,000 returned home. To those reading his letters, there could be no doubt cast upon the magnificence of his victory.

---

[29] Caesar, Julius. *Commentaries on the Gallic War.*
[30] Ibid.

Chapter 5 - Ariovistus, the German King

Ariovistus the king of the Germans, had settled in their territories, and had seized upon a third of their land, which was the best in the whole of Gaul, and was now ordering them to depart from another third part...The consequence would be that in a few years they would all be driven from the territories of Gaul, and all the Germans would cross the Rhine.

(Julius Caesar, *Commentaries on the Gallic War*)

The Roman Republic was not the only European force against whom the Gauls were forced to defend their territory and way of life. To the east of Gaul and the north of Italy proper, Germanic tribes ruled—and some of these also wanted a stake in the land claims of Gaul. One such ruler, Ariovistus, observed the events of 58 BCE shrewdly, plotting how to best take advantage of the situation. He decided to unite the Germanic tribes and Gauls together to fight back against the encroaching Roman Republic.

Ariovistus was not unknown to the people of Gaul, as some had come to him for help in an earlier war against the Aedui. Because of his previous alliance with the Arverni and Sequani people of Gaul, Ariovistus was well positioned to incite an anti-Roman movement in Gallic lands. He was also in an ideal position to begin moving his own people into Gaul since both the local tribes and the watchful Romans were on officially friendly terms with him. Ariovistus had actually been bestowed with the titles of Friend of Rome and King of Germany in 59 BCE by the Roman Senate.[31] Caesar was quick to point this out when the two met face to face two years later to discuss terms.

As soon as Caesar and his legions had defeated the Helvetii and stopped the mass migration of their people, he was compelled to deal with a new mass group of migrants moving in from Germany. He'd received word that the German Suevi were fighting with the Aedui at the Vosges, so he set off some 280 kilometers (174 miles) northeast to confront them. Along the way, the Romans met with many Gauls in the villages where they stopped to procure grain and supplies, and they were repeatedly told of the immense stature and strength of their German opponents.

The Roman legions became distracted and terrified as these rumors flew through the ranks, and in Caesar's letters home, he described how many of his men requested permission to return to their homes. Others fell to tears at the thought of approaching Ariovistus and his army of giant men, and eventually, the morale of the legions was so downtrodden that even officers began to tell Caesar the battle was not feasible. In *Commentaries on the Gallic War*, Caesar wrote:

> Some actually told Caesar that when he gave the order to strike the camp and advance, the men would not obey and would be too terrified to move. Observing the state of affairs, Caesar called a meeting to which the centurions of all offices and grades were summoned, and rated them severely for presuming to suppose that it was their business to inquire or even to consider where they were going, or on what errand.

---

[31] Shotter, David. *The Fall of the Roman Republic.* 2005.

Before engaging on the battlefield, Caesar and the German king Ariovistus exchanged a series of messages. The leaders met on horseback to parlay while their lines of cavalry faced one another, stones hurled regularly from the Germans toward the Romans. Caesar refused to let his soldiers be provoked into starting a fight then and there, but he also did not yield to the demands of Ariovistus to leave Gaul to its own devices.

Caesar was firm but diplomatic with the German king, acknowledging the political friendship the two of them enjoyed and calling upon Ariovistus to cease the movement of his people into Gaul. The reply from Ariovistus was incredulous; the German king told Caesar that the migration was his own business and Rome had no right to interfere. Caesar insisted that since the migrant Germans were engaging in pillage and warfare against the Aedui, it was his obligation as a governor and protector of Rome and its allies to move against the intruders. To this, Ariovistus claimed that it was his right as a king to conquer other people and demand taxation.

Caesar described Ariovistus as an overconfident leader, particularly in his belief that the Roman Senate would hold firm on its offer of friendship despite these violent forays into allied territory. Ariovistus went as far as to insinuate that if he killed Julius Caesar, he would even gain the loyalty of many members of the Senate. The parlay came to an end quickly after that, and Caesar made haste to leave with his cavalry as the German side had become more unruly during the discussion and seemed ready to instigate war at any second.

The next day, Ariovistus sent word to Caesar that he desired another parlay. Weary and untrusting of his rival, the governor instead sent two of his men, Gaius Valerius Procillus and Marcus Mettius, to meet with the king. When Procillus and Mettius saw the Germans preparing their battle lines, they were captured and put in chains.

Caesar prepared over the next few days to meet Ariovistus in battle, but the German lines refused to present themselves. Apparently, it was the strategy of the opposing king to move slightly forward each day, stealthily line by line, only engaging in small fights without bringing forth the bulk of his army. More importantly, he placed some of his own troops across the supply line of the Romans, cutting off their food and water resources. By forcing the Romans to engage in small skirmishes over the following days, Ariovistus ensured that his enemy was hungry and tired for the real battle.

Caesar postulated that the reason the Germans would not engage in proper battle during that time was due to them having been warned by their wise women that they should not fight before the new moon. That may or may not have been true, but the fact was that Ariovistus had more troops, and they had the Romans surrounded. Ariovistus, therefore, had the luxury of attacking whenever he pleased.

The Roman leader was outnumbered and cut off from the supplies, but he had yet to run out of food. He knew that he must force the Germans to fight immediately to avoid being starved into defeat or surrender. Using his best lines of men as a shield some 550 meters (600 yards) from the German camp, Caesar ordered a secondary Roman camp to be built. He stationed two of his legions there and four at the original camp. The next day, auxiliary units provided cover while all six legions crept up into a battle line, *triplex acies* formation. *Triplex acies* was a classic Roman military tactic, in which the veteran warriors were placed in the third battle line to act as a barrier and anchor. If the first two ranks became overwhelmed, they could fall back behind the veteran lines and regroup or retreat in the most orderly fashion possible.

In this formation, the Roman army advanced on the German camp. Quickly, Ariovistus' men formed a phalanx, moving in front of a wagon train full of women and children. Caesar remarked that this was standard military operation for the Germans and speculated that it was meant to be motivational, as the women and children screamed and sobbed as the fighting ensued.

The Germans responded to the advancement of the legions so quickly, wrote Caesar, that the Romans had no time to throw their javelins. The soldiers dropped their long-range weapons and brandished their swords, engaging immediately in hand-to-hand combat. Some of the men in the Roman front lines jumped onto the Germans' shield wall to pry the defensive instruments out of the hands of their enemies and stab them to death from above.

Ultimately, Caesar's forces were victorious. The Germans were routed, and those who could still escape ran 24 kilometers (15 miles) to the Rhine River, crossing it by boat or by swimming. Procillus and Mettius, who had remained in chains for the duration of the battle, were removed and joyfully welcomed back into the Roman ranks. Thousands of German men, women, and children were left behind and taken prisoner by Caesar's men. This proved to be the best prize of all since Caesar could sell them as slaves at an incredible profit to himself.

In the aftermath of the Battle of Vosges, the German migrants returned to their homeland, and it seems that Ariovistus lost his authority there. He died just a few years later due to unclear circumstances.

Chapter 6 – Battle of the Sabis

Of all these [Gauls] the Belgae are the bravest, because they are furthest from the civilization and refinement of [our] Province.

(Julius Caesar)

Having successfully been engaged in two important campaigns during his first year as governor of Transalpine and Cisalpine Gaul, Caesar stationed his legions with the Sequani for the winter to give them their due rest. It was customary for the generals of his day to do battle only in the warmer months of the year, so he left his troops under the authority of Titus Labienus and took his own refuge elsewhere in Hither Gaul. There, Caesar received repeated reports from various sources that the Belgic people of far northern Gaul were conspiring against him.

The Belgae were an agricultural people, many of whom had migrated across the English Channel into Iron Age Britannia. There, they helped revolutionize farming with their heavy plow, as well as introduced the potter's wheel to the people living there.[32] Originally of Germanic heritage, the Belgae still shared a border with

[32] "Belgae, Ancient People." *Encyclopedia Britannica.* Web.

Germania. It is unclear how long they had been living in the western part of Europe, but it had to have been a significant amount of time for Caesar to relate to them as Gallic instead of Germanic.

When the weather grew warm again in the summer of 57 BCE, Caesar raised two more legions in Cisalpine Gaul.[33] While he waited for these additional troops to finish their training, Caesar sent envoys to the Gallic people with whom he was allied and found that they all reported the Belgae were gathering an army against him. Upon hearing this news, Caesar gathered his men from their winter retreat and marched upon the new enemy.

Realizing that the Belgae had loyalties divided into a variety of sub-groups, Caesar considered his strategy while assembling his men. If he could avoid a battle against the entire unified force of the Belgae, whom he had heard numbered among 300,000, his own odds of an easy victory increased greatly. Caesar therefore ordered the forces of the Aedui to attack the Bellovaci while he prepared to meet with the remaining bulk of the enemy troops. On the banks of the Aisne River, the Romans made their camp and placed guards at the bridge by which they were to receive provisions. The camp was fortified by a high rampart and a wide ditch.

The Belgae began their march upon the nearby town of Bibrax, and after a day of siege upon the walls and fortifications of the community, they halted for the night and slunk back to their camp. Caesar noted that they laid siege in the same style as the Germans. Upon night falling, messengers from Bibrax ran to Caesar's camp and urged him to send a relief force to the town for the next day's expected siege. He complied, supplying the defensive forces of the Remi tribe with archers and slingers.

The influx of these Roman warriors into Bibrax changed the course of the attacking Belgae, who then determined to leave the town and merely burn and pillage the surrounding area. Once they were

---

[33] Caesar, Julius. *Commentaries on the Gallic War.*

satisfied with that, they moved onto Caesar's camp and made their own camp within about two miles of the Romans. Caesar remarked in his letters that the smoke from the enemy campfires indicated that their camp was at least eight miles wide.

The obvious size of the enemy encampment gave Caesar pause. He considered whether there was some way he could refuse the oncoming battle and spare himself what would likely be considerable losses. Before making a firm decision one way or the other, Caesar sent his cavalry to fight in a series of small-scale skirmishes to ascertain which side had superior technique and prowess. It was a move very similar to the one used on the Romans by Ariovistus the previous year, and it served to convince Caesar that his own forces did indeed have the strength to overcome the Belgae.

Determinedly, Caesar prepared his battlegrounds. The space between the two army encampments contained a shallow hill upon which he envisioned his six legions. He would station the two newest legions trained in Cisalpine Gaul at the camp while entreating the enemy to surround his veterans on the hill. His newest soldiers could flood in from the flank if it proved necessary. Having dug a series of trenches on either side of the hill, the general was ready.

The Belgic army made its first move, and instead of placing itself within the prepared grounds, they attempted to cross the Aisne some distance from Caesar's camp. In doing so, they hoped to cut off the Romans' supply chain at the bridge and lay waste to the villages of the Remi who were supplying the Romans. Caesar ordered some of his number in the direction of the bridge, and after what he described as a "severe struggle," he was successful in fighting off the enemy and keeping the supply line and bridge encampment secure. The Belgae were forced to withdraw entirely to their own lands.

While the Belgae retreated, Caesar followed them several days while attacking sporadically from the rear. Along the route, he decided to take advantage of their passing close by an undefended town called

Noviodunum so that his soldiers could take it by force. The town quickly surrendered and gave hostages to Caesar so that he would allow them to keep their home in peace. As the Belgae continued to make haste for their home, the Romans continued to sack Gallic towns as they saw fit, stopping only to confer with their friends, the Aedui and the Remi.

Chapter 7 - The Germanic War

They have plundered the world, stripping naked the land in their hunger... they are driven by greed, if their enemy be rich; by ambition, if poor... They ravage, they slaughter, they seize by false pretenses, and all of this they hail as the construction of empire. And when in their wake nothing remains but a desert, they call that peace.

(Tacitus, *The Agricola and The Germania*)

In the year 55 BCE, Caesar's two political allies were simultaneously elected for the post of Roman consul, a position that was always proffered in pairs. With both Pompey and Crassus at the head of the government, the *Lex Trebonia* law was passed to grant both consuls a five-year governorship of Spain and Syria, respectively.[34] For Julius Caesar, the consuls granted a five-year extension to his original governorship of the provinces of Cisalpine Gaul, Transalpine Gaul, and Illyricum. While Crassus made ready to invade Parthia and Pompey built Rome's first permanent theater, Caesar was engaged once more with invading Germans.

---

[34] Gruen, Erich S. *The Last Generation of the Roman Republic*. 1974.

It was the Usipetes and Tencteri tribes this time who made their way across the Rhine River intent on finding land to settle for themselves in Gaul. Their migrations were pressed by the continued attacks of the Suevi in Germany, whose endless harassment made the fundamental industry of agriculture quite difficult. Caesar described the Suevi as the most fearsome group of Germania, with legions upon legions of warriors and an annual habit of sending a thousand armed men into the world for the sole purpose of warfare.

Caesar may have had a small amount of empathy for the fleeing tribes of the Usipetes and Tencteri, but it was not enough to allow them to settle in Gaul. Determining to not allow the Gauls to settle the matter among themselves, Caesar returned to the army from his winter retreat to take on the fresh wave of German migrants. Once there, he found that certain Gauls had been in contact with the migrants and had promised them that all their needs would be met after crossing the Rhine. Of course, this would be at the detriment of the Gallic tribes who had not entered into such negotiations.

Caesar summoned the leaders of the Gallic tribes to a meeting where he impressed upon them the need for unity and defensive tactics. Feigning ignorance to the previous political alliances that had been made between some of those leaders and the Usipetes and Tencteri, Caesar easily led everyone assembled to the conclusion that they would band together. This way, the governor was careful to avoid provoking a clash between members of the meeting who had previously endangered the others; it was both a move to unite Gaul against its enemies and under the leadership of Roman authority.

Supplies were gathered and the warriors were readied before Caesar led them out to meet the Germans. Upon doing so, he received an envoy from the enemy ranks who delivered the following message:

> The Germans neither make war upon the Roman people first, nor do they decline, if they are provoked, to engage with them in arms; for that this was the custom of the Germans handed down to them from their forefathers, to resist

whatsoever people make war upon them and not to avert it by entreaty...they had come hither reluctantly, having been expelled from their country. If the Romans were disposed to accept their friendship, they might be serviceable allies to them; and let them either assign them lands, or permit them to retain those which they had acquired by their arms; that they are inferior to the Suevi alone, to whom not even the immortal gods can show themselves equal; that there was none at all besides on earth whom they could not conquer.

Caesar responded that there was not enough land to offer them any without hindering the existing communities within Gaul but that they might try to move into the Ubii lands and help that people defend it from the Suevi. The envoys agreed to entreat the Ubii to such an arrangement, asking that Caesar not advance his army or attack them until word could be sent back in reply. Caesar agreed only to advance far enough to find water for his troops, but he allowed his cavalry to march ahead with orders not to provoke a fight. He remarks in his letters that once the Germans saw the cavalry approach, they began to attack.

The battle was short-lived but provocative. More than 70 of the Romans' horses were killed by the enemy, as well as a number of the mounted warriors.[35] Many of their horses, riderless and terrified, galloped back from where they had come and met upon Caesar and the rest of his troops a few miles beyond the battlefield. Furious, Caesar readied himself and the legions to prepare for war the next day.

Before any retaliatory movement could be made, however, a large gathering of Germans approached Caesar's camp peacefully. Comprised of people whom Caesar described as "princes and old men," these people apologized profusely for the attack and claimed to have had no part in it. Furthermore, they wished for peace and the chance to negotiate properly. Unbelieving of the same rhetoric this

---

[35] Caesar, Julius. *Commentaries on the Gallic War.*

second time, Caesar had the men arrested and started to have the troops march forward the eight miles to where the enemy still stood. According to his letters, there were more than 400,000 Germans assembled there, including women and children among the wagons and baggage.

The German camp was in a tumult and completely unprepared for such a swift attack. Though some of their warriors were able to find weapons and fight for a time, it was not enough. The Romans beat them back decisively until they fled in all directions, many hurling themselves in the Rhine in an attempt to escape. Without losing a single Roman soldier, Caesar turned from the emptied camp and returned to his own, telling the imprisoned Germans there that they were free to follow their own people if they wished. None did so.

While the Romans rested and the freed Germans reflected on the turn of events, Caesar considered how best to follow up the day's battle. He'd seen the same circumstances repeat itself again and again, and he observed that there must be some way to convince the people in Germania to stay on their side of the Rhine. Thus, he conceived of a plan to follow his enemy into Germania and stop the invasions at their source. To that end, the Romans marched after their surviving foes and crossed into Germania, having procured the promise of ships from the allied Ubii people.

The foes on the other side of the border were keen horsemen, noted Caesar, and they were able to take sickly animals and turn them into healthy, valuable workers. In Caesar's letters to the Roman Senate, he told his audience how the German horses were so well trained that they would stand still in place during battle after their rider had jumped into the fray, awaiting his return. Aware that his own cavalry was outmatched, Caesar had to rely on the expertise of his infantry. He bade his legions to build a bridge over the Rhine and move over it during a ten-day process before then moving confidently into Germania.

Pressing eastward, Caesar frequently met with envoys asking for peace between the Romans and their own communities. To these, Caesar had only one answer: Send hostages and the alliance will be made.[36] Hostages were his preferred method of cementing friendships, particularly with new acquaintances. The more important the hostage, the more serious the claim of peace from the foreign tribe.

Germans near the Rhine had already seen the retreating Tencteri and Usipetes warriors, however, and they were quick to desert their communities and go into hiding to avoid confrontation. Caesar did not care where the Germans were hiding; he meant only to strike fear into their hearts so that they would not even think of crossing into Gaul anytime soon. Any thought of conquest and rule in those lands was probably negated by the fact that the area was so politically divided, poor in precious metals, and, by Roman standards, simply barbaric. The Romans burned all the villages and homes they could find, and after 18 days in Germania, they returned home and cut down the bridge they'd used to get there.[37]

---

[36] Caesar, Julius. *Commentaries on the Gallic War.*
[37] Ibid.

Chapter 8 – United Gaul Versus Caesar of Rome

Two years passed in which neither Pompey, Crassus, or Caesar were elected as consuls; however, they were all still employed as governors within their respective provinces. In 52 BCE, Pompey had been made consul once more, but Crassus had been killed in his own military campaign against Parthia. In Gaul, a great revolt had been building against Caesar—and by extension, Rome—at the hands of Vercingetorix.

Vercingetorix became the leader of the Gallic Arverni tribe that very same year, and he had one pressing goal in mind: the expulsion of Rome from Gallic lands. He took pains to convince his people and kingly peers that they must shake off the dominance of the Romans. Seeking sovereignty in Gaul, Vercingetorix stepped up to lead a rebellion. It was a difficult time for Caesar, who had planned to keep his legions resting in their winter quarters for several more weeks. But on the other hand, he did not want to lose the kinship of the Aedui by allowing them to become overrun with revolutionary Gauls with whom they were not united.

Furthermore, Caesar could not be sure to what degree the followers of Vercingetorix gave their loyalty. Vercingetorix was the son of a slain Gallic king who had been killed by his own people for the dishonorable ambition of ruling over all the tribes. After the death of his father, Vercingetorix had been exiled from his homeland for a short time before supporters welcomed him back. Vercingetorix immediately expelled his enemies from Arverni and gathered an army. If he had the same intentions as his father—and it very well seemed that he might—then perhaps he might fail by his own hand without Caesar having to do a thing.

Caesar chose to bring all but two of his legions to meet Vercingetorix's men in battle. Desiring a decisive fight, Caesar knew he would have to draw out the enemy leader and force him to procure all his warriors. To lure out his opponent, Caesar sacked the towns of Vellaunodunum, Genabum, and Noviodunum on his way to Gergovia, the realm's capital city which lay in modern-day central France. In the latter, he collected hostages, horses, and weapons from the towns' citizens in exchange for peace and an alliance. As planned, Vercingetorix moved to meet Caesar's forces near Noviodunum.

When the people of the town spotted their king's cavalry in the distance, they rejoiced and quickly abandoned the peace they had negotiated with the Romans. Fortifying themselves, the Noviodunumites grabbed what remained of their weaponry, but Caesar's centurions—still in the process of carrying out the seizure of weapons—were able to escape unharmed. Caesar sent out his own cavalry to meet that of Vercingetorix's and succeeded in turning the enemy line back to seek out its main body. As the Gallic cavalry retreated, the townspeople once more surrendered to Caesar, quickly offering hostages to him.

Vercingetorix called his advisors for a strategy meeting and decided to make it impossible for the traveling Roman army to feed and sustain itself within Gaul. On the orders of Vercingetorix, dozens of unfortified villages were burned to the ground to prevent Caesar's army from sacking them for foodstuffs to feed their soldiers and horses. Towns with fortifications and the means to protect themselves were left to stand only if the king believed they were capable of withstanding a siege.

This action did indeed leave the Romans with little food. Corn was their main food supplement, which they had been receiving from the Aedui and Boii peoples, but with their own villages burned and stores pillaged, those tribes could scarcely feed themselves.[38] Before hunger got the better of his army, Caesar marched his legions to the large town of Avaricum. Still standing, thanks to its defensive architecture, Avaricum nevertheless fell to the Roman siege and provided Caesar's army with all the supplies they needed to replenish their stocks. At long last, the Romans set off for Gergovia.

Gergovia was not an easy target. The city stood 1,200 feet high on the plateau of a mountain overlooking a large plain. The plateau was 2.2 kilometers (1.5 miles) in length by 535 meters (1,755 feet) in width, and there was only one entrance. The city could be defended by a relatively small guard thanks to its physical location, a feature that Vercingetorix had been relying on to keep it safe.

Guessing that his enemy was headed to the capital, Vercingetorix placed his troops on the opposite side of the river Elave, the modern-day Loire River, as the Romans and moved with the enemy, burning all of the bridges before Caesar could reach them and access Gergovia. When Caesar saw the succession of burning bridges, he formulated a plan to trick the enemy and gain access. First, he split his entire army into two parts, the first of which contained two-thirds of the men and the second of which contained the remaining third. He ordered the largest to continue marching south while the third hid from sight. When the troops on the other side of the river had moved on, the remaining Romans hurriedly rebuilt the bridge. When it was ready, Caesar sent for the rest of the troops and pushed ahead, across the river.

---

[38] Ibid.

Despite managing to cross the river, Caesar's army was beaten back into retreat by that of Vercingetorix and an Aedui group that had switched allegiance. Caesar managed to convince the Aedui to rejoin him and lay siege to Gergovia, but their combined forces could not gain the high ground. With supplies running low once more, Rome was forced to retreat into Aedui territory.

Chapter 9 – The Battle of Alesia

By September of 52 B.C., Caesar was about to conquer of all of Gaul with one final siege and battle, the Siege of Alesia.

(Joseph M. Durante)[39]

After the success of the Gauls at Gergovia, Caesar abandoned his plan to invade the capital. Instead, he followed his enemy to another fortified city, that of Alesia, in order to defeat them there. It was the summer of 52 BCE when the two armies met at Alesia, and the army of the Gallic king had been much enhanced following his great victory at Gergovia. Unfortunately for Vercingetorix, however, Caesar had already defeated his cavalry upon approaching the city.

In Caesar's letters home, he said that he camped outside the city and performed a great deal of reconnaissance upon its fortifications before coming up with a plan of attack. The Gauls were terrified, Caesar went on, since their skilled cavalry had been broken and he was now camped within sight of the walls. Like Gergovia, the city of Alesia was perched on the top of a high hill and did not present an easy challenge. In making preparations for war, the Romans camped at the foot of the hill for several months.

---

[39] Durante, Joseph M. "The Battle of Alesia: The Roman Siege That Completed Julius Caesar's Conquest of Gaul." *War History Online.* Web. 13 September 2017.

Caesar's strategy involved what he called circumvallation. The method was characterized by encircling a city with a series of defensive forts so as to make it impossible for citizens within the circle to send messages or receive supplies.[40] At the foot of the hill of Alesia, the Romans built 23 outposts around a total distance of 18 kilometers (11 miles).[41] Each small fort could hold a sentry soldier, and these guards were refreshed regularly. The outposts were occupied all day and all night, and the plain stretching out beyond the Roman camp was defended by hired German mercenaries and cavalry.

The Gauls were not simply standing aside and waiting for the Romans to finish surrounding the city with fortified camps, but they had a great deal of trouble attacking the circumvallation without giving away an entrance to Alesia. Skirmishes were fought continuously, but despite this, the building project moved forward. Seeing that his troops were unable to shift the Romans from their purpose, Vercingetorix sent members of his cavalry out from the city to return to their home states and try to find more willing men to join the fight. According to Caesar, by that time the Gauls within Alesia had barely enough supplies of corn to feed them for 30 days. He wrote home that he learned such private information about his enemy from the deserters of the Gallic army.

While the enemy cavalry was abroad gathering reinforcements and more food, Caesar set some of his own men to the task of digging trenches to surround the city. When they were complete, he connected them to the river and thereby constructed a considerable moat. On the bank of the moat, he built ramparts nearly 4 meters (12 feet) in height, complete with battlements that had sharp stakes to prevent enemy climbers. To stave off the Gauls from preventing all this work from happening, more trenches were dug, in which stakes

[40] Knighton, Andrew. "Circumvallation: How the Romans Mastered Surrounding Towns to Conquer Populations." *War History Online.* 18 November 2016.

[41] Caesar, Julius. *Commentaries on the Gallic War.*

were set, pointing upwards. Any foray into the trench would likely result in impalement.

Within the month, the Gauls were running out of food. They sent out the aged men, the sick people, women, and children from the city to save resources for the fighting men within. Caesar wrote that he believed the Gauls wanted him to feed these people and keep them under his authority, but he didn't allow them into his fortifications. They were forced to fend for themselves and look for shelter elsewhere.

It was early September 52 BCE before the Romans and the Gauls met in the ultimate battle for Alesia. The Gallic reinforcements had arrived, and Caesar was provided with relief legions brought by his fellow Romans, Marc Antony and Gaius Trebonius. The numbers probably totaled about 75,000 fighting for Rome and 80,000 for Vercingetorix.[42]

The Gauls focused their attacks on the weak spots of the Roman fortifications, which lay on the north side of the surrounding hills. It was a lengthy process thanks to the multitude of trenches that lay between the city wall and the surrounding forts, which had the desired effect of giving the Romans time to cut the enemy forces down as they attempted to advance. Ultimately, the Gauls were trapped within the limits of Alesia, and despite having the higher ground, there was no way to beat back the Roman legions.

Caesar's, Antony's, and Trebonius' legions were forced to fight the Gauls within the city and also those surrounding them and their ramparts. It was an almost impossible feat, but thanks to the extensive preparations and painstakingly constructed trenches, towers, ramparts, and forts, Caesar proved victorious at last. While Roman soldiers slaughtered the cavalry and outlying armies of Vercingetorix ceaselessly, deserters fled the city in droves.

---

[42] Delbruck, Hans. Translated by Walter J. Renfroe Jr. *The Barbarian Invasions.* 1990.

Vercingetorix finally admitted defeat on October 3, 52 BCE, and instructed his people to offer him up to Caesar as a war prize.[43] Caesar received his customary hostages happily and in doing so brought an end to the most prominent of the Gallic revolutions against him. Vercingetorix was taken to Rome, where he was imprisoned lavishly at Caesar's expense for almost six years before being executed.[44]

---

[43] Caesar, Julius. *Commentaries on the Gallic War.*

[44] Mace, James. M. *Soldier of Rome.* 2008.

Chapter 10 - Crossing the Rubicon

On January 10, 49 B.C., on the banks of the Rubicon River in southern Gaul (near the modern-day city of Ravenna), Julius Caesar and the soldiers of the 13th Legion waited and weighed their options.

(National Geographic History[45])

The large-scale Gallic revolts had come to an end, but Caesar's pacification of Gaul was not without its share of local protestations. There were uprisings by the Carnutes and Bellovaci in 51 BCE, during which the Roman Army lay siege to the city of Uxellodunum. Back in Rome, tensions rose between Caesar and Pompey as their political alliance came to an uncomfortable end. Caesar's daughter and Pompey's wife, Julia, had died three years earlier and left Pompey with little reason to continue his controversial support of Julius Caesar and the Gallic Wars.

Switching political sides, Pompey had ceased to support the Populares ideals for government and began to promote those of the Optimates. He and Caesar were officially at odds, and that left Caesar without either of his original allies from the First

[45] Redonet, Fernando Lillo. "How Julius Caesar Started a Big War by Crossing a Small Stream." *National Geographic History.* March/April 2017.

Triumvirate. Marc Antony became his most important ally at that point, but neither of them could beat the authority of Pompey the Great in Rome. Pompey and the Senate, having decided that Caesar held command over too many Roman soldiers, demanded that he give up two of his legions. Pompey claimed to need those two legions for the war against the Parthians, which had been ongoing in the eastern provinces since 66 BCE. If Caesar agreed, the Senate would allow him to run for consul in 48 BCE.[46]

It was important that Caesar become consul that year because his term as governor of Gaul was nearly done. If he found himself without a governorship or a consulship, he would return to Rome as a citizen with no authority and therefore be at the mercy of his many enemies within the Senate. Though Caesar continued to enjoy high popularity with the Roman public, he had powerful enemies in the government who believed he had committed a series of war crimes in Gaul. If they had their way, Caesar could be executed.

Knowing that his main political enemy was Pompey, Caesar told the Senate that he would willingly give up his legions if Pompey did the same. Though the proposition was considered, it did not go forward. While he considered his options though, Caesar formally unified the communities he'd conquered in Gaul under Roman rule and extended the map of the Roman Republic.[47]

With the Roman Senate urging him to give up his governorship and return to Rome, Julius Caesar faced a tough choice. The Triumvirate was gone; he could no longer rely on the clever politicking of Pompey the Great on his behalf. Returning to Rome as a citizen with no army meant that Caesar would be tried and punished by the Senate for war crimes against the Gauls and for disobedience to the Senate and Roman law. He'd lose everything and probably be executed by the state, despite his popularity among the plebeians of

---

[46] "A Timeline of the Life of Julius Caesar." *San Jose State University*. Web.

[47] Ibid.

Rome. On the other hand, to keep his power and territory, there was only one option: remain with the army he'd cultivated in Gaul.

The Rubicon River beckoned and, just across it, the official territory of the Roman Republic. To enter Rome with a foreign army was instantly indicative of war, and Caesar knew this all too well. This action specifically declared war on the Senate and could be considered treason and an invasion of Italy. Caesar also knew that, thanks to the way the Roman military worked, his legions had developed a loyalty toward him and not to the Senate. Some of his soldiers had been serving under his command for ten years, and they were happy to follow him into whatever challenge he deemed appropriate.

In January of 49 BCE, Caesar's active legion, the XIII, followed him to the Rubicon in the frigid, snowy air of winter and awaited their instructions.[48] The rest of his forces, as many as eight legions, were still positioned in Gaul.[49] Finally, the war hero made his decision; they crossed the freezing stream of water and unofficially declared war on their own government. Anxious to meet his challengers face to face, Caesar led his loyal warriors straight to Rome, apparently stating that "the die is cast."

---

[48] McPike, Mary. *A Study of Suetonius' Account of Caesar's Crossing of the Rubicon.* 1924.
[49] Greenhalgh, P. A. L. *Pompey: the republican prince.* 1981.

Chapter 11 - Caesar's Civil War

Men in public life did their best to avoid accidental events or actions from being seen as unlucky. On a famous occasion during the civil war, Caesar tripped when disembarking from a ship on the shores of Africa and fell flat on his face. With his talent for improvisation, he spread out his arms and embraced the earth as a symbol of conquest. By quick thinking he turned a terrible omen of failure into one of victory.

(Anthony Everitt)[50]

The confrontation known as the Great Roman Civil War, or Caesar's Civil War, came to be known as the culmination of the internal strife within the Roman Republic which changed the republic into the Roman Empire.

The Senate assumed that there would be troops sent from Italy's towns in response to Caesar's march toward them. They believed that the people supported the Senate and its authority over Italy; there was, however, little senatorial support and Italy's communities

---

[50] Everitt, Anthony. *Cicero: The Life and Times of Rome's Greatest Politician.* 2002.

outside of Rome proper were disinclined to send their soldiers and resources to the capital for the impending political fight.

The stakes were high for the soldiers backing Caesar; if the campaign failed, they were certain to lose their military pensions for committing treason.[51] As an incentive, Caesar doubled the salaries for his soldiers.[52] With this military support, combined with the lack of support for the Senate, Caesar was able to continue his march toward Rome, entering the capital of the republic for the first time in ten years.

Pompey had promised the senators and the public that if Caesar did dare to march south with his army, he would assemble his own legions and protect the republic. Unfortunately, he could not gather enough troops on such short notice, and Caesar's single legion occupied Rome as Pompey retreated to the nearby southern city of Capua. He did not wait for Caesar to meet him at Capua; he and his soldiers retreated and headed across the Adriatic Sea to prepare their battle strategies in Macedonia.

Pompey probably expected that Caesar would pursue him there, but in fact, Caesar moved in the opposite direction toward Spain. On the way, he moved back through Gaul where he gathered some more of his legions for the war. Once in Spain, Caesar attacked Pompey's forces in the absence of their governor in 49 BCE. In a series of maneuvers designed to cut the Roman soldiers from Spain off from their sources of food and water, Caesar successfully wore out his opponents. They surrendered and were disbanded.[53] Having forcibly removed his most authoritative critics from Italy and Spain, Caesar returned to Rome that same year. There he was appointed as dictator, oversaw his own election to be a consul again, and resigned his dictatorship, all within the span of under two weeks. Perhaps an

---

[51] Ibid.

[52] Southern, Pat. *The Roman Army: A Social and Institutional History.* 2007.

[53] "Caesar in Spain." *UNRV History of Rome.* Web.

absurd turn of events for Pompey's senatorial supporters who wanted to strip Caesar of all his power, the election of a so-called warmonger as head of government occurred simply because Caesar had the majority of the popular vote. Julius Caesar was hailed as a war hero and a friend of the common people, in no small part thanks to his self-indulgent marketing campaign of letter-writing during the Gallic Wars. Furthermore, the people of Rome were terrified of war coming to their city and believed that by giving Caesar the title he sought, they were protecting their own interests.

Finally crossing the Adriatic Sea to meet Pompey's forces in Macedonia, Caesar led his army to Dyrrachium.[54] Caesar was at an immediate disadvantage because he had only enough ships to move half of his army at once. He had planned to move one half to the eastern side of the Adriatic and then send the ships back to Italy to pick up and deliver the remaining half; however, Pompey's soldiers managed to cut off these ships from performing the second step. Not only did this leave Caesar without half of his army, but it cut him off from his supply stations in Italy. Pompey was the favored warlord of the east Adriatic, and therefore, it would not be possible to find food, water, and weapons among the people of Macedonia and nearby Greece.[55]

The following map illustrates the path Pompey took out of Italy to evade Caesar, as well as the path Caesar eventually took to follow him. [56]

[54] Mitchell, William Augustus. *Outlines of the World's Military History*. 1940.

[55] Welch, Kathryn. *Magnus Pius*. 2012.

[56] Map for Pompey's flight to Egypt. Creator: Linguae. License: Creative Commons Attribution-Share Alike 4.0 International license.

Caesar's forces made several attempts to evade the naval blockade, but all were fruitless until Marc Antony managed to pass through and collect four more legions from Italy and land them at Nympheum.[57] Some miles north of Caesar's camp, Antony waited with the new troops while both Caesar and Pompey moved to meet him. As both parties were able to move northward swiftly, Pompey pulled back closer to Dyrrachium to avoid being caught between Antony and Caesar.

On the western coast of the battleground, Pompey still had the advantage over his enemy. His navy was larger and stronger, and at his back, he could see any approach from a distance thanks to the hilly landscape. Caesar began digging trenches and building fortifications immediately, but these were no surprise to his Roman opponent. Pompey ordered the same fortifications built beyond his own camp, creating a terrifying series of ditches and armed guard towers between the main bodies of both armies. On July 10, 48 BCE,

[57] Belfiglio, Valentine. J. *A Study of Ancient Roman Amphibious and Offensive Sea-ground Task Force Operations.* 2001.

the former members of the First Triumvirate fought their first head-to-head battle, the Battle of Dyrrachium.[58]

Though Caesar's tactics were strong and his men were experienced, he was betrayed by two defectors who told Pompey where to find the unfinished section of his opponent's wall.[59] Pompey attacked the spot and found it was indeed weaker than the rest of Caesar's fortifications. Reinforcements were sent swiftly, but Pompey had far more soldiers at his command than Caesar did, and eventually, the sheer multitudes of Pompey's forces forced the retreat of the Caesarion forces. They moved south and were not pursued by Pompey, who believed the retreat was a trick of Caesar's designed to lure him into a trap.[60]

The Battle of Dyrrachium was a victory for Pompey, although he did not realize it until it was too late to capitalize on his position. Had he ordered his soldiers to pursue the retreating army of Caesar, he may have forced them to surrender, forever changing the course of history. In reality, Caesar regrouped at Pharsalus and decisively defeated Pompey's forces there. Defeated, Pompey the Great fled to Egypt, and his legions dispersed.

Officers of the ruling Egyptian king, Ptolemy XIII, had Pompey killed in September of 48 BCE.[61] Caesar arrived shortly afterward to speak with his old ally, and upon finding him dead, he began to interfere with the Egyptian civil war that was brewing. With no serious contenders for the consulship of Rome other than Pompey's own nemesis, Julius Caesar was elected head of the Roman Republic in 46 and 45 BCE, and in 44 BCE, he was made dictator for life.

---

[58] Rogers, Jay. *In the Days of These Kings*. 2019.

[59] Cartwright, Mark. "The Battle of Pharsalus." *Ancient History Encyclopedia*. Web. 13 June 2014.

[60] Holmes, Thomas Rice. *The Roman Republic and the Founder of the Empire*. 1923.

[61] *"Pompey the Great." Encyclopedia Britannica*. Web.

Thanks to his military prowess and ambition, Caesar had added all of Gaul to the republic and earned the loyalty of Romans and the respect of foreign warlords and kings. The Gallic Wars were his crowning glory and the reason for his ongoing dictatorship of a nation that was supposed to be a fiercely proud republic.

Part 4: Sarmatians and Scythians

A Captivating Guide to the Barbarians of Iranian Origins and How These Ancient Tribes Fought Against the Roman Empire, Goths, Huns, and Persians

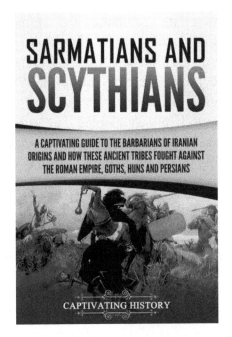

Introduction

Masters of the horse, the Scythians and Sarmatians opened the Eurasian Steppe to nomadic civilizations like it had never seen before. Following in the footsteps of the Cimmerians, a group of tribes sharing a common culture called the Steppe their home, adapting themselves to its harshness. Born out of this environment, a very particular way to live was adopted and later spread to peoples of Central Asia—the pastoral nomadic lifestyle. It would be the bane of organized armies of great empires, as the excellent mobility granted by their superior horse-riding skills were more than a match for the slow infantry that formed the backbone of the sedentary civilizations' armies.

The tale of the Scythians and Sarmatians have lasted through history, and although they had not one written historical record of their own, their presence was registered by dozens of classical historians. More importantly, though, their precious burial tombs still retained some of the civilizational remains of this extraordinary group of peoples.

The Scythians and Sarmatians had been deeply connected since their origin. The first Sarmatian people, the Sauromatae, were a part of the greater Scythian cultural group and spoke a dialect of the Scythian language. When the great Persian army invaded the Scythian territory in 513 BCE, the Sauromatae were listed among the allies of the Scythians, so we know they had friendly relations to some degree. However, later Sarmatian tribes wouldn't be so kind to the Scythians, and they eventually integrated part of them by subjugation. However, they both shared a fairly similar culture, and aside from the same language, they shared a common religious structure and practices, similar tribal organization, and similar clothing.

The Indo-European peoples commonly called as Scythians spanned the territory ranging from modern-day Romania to modern-day China. However, the Scythians and the Sarmatians mainly occupied the northern coast of the Black Sea, from modern-day Romania to the Volga River in modern-day southern Russia. The Scythians existed between, at least, the mid-8th century BCE and the 3rd century CE, while the Sarmatians (if we count the Sauromatae) existed between the 5th century BCE and the 5th century CE.

So, to tell the history of the Scythians and Sarmatians is to try to piece together a puzzle with a considerable amount of missing pieces, and it becomes even harder when one takes into account that some of the existing pieces have raised doubt about their veracity, as is the case with Herodotus, a Greek historian who lived around 484 to 425 BCE, who tells us about the Scythians in his *Histories*.

The goal of this book is then to gather and sort through the sources and present a concise but informative and accurate account of the history and legacy of the Scythians and Sarmatians.

Part I: The Scythians

Chapter 1 – Origins of the Scythians

The evidence for the existence of wagon nomadism, that is nomadic peoples that developed and used wagons for transportation of their belongings over large-distance migrations or nomadic behavior, can be traced as far back as the Bronze Age, but it is in the first millennium BCE that the archaeological data points to an increase of nomadic horse breeders in the northern Pontic region. It is only from the 8th century BCE onward that we start to know the name of the peoples who inhabited there, the Cimmerians and the Scythians, through the historical data. It is thought that the Scythians originated through the wave migrations of several ancient, related populations of the Indo-Iranian language group that came from Central Asia/southern Siberia.[62]

Geographically the full extent of the presence of the Scythians is not entirely known. However, it's known that they occupied a region ranging from the river Danube in the west to the river Don in the east and to the Black Sea in the south. This region was the core of their civilization. Nevertheless, at certain times of expansion, this border

---

[62] Bonfante, Larrisa – *The Barbarians of Ancient Europe: Realities and Interactions*. New York: Cambridge University Press, 2011. p. 110

could go farther and include the Caucasus and the Dobruja regions, to the southeast and west, respectively.[63]

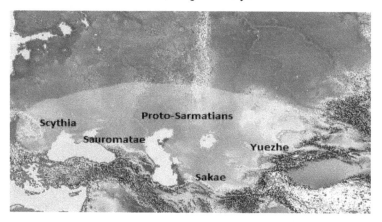

Figure 2 – Estimated maximum extent of the Scythians, 500 BCE. Although they have different names, culturally they are all very similar to the point that they are all regarded as Scythian peoples.

It is thought that the geographical area occupied by the Scythians had an abundance of fertile soil and rivers, which provided optimal pasture lands for the Scythian nomadic horse-breeding civilization. However, reconstructing the landscape of the Scythians' home still remains a problem to solve among archaeologists.[64]

Their introduction in the historical records starts out with warfare, as their raids into the Near East's civilizations are registered in both cuneiform documents of Assyro-Babylonian origin and in the works of some authors of classical antiquity. Evidence of Scythian invasions is not only confirmed by the historical records but with archaeological findings of arrowheads, horse gear, and other items of Scythian origin as well. Archaeological data of the destruction of Urartian towns and fortresses also corroborate the Scythian

---

[63] Bonfante, Larrisa – *The Barbarians of Ancient Europe…* p. 109

[64] Bonfante, Larrisa – *The Barbarians of Ancient Europe…* p. 109

incursions into the Near East and the importance they played as a political destabilizer in the region.[65]

The Caucasus region was their entrance into the Near East, and their presence on the local tribes there is evident by the archaeological data. Scythian burial sites (*kurgans*) of a tribal chief and their mounted bodyguard were found in this region, and Scythian items are a frequent find in archaeological sites of local tribes.[66]

From this point onward, the Scythian peoples would influence the politics of the Near East and the Black Sea as they kept raiding their lands. However, during this process, the Scythians would also assimilate into their own culture the aspects they liked about other civilizations they contacted. Scythian material culture was enriched by their connection with the wealthy sedentary civilizations in both their complexity and material value. The luxury of the Near Eastern sedentary civilizations was captivating to the nomadic steppe tribes, and so, a process of cultural absorption started.[67]

---

[65] Bonfante, Larrisa – *The Barbarians of Ancient Europe...* p. 111. SINOR, Denis – *The Cambridge History of Early Inner Asia.* New York: Cambridge University Press, 1990. p. 99 & 100.

[66] Sinor, Denis – *The Cambridge History of Early Inner Asia.* New York: Cambridge University Press, 1990. p. 100.

[67] Sinor, Denis – *The Cambridge History of Early Inner Asia.* New York: Cambridge University Press, 1990. p. 100 & 101.

Chapter 2 – Art, Culture, and Religion

The Scythians had a language system of Indo-Iranian origin that influenced other nomadic Indo-Iranian peoples, like the Sarmatians, to an extent. Since they did not have any written records, any study on their language relies heavily on the Scythian words classical authors wrote down in their books, so it's very difficult to reconstruct how exactly they would have spoken.

Since we can't rely on original sources by the Scythians, some of our knowledge of their culture and religion is based on the artifacts found in archaeological sites. For instance, Scythian art reflected much of what their way of life looked like with a focus on the representation of animals (stags, birds, bears, etc.) with an emphasis on horses. This art was not only on physical objects but also on their own bodies, as they would tattoo these natural and animal iconographies. The early period of Scythian history featured Near Eastern, especially Assyro-Babylonian, influences on their artistic output as they came into contact with them via military incursions and raids. However, from the sixth century BCE onward, the Greek cultural influence can already be seen in their material culture, reaching an apex in the fourth century BCE.[68]

The absorption of Greek culture promoted by trade, especially in the fourth century BCE, reflected in the art style of their pieces. Gold ornaments, jewelry, hair combs, jugs, and other items began to feature a more pictorial and scenic style with decors of Scythian daily life or metaphysical events.[69]

The Scythian cultural enrichment during this phase wasn't synonymous with the enrichment of every individual but only of the chiefs or aristocracy who would be benefited by the cultural exchange that the Scythians had with other civilizations, at least in a "perpetual" sense, as the precious items of art would accompany the aristocratic Scythians in the afterlife.[70]

As commerce enriched them and the Greek cultural influence increased amongst the Scythian tribes, the nomadic or semi-nomadic tribes became more sedentary and settled in the northern Black Sea area, near Greek towns. A gradual change of the traditional burial method, with the *kurgans*, can also be seen during the fifth and fourth centuries. The conventional process of laying the body in a grave was done on a mattress or a primitive couch made of plant fibers; however, following Greek influence, the practice of using sarcophagi became more and more common, especially for the aristocratic members of society. In zones where the Greeks had direct contact with the Scythians, for example, Crimea, the royal and

---

[68] Jacobson, Esther – *The Art of the Scythians: The Interpenetration of cultures at the edge of the Hellenic world.* Leiden: E.J. Brill, 1995. Ch. 3. SINOR, Denis – *The Cambridge History of Early Inner Asia.* New York: Cambridge University Press, 1990. p. 109.

[69] Jacobson, Esther – *The Art of the Scythians...* Ch. 3.

[70] Sinor, Denis – *The Cambridge History of Early...* p. 109.

noble burials of the fifth and fourth centuries had the body laid in a sarcophagus.[71]

The Scythian religion was heavily influenced by the Indo-Iranian gods, and at the center of their pantheon was the goddess Tabiti who, according to Herodotus, was responsible for a safe and well-functioning household. The priest class, the Enarei, were thought by the Scythians to have the gift of prophecy, given to them by the goddess Argimpasa, queen of the heavens and mistress of the animals. To tell the future, the Enarei would use strips cut from the bark of the linden tree.

The Enarei also had the power to heal the Scythian king by divination, at least in Herodotus' narrative. To cure the king, the Enarei supposedly would find any men who had falsely sworn loyalty to the king, treating this treason as the cause of his disease, and then they would kill them. With the traitors punished for their treason, the king's health would, apparently, improve. [72] This passage by Herodotus tells us more than how the Enarei supposedly cured the king; it also gives us a clear idea of how much influence these priests held in Scythian society. By crossing the archaeological data with these narratives, we can confirm that religion indeed played a significant role in everyday life, and the Enarei had a critical role in it, so much so that they were buried with riches and precious ceremonial artifacts.

Herodotus also remarks that the Enarei dressed in the clothes of women and were hermaphrodites, as they were cursed by the goddess Aphrodite. In his *Histories*, Herodotus talks about this curse as a way to explain the "unusual Scythian femininity":

> So these Scythians who had plundered the temple at Ascalon, and their descendants forever, were smitten by the

---

[71] Bonfante, Larrisa – *The Barbarians of Ancient Europe*... p. 85

[72] Herodotus – *Histories*. Book 4.68

divinity with a disease which made them women instead of men: and the Scythians say that it was for this reason that they were diseased, and that for this reason travellers who visit Scythia now, see among them the affection of those who by the Scythians are called ENAREI.[73]

Although this curse is a myth, the fact that the scythians believed it was true could have impacted the importance their society placed on women and that venerating them would please the gods and, thus, protect them from further punishment. However, the likely explanation of why the scythians had a matriarchal society lies at the cultural heart of the indo-iranian primordial tribe from whom they originated. That culture probably had a social structure where women not only had a prominent place of power but more importantly, they had a deep connection with the divine forces. This is why both scythian and sarmatian tribes share this societal feature. The Enarei were responsible for religious rituals as well, and besides animal sacrifices, which would include various types of livestock and in important occasions horses, the Scythians also used hemp and alcohol in these rituals to get into a spiritual trance.[74] Another religious ritual that the Sarmatians would also come to share with the Scythians was the practice of worshiping a god of war, who Herodotus equates to the Greek god Ares, by placing offerings onto small mounds made of brushwood where an iron sword was placed. The Scythians, in fact, unlike the Sarmatians, had a proper temple or earth mound, which was specifically dedicated to this kind of worship, meaning their place of worship would be semi-stationary and would be placed in locations reserved for these types of rituals.

---

[73] Herodotus – *Histories*. Book 1.105.

[74] Herodotus – *Histories*. Book 4.

Chapter 3 – Economy and Society

Scythians in the seventh century BCE lived in a communal tribal organization where social disparities between individuals wouldn't be very noticeable. However, as time went on and the Scythians secured more and more land and wealth, the accumulation of riches started to occur, primarily amongst the individuals with higher social standing who essentially became the aristocracy of said tribe. According to Herodotus, there were different types of Scythians, such as the Gargarii of the south of Ukraine (the Agricultural Scythians) and the so-called Royal Scythians who predominantly kept in the Crimean region. We don't know exactly how many individual tribes part of the Scythian cultural group were, but we do know that they weren't politically homogeneous and that they were made of smaller tribal groups who at some points would answer to a high-king who everyone would recognize either by their own volition or by subjugation. Some historians now theorize that the Gargarii weren't Scythians at all but were instead a kind of serf under Scythian domination and thus had to work for them. This reasoning justifies why they were sedentary and focused primarily on agricultural, something the Scythian nomads weren't very fond of. The Royal Scythians were named that way by Herodotus because most of the high-kings of the Scythian confederation came from this tribe, and this tells us that the Royal Scythians maintained a dominant position over the other tribes during an extended period.

It's still unclear if there were periods where there weren't any Scythian high-kings or if the high-king wasn't recognized as such by all of the tribal chieftains. Usually, a high-king from a dominant tribe would rule smaller tribal chieftains, who would then answer to him in a bond, similar to vassalage. This royal power was hereditary, and subject Scythian tribes would pay tribute and provide servants to the ruling tribe. Slaves were part of the Scythian society, but the evidence points to them being only domestic slaves and not used for other societal purposes.[75]

Furthermore, there is evidence that women would have had more significant participation in Scythian society than their Greek counterparts, occupying important societal roles and also fighting alongside men on the battlefield, thus being revered as great warriors. This is a feature shared by the other Indo-Iranian peoples like the Sarmatians, and at least in the Scythians' case, it would influence their pantheon of gods, in which goddesses like Argimpasa would have held a pivotal role in their beliefs. Scholars are not entirely sure if the Enarei priesthood would be held specifically by women or only by hermaphrodites, but either way, the Scythians venerated feminine characteristics. This can be seen in Scythian gold art where they depict humanoids who tend to be feminine.[76]

Scythian clothing was unisex, and both men and women wore kurtas, trousers, high boots or leather shoes, and a tunic with a round neck and long side openings, designed for horse riding. The kurtas, a loose collarless shirt, would have been made of woolen cloth, hemp, deerskin, or thick felt. Both commoners and aristocrats wore the same type of clothing, but the materials were different. As the Scythian civilization started to become richer, the aristocrats used

---

[75] Sinor, Denis – *The Cambridge History of Early....* p. 104

[76] Bonfante, Larrisa – *The Barbarians of Ancient Europe...* p. 120

important materials for their clothing like silk or linen, oftentimes decorated with gold.[77]

The gold and precious loot accumulated by raids and pillages would have reaped great rewards for the Scythian aristocracy, a much more lucrative and significant economic activity would come to them from the Aegean Sea, particularly in the fourth century BCE. The Greek city-states required greats amounts of cereal crops, particularly during the Peloponnesian War, and would import them from the Scythians of the Bosporus. The Scythian aristocracy willing to accumulate Greek wealth would act as a mediator between the tribes of the East European forest-steppe, a perfect area for agriculture, and the Greeks. The aristocracy reaped excellent rewards from this "exploitation" of the agricultural Scythian communities, and this economic situation would be one of the forces behind the sedentarization of both the agrarian tribes and of the enriching aristocracy as well as one of the causes of the social gradation of wealth inequality between the common Scythian and the aristocracy.[78]

Aside from the exploitation of the agricultural Scythians, the Royal Scythians would also trade the products of their hunts and their animal husbandry, including pelts, furs, and other animal parts that were highly sought after by Mediterranean traders. Livestock and horses could have been something that they possibly traded with the Greek colonies of the Black Sea since the Scythians were predominantly animal breeders. With the result of their commerce, the Scythians would be able to buy precious manufactured materials such as jewelry, weapons, armor, and vases.

---

[77] Encyclopedia Iranica – *Clothing of the Iranian Tribes on the Pontic Steppes and in the Caucasus* [Online] [Read 21/06/2019] Available at: **http://www.iranicaonline.org/articles/clothing-vii**

[78] Sinor, Denis – *The Cambridge History of Early....* p. 105

As a semi-nomadic group of tribes, the Scythians didn't have a centralized currency or financial system. Evidence of Scythian coin production has been found, and Strabo tells us of King Scilurus (who ruled in the latter half of the second century BCE) minting coins in the city of Olbia. These coins would come in two forms, either the primitive dolphin-shaped or arrowhead currency used for trading before the fifth century BCE or the imitations of Greek coins or Roman denarius, the Roman standard silver coin. They would also use Roman, Greek, or Pontic coins which they obtained through conquest or mercenary duties.

Scythian society was constructed around warfare, and the types of rituals they had and the items they carried to their grave show that being a victorious warrior had an impact on the social standing of an individual. Powerful commanders would take many precious items and artifacts to their graves, some acquired in faraway lands, and the most prestigious of the noblemen would even be buried with some of their warriors, servants, and horses.

Chapter 4 – Warfare and Conquest

The start of the known Scythian conquests comes in the form of their incursions into the Caucasus and Near East, which was already discussed in the first chapter of this book. However, perhaps the most significant military achievement of early Scythian history is the epic tale of how they managed to defeat the military incursion of the mighty Persian king, Darius I, into Scythia around 513 BCE. King Darius I, alongside his great army (700,000 according to Herodotus, but in reality, it would have been substantially less), tried to subdue the Scythian tribes and thus stabilize his empire's border region with Scythia. He was met with a tribe of fast horse warriors that used guerilla tactics to weaken his army, avoiding open confrontation. They also applied scorched earth tactics, destroying and burning everything as they evaded Darius' army, making it so that Darius I couldn't live off their lands. This lasted the whole campaign, and the two forces would not engage each other in direct confrontation, at least as far as we know. However, Darius' efforts would be somewhat effective as they managed to subdue the subject peoples of the Scythians, such as the Budini, along the Black Sea coast. And while the scorched earth tactics may have been effective in helping to end the Persian attack, according to Herodotus, the Scythians ended up destroying most of their better lands. At the end of the Persian incursion, the Persians effectively controlled the major ports of the Black Sea, such as the city of Olbia, although this came at the cost of many Persian lives by the lack of supplies and the tactics of attrition on the part of the Scythians. The end of this military debacle would also bring about "written silence," since the Scythians would not be mentioned again in the classical sources until the campaigns of Philip II of Macedon in 329 BCE.[79]

Figure 2 – Estimated path of Darius I's military incursion into Scythia, 513 BCE. The Scythian region represents the extension of the Indo-European tribes commonly referred to as Scythians because of their cultural similarity. Darius I's incursion was primarily against the European Scythians.

In 339 BCE, the Scythian king Ateas, a 90-year-old, became known for his military incursions into Thracia. He was successful at first and managed to conquer important areas from the Getae, a Thracian tribe that occupied the small area south of the Danube, as the fortified settlement of Eumolpia (modern-day Plovdiv, Bulgaria), but he was ultimately defeated and killed by the Macedonian king Philip II. The aftermath of Ateas' defeat was the capture of 20,000 women and 20,000 horses by the Macedonian king.[80]

---

[79] Sinor, Denis – *The Cambridge History of Early*.... p. 101

[80] Sinor, Denis – *The Cambridge History of Early*.... p. 106

Although this defeat weakened the Scythian hold on their western territories and the Getae managed to cross the Danube into their lands, their civilization would still thrive until the latter half of the third century when their hold on the Eurasian Steppe was seriously challenged by the Sarmatians and the Celts. This effectively ended the Scythian domination in the Eurasian Steppe and pushed them into two smaller and sperate kingdoms, known as the Crimean Little Scythia and the Thracian Little Scythia, which will be explained in more detail in the next chapter.[81]

In 329 BCE, a young Macedonian general named Alexander conquered the whole Persian Empire, which was under the rule of Darius III. After this, he sought to solidify his conquests and expand into India. At the southern bank of the river Jaxartes (modern-day Syr Darya), Alexander had built a city to delimitate the border of his empire. The city was called Alexandria Eschate (located in modern-day Khujand, Tajikistan). The local population of Sogdians, an ancient Iranian civilization, did not like this intrusion into their land and revolted. The peoples that lived across the Jaxartes, the Scythians or Sacae, saw this revolt as a great opportunity to loot and pillage the Greeks, so they joined forces with the Sogdians. To end this instability on his northern borders, Alexander took the matter into his own hands and personally led the battle against the Scythians and Sogdians.

Since the Jaxartes was wider than a bow shot, the Greek troops should have been able to board their ships and rafts in safety. However, their crossing would be within the Scythian fire range, meaning they could potentially be hit by incoming arrows. To prevent this, a plan was devised: The Greek catapult would be placed right next to the shore where they would then have the range to hit the Scythian forces and continuously fire until the whole army had crossed safely. The plan worked, and in the first round of catapult fire, a Scythian leader was killed, alongside many other Scythians.

---

[81] Sinor, Denis – *The Cambridge History of Early....* p. 107

The Greek archers were the first to cross so that they could protect the rest of the army by keeping the Scythian forces at a distance. After them followed the cavalry and finally the infantry. To force the Scythians into direct confrontation, Alexander sent his auxiliary light cavalry forces to bait the Scythians into an attack. This was successful, and the Scythians surrounded the auxiliary cavalry and engaged in close-quarters combat. Now the rest of Alexander's army had a chance to engage the Scythians and defeat them, which they did. The infantry and archers quickly surrounded the Scythian forces, catching those who sought to flee the onslaught and defeating the main Scythian army. The aftermath of this battle resulted in 1,200 Scythians killed and 1,800 horses captured.

The last detailed account of a Scythian battle in the written classical sources took place between 310 and 309 BCE when the Scythians intervened in the Bosporan Civil War, a dynastic dispute among the heirs of the Bosporan Kingdom. Satyrus II, the eldest heir, inherited the throne, but his brother Eumelos contested his claim. Fearing persecution from his older brother, Eumelos fled the capital and was offered refuge by the Siraces, a tribe of the Sarmatians, who seized the opportunity to gain influence in the Bosporus and try to take lands from the Scythians. The king of the Siraces, Aripharnes, and Eumelos allied with one another and gathered a force of 20,000 horsemen and 22,000 foot soldiers. Satyrus responded by mobilizing an army of 2,000 Greek troops and a similar number of Thracian mercenaries. However, the core of Satyrus' army was made up of 10,000 Scythian horsemen and 20,000 Scythian foot soldiers.

The Bosporan army (34,000) was at a disadvantage and was outnumbered by the Siraces (42,000). This situation was aggravated by the lack of forage for the Scythian horses, which had to be carried by wagon in a long and slow supply train. When they reached the Siracen army, they found the enemy on the northern bank of the river Thatis, ready to engage in battle in a more advantageous position. Satyrus made the bold move of crossing the river to attack them, using the wagon supply train to make a fortified camp which they could defend until the whole army had crossed. This move was surprisingly successful, and once all the forces were ready, he immediately drew them to the front of the makeshift fort. Ready to face the Siraces, Satyrus placed the Greek and Thracian troops in the right wing of his battle line, some of the Scythian cavalry and infantry in the left wing, and heavy Scythian cavalry in the center. We know little of the Siracen battle line, however. We can only assume that Eumelos and their cavalry were on the left flank, facing the Greek and Thracian mercenaries, with the infantry on the right wing. Aripharnes was at the center, also with heavy cavalry.

The battle was fierce, and both sides suffered heavy losses as soon as it began. Eumelos met with success against the Greek and Thracian mercenaries, causing them to waver, but, at the same time, Satyrus and the Scythians had managed to defeat Aripharnes' heavy cavalry. The Bosporan king, watching his left side collapse, quickly moved behind Eumelos' rear and charged in an all-out attack, smashing him between the Greeks and Scythians. Having been defeated, the surviving Siraces fled the battlefield and took refuge at a nearby fortress. The Scythian-Bosporan combined might was victorious.

This battle exemplifies the speed at which the Scythian forces could move and rearrange their positions to suit their needs. The might of their cavalry and the speed at which they conducted their attacks were difficult to counter in the ancient battlefield and was generally very effective against heavy infantry.

Scythian warfare was typically done on horseback, and thus, their army had a lot of cavalries. This gave them an advantage over traditional armies of the complex civilizations of the Near East that were overly dependent on infantry. Mounted archers were vital in the Scythian army as they gave them sufficient range to keep them free from engaging with the enemy but could also kill somewhat effectively. Their practice with the bow on horseback made them skilled shooters, but it was the fast-repeated volleys of arrows that did more significant damage. They would use guerrilla tactics to deceive their enemies while bombarding them with volley after volley of arrows and darts, and after the enemy broke their unit cohesion, the Scythians would charge in with lances and close-quarter weapons.[82] Herodotus stated that the Scythians "who have neither cities founded nor walls built, but carry their houses with them and are mounted archers, living not by the plow but by cattle, and whose dwellings are upon carts, these assuredly are invincible and impossible to approach."[83]

The most famous representation of Scythian armor is that of the scale armor, but early Scythian attempts at defensive wares were much simpler and consisted of animal leather or hide which, in some case, were covered by plates of iron or bronze. Only after their contact with Mesopotamian smiths and armorers would the Scythians develop the much more effective scale armor, which better protected the torso against spear or arrow penetration. Scale armor would prove so popular amongst the Scythian ranks that it remained the main armor of the Scythian armies until their disappearance in the fourth century CE.[84]

The helmet also naturally evolved as the Scythians came into contact with new types of warfare and new models made by other civilizations. Around the sixth century BCE, the Scythians used a cast-bronze helmet which gave good protection to the lower parts and the back of the head. This type of helmet is commonly named the "Kuban helmet," as it was found in archaeological excavations around the Kuban area (a region in modern-day southern Russia). However, from the fifth century BCE to the third century CE, along with their body armor, the Scythians would use a scale helmet. This piece of headgear constituted of a pointed leather cap which was then covered with overlapping metal scales. This scale type of construction, like the body armor, gave good protection against

---

[82] Chernenko, E.V. – *The Scythians 700-300 BC*. Oxford: Osprey Publishing, 1983.

[83] Herodotus – *Histories*. Book 4. 46.

[84] Chernenko, E.V. – *The Scythians...* p. 7.

sword and spear attacks, and so, it was widely used among the Scythians. Alongside the adoption of the scale helmet, another model would be adopted by the Scythian aristocracy—Greek helmets of either Corinthian, Chalcidian, or Attic origins.[85]

Scythian weaponry consisted of three types: long-range melee weapons (spears and lances), close-range melee weapons (daggers and swords), and mobile projectile weapons (javelins and bows). Spears would be used extensively by mounted or foot warriors to thrust their enemy at a safe distance and for throwing. They would be between 170 to 180 centimeters (5.5 to almost 6 feet) long. Evidence of longer spears and lances was found in some Scythian burial mounds, but it has such a rare occurrence that historians think that these types of weapons (that could reach up to three meters long) were only used by specialized cavalry units, due to requiring higher skill to maneuver them successfully.[86]

Swords and daggers were used by the Scythians, but it was more of an important tool for rituals and religious practices than combat. Some of the most impressive Scythian swords found to this day in archaeological excavations are merely ceremonial ones, made of gold and adorned with the Scythian animal art style. That is not to say that they didn't use the sword in combat; in fact, there is evidence that they used two types of swords, short and long ones, with the latter having more practical use in mounted combat due to its longer range.[87]

Other weapons used by mounted warriors include the javelin, which was basically a smaller spear that had a small, sharp pyramid head.

[85] Chernenko, E.V. – *The Scythians...* p. 7

[86] Chernenko, E.V. – *The Scythians...* p. 17

[87] Chernenko, E.V. – *The Scythians...* p. 14

While it was mainly used to disable shields or slightly injure the enemy, it still could kill or gravely injure someone.[88]

Lastly, the bow was, without a doubt, the most popular weapon used by the Scythians, and arrowheads were found in burial mounds of commoners and kings alike. It was the essential weapon for these warriors. The bow had a curved structure, and its length was up to 120 centimeters (a little less than 4 feet). The bow was mighty, but stiff and considerable strength would have been needed to master its use. Once mastered, the bow revealed to be a potent long-range projectile weapon that could shoot arrows up to a distance of 200 or more yards. The arrows were made of a reed or branch staff and a metal or bone tip, with the fletching made from birds' feathers.[89]

The people conquered by the Scythians would meet a ruthless and powerful foe, which, according to Herodotus, would not have mercy upon them and would practice human sacrifices. Historians cannot say for sure if the bloody practices Herodotus describes of their captives are true or if he is just portraying the Scythians as inhumane and barbarians to transmit the idea that the Greeks were culturally superior. Either way, the following excerpt of Herodotus' *Histories* remains a compelling read and can give us some idea of what the Scythian customs were:

> That which relates to war is thus ordered with them:—When a Scythian has slain his first man, he drinks some of his blood: and of all those whom he slays in the battle he bears the heads to the king; for if he has brought a head he shares in the spoil which they have taken, but otherwise not. And he takes off the skin of the head by cutting it round about the ears and then taking hold of the scalp and shaking it off; afterwards he scrapes off the flesh with the rib of an ox, and works the skin about with his hands; and when he has thus

---

[88] Chernenko, E.V. – *The Scythians...* p. 19

[89] Chernenko, E.V. – *The Scythians...* p. 11 & 12

tempered it, he keeps it as a napkin to wipe the hands upon, and hangs it from the bridle of the horse on which he himself rides, and takes pride in it; for whosoever has the greatest number of skins to wipe the hands upon, he is judged to be the bravest man. Many also make cloaks to wear of the skins stripped off, sewing them together like shepherds' cloaks of skins; and many take the skin together with the finger-nails off the right hands of their enemies when they are dead, and make them into covers for their quivers: now human skin it seems is both thick and glossy in appearance, more brilliantly white than any other skin. Many also take the skins off the whole bodies of men and stretch them on pieces of wood and carry them about on their horses...(...)Once every year each ruler of a district mixes in his own district a bowl of wine, from which those of the Scythians drink by whom enemies have been slain; but those by whom this has not been done do not taste of the wine, but sit apart dishonoured; and this is the greatest of all disgraces among them: but those of them who have slain a very great number of men, drink with two cups together at the same time.[90]

---

[90] Herodotus – *Histories*. Book 4. 64-66

Chapter 5 – End of the Scythians

The tale of the end of the Scythians comes to us via the Greek philosopher and historian Strabo. According to him, from the second century BCE to the first century CE, two minor Scythian kingdoms resisted the onslaught from the Celts and Sarmatians. One of them was situated south of the Danube River and is thought to have been formed by the Scythians who remained after King Ateas' defeat after the other Scythians returned to the northern Black Sea coast. The other minor Scythian kingdom was located in what is known today as the peninsula of Crimea and went as far north as the region of Taurida (modern-day South Ukraine). Neapolis, the capital of the Crimean kingdom, was where the Scythian royal and aristocratic headquarters were based and from where the Scythian high-king would have ruled the Scythian confederation.[91]

The Crimean kingdom had significant cultural and economic development in the second century BCE. In a measure to centralize their Mediterranean trade and stop dealing with the Greek mediators,

---

[91] Sinor, Denis – *The Cambridge History of Early....* p. 107

they successfully attacked the Greek towns of the northwest Chersonesus Taurica (the Greek Crimean colonies). Commanded by King Scilurus, the Scythians managed to conquer all of the northwestern Crimean Greek colonies, some being completely devastated and razed to the ground while others became occupied by the Scythians who built their fortresses on their ruins. The ones who didn't want to end in ruin submitted to Scythian domination, like the town of Olbia where King Scilurus made his coins.[92]

The effort made by Scilurus to expand their power and drive out the Greek commercial mediators was complemented by what the evidence points out as being the existence of a Scythian fleet, which would have allowed Scythian merchants to safely conduct trade of their agricultural goods directly with the Mediterranean.[93]

The death of Scilurus and the succession of his son Palacus would mark a turning point of the Scythian offensive toward the Greek colonies as the remaining ones would turn to the Pontic kingdom for help. Mithridates VI, also known as Mithridates the Great, the king of Pontus, answered the Greek call for help and sent an army commanded by the general Diophantus. The Pontic army delivered a bitter defeat to the Scythian and Sarmatian combined force, as Palacus had enlisted the Roxolani, a Sarmatian tribe, to help deal with the Pontic army, and managed to protect the Greek domains, although the Greeks wouldn't fully recuperate all the territories they had lost under the reign of Scilurus.[94]

The defeat at the hands of the Pontic army was brutal, but open hostilities would resume again later in the first century CE, at which point the Greek Chersonese sought help from the Romans. A Roman expedition was then mounted to liberate the Greeks from constant

---

[92] Sinor, Denis – *The Cambridge History of Early.... *p. 108

[93] Sinor, Denis – *The Cambridge History of Early.... *p. 108

[94] Sinor, Denis – *The Cambridge History of Early.... *p. 108

harassment that culminated in the year 63 CE with a Scythian defeat. Archaeological evidence ranging from the first to the second century CE point to the destruction of Scythian forts by the Roman military presence in the area.[95]

The Scythians, after all of these military failures, weren't totally driven off their lands, and evidence shows that they still persisted through the second and beginning of the third centuries CE. It is by the middle of the third century CE that we can no longer find evidence of a culturally distinct Scythian population. They were assimilated by the Goths and other nomadic peoples that passed through the Bosporus region, and they lost their cultural and linguistic cohesion, marking the de facto end of what we broadly call the Scythians.

---

[95] Sinor, Denis – *The Cambridge History of Early…*. p. 108

Part II: The Sarmatians

Chapter 6 – Origins of the Sarmatians

The first reference to the term "Sauromatae" comes via the Greek writer Herodotus in his *Histories* to describe a nomadic people that lived south of the river Don and the Volga. He refers to them as being the sons of a Scythian father and an Amazon mother, which to him justified why they spoke a "broken-dialect" of the Scythian language. The basis of this affirmation is, of course, only mythical; however, by analyzing and cross-referencing the various classical authors and the archaeological data, academics have been able to conclude that both Scythian and Sauromatae tribes originated from the peoples of the Bronze Age Srubnaya culture, located on the northern shore of the Black Sea and covering a large part of the Pontic-Caspian steppe (from modern-day northeastern Bulgaria through Romania, Moldova, Ukraine, and southern Russia to western Kazakhstan). Some of the tribes of the Srubnaya culture cooperated with tribes from the Andronovo culture, whose presence covered almost all of modern-day Kazakhstan, and were influenced by them culturally, which can explain why the Sauromatae spoke a "broken-dialect" of the Scythian language.[96]

The Sauromatae, like the Scythians, were not a single unified entity but rather a group of different tribes that shared a common cultural background. They mostly stayed in the territory southeast of the river Don between the sixth and seventh century BCE, but starting at the end of the fifth century, the Sauromatae crossed the Don and established themselves in the coast of the Azov Sea.

The close proximity between the Sauromatae and the Scythians, both in geographic and cultural terms, transpired in peaceful cooperation between the two groups of peoples. So much so that when the Persian emperor Darius I sent a military incursion to end the Scythian menace, the Sauromatae were counted amongst the Scythian allies.[97]

Although the Sauromatae shared a genetic link with the later Sarmatians, they are not the same thing, and a direct line of development can't be established between the two peoples more clearly because the Sarmatians developed differently than the Sauromatae even though the two eventually crossed paths and intermixed with each other.[98]

The Proto-Sarmatian group of peoples originated in the area south of the Ural Mountains and ultimately, between the fourth and third centuries BCE, migrated to the region south of the Volga and southeast of the Don, conquering the Sauromatae that lived there. The mixing of these peoples, the Sarmatians, and the Sauromatae, is at the core of the origin of the Sarmatian tribes we later see

---

[96] Sinor, Denis – *The Cambridge History of Early....* p. 110

[97] Brzezinski, R; Mielczarek, M – *The Sarmatians 600 BC–AD 450* Oxford: Osprey Publishing, 2002. p. 7

[98] Brzezinski, R; Mielczarek, M – *The Sarmatians.* p. 6 & 7; SINOR, Denis – *The Cambridge History of Early....* p. 112

mentioned in the sources of antiquity—the Aorsi, Siraces, Roxolani, Alans, and the Iazyges.[99]

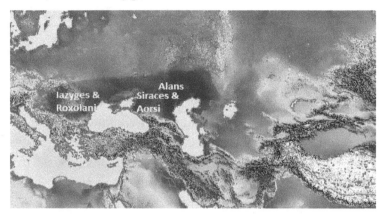

Figure 3 – Estimated maximum extension of the Sarmatians and the main tribe's location in the 1ˢᵗ century CE. The Alans originated only in the 1ˢᵗ century CE and assimilated the Aorsi and probably the remaining Siraces.

The Siraces were Sarmatians that migrated to the Black Sea/Sea of Azov coast, south of the Don, in the late fifth century BCE. They often appear in classical works alongside the Bosporan Kingdom, who they maintained close relations with. At one point, Strabo mentions that the Siraces during the reign of King Abeacus were able to raise around 20,000 riders. From what we can conclude though, they were a relatively smaller tribe, so we can't confirm that this is accurate. The close proximity they maintained between the Pontic and Bosporan Kingdoms made them the most Hellenized of the Sarmatians, and although most of their aristocracy kept a semi-nomadic lifestyle, most of the population was sedentary.[100]

The Aorsi lived in the open plateau south of the Don and northeast of the Siraces. Strabo indicates that the Aorsi was one of the most prominent Sarmatian peoples and was, in fact, divided between the lower and upper Aorsi. The lower Aorsi was described as being able

---

[99] Sinor, Denis – *The Cambridge History of Early....* p. 112

[100] Brzezinski, R; Mielczarek, M – *The Sarmatians.* p. 7

to field around 200,000 riders and lived in the plateau south of the Don. The upper Aorsi occupied a more significant area consisting of all the coast of the Caspian Sea, and modern studies have traced their influence all the way to the Aral Sea.[101]

The Roxolani and Iazyges were in the vanguard of the Sarmatian move westward, and all evidence points to them as being the first Sarmatians to cross the river Don. The two tribes were located in different geographical zones; the Roxolani mostly kept themselves in the region south of Ukraine of the forest-steppe, while the Iazyges kept to the Crimean territories and the coast of the Black Sea/Azov Sea. Their gradual advancement westward of the Don started in the second century BCE and lasted until the Roxolani had reached the region of Moesia in the first century CE and threatened the eastern region of the Roman Empire.[102]

The Alans were the last of what we call the Sarmatian tribes to appear in the Black Sea region coming from Central Asia in the mid-first century CE. They are described as not being wholly Sarmatian and are thought to have had a tribal composition of both Central Asian and Sarmatian origins. Some authors of antiquity point to the Sarmatian part of the Alans having originated in the tribe of the Massagetae, who had mixed with several Saka peoples and other Central Asians. [103]

---

[101] Brzezinski, R; Mielczarek, M – *The Sarmatians*. p. 7 & 8

[102] Brzezinski, R; Mielczarek, M – *The Sarmatians*. p. 8

[103] Brzezinski, R; Mielczarek, M – *The Sarmatians*. p. 10

Chapter 7 – Art, Culture, and Religion

The absence of Sarmatian written sources makes it somewhat difficult to pinpoint what exactly their culture and religion were like. From the archaeological data and the classical sources, we can infer some information about the way these people lived and their cultural traditions.

Some historians have the opinion that the cultural output of the Sarmatians was less developed than the Scythians, meaning that the archaeological materials that have been found are often less complex in detail and less rich. The frequency of the richer artifacts is also less than the Scythians.[104]

Nevertheless, the Sarmatian artifacts are still impressive in their own right and are the physical proof of their artistical achievements. Today, we can find some of them in the Sarmatian collection of the State Hermitage Museum in St. Petersburg, Russia, that boast an extensive and magnificent collection of precious artifacts. There are multiple kinds of gold Sarmatian artifacts, including golden torques, perfume flasks, and diadems; these all share the same art style—the

---

[104] Sinor, Denis – *The Cambridge History of Early….* p. 111

so-called polychrome Sarmatian animal style. Notable for the representation of the heads and bodies of animals in their ornaments, the polychrome Sarmatian style was the result of the deep connection the Sarmatians had with nature and the importance it had to them.[105]

The few Sarmatian art pieces that made their way to us are here thanks to the burial rituals which, similar to the Scythians, constituted of underground structures beneath an earthen mound where they buried their dead in rectangular rooms and included personal items, gifts, and offerings. In the burial mounds of the important Sarmatian individuals, various gold items, like bracelets, torques, or even belt buckles, have been found, displaying their wealth. If the individual was female, then precious jewelry pieces like rings or necklaces made of gold accompanied the dead.[106]

The Sarmatian animal art style is also indicative of their religious veneration with nature and their use of animal and ritualistic sacrifices. Although not much is known about their specific gods or goddesses, we know some tidbits of information. We know that through historical evidence from the Alan tribe that the Sarmatians probably worshiped a pantheon of seven gods—the norm amongst tribes of Indo-Iranian origins. Amongst their pantheon, historians are almost certain that the Sarmatians worshiped a god of water and a goddess of fire, which was also very common amongst Indo-Iranian tribes. One particular religious practice that we know of through the records of the Roman Ammianus Marcellinus is the worship of a god, similar to the Roman god Mars; this ritual was consummated by

---

[105] The State Hermitage Museum. *Treasures from the Sarmatians*. HermitageMuseum.org. 24 May 2019

< https://www.hermitagemuseum.org>

[106] The State Hermitage Museum. *Treasures from the Sarmatians*. HermitageMuseum.org. 24 May 2019

< https://www.hermitagemuseum.org>

driving a sword into a small earth mound. In a representation of the erection of the "axis mundi" (in ancient religions, the axis mundi represented the "umbilical cord" that unites the world of gods with the world of humans, and erecting an axis mundi meant to create a site where this "umbilical cord" could exist), the ritual likely symbolized the connection of the people with their gods, a practice that the Sarmatians shared with their Scythian cousins, who, unlike them, had specially dedicated altars for this specific ritual. Outside of these altars, we don't have any archaeological data of Sarmatian buildings that were used specifically as temples, which suggests they didn't have any.[107]

Sarmatian burials and religion were interconnected since the burial of a deceased individual was done according to their religious beliefs. Aside from preparing a journey to some kind of afterlife, evidence of their worship of fire can be found in their burial mounds. Remnants of a ritual bonfire, which was used to cover the graves, have been found, as well as a ring made of its ash inside the grave. The prevalent role of fire with Sarmatian graves is not fully understood, but it gives us a clear indication that to these people fire was essential for the burial ritual. The close proximity of the burial mounds suggests that the Sarmatians practiced some type of ancestor veneration and that Sarmatians liked to be buried close to their ancestors. Of course, this doesn't necessarily mean that ancestor veneration was an essential part of their religious customs but was rather a cultural practice that was of vital importance to these peoples.[108]

In burial mounds of some Sarmatian women, what would be considered a small portable altar— a small stone plate—that was used for various ritual activities, such as igniting ritual fires or

[107] Encyclopedia of Religion. *Sarmatian Religion*. Encyclopedia.com. 3 Jun. 2019<https://www.encyclopedia.com>.

[108] Encyclopedia of Religion. *Sarmatian Religion*. Encyclopedia.com. 3 Jun. 2019<https://www.encyclopedia.com>.

grinding chalk, has been found. The fact that these portable altars have only been found, so far, in burial mounds of women indicates that only women could be priestesses or, at the very least, that they were the only ones that could use them religiously.[109]

The Sarmatians practiced cultural body deformation, and although we are not totally sure if the accounts by the Roman geographer Pomponius Mela (15–45 CE) of breast cauterization in women are true, we do have archaeological evidence that the Alans practiced head elongation. In their infancy, Alan children could be bandaged in the head so that they would have an elongated cranial structure when they were older. The purpose of this practice, outside a culture sense of "fashion," is not very well understood, but the frequency of elongated skulls in the archaeological data dated between the fourth and fifth centuries CE points to this practice being popularized by Hunnic influences.[110]

Body tattoos were also a common practice among Sarmatian peoples, and, according to the Roman philosopher and historian Sextus Empiricus (160–210 CE), they were tattooed in their infancy. The tattoos would have been likely made in the Sarmatian animal style, given the importance it had to the Sarmatians culturally.

All of what we know of the art, culture, and religion of the Sarmatians corroborate the narrative that historically the Scythians and the Sarmatians had very close cultural ties, not only in linguistic terms but also in cultural practices.

---

[109] Encyclopedia of Religion. *Sarmatian Religion*. Encyclopedia.com. 3 Jun. 2019<https://www.encyclopedia.com>.

[110] Brzezinski, R; Mielczarek, M – *The Sarmatians*. p. 13

Chapter 8 – Economy and Society

Economically, the Sarmatians weren't too different from the Scythians. As a semi-nomadic group of tribes, these peoples would depend on agriculture and animal husbandry to not only sustain themselves but to also trade with other civilizations. Hunting played a large part in their economy since the furs and pelts they gathered would garner a high price in the Mediterranean and Pontic areas. Some of their material wealth and precious artifacts would come from raiding and warfare, as their high mobility would give them the capability of gathering quick pillaging parties to gain loot from neighboring settlements. This form of warfare was the result of their mastery of horse riding and their reliance on the horse for their martial activities, which made them have a cavalry that was much larger than other civilizations at this time.[111]

Another point to consider in terms of their economic structure and something that can't be disregarded was their work as mercenaries on the payroll of wealthy empires or kingdoms, such as the Bosporan Kingdom and the Roman Empire. Not only would they be paid handsomely for their services, but their loyalty and good behavior

---

[111] Sinor, Denis – *The Cambridge History of Early…*. p. 115

would be rewarded with precious gifts made of gold or other valuable materials.[112]

The upper Aorsi, and later the Alans, had access to other types of riches since the important trade routes that came to the Black Sea from Mesopotamia and India gave them a type of material wealth that other Sarmatian tribes couldn't manage to achieve. Strabo describes this well in his passage:

> But the upper Aorsi sent a still larger number, for they held dominion over more land, and, one may almost say, ruled over most of the Caspian coast; and consequently, they could import on camels the Indian and Babylonian merchandise, receiving it in their turn from the Armenians and the Medes, and also, owing to their wealth, could wear golden ornaments.[113]

The Sarmatians had no official coinage or complex financial system. Instead, they would trade either by bartering or using coins from other civilizations, such as Roman and Greek coins. In the Black Sea region, cities from other kingdoms like the Greek Olbia and Bosporan Chersonesus would be responsible for coin mintage, and when these types of towns would be conquered by the Sarmatians or the Scythians, they would use it to strike their own coins, which imitated Greek ones.[114]

The Sarmatians were a tribal society and shared many features with other similar contemporary civilizations, primarily the Scythians. The Sarmatians were divided amongst many tribes that together had a familiar culture and language, but each tribe was independent and

---

[112] Brzezinski, R; Mielczarek, M – *The Sarmatians*. p. 15

[113] Strabo – *Geography*. Book 6. 8 [Online] [Read 26/05/2019] Available at: **http://penelope.uchicago.edu/Thayer/E/Roman/Texts/Strabo/11E*.html**

[114] Grumeza, Lavinia – *Roman Coins in Sarmatian Graves from the Territory of Banat (2nd-4th centuries AD)*. Analele Banatului Archeologie-Istorie. Cluj-Napoca: Editura MEGA. ISSN 1221-678X. Nº 21 (2013). p. 117-128.

had a "king" or "chief" figure. On certain occasions, these leaders would unite to rule over great confederations of peoples, as was the case with the Alans, Roxolani, Iazyges, Aorsi, and Siraces. All of these tribes were confederations and were formed either by the subjugation of many smaller tribes or by tribal initiative, meaning that the tribes would have come together by their own volition and then elect a king from a tribe that everyone respected. We are not entirely sure why they created confederations due to a tribal initiative; presumably, it was to become stronger as a cultural group or to seek the opportunities a tribe could have in such confederations, such as ease of access to better loot. It is thought that all the Sarmatian confederations mentioned above were created by free tribal aggregation, but they all, at some point or another, integrated smaller tribes forcefully.

This was not the only thing that the Sarmatians shared in common with the Scythians, as they also wore similar clothing. Both men and women would wear short cloaks, caftans (a traditional type of shirt) that opened in the front, loose trousers, and headdresses with one or two disks over the forehead. They wore high boots, leather stockings, shoes with a pointy front, or high felt boots. Women could also be seen wearing a sleeveless dress fastened at each shoulder with a fibula. To this day, caftans are still worn in the regions the Sarmatians influenced. The difference between aristocratic and commoner clothing was the materials from which the wares were made. Sarmatian aristocrats wore clothing made from silk and linen that was decorated with gold ornaments; all of these were imported materials from the Mediterranean civilizations.[115] Sarmatians would primarily trade natural goods for manufactured ones from their Mediterranean trading partners. From Greek clothing and helmets to jewelry, the Sarmatians would seek these goods, and in exchange,

---

[115] Encyclopedia Iranica – *Clothing of the Iranian Tribes on the Pontic Steppes and in the Caucasus* [Online] [Read 21/06/2019] Available at: **http://www.iranicaonline.org/articles/clothing-vii**

they would sell or barter pelts, furs, domestic animal products, and agricultural goods.

As stated above, the disparity of wealth between the regular people and the aristocracy wasn´t as accentuated as in the Scythian society, or at least when it comes to the burial mounds, and so, historians assume that very few individuals would obtain more wealth than the others and that it wasn't so much as to leave a large wealth gap. However, this is true only for the few centuries of their presence in the Black Sea area because as they became successful by the fourth to the first century BCE, wealth came pouring in, and only those with the most power would gain the more significant share. This wealth disparity would increase over time, as each figurehead would break tribal communal traditions and accumulate wealth for themselves.[116]

Sarmatian societal roles placed women in a place of great influence, similar to the Scythians. Not only did women participate in some form of the priesthood and hold religious importance, but they would also fight alongside men on the battlefield. A large number of burial mounds with graves of women warriors have been found, attesting to the equal role of women and men in warfare. Some burial mounds have been found where women were buried in a central position and accompanied by many riches, so we know that Sarmatian women could hold positions of societal importance and had the power to accumulate vast sums of wealth. The Greek tales of the mythical Amazonian warriors originated from the Sarmatian tribes since, according to some classical authors such as Hippocrates and Pomponius Mela, Sarmatian women could only marry after they had faced an enemy on the battlefield.[117]

The account of the classical writer Pomponius Mela goes as follows:

---

[116] Sinor, Denis – *The Cambridge History of Early....* p. 116

[117] Sinor, Denis – *The Cambridge History of Early....* p. 111 & 112. Brzezinski, R; Mielczarek, M – *The Sarmatians.* p. 43

They are warlike, free, unconquered, and so savage and cruel that women also go to war side by side with men; and so that women may be suited for action, their right breast is cauterized as soon as they are born. As a result, that breast, now exposed and ready to withstand blows, develops like a man's chest. Archery, horseback riding, and hunting are a girl's pursuits; to kill the enemy is a woman's military duty, so much so that not to have struck one down is considered a scandal, and virginity is the punishment for those women.[118]

Slavery was a part of Sarmatian society, but evidence points to the fact that the Sarmatians only used slaves domestically or as an object to trade.[119] However, they would maintain certain conquered peoples as serfs who did most of the agricultural work for them. Evidence points to people like the Limigantes, who lived at the intersection of modern-day Romania, Hungary, and Serbia, of having that societal and economic task.

[118] Mela, Pomponius – *De Situ Orbis*. Transl. F.E. Romer. Michigan: University of Michigan.1998 p.110

[119] Sinor, Denis – *The Cambridge History of Early*.... p. 116

Chapter 9 – Warfare and Conquest

Warfare and conflict were an essential part of the Sarmatian society, and their culture, economy, and society were built around warfare, pillaging, and conquering. From hunting to looting, the Sarmatians knew that to survive in the steppes, one had to be not only mobile but bold and strong. From the fourth century BCE onward, their fame as formidable and ruthless warriors grew, and soon enough, they would be hired as mercenaries by the Pontic and Bosporan Kingdoms and later the Romans.

The first written account of the Sauromatae in the classical sources is about their participation with the Scythian force against the Persian king Darius I in 513 BCE. It's no mere coincidence that when the classical authors mentioned them later in their texts that it had to do mostly with their conflicts and the way they fought. The extent of their collaboration is not entirely known, but Herodotus mentions them as allies of the Scythians.[120]

The Sarmatian tribes had many military encounters throughout their written history. The Aorsi fought on the Roman side in the Roman-Bosporan War in 49 CE, and the Siraces fought on the opposite side. This Bosporan conflict was created when the Bosporan king Aspurgus died and left the kingdom to his son, Mithridates III. The claim of Mithridates was strengthened when the Roman emperor

---

[120] Brzezinski, R; Mielczarek, M – *The Sarmatians.* p. 7

Claudius made him ruler of all the Bosporan territories, although they remained as a client-state of the Romans. However, in 45 CE, for reasons we don't fully understand, Claudius deposed Mithridates and placed Cotys I, Mithridates' younger brother, on the throne. To protect his new client-king, Emperor Claudius placed Gaius Julius Aquila in charge of a few Roman cohorts.

Mithridates couldn't stand idly by and watch his treasonous brother claim the throne that he felt was his, so he sought help from a neighboring Sarmatian tribe, the Siraces, who was under King Zorsines. Cotys feared an impending invasion and turned to Gaius Julius Aquila and his cohorts for help. Gaius was a shrewd general, and seeing that Mithridates' forces were much larger in number than theirs, he quickly enlisted the help of another Sarmatian tribe, the Aorsi, who was under King Eunones. As soon as their forces were prepared, Eunones and Aquila attacked the opposing side. The Roman forces began to lay siege to the Bosporan cities under Mithridates' control, such as Artezian, while the Aorsi invaded the Siracen territories and laid siege to the settlement of Uspe. This Siracen city had weak defenses, which enabled the Aorsi to construct tall towers which they could use to harass the defenders with arrows and darts. Uspe's defense was unsustainable and quickly fell to Aorsi control. The siege would only last one day, according to the Roman historian Tacitus, and it would result in the surrender of the Siraces.

When Mithridates received word of his ally's surrender and seeing that his forces were dwindling, he decided to surrender personally to King Eunones, since he knew that the Romans and his brother would kill him. Tacitus describes that Mithridates went to Eunones' court and kneeled before him, saying, "Mithridates, whom the Romans have sought so many years by land and sea, stands before you by his own choice. Deal as you please with the descendant of the great Achaemenes, the only glory of which enemies have not robbed me." The king of the Aorsi was impressed by his courage and, considering that the Aorsi was the only tribe capable of protecting him against

Roman aggression, allowed Mithridates to take refuge in the Sarmatian court. However, Eunones could not put his alliance with the Romans at risk to protect a deposed prince and wrote to the Roman emperor informing him of Mithridates' presence in his court but also asked that he show mercy to the deposed Bosporan king. Claudius showed his mercy but ordered Mithridates to be sent to Rome. After an audience with the emperor, Mithridates was let go and forgiven.[121]

The Aorsi-Roman force secured a victory for their coalition and brought such devastation to the Siraces that they would only appear once more in the classic books as a co-belligerent in the Bosporan conflict of 193 CE. After that, they vanish from written history. Although the Aorsi chose the winning side in the Roman-Bosporan War in 49 CE, some decades later, they would be conquered and assimilated by the powerful Alans who had recently arrived in the Black Sea area.[122]

The Iazyges and Roxolani, who had crossed the Don in the second century BCE, were in an advantageous position in the first century BCE, having close proximity to the Roman border and thus access to direct diplomatic relations with the Roman Empire as well as the possibility to loot some of their wealthier cities. For the duration of the first century CE, the Iazyges were relatively friendly with the Romans and helped them in their military agendas. However, the Roxolani conducted a series of raids on Roman Moesia from 62 to 86 CE, even managing to destroy a Roman legion. This destruction reminded the Roman generals that the Sarmatian peoples were a serious foe, and even their superior army structure couldn't compete with the large numbers of cavalrymen the Sarmatians had in their hosts.

---

[121] Tacitus – *The Annals*. Book XII. [Online] [Read 20/06/2019] Available at: **http://classics.mit.edu/Tacitus/annals.8.xii.html**

[122] Brzezinski, R; Mielczarek, M – *The Sarmatians*. p. 8

The Roxolani also participated in the Dacian Wars, siding with the Dacian peoples against the Roman invaders. In this war, the Romans enlisted the help of the Iazyges who had been receptive toward them previously. At the end of the Dacian Wars, Roman emperor Trajan won the conflict against the Dacian-Roxolani combined force and managed to antagonize both Sarmatian tribes (Roxolani and Iazyges) by establishing and demarcating the imperial province of Dacia, infringing on Sarmatian control in the area. They would engage in many conflicts with the Roman Empire after this, only being temporarily pacified when Roman Emperor Hadrian allowed them to coexist in Roman-controlled Dacia. In this pacification process, the Roxolani king, Rasparagnus, was given Roman citizenship, and subsidies were paid to the Roxolani to maintain some stability with the borders. The Marcomannic Wars (166–180 CE) during the reign of Roman Emperor Marcus Aurelius marked a reopening of their hostilities with the Sarmatians as the Iazyges joined with Germanic forces to invade the Roman provinces of Pannonia, Dacia, Noricum, and all the way to Italia and Achaia (Greece). Marcus Aurelius ultimately defeated them, and peace was made. The truce between the two would be finalized by the handing over of 8,000 Sarmatian horsemen. For this victory, Marcus Aurelius would adopt the title of "Sarmaticus," a title that openly displayed to the Romans that Aurelius was the one to subdue and achieve great victories against the Sarmatians.[123]

The first Alanic military conflict that is mentioned in classical literature is the Alanic incursion into Parthia in 72 CE. What essentially was a looting military incursion by the Alans nearly resulted in the capture of Armenian King Tiridates I in battle. He escaped and was successful in his attempt to defend his homeland from Sarmatian sacking.

In 135 CE, another account of an Alanic looting incursion is mentioned, this time into Asia Minor via the Caucasus Mountains.

---

[123] Brzezinski, R; Mielczarek, M – *The Sarmatians*. p. 9

This endeavor was eventually driven back by Arrian, the Roman governor of the province of Cappadocia, a region in modern-day Turkey. The beginning of the second century CE would mark the Alanic arrival in the Black Sea area where they assimilated and conquered the local Sarmatians such as the Aorsi.[124]

The military organization of the Sarmatian units from the seventh to the fourth century BCE was of tribal origin and would require all men and women who could fight to report to the battlefield where individuals of power would command their small local groups. These individuals would then answer to the commands of the tribal king or chief. From the fourth century onward, the Sarmatians developed a social structure around warfare, and warriors would only be the ones explicitly chosen to fight on the battlefield, whether they were men or women, not just all able-bodied individuals. A warrior "caste" thus arose.[125] The Greek author Lucian gives us an idea of how the hordes of Sarmatian warriors were raised:

> Our custom of the hide is as follows. When a man has been injured by another, and desires vengeance, but feels that he is no match for his opponent, he sacrifices an ox, cuts up the flesh and cooks it, and spreads out the hide upon the ground. On this hide, he takes his seat, holding his hands behind him, so as to suggest that his arms are tied in that position, this being the natural attitude of a suppliant among us. Meanwhile, the flesh of the ox has been laid out; and the man's relations and any others who feel so disposed come up and take a portion thereof, and, setting their right foot on the hide, promise whatever assistance is in their power: one will engage to furnish and maintain five horsemen, another ten, a third some larger number; while others, according to their ability, promise heavy or light-armed infantry, and the

---

[124] Brzezinski, R; Mielczarek, M – *The Sarmatians*. p. 10

[125] Brzezinski, R; Mielczarek, M – *The Sarmatians*. p. 14

poorest, who have nothing else to give, offer their own personal services. The number of persons assembled on the hide is sometimes very considerable; nor could any troops be more reliable or more invincible than those which are collected in this manner, being as they are under a vow; for the act of stepping on to the hide constitutes an oath. By this means, then, Arsacomas raised something like 5,000 cavalry and 20,000 heavy and light-armed.[126]

Although one could say that the Sarmatians dedicated themselves professionally to warfare, considering their civilization and culture depended on it, they didn't have a professional army structure like the Roman Empire did. The Sarmatian method of raising an army was similar to those of the Celts or the Gauls where individuals pled their loyalty to one man or cause, who in turn promised them booty and plunder. However, this is only true of their military organization until the second century CE, since Sarmatian society became more hierarchical from the second to the fourth century CE, and warriors were chosen and trained according to their skills. As such, between those centuries, a special kind of Sarmatian cavalry unit, the armored lancer, was formed to help support the Sarmatian armies with the use of the long lance.[127]

The cavalry was at the core of the Sarmatian army, and the most common unit of the cavalry was the light-armored horse archer; they would be accompanied by better-armored lancers who constituted the minority of the forces. Some historical records state that they used infantry, but it is likely that either it was constituted mainly of non-Sarmatian peoples (i.e., assimilated peoples) or of poorer Sarmatians who could not afford to own a horse.[128] The Alans, for

---

[126] The Works of Lucian of Samosata. Translated by Fowler, H W and F G. Oxford: The Clarendon Press. 1905. [Online] [29/05/2019]. Available at: **https://lucianofsamosata.info/Toxaris.html**. Entry 48.

[127] Brzezinski, R; Mielczarek, M – *The Sarmatians*. p. 15

[128] Brzezinski, R; Mielczarek, M – *The Sarmatians*. p. 19 & 20

instance, had an aversion of being on foot and considered it beneath them, which is confirmed by Ammianus Marcellinus who states, "Therefore, all those who through age or sex are unfit for war remain close by the wagons and are occupied in light tasks; but the young men grow up in the habit of riding from their earliest boyhood and regard it as contemptible to go on foot…"[129]

The armor the Sarmatian soldiers used was made of mostly leather, hide, or iron. Bronze armor would be used by only the richest warriors since it was expensive and difficult to make. The famous scale armor of iron and bronze, a characteristic that they also shared with the Scythians, has been found in archaeological findings amongst the Sauromatae of the sixth century BCE. However, only the wealthiest of warriors would be able to afford it. The less wealthy would sew individual scales to their hide or leather armor. A different type of armor, the mail, has only been found in archaeological findings of the first century CE. The Sarmatians first used mail armor to complement the use of scale armor in the torso area, which was less technologically advanced, and would also use mail armor to cover their arms and legs. Only in the second century CE do we find complete sets of mail armor being used by the Sarmatians. Around this century, another type of scale armor also appeared one that was less resource-demanding and made from local materials like horns or horse hooves that were then enclosed in the scale form. [130]

The helmets of the Sarmatian aristocracy, like their armor, would be made of metal, and the earliest of these was the Greek Corinthian helmets that were modified to not restrict the vision of the wearer as much. From the second century CE to the fourth CE, around the Black Sea area, another Greek helmet would replace the Corinthian,

---

[129] Marcellinus, Ammianus – *Rerum Gestarum*. Book 31. 2.20 [Online] [Read 30/05/2019] Available at: **http://penelope.uchicago.edu/Thayer/E/Roman/Texts/Ammian/home.html**

[130] Brzezinski, R; Mielczarek, M – *The Sarmatians.* p. 20 & 21

the Greek pileus, as well as other Celtic and Italo-Etruscan varieties. The Greek pileus was a very basic helmet, essentially consisting of a cone-shaped metal hat that only protected the individual's cranium. At the end of the first century CE, one peculiar helmet gained considerable popularity. It was made of curved iron plates that were placed beneath an iron skeleton made of three or four vertical bands and riveted to two horizontal hoops; it is often portrayed as the precursor of the medieval Spangenhelm.[131]

The Sarmatians used three main weapons: the spear/lance, the sword, and the bow. The spear and long lance would be used on horseback and would allow the user to kill their enemy at a safe distance, especially with the case of the long lance. The Iranian *acinaces*, also spelled *akinakes*, was a short sword (35-45 centimeters, or between 14 and 18 inches) they used, although there were swords that were longer (around 70 centimeters, or a little over 2 feet). The latter would be especially useful for horseback combat since that required weapons with a longer range. The primitive bow of the early Sarmatian period would consist of various pieces of wood glued together and was usually no longer than 80 centimeters (a little over 2.5 feet) in length. It was only from the first century CE onward that the Sarmatians adopted the so-called Hunnic bow that was larger, measuring 120 centimeters (almost 4 feet) in length, and was made of much stronger composite materials.[132]

---

[131] Brzezinski, R; Mielczarek, M – *The Sarmatians*. p. 22

[132] Brzezinski, R; Mielczarek, M – *The Sarmatians*. p. 24-34

Chapter 10 – End of the Sarmatians

The Sarmatian period ends in a very similar way as the Scythian one did, with the vast migration of the Goths from Scandinavia and Eastern Europe. They swept the Black Sea area westward and either destroyed entire tribes or integrated tribes who they conquered on their way. Let's take a look at how each Sarmatian tribe ended their period of glory around the Black Sea region.

As mentioned before, the Sauromatae ended with the arrival and conquest/assimilation of them by the Siraces and Aorsi in the 5th to 4th century BCE; the Siraces vanished after the Bosporan conflict of 193 CE, perhaps assimilated by the Aorsi; and the Aorsi would end with the arrival of the Alans in the Black Sea area in the mid-first century CE, being conquered/assimilated by them.

The Iazyges and Roxolani, who had crossed the Don well before the Alans arrived, survived some conflicts with the Roman Empire but were ultimately assimilated into the empire between the third and fourth centuries CE, who then used their territories as a natural barrier against the hordes of Gothic invaders. This act established Dacia and Pannonia as the land of the Danubian Sarmatians, where they maintained some degree of cultural identity and autonomy but were regarded as part of the Roman Empire.[133] By the mid-5th century CE, both tribes were conquered and assimilated into the Huns.

Lastly, the Alans were driven out of their position of dominance over the northern Black Sea area when the Gothic peoples arrived in the first half of the third century. This moment marked the beginning of a process that scattered the various Alanic tribes which constituted the Alanic federation decades before the invasions of the Goths. By the time of the Gothic invasions or migration to the Black Sea area, the first split occurred, and some Alans stayed with the Gothic peoples and were assimilated by them while the larger group of Alans retreated to the east of the Don.

The Goths, who since the first century CE had been migrating in waves from their ancestral lands in Scandinavia to Central and Eastern Europe, were, in the fourth century, divided amongst two major groups: the Visigoths and the Ostrogoths. The Visigoths, who were Roman *foederati* (similar to vassals), occupied the area of the Danube River, while the Ostrogoths, who had much more contact with the Huns, occupied the northern Black Sea coast. These peoples had already assimilated the majority of the Sarmatian communities that lived in the Black Sea area, either politically, in the sense that some tribes were under the rule of the Gothic kings, or demographically, where they integrated most of the ethnic Sarmatians into their own cultural group.

The part of the Alans who managed to escape west at the time of the Hunnic arrival into the Black Sea area would be found with all types of tribes, including the Goths and other Germanic tribes. In 378, we know that a group of Alans participated in the Battle of Adrianople on the side of the Visigothic revolt against the Romans. This battle resulted in a victory for the Visigoths thanks to the swift action of the Alanic cavalry, which not only intercepted the Roman cavalry

---

[133] Brzezinski, R; Mielczarek, M – *The Sarmatians*. p. 7 & 8.

but also flanked the Roman infantry, allowing the Visigothic infantry to engage more easily with the Roman battle line. This Gothic and Alanic victory would start the beginning of the end of the hegemony of the Roman Empire in Europe, as the defeat of Adrianople was, at the time, the worst Roman defeat since the Battle of Edessa against the Persian Sassanids in 260 CE.

The last semi-autonomous Alanic group we have a record of is the one that crossed the Rhine with the Germanic Vandals and Suebi and managed to reach Spain and North Africa, at which point they were assimilated by the Vandals. In 418, Attaces, the Alanic king, was killed in battle against the Visigoths. The surviving Alans appealed to Gunderic, the Vandal king, to accept the crown of the Alans. He agreed and adopted the use of the title of "Rex Vandalorum et Alanorum" as a way of demonstrating his control over the Alanic peoples that still lived with the Vandals.

In the fourth century CE, a confederation of nomadic peoples, the Huns, was coming from the east into the Black Sea area, and they were much more numerous than any Sarmatian and Gothic tribal confederation that lived there. They apparently operated with vicious cruelty and were formidable mounted warriors that relied on their powerful horse archers to inflict heavy casualties to infantry forces before they could engage them. The threat the Huns posed to the Goths made them migrate into the Roman Empire together with some of the Alans. However, other Alanic tribes managed to coexist to an extent with the Hunnic peoples. This, however, wouldn't last for long, and in the late fourth century CE, the remaining Alans that still lived in the Black Sea region were conquered by the Huns, either being killed or assimilated. Unfortunately, we don't have any type of information on how the battles between the Alans and the Huns were conducted or where they took place. The Alans under Hunnic rule would accompany them in their ravaging of the Roman Empire in the 5th century CE under the rule of Attila the Hun. Eventually, the Alans became so assimilated into the Huns that classical historians could no longer make a distinction between the two. The ones who managed to survive went with the Goths, traveled farther west to merge with the Vandals and Suebi, or were integrated into the Roman Empire. The arrival of the Huns in the fourth century CE permanently marked the end of the Alans as a confederation and as a social unit. Only one of the scattered Alanic tribes managed to survive the Hunnic invasion and maintain some semblance of cultural identity, who were those that fled south to the Caucasus Mountains and managed to survive to the modern day in the form of the Ossetians.[134]

The demise of the Alans marked the end of Indo-Iranian domination of the northern Black Sea, but the remains of their presence would be preserved through historical artifacts and writings from primary sources. Today, we cannot only admire their material culture and artistic output in museums and expositions, but we can also continue to write about their history so that they may never be entirely lost to time again.

---

[134] Brzezinski, R; Mielczarek, M – *The Sarmatians*. p. 24-34. Sinor, Denis – *The Cambridge History of Early....* p. 112

Conclusion

The Indo-Iranian peoples of the Scythian and Sarmatian tribes shared more similarities throughout their existence than many people think. Not only did they share the same language, but they also shared the same nomadic or semi-nomadic way of life, a similar art style, the related culture of warfare and horseback riding, the high placement of women in their societal hierarchy, similar economic structures, and much more. Although they were different people, more things brought them together than placed them apart.

Even though they are no longer around as a unified cultural group, their legacy as ruthless warriors and nomadic herders lives on to this day, thanks to the writers of antiquity who, good or bad, wrote about their way of life. In a way, they never ceased to exist.

The Scythians and Sarmatians, due to not having a written record and being mostly lost through time as they were assimilated by conquering peoples, don't have the popularity amongst the general public that they should have, especially Western audiences. Many academic works have been written in Russian, Romanian, and Polish, among others, but the English translation of these works is very sparse, which means that researching this topic is particularly tricky to non-Eastern Europeans. Perhaps the lack of interest among the international public, outside of a few cases, keeps the academic papers and books about these Indo-Iranian peoples from being published, even though the literary world would only be enriched by these translations.

Part 5: The Goths

A Captivating Guide to the Visigoths and Ostrogoths Who Sacked Rome and Played an Essential Role in the Fall of the Western Roman Empire

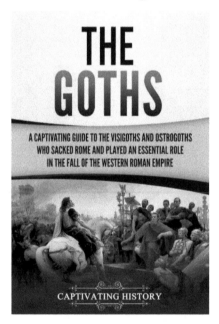

Introduction

When J. R. R. Tolkien was writing his best-known work, *The Lord of the Rings*, between 1937 and 1949, he drew inspiration from various sources, with the largest well of inspiration being European folklore. However, according to some sources, he would also use real-life historical figures and base his characters on them. Take Théoden, for example. Théoden was an aging king of Rohan who, after Gandalf the wizard helped him strip the yoke of Grima Wormtongue, rode into battle and died being crushed by his horse. The men picked him up and carried him into battle nonetheless, singing praises to him and shedding tears. Scholars claim that Tolkien based Théoden on a real-life king who also died by being trampled by his troops' horses but who was known for his bravery and who dealt a mighty defeat to a superior foe in the process. That king was Theodoric I, the battle was at the Catalaunian Plains, and the king himself was a Goth.

No, not the kind of Goth you might be imagining, dear reader. Centuries of Gothic subculture have left us with angsty teenagers wearing dark makeup, skin-tight leather outfits, and white face paint. But before that, the term "Gothic" referred to a particular type of literature, made popular by the 1764 novel *The Castle of Otranto* by Horace Walpole. It began a whole generation of prose and poetry that dealt with old architecture, churches, mysterious men and women, the supernatural, and the underlying element of fear. Yet even Gothic literature had to start from something. And since we've already mentioned architecture, it's instrumental to mention Gothic art and Gothic architecture. This particular movement was popular in pre-Renaissance Europe, taking some of the elements of Romantic architecture and art and putting a more "barbaric" spin on them. There are far too many churches, cathedrals, basilicas, and other buildings that were made in this style, but even that style had to derive its name from something. And if the terms "barbarian art" and "Gothic" are anything to go by, then the culprit is definitely the Goths.

Middle school level history will probably only mention the Goths in passing. You'll learn that they were divided into the Ostrogoths and the Visigoths at some point and that they were in the Roman service for a while. We won't blame you if that's the case. After all, for a long period of history, even proper historians avoided talking about the Goths. During the rise of the Nazi regime in Germany, Gothic and Arian ideas were freely interconnected with the totalitarian ideas of racial and national supremacy of Hitler's people. In fact, far too many people will think of swastikas and concentration camps if you so much as mention the term "Arian" to them. It's a huge shame that that's the case because those two terms are interconnected and make a huge part of European history. But we know better, dear reader. We will delve into the fascinating world of the Goths with a scientific lens, exploring everything we can about how they came about, where they lived, what they did, and how they died off. We will look into the nitty-gritty details of their everyday life, as well as some major historical events that were affected by Goths of any variety. Do strap yourselves in—there are quite a few of those.

Ancient and early medieval European history are replete with scant, contradicting, or even irrelevant information. Therefore, reconstructing an entire ethnic profile of a bygone people can be a daunting task. So, it shouldn't surprise you to spot some irregularities or unanswered questions in this book. But don't be afraid; even some of the greatest historians who studied the Goths, such as Herwig Wolfram, couldn't learn everything they needed to know (let alone everything they wanted to know) about the Goths. Hopefully, we will manage to rekindle some of that interest with this lovely volume you have before you. So, without further ado, let's delve into the world of the Goths.

Chapter 1 – Who Were the Goths? Names, Origins, and Early Settlements

One of the most common questions people ask historians is "Where do the Goths come from?" We know where they lived, what they did, and how they affected the course of human history, but we generally don't know anything concrete about their early days. Unlike the Sumerians, the Akkadians, the Babylonians, the Hebrews, and numerous other people groups, we can't exactly place the origin of the Goths, including how they got their name. Of course, there are plenty of different theories out there about the subject, but each and every one of them is debated fiercely by historians and archeologists even today.

The Names of Goths

The word "Goth" was, at certain points in history, a mere umbrella term for a wide swathe of different Germanic peoples. This isn't particularly odd since the Romans (and really any other people group in power) had the habit of not calling individual tribes by their actual name if they were replacing a tribe near the borders of their realm. For example, the Goths themselves were, at one point, called "Suevi," despite the fact that the Suevi (often called Suebi) was an entirely different people group. The same thing happened when they were called "Scythians."

In other words, when an ancient person would refer to the Goths, they would be talking about the Goths, Vandals, Rugians, Gepids, Scirii, Burgundians, and Alans, to name a few. But even the Goths themselves came in two distinct people groups (though why they came to be two groups is something we'll cover in later chapters). At the time, more specifically during the early and mid-4th century, they were known as the Greutungi and the Tervingi, but with the gradual rise of their prominence in Roman politics, they acquired different names. The Greutungi would bear the name Ostrogoths, later identified as the "Eastern Goths," whereas the Tervingi would gain the name Vesi, but even that was later changed (albeit by the Roman statesman Cassiodorus who had entered the service of the then-king of the Ostrogoths, Theoderic the Great) to Visigoths, the "Western Goths." Despite being essentially the same people, and even sharing rulers at a few points in history, the two tribes were very distinct, and the history of the Goths can't really be viewed in any other way than being the history of these two powerful and influential groups.

When it comes to the term "Goth" itself, the picture becomes a bit blurry. Historians have tried to link many "original names" to the tribe, such as Guti, Gutones, Gauts, Geti, and Getae. However, none of them have proven to be conclusively the same as the Goths of late antiquity, or even their ancestors. In Ostrogothic Italy, for instance, they called themselves the Gut-Thiuda, meaning "Gothic men," with many other variations existing in other languages such as Norse, Greek, and Latin.

One interesting theory is that the Goths got their name from a supposed major deity and the progenitor of the Gothic Amali royal dynasty, a god called Gaut or even Gapt. While not conclusive, it does offer good insight into how important the Amali actually were to the Goths if they were willing to name an entire people group after their first ruler.

Origins of the Goths and Early Settlements

The etymology of the term "Goth" does raise a lot of hot debates, but they are nowhere near as heated, diverse, or even controversial as the debates about where the Goths actually originated from. Many different places in Europe were suggested as their original homeland, but we can't claim with any level of certainty that they are accurate. One common example is the Scandinavian Gothic "original homeland." Despite a severe lack of physical evidence, many scholars still argue that the Goths came from the region that makes up modern-day Sweden. The 6th-century Eastern Roman historian Jordanes called this original Gothic homeland Scandza.

If we did lend some credence to this theory, we can assume that the people group which would develop into the Goths came from Scandinavia to mainland Europe in the early 1st century CE. We actually have some evidence of an early Gothic settlement in modern-day Poland, as part of the so-called Wielbark culture. However, the site, which contains over 3,000 ancient tombs, didn't just "house" Goths. There's also evidence of Gepids, Rugians, and Venedi inhabiting the area, suggesting that all of these tribes (the Goths included) merely came here and settled an area where an earlier culture had lived. Whatever the case might be, the Goths (called Gutones by early historians) lived in the area and had to deal with other tribes on a daily basis. Three tribal groups in particular would wage wars and/or trade with the Gutones. The first were the Vandals, the second the Marcomanni, and the third were the Rugians and Lemovians (it's debated whether or not these two were the same tribe or if we should classify them separately). In later centuries, the Goths would begin to migrate eastward, inhabiting lands close to the Black Sea. This new culture was a melting pot of different influences. Other than the Goths, we also see traces of the Slavs,

Dacians, and Sarmatians. Archeologists have dubbed it the Sântana de Mureș/Chernyakhov culture. The first part of the name comes from the commune in Romania where archeological localities of this culture are located. The second part is Soviet/Russian in origin, and it refers to the Black Sea.

It was here that the Romans first came into direct contact with the Goths, who called them the Scythians. We can safely say that they fully settled in this region in the first half of the 3rd century CE and that they were openly hostile to the Roman Empire. A Gothic ruler, Cniva, actually led a combined attack against the Romans with different tribes and possibly even Roman defectors among his units; it was an attack that would forever intertwine the fates of both the Romans and the Goths.

The region of Götaland in Sweden, with the island of Gotland in the east; some scholars still consider this region the original Gothic homeland.[i]

Chapter 2 – History of the Goths: Relations with Romans, Gothic Kingdoms

Goths and Romans

As mentioned in the previous chapter, Cniva was the first Gothic king (though the term "king" is debatable in this sense) to lead a successful attack on the Romans, winning the siege of the city of Philippopolis (today's Plovdiv in Bulgaria) in 250. But it would be the following year that really brought Cniva fame among the Goths and infamy among the Romans. During the Battle of Abritus (today's Razgrad in Bulgaria), Cniva crushed the Roman forces and killed both Emperor Decius and his co-emperor and son, Herennius Etruscus. The new emperor, Trebonianus Gallus, allowed Cniva to leave with all of his spoils and even agreed to pay him a tribute so that he wouldn't invade the empire in the future. This was a resounding success for the Goths, but more importantly, it was an evident sign that the Goths would become a prominent sociopolitical factor in southern and southeastern Europe.

Half a decade later, the Goths would begin to launch successful naval attacks against the Romans. It wouldn't be until Claudius

Gothicus, also known as Claudius II, became emperor of Rome in 268 that the battles between these two peoples would flip to Roman advantage. The emperor fought in several campaigns against a coalition of Germanic tribes known as the Alamanni, whom he defeated at the Battle of Lake Benacus. Immediately after this campaign, he turned his attention to the Goths, though they attacked first with the intention of invading Italy. It was in either late 268 or early 269 that Claudius' forces, led by his skilled commander Aurelian, crushed the Goths at the Battle of Naissus (modern-day Niš in Serbia). The death of Claudius in 270 brought about the issue of succession. By all accounts, Claudius' brother Quintillus was to take the throne, which he did with lots of support from the Senate. But the Roman army didn't accept him. Instead, they chose Aurelian as their emperor in Sirmium (Sremska Mitrovica, Serbia), and the two "emperors" clashed in battle. Aurelian took a decisive victory and became the legitimate emperor of Rome.

Aurelian's skill in combat was well known to the Romans. It was he who led the charge against the Alamanni while Claudius was still alive, and it was he who crushed the Goths at Naissus. But one more battle with the Goths would cement his name as a major military commander, and it took place in 271. Aurelian decimated the Gothic forces, killed their leader Cannabaudes, and forced them all beyond the Danube River. However, he relinquished all of the former territory of Dacia, a prominent Roman province in the Balkans and one of the first areas that the Goths inhabited en masse.

The Goths would fight Rome on several other occasions with varying success. In 275, they launched their last naval attack on Asia Minor, but the very next year, they were crushed by Emperor Marcus Claudius Tacitus. Half a century later, in 332, Emperor Constantine would systematically help the Sarmatians move to the northern banks of the Danube River. The Sarmatians were the first line of defense against the Goths, who were still raiding from time to time. According to local sources, the Goths lost over 100,000 people during these Sarmatian migrations. Constantine even captured a certain Ariaricus, who was supposedly the son of the reiks in charge of the Goths (we will get into the title of "reiks" and its relation to the term "king" a bit later). Even as early as this point, the Goths would have had a complicated relationship with the Romans. The vast majority of them acted independently and attacked the Roman borders frequently, but there were also scores of Goths who willingly fought for the enemy. Later history would prove to be just as complicated when it came to the issue of Goths being both allies and enemies of the Roman Empire.

The Goths didn't find any success in war until their rebellion which constituted the Gothic Wars of 376-382. During this time, the emperor who controlled the eastern part of the Roman Empire was Valens. During his reign, he had to put down a rebellion by Procopius, a Roman official who declared himself emperor in Constantinople. While Valens had to deal with Procopius, the Goths were preparing to rebel, which they did in tandem with a few other tribes in the Balkans (such as the Alans and Thracians). The barbarians and the Romans would clash in 378 at the Battle of Adrianople. During this battle, the Gothic chieftain Fritigern took a decisive victory and annihilated two-thirds of the Roman army. Valens also died at this time, and there are at least three versions on how it happened. The two most commonly mentioned were either him dying in battle or being burned alive while lying in a hut he had been carried to The battle was a humiliation that the Romans didn't expect, and many historians see this event as the prelude to the decline and fall of the Western Roman Empire (despite the battle taking place at Adrianople, which is in the Balkans which at the time was located in the eastern half of the empire).

But it didn't stop with Adrianople. The Goths were massacred in the streets in retaliation by Roman military officials, both soldiers and civilians. This prompted the Goths to rebel even harder, killing and looting everything Roman they could find. It was the task of the successor emperor, Theodosius I, to subdue the Goths, which he surprisingly did. At first, he would offer different Gothic tribes to either defect to Rome or be wiped out. His biggest diplomatic success that involved this tactic was when he negotiated with Athanaric, one of the most prominent Visigothic chieftains and military tacticians at the time. While Athanaric himself died before he could definitively accept Theodosius' offer, his successors became ardent supporters of the Roman Empire. Theodosius even arranged for the late chieftain to get a huge, extravagant funeral, which awed the other Visigothic rulers at the time. In 382, the emperor turned his attention to the Ostrogoths, defeating their leaders in battle and sparing the survivors who surrendered. It was during this year that most of the Goths were allowed to settle south of the Danube border, with some moving into Asia Minor. Thanks to this maneuver, the Goths would become increasingly Romanized, while the Roman troops became more Germanic.

During this time, the Huns, a nomadic tribe from the east, were invading the Pannonian Basin and becoming a threat to the local tribes, the Goths included. The Goths were already undergoing a division, with the river Dniester serving as the de facto border between them. The Tervingi/Visigoths were loyal to the Roman Empire and became its foederati (semi-independent territories whose armies were tasked with defending Rome but who also received monetary and territorial benefits from the empire) whereas the Greutungi/Ostrogoths had to deal with the Huns.

Missorium of Theodosius I, Museum of Mérida, Spain. Note the Gothic soldiers left of the emperor, who is in the middle[ii]

Goths and Other Tribes

The Gothic people moved quite a bit throughout their several centuries of historical prominence. This allowed them to form relations with different tribes in their close vicinity, whether those tribes were under Roman rule or their direct enemies.

Probably the earliest tribe that we might ascribe as friendly to the Goths were the Taifals or the Taifali. This group would settle Dacia with the Goths, and as early as the 3rd century, they'd raid and attack the Romans under Gothic "kings." However, as time passed, the Taifals, like any other tribe close to the Roman borders, would enter into the service of the Roman Empire. After the fall of Rome, the Taifals were already under the service of Gaul. They more or less disappeared from history in the mid-to-late 6th century.

The relationship between the Taifals and the Goths was varied, to say the least. Since they were both Germanic in origin, they cooperated on many military outings against Rome. However, nothing really bound the Taifals to the Goths at the time, which is why they would fight against them whenever a significant number of Taifals entered Roman service.

When separate Gothic kingdoms formed, each of them had different tribes to deal with daily. The Ostrogoths, for instance, had a brutal and unrelenting enemy in the Huns. When it comes to the Balkans, historians argue that the Huns were a sort of "mortal enemy" to the Gothic people. The Goths would even use the Huns as parts of their curses and would accuse women of witchcraft and bearing children to the Huns. Fights between the invading nomads and the Goths in Dacia would be frequent and extremely bloody, which led to a kind of collapse of the Ostrogoths on a few occasions. Bizarrely, though, some Ostrogoths would outright join the Huns, either by means of surrender or by defecting from the tribe.

On the other hand, the Visigothic kingdom of Toulouse (which we will cover in more detail a little later) had other tribes that they were in touch with. Within the kingdom itself, several different people groups enjoyed civic freedom. Aside from the Goths and those Romans who willingly entered the services of their former barbarian foederati, the kingdom was composed of Syrians, Greeks, Bretons, and Basques, with a strong population of migrant barbarians such as Thracians, Galindians, Alans, Vandals, Taifals, some Gauls, Heruli, Warni, Thuringians, Saxons, Sarmatians, Suevi, and even Ostrogoths who fled from either the Romans or Huns. The Goths and the Romans, of course, held the highest power in the land, but they were very distinct, especially in terms of Christianity (Roman Christians vs. Gothic Arian Christians). Outside of the kingdom, the biggest threat to the Visigoths were the people of Gaul and, especially, the Franks. The Franks would be the ones to destroy the Visigothic kingdom, but before we move on to how the Gothic kingdoms fell, we should take a look at how they came about.

Gothic Kingdoms

Our history has known the Goths by two major names. They are either known as the Greutungi or the Tervingi or, thanks to

Cassiodorus, the Ostrogoths and the Visigoths. Each of these kingdoms had a vibrant history that occurred alongside the fall of the Western Roman Empire and the rise of the West Germanic kingdoms in western and central Europe.

Before we move on to individual kingdoms, we should stress how we're going to approach both of them. Instead of going over every minute detail about each kingdom, we will treat you with a summary of how they came about. Each summary will start with their formative years and conclude with their fall. Finally, we will focus on the kings of the most venerated dynasties of both the Ostrogoths and the Visigoths in an individual chapter following this one.

Why the disclaimer? Well, the history of these two kingdoms is very messy and quite daunting, even for a seasoned historian. This way we can provide you with the most interesting details of the early Gothic kingdoms and how they shaped the political and social landscape of Mediterranean Europe, especially the Balkans, late antiquity Italy, and the Iberian Peninsula.

Ostrogoths

Ostrogoths are indeed interesting on the face of it, especially if we look at their lineage. Many different rulers claimed divine origins throughout Europe, and the rulers of the Eastern Goths were no exception. As we said, the Goths didn't really have a hereditary system of rule, but that didn't stop them from having their dynasties, and the mightiest house to rule the Eastern Goths were the Amali.

Historically speaking, it's hard to trace some of the older rulers of this dynasty. It would be interesting if we could since one of the ancestors, right under Amal (the so-called Father of the Amali), was called Ostrogotha. Of course, the name itself could have been a contemporary construction during the time when Cassiodorus wrote his major work, the *Origo Gothica*, or the history of the Gothic people. Be that as it may, we can't say for certain if the first ten or so rulers of the Amali dynasty even existed as actual, non-mythical figures. The first Ostrogothic ruler for whom we have some kind of confirmation of historicity is Ermanaric. According to Roman sources, most notably the *Res Gestae* (Latin for "Things Done") by ancient historian Ammianus Marcellinus and *Getica*, a work by the Roman historian Jordanes which claims to be the summary of *Origo Gothica*, Ermanaric ruled a wide portion of land known as Oium. Supposedly, this land was a section of Scythia which the Goths had recently moved into during the time of Ermanaric's direct ancestors. Experts disagree on just how much territory this reiks had under his belt, but they're fairly sure that he was a prominent political force in the region.

Ermanaric ruled the Gothic lands (according to some historians, they stretched from the Baltic Sea to the Black Sea) until his death. He was then succeeded by his brother Vithimiris, who more than likely ruled around the year 375 or 376, according to Marcellinus. Jordanes, on the other hand, claims that the ruler who took over after Ermanaric was a different king, Vinitharius.

If we take Marcellinus at his word, Vithimiris would die in 376 fighting against the Huns, so his kingdom was ruled by two chieftains, Alatheus and Saphrax, who served as regents for Vithimiris' infant son, Vitheric. Both of these men would prove themselves as capable soldiers, and Alatheus would distinguish himself at the Battle of Adrianople in 378, where they were allies with the Tervingi chieftain Fritigern. We don't know for sure what happened to Saphrax, but Alatheus would continue to lead military campaigns against the Roman Empire, eventually dying in battle in 386 when his army tried to invade the Roman territories south of the Danube.

If we take Jordanes at his word, however, we find a few more rulers such as the aforementioned Vinitahrius (the so-called Conqueror of the Antes). Each of these rulers supposedly led the Goths during the reign of Attila the Hun (434-453), though there are other sources mentioning other rulers such as a certain Videric (or Vettericus), son of Berimund and grandson of Thorismund. Thorismund was supposedly the son of Hunimund the Younger, who in turn was the son of Ermanaric. This section of the Amali family tree is indeed convoluted, and this is only one branch. Ermanaric's supposed descendants would eventually take hold of the Ostrogothic lands through marriage, which we will cover a little later. For now, let's focus on Vandalarius. According to the early sources, he had three "sons": Valamir, Theodemir, and Vidimer. In truth, these three chieftains were merely brothers-in-law. Valamir succeeded the previous reiks, starting off as a loyal vassal to Attila the Hun and completely taking control of the Gothic lands many years after Attila's death. His reign ended either in 468 or 469. Both Vidimer and Theodemir ruled after him, with the latter's reign ending in 475. Theodemir's son and heir Theoderic (or Theodoric) would be one of the greatest rulers in Ostrogothic history (and Gothic history in general).

The Ostrogothic kingdom had its roots in the Balkans. However, at its peak between 493 and 526, it encompassed the whole of Italy and Dalmatia, covering parts of today's Italy, Austria, Slovenia, Croatia, Bosnia and Herzegovina, and Switzerland. Moreover, Theoderic was the king of both the Ostrogoths and the Visigoths at one point, cementing the reign of the Amali dynasty over all Goths. After his death, the kingdom would wane and fall due to dynastic disputes. It would see its end when Byzantine Emperor Justinian I began his conquest of the former Western Roman territories. Archeologists and historians aren't in full agreement over the year, but it's generally thought that 553 was the year when the Battle of Mons Lactarius took place. During this battle, the last of the Ostrogothic kings died, and the Eastern Goths lost their independence for good.

Visigoths

While the Eastern Goths fought against the Huns, the Western Goths were forced to flee. In the year 376, a large contingent of Goths left Dacia to evade attacks from the Huns and settled south of the Danube, accepting Roman rule. However, their relations with the Romans quickly soured, which led to massive rebellions and wars.

The year 378 and the Battle of Adrianople would prove to be a defining year for all the Gothic tribes, with a decisive victory against Rome and the murder of Emperor Valens, but it was four years later that the seeds of division between the two Gothic tribes would be sown. Emperor Theodosius I officially settled the ancestors of the Visigoths in the province of Moesia, making them the foederati of the empire. Their task was to safeguard the northern border against the invading tribes. In exchange for their service, the Goths were given lands and titles. Bit by bit, these once pagan tribes began to convert to a new form of monotheism, known as Arian Christianity. A little over a decade later, in 395, they would follow Alaric into the territory of today's Greece. By 401, Alaric had already begun to raid Italy, with large numbers of his Goths beginning to settle the peninsula. Alaric has the honor to be known as the first Visigothic ruler whom we can historically verify and is commonly referred to as the founder of the Balthi dynasty, the royal house of the Visigoths.

Alaric would also be the first ruler in late antiquity to completely sack Rome in 410. Because of his exploits, he became a major threat to the empire, and his death (which happened the same year) only barely felt like a relief. In the next two to three years, his successor, Athaulf, would take the Western Goths even farther west, settling them in Gaul (modern-day France) and the territories of modern-day Spain.

The Visigoths had a tumultuous history during this period. Their own relations to Rome were dodgy and shifted often. However, the monarchs that followed Athaulf cemented Gothic power on the Iberian Peninsula, as well as its supremacy over the waning Roman Empire. Athaulf was succeeded by a chieftain called Sigeric, who only ruled seven days. He was succeeded by Wallia, who was in turn succeeded by Athaulf's nephew, Theodoric I. It would be Theodoric who would be the first chieftain history recognizes as a king rather than a mere reiks. This monarch's history is filled with military successes and expansions, and his life ended in the most glorious way possible—he was the king who defeated Attila the Hun at the Battle of the Catalaunian Plains and made him retreat, a battle where the Gothic king lost his life in the thick of the fray.

Theodoric's sons would prove to be just as famed as their father, but an infamous tradition of fratricide marked the Balthi at the time. Theodoric's eldest son Thorismund, for example, succeeded him in 451, but as early as 453, he was usurped by his younger brother Theodoric II and killed. Theodoric ruled for thirteen years, having both lost and reclaimed the region of Septimania (today's French Riviera that encompasses the French Mediterranean coast) in wars against the Romans. During his defeat, the Visigoths retreated as far west as the region of Aquitania (southwestern France). This particular move by the Goths would prove to be important because of what Euric, the younger brother of Theodoric II, was going to do. Namely, Euric killed his brother in 466 and assumed the Visigothic throne, ruling for eighteen long years of prosperity. During his time, the Visigoths invaded and conquered most of the Iberian Peninsula, with the city of Toulouse as their capital. In 475, Euric would officially declare himself an independent ruler, severing ties with the Roman Empire.

Euric's reign was plentiful. He codified the first Gothic laws, whose fragments survive to this day. In addition, he was a staunch Arian Christian, and the Church flourished under his dominion. He would be succeeded by his son Alaric II, who himself codified his own code of law. An ally of Ostrogothic King Theoderic the Great, he married his daughter Theodegotha and had a son with her called Amalaric, who would rule the Visigoths from 526 to 531. But Alaric also had an illegitimate son, Gesalec, who was elected by the people to rule after Alaric's death in 507 in the Battle of Vouillé against the Frankish king Clovis.

Alaric's death was the de facto end of the Balthi-led Visigothic power. They still maintained control of Septimania, however, with Narbonne as their capital. But they never reclaimed the vast territories that both Euric and Alaric II controlled. As the centuries passed, the Visigoths living in the remnants of Euric's kingdom converted from Arianism to Catholicism. The kingdom would begin its rapid decline after the Battle of Guadalete in 711, where the Gothic Christians lost to the Muslim Umayyad Caliphate led by the commander Ṭāriq ibn Ziyad. Some kings held out until 721 and the conquest of Narbonne; after that, nearly the entire Iberian Peninsula submitted to Muslim rule.

At its height, the Visigothic kingdom (also known as the Kingdom of Toulouse or the Kingdom of Toledo) stretched from the south of Spain to the southwest of France, excluding some territories that belonged to what is now modern-day Portugal and parts of northern Spain. It was a true European powerhouse at the time, and its influence still echoes in the region. The kingdom also established the Visigoths as a political and religious force, with its rulers surviving the fall of the Western Roman Empire and the rise of other barbarian kingdoms in the Mediterranean.

Relief detail of the Ludovisi Battle sarcophagus, National Museum of Rome. The scene depicts Romans and Goths in battle[iii]

Chapter 3 – Ostrogothic and Visigothic Rulers

The term "king" doesn't really apply to a Gothic ruler. While we will go into more detail about this when we cover the social hierarchy of the Goths, we will only briefly mention that the title "reiks" isn't necessarily the same as the title of king. Of course, many rulers who styled themselves as reiks were also historically Gothic kings. So, to make things a bit easier, we will use the title of "king" interchangeably with that of "reiks" for all of the rulers below.

Both the Amali and the Balthi dynasties produced statesmen of incredible skill and fervor. It's actually rather stunning that a tribe whose origins are modest at best was able to achieve such prominence that they would be able to outshine even a powerhouse like the Roman Empire. Some of these kings were also direct participants or direct witnesses to some of the most famous historical events of early Europe. As such, they are definitely worth a detailed, thorough read.

Ostrogothic Rulers

Ermanaric

Although not the progenitor of the Amali dynasty, Ermanaric is certainly a ruler that left his mark on the ancient world. Supposedly, he was in charge of a massive territory that took up a large section of today's Ukraine. If we are to believe the ancient sources, that territory would stretch from the Danube River in the Balkans to the Baltic Sea in the north, as well as between the rivers Dniester and Don.

According to Marcellinus, Ermanaric took his own life when the Huns began to invade and plunder his kingdom. Other sources mention conspiracies to poison the Gothic ruler and other potential ways that could have ended his life, but the veracity of these claims holds little historical weight.

There is more legend than fact written down and passed on when it comes to Ermanaric. He supposedly conquered many different tribes like the Heruli, the Venedi, and the Aestii, as well as securing an alliance with the Western Goths (though it's far more likely that he forced them to submit as well) and driving the Vandals out of Dacia. Because of his many military achievements, he became a legendary king in many different European cultures. The Anglo-Saxons and the Scandinavians especially grew fond of the famed Amali ruler, and he was shown as being a powerful but ruthless king. Whatever the case might be, Ermanaric is the first historically known Amali monarch among the Goths, but he would definitely not be the last.

Valamir

Valamir, according to tradition, ruled the Ostrogoths after a 40-year-long interregnum, i.e., a period without a ruler. He is supposedly the first ruler to hold dominion over a large portion of the Goths in the Balkans after his relative Thorismund, the grandson of Ermanaric. However, historically speaking (and if we take all of the sources into consideration), it's highly likely that the rulers who came before Valamir were vassals to the Huns, who were now a major force in Pannonia and at their peak under the reign of Attila. Valamir's father was a ruler called Vandalarius, while his brothers-in-law (and his short-lived successors) were Theodemir and Vidimer.

Valamir became a powerful warrior while he was in Attila's vassalage. In 447, he would raid the lands below the Danube alongside the Huns and distinguish himself as a strong ally. In the Battle of the Catalaunian Plains, he was one of many commanders that led Attila's army. It seemed as if Valamir would continue his loyal service to the Huns, but Attila's death in 453 changed all of that. Shortly after this event, Valamir began to openly solidify his position as ruler after Emperor Marcian settled the Goths in Pannonia. Valamir rebelled against Attila's sons and continually defeated them in a series of battles. Between the years 456 and 457, he would finally crush them and win independence for the Goths.

But Valamir was having both external and internal problems when it came to his rule as an independent monarch. Namely, an Amali collaborator of the Eastern Romans appeared in the form of one Theodoric Strabo. Strabo is a Roman term for people who were crossed-eyed, which would translate his name to "Theodoric The Squinter." Strabo was on good terms with the Romans and their emperor, Leo I, and he would receive large tributes as a reward for his service. Valamir's Goths, on the other hand, didn't receive their share in 459. This prompted a series of attacks on the province known as Illyricum, and these attacks would not end until three years later. Emperor Leo agreed to pay Valamir's men 300 pounds of gold on a yearly basis to maintain good graces with the Goths.

In 469, there was tension brewing between the Ostrogoths and a lot of minor Germanic tribes. This coalition of tribes was led by the Suevi chieftain Hunimund, the Scirii chieftains Onoulf and Edeko, and a certain Alaric, and the tribes in question were the Suevi, the Scirii, the Sarmatians, the Rugians, the Gepids, and possibly the Heruli. Of course, the Roman Empire officially supported the anti-Gothic coalition, hoping to crush the Goths and gain a huge swath of territory. Theodemir, the brother-in-law of Valamir, was the chief commander of the Goths. The two sides would clash in the Battle of Bolia, and while we might not know the exact number of casualties, the historical consequences of this war tell us enough. Namely, the Goths crushed the coalition of tribes and practically ended the Scirii for good. However, there was one important casualty during this war: the reiks himself. Valamir was thrown off his horse during a raid by the Scirii a little before the battle. He was subsequently killed, allowing Theodemir to take control of the land.

Theoderic the Great

Coin depicting Theoderic the Great, Palazzo Massimo, Rome[iv]

There is little debate when it comes to the question of the most famed Gothic ruler in all of history. Proper Ostrogothic history might even be said to begin with the son of Theodemir, with a man who would come to raise the Goths from a disjointed barbarian tribe to a major political force in all of Europe.

Theoderic was, almost prophetically, born in 454, the very year after Attila's death. At the age of seven, he was sent to Constantinople as a hostage to Emperor Leo I; this was done so that the emperor could ensure that the boy's father, the aforementioned Theodemir, would honor his part of the treaty. However, this situation proved to be beneficial to the young Goth. He would gain an education from the best teachers the Great Palace of Constantinople had to offer. As such, he learned and spoke both Greek and Latin, though we can't say with what fluency he did so. Emperor Leo admired the young man, as did his successor, Emperor Zeno.

After 471, Theoderic was no longer a hostage to the Romans. Eight years later, he would settle the Goths in Epirus with the help of his cousin and a skilled warrior, Sidimund. It's worth noting that Sidimund was in the service of Valamir, Theoderic's uncle-in-law, making him a commander with noteworthy battle experience.

The year 483 saw the young Theoderic become the Roman "Master of Soldiers." The next year, he was elected as a consul during a lavish ceremony which Emperor Zeno presided over. But Theoderic would eventually return to his people in 485, and sure enough, three years later, he became the king of the Ostrogoths.

Theoderic would claim his first major historical footnote during the early days of his reign over the Eastern Goths. It had been twelve years since the Western Roman Empire fell to Odoacer and his troops. The Germanic king's ruthless reign left former Roman citizens in Italy essentially without any human rights. In addition, he would often go after the Byzantine lands near the borders of his new kingdom. Zeno, wanting to calm the now restless Goths and to rid himself of Odoacer, proposed that Theoderic invade Italy, an endeavor which he gladly accepted.

At first, Theoderic won a few minor battles, such as the ones in Isonzo and Verona in 489. The Battle of Faenza was his first major defeat against the Italian king, but he quickly got back on his feet at the Battle of the Adda River in 490. For the next three years, Theoderic would lay siege to Ravenna, which was the capital of Odoacer's Italy at the time. Both monarchs agreed to a peace treaty which was to be marked by a banquet on March 15, 493. During this banquet, Theoderic performed a deed that got him into the history books. He proposed a toast to Odoacer but then jumped at the defeated king and struck his collarbone with his sword. With this action, Theoderic became the man who defeated the destroyer of the Western Roman Empire. Italy now belonged to the Amali.

Theoderic's reign in Italy was a breath of fresh air to the residents. The Romans retained their rights, and the Gothic king maintained good relations with the Byzantine emperor. The Romans lived under their own law and customs while the Goths, now the ruling class, lived under theirs. Even other minor religious groups were allowed to practice their faith. In the year 519, an angry mob burned Ravenna's synagogues. However, Theoderic ordered the people of the city to pay for the complete rebuilding and restoration of these sacred Jewish places.

Theoderic saw the importance of allies early on, so he began to form relations with different tribal kings by way of marriage. He himself married Audofleda, the sister of the Frankish ruler Clovis I. His own sister Amalafrida was married off to an incompetent Vandal king called Thrasamund, with whom she had two children that we know of. However, the marriages of Theoderic's daughters were far more intriguing and important to the Goths. Theodegotha, his oldest daughter, married the Visigothic king Alaric II, with whom she had one son, Amalaric. With that move, Theoderic was essentially ruling over the Visigoths by proxy, since he was the regent of his infant son after Alaric was killed in a battle in 507. His second daughter, Ostrogotho, married Sigismund, the king of the Burgundians at the time. Sigismund would eventually order his men to kill their son Sigeric in 522, shutting down the Amali dynasty's potential claim to the Burgundian throne. Sigismund's second wife, according to the medieval Gallo-Roman historian Gregory of Tours, supposedly asked him to deal with Sigeric because he was plotting against the Burgundian throne and that he even had ambitions to inherit Theoderic's throne in Italy.

And the marriage of his youngest daughter, Amalasuintha, proved to be the least fruitful in terms of establishing a long-term dynasty. Amalasuintha married an Ostrogothic noble who lived in Iberia at the time. This man was named Eutharic, and, based on tradition at least, he was the distant relative of Ermanaric, which technically made him an Amali noble and the right person to inherit Theoderic's throne. However, Eutharic died in either 522 or 523 while Theoderic was still very much alive.

While his kingdom was in disarray at this point, Theoderic wasn't one to give up. When his grandson Sigeric was killed, the king of the Ostrogoths invaded the Burgundian lands and in 523 annexed the southern parts of the barbarian kingdom. Sigismund himself was a prisoner, and his brother, Godomar, ruled what was left of the Burgundian territory. With this campaign, Theoderic's kingdom was at its territorial peak. Sadly, the following year would see the Vandal king Hilderic capturing Theoderic's sister Amalafrida and killing her Gothic guards. From that point until the end of his life in 526, Theoderic was planning an expedition to free her.

Theoderic was known for his military prowess, his acute sense of politics, and for his just attitude toward the many different ethnic groups that lived within the borders of his kingdom. However, he was also a renowned builder as well as a renovator of old Roman architectural sites. Ravenna saw the majority of his rebuilding efforts, where he reconstructed an old aqueduct which provided fresh water for the city. Ravenna was also the home of his now-famous Palace of Theoderic, which contained a small church and an equestrian statue of the king. In addition, he issued the building of Hagia Anastasis, an Arian cathedral, as well as three other churches. Ravenna also holds his mausoleum, a rare architectural feat of its time.

Rome was also a city that the king loved to reconstruct and "repopulate" with new buildings. He rebuilt the city walls, the granary, the sewage system, the aqueducts, the Senate's Curia, and the Theater of Pompey. The Senate itself gifted Theoderic with a golden statue of himself as gratitude for his work on the walls. Possibly his biggest undertaking in the city was the reconstruction of the Palace of Domitian on Palatine Hill. His endeavors in these fields were so well known that even people in Syria were singing praises of the Gothic king.

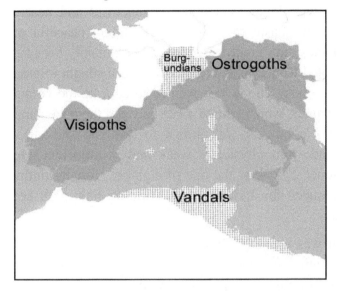

Theoderic's kingdom at its peak, c. 523. The solid pink territory is directly ruled by Theoderic, whereas the gradient territories represent his vassals[v]

Amalasuintha

Amalasuintha is an odd addition to this list, but she was incredibly influential to the events that would follow the death of her father and the dissolution of Ostrogothic Italy. During Theoderic's reign, she was married to Eutharic, an Amali noble from the branch of Ermanaric. This was done specifically because Theoderic wanted an heir with a pure Gothic royal bloodline, making Eutharic the perfect choice. However, Eutharic himself died during Theoderic's reign, so he was unable to succeed the great Ostrogothic monarch.

With both her husband and her father gone, Amalasuintha was effectively the ruler of the Ostrogoths in 526 since her son, Athalaric, was only a ten-year-old child at the time. The Gothic queen also had a daughter, Matasuntha, who would go on to marry one of the later Gothic kings roughly a year after her mother's death.

Athalaric was a king in name only. Over 90% of the political decisions were coming from Amalasuintha, and nearly every decree or legal document was done through her engagement and nearly none of his. While Amalasuintha's reign was largely peaceful at first, the Gothic nobles didn't take too kindly to her, mainly because she held deeply rooted Roman values and virtues and sought to pass them onto the young heir. The nobles wanted to educate the young king in their own values, which caused a rift between the queen and the nobility. Athalaric himself was drawn to drinking and other excesses which made him physically weak and incompetent. He would die on October 2, 534, at the age of eighteen. Amalasuintha would remain the queen for another year, co-ruling Italy with her cousin Theodahad.

The Gothic queen was a model woman during her time. She was fluent in Greek, Latin, and Gothic, and she also had extensive knowledge in philosophy and politics. With her affinities to everything Roman, it is no wonder that she was in frequent diplomatic contact with Byzantine Emperor Justinian I, known as the greatest ruler that the court of Constantinople ever had. Justinian and Amalasuintha maintained good relations throughout her reign, and she even wanted to move to Constantinople with a vast part of the Gothic treasury.

But not all of Amalasuintha's decisions were wise. Her co-ruling with Theodahad, for instance, was a move that looked good on the surface. As the firstborn of Amalafrida and the nephew of Theoderic the Great, Theodahad was respected by the Gothic nobility, so his co-regency of Ravenna with his cousin would turn Amalasuintha's detractors into allies. However, Theodahad more than likely sided with the Gothic nobles because Amalasuintha was imprisoned in 535 and taken to the island of Martana, a landmass in Lake Bolsena. She was murdered there the same year, leaving Theodahad as the sole ruler of Ravenna. Historians aren't in agreement about Theodahad's involvement with the killing of Amalasuintha; some say he was responsible, while others claim he can only be involved to the extent of ordering her imprisonment.

Her death was the event that initiated the Gothic War, which lasted until 554 when Italy was crushed by the Byzantines. Justinian's ambitions to return Rome to its former glory were slowly coming into fruition, and the catalyst for all of it was the death of the Gothic queen at the hands of her own people.

Woodcut of Amalasuintha, The Nuremberg Chronicle, 1493[vi]

Theodahad

Theodahad ruled in Ravenna for a very short period, between 534 and 536. He was an elderly man at the time of his ascension and preferred poetry and Neoplatonic philosophy over matters of war. While he was far from being the first ruler to have this disposition, he was ruling the kingdom during its notable downfall. The Byzantines were not happy with the death of Amalasuintha, an event which Theodahad might have had nothing to do with. Nevertheless,

Justinian's troops, led by his famed general Belisarius, began invading Italy promptly, and it was the general's successful invasion of Naples that sealed the Gothic king's fate, considering he hadn't sent any help to the natives of this city. With the civil unrest and the threat of Justinian quite literally at their door, the Goths wanted Theodahad out. One Ostrogothic noble, Vitiges, was declared the new king of Ravenna. His marriage to Amalasuintha's daughter Matasuntha cemented his claim to the throne. His very first act after the marriage was to depose and kill Theodahad, to the joy of the local Gothic nobility and people alike.

It's a little sad to see just how inconsequential Theodahad's reign had been. If we look at the rulers that followed, we come to a startling realization that Theodahad was the last Amali king to rule over the Ostrogothic people. A powerful dynasty that crushed numerous tribes and kingdoms and rose to hold a vast area of southwestern Europe for a time ended with an elderly monarch who ruled for no more than two years.

Ostrogothic Kings After the Amali

With Theodahad deposed and killed, the reign over what was left of Italy went to Vitiges, the first non-Amali ruler to sit on Ravenna's throne. He would merely be the first of five kings to reign over a failing kingdom during Justinian's conquest, collectively known as the Gothic War, which lasted from 535 to 554.

During its early stages, Vitiges was already married to Matasuntha, giving himself at least a tenuous link to the Amali dynasty. He immediately had a massive problem on his hands, though, that being the siege of Rome by the Byzantines. The two armies would clash for control of the city from 537 to 538, an endeavor which ended with Justinian's victory and Vitiges' retreat. A huge chunk of the Byzantine army was made up of Huns and Slavs, two tribes that had historically clashed with the Goths frequently while the Roman Empire was, at least nominally, still a single realm. But it wasn't just manpower that defeated Vitiges. Justinian's troops were better trained than their Ostrogothic opponents, and Belisarius was an experienced military commander who had already won a host of different battles.

Losing Rome, Vitiges would begin his retreat to Arminium (modern-day Rimini, Italy), but Belisarius took this city as well—not through battle, but rather through intimidation. When his army was joined by 2,000 Heruli bannermen led by an Armenian eunuch called Narses, the Byzantine general divided his troops into three separate garrisons, all of which began to surround the city. Vitiges had no other option but to flee. The same year would see the fall of towns such as Aemilia and Urbinum.

The first victories for the Goths came between 538 and 539 when the Byzantines unsuccessfully tried to take Mediolanum (modern Milan). This endeavor saw the removal of Narses from the position of commander and gave Belisarius complete control over the armies. Another somewhat interesting defeat came to both the Byzantines and the Goths when a huge host of Franks descended from the Alps and attacked the two armies. They were victorious, but an outbreak of dysentery halved their ranks and forced them to retreat. This event gave both armies some time to recuperate and draw up new battle plans.

Ravenna was the final destination for the Byzantines and the last place of refuge for Vitiges. During the war, he tried to find allies in different rulers, even going so far as to contact the Persians and ask them to attack the eastern frontier of Byzantium. Sadly, all his efforts, thus far, had failed, and Vitiges was all but deposed. Justinian's court offered terms with the empire keeping parts of Italy south of the river Po and the rest remaining under the Goths. While both the Ostrogothic nobility and the Byzantine generals accepted these terms, Belisarius did not. However, when he was in Ravenna, he was offered the title of Western emperor, which he falsely accepted. Vitiges was made a patrician, but that didn't stop Belisarius from taking both him and Matasuntha as hostages to Constantinople in late 540. Vitiges died childless in 542, while

Matasuntha married a Byzantine patrician called Germanus, who was a cousin of Emperor Justinian. The two had a single son, also called Germanus, who was born in 551.

The vacant spot of the king of the Ostrogoths had to be filled. A lot of Gothic nobles wanted to see Uraias, who was stationed in the town of Ticinum (modern Pavia), succeed Vitiges. This made sense as Uraias was both the greatest military commander in the Ostrogothic army and the nephew of the previous king. But Uraias refused the throne in favor of Ildibad, who controlled Verona. Ildibad himself was a Visigoth, a nephew of the first non-Balthi Visigothic king Theudis. They both controlled the only specks of free Gothic land, but Ildibad, upon ascending the throne, quickly expanded his reach to Venetia and Liguria. One of his best-known victories in battle was that of Treviso, where he crushed the local Roman military commander Vitalius. To add insult to injury, Vitalius was also aided by a large contingent of Heruli, whose leader was killed in combat. Ildibad's authority over the valley of the Po River grew with each victory, and his own nephew, Totila, became the military commander of Treviso.

The very next year, 541, saw Ildibad murdering Uraias under the suspicion that his uncle's clan was plotting to remove him from power. Later that year, Ildibad himself was murdered at a banquet. Since there was no suitable heir, Eraric was elected as the successor to the now-late Visigothic noble. Eraric was a Rugian, and his tribe was one of the many allies that the post-Amali Ostrogoths had. However, he was far from being the best choice of monarch to succeed Ildibad. Namely, he had secretly been planning to surrender the kingdom to the Byzantines, a plot which was thwarted by the Goths. Totila, the nephew of the late Ildibad, vied for power in Ravenna and demanded the death of Eraric, a demand which he saw come true that very same year. With Totila at the helm, the Ostrogoths would see ten years of relative stability and revival.

Totila's skills as a commander were shown early on when he began to push back the Byzantine army. Soon after, he would take control of the southern Italian Peninsula, getting ready for bigger and harder sieges. One such siege was of the city of Naples in 543, which ended with the city opening its gates to the king due to starvation. Totila would go on to lead two different sieges of Rome. The first one in 546 was successful; it was also helped by tactical starvation of the inhabitants, but the city remained steadfast and quickly rebuilt its walls. During the second siege, in Totila's absence, the Ostrogoths were defeated by Belisarius but the success was short-lived as the Byzantine general was recalled from Rome. During the third siege in 549/550, the city opened its gates to Totila, this time thanks to a few starving Romans who defected to the Ostrogothic king.

Next, Totila conquered Sicily, Sardinia, and Corsica, after which he shifted his attention to Greece. Under Justinian's orders, General Narses advanced against the Goths, and the two armies clashed during the Battle of Taginae in 552. Totila was killed in combat, and his death was the final nail in the coffin of the Ostrogothic kingdom.

The last known king of the Ostrogoths was Totila's distant relative and army commander Teia. Teia ruled for only about half a year, and his rule was marked with difficult battles, retreats, and skirmishes. His capital was Pavia, but he would meet his end close to modern-day Naples during the now-famous Battle of Mons Lactarius. General Narses crushed the Gothic forces, and Teia himself was killed in combat, just like his predecessor. Most of the Gothic generals were killed in combat as well, and those that survived sought an armistice. A mere year later, in 554, all of the Gothic lands were subjugated, and the people began to assimilate with the local Italians.

Visigothic Rulers

Alaric I

Though merely a reiks, Alaric I had proven himself to be a capable ruler well before the Kingdom of Toulouse was established. Possibly his greatest achievement was the sack of Rome in 410. It was the first time a foreign invader had captured the city in approximately 800 years. However, the sack itself wasn't as devastating as many other sieges that came before or after it. The Gothic armies merely burned a few buildings and plundered them for riches. The Roman citizens themselves were spared any inhumane acts. In addition, the basilicas of St. Peter and Paul were nominated as sacred places not to be disturbed (other than plundering).

Sadly, Alaric would meet his end the very same year he sacked Rome. While he was in Calabria in the south of Italy, Alaric wanted to invade Africa. However, most of his ships were battered during a storm while he sailed south with his troops. The reiks himself died in Cosenza, more than likely from a fever.

Alaric's name became legendary, so much so that a few rulers were either named after him or had a name that was some variation of his.

Athaulf

Athaulf was a brother-in-law to Alaric and was unanimously elected as reiks immediately after his death. Athaulf's reign was mired in controversy, political intrigue, and complicated relations of Roman emperors and pretenders to the throne. However, he was the first Visigothic ruler to secure territorial autonomy and political prestige to the Gothic tribes.

Athaulf and the contemporary emperor of Rome, named Honorius, had a complicated relationship. At first, Athaulf would frequently support pretenders to Honorius' throne, such as Priscus Attalus, a man whom Alaric had made emperor in Rome to rival Honorius' rule in Ravenna. In addition, the Visigothic ruler had an important hostage, the emperor's half-sister Galla Placidia, which might have secured him gold and territorial autonomy from Ravenna. During his trip to Gaul, where he would have joined forces with the local usurper Jovinus, Athaulf came across Honorius' Gothic commander Sarus. This was a significant encounter since Sarus and Alaric had had a long-standing rivalry, which Athaulf deepened by murdering Sarus. Once again, Honorius had an additional reason to go to war against the Visigothic leader. But then things took an unexpected turn. Jovinus declared his own brother Sebastianus as co-emperor, an action which Athaulf didn't approve of nor knew about. Enraged, Athaulf allied himself with the emperor in Ravenna and crushed the two usurpers, first capturing Sebastianus in battle and later capturing Jovinus in the siege of Valentia in 413.

The very next year, Athaulf took Galla Placidia's hand in marriage. This move cemented the relationship between the Western Roman Empire and Athaulf's Visigothic people. Placidia gave birth to their son, Theodosius, but the child died in infancy a mere year later.

During 415, the final year of his life, Athaulf had already been ruling over Narbonne and Toulouse, which he took in 413. His relations with the Roman Empire soured thanks to Honorius' general, Constantius, a man who would later be crowned Emperor Constantius III. Athaulf and Galla Placidia were traveling west, and while in Barcelona, the Visigothic reiks decided to take one of Sarus' men into his service. The same man killed him in his bath, which prompted the ascension of Sarus' brother, Sigeric, to the position of king. But Sigeric would "rule" for a grand total of seven days, promptly getting killed and being replaced by a non-Balthi ruler, Wallia. During his reign, Galla Placidia returned to Ravenna in 417 and married Constantius III, the same general who had a major falling out with the Visigoths.

Theodoric I

Wallia ruled for only three years, after which he was succeeded by Theodoric I. Although he was an illegitimate son of Alaric, he was nonetheless elected as a monarch of the Visigothic people. It's interesting to note that an illegitimate son would go on to become one of the most glorious rulers of his time. The famous Battle of the Catalaunian Plains, where his efforts helped crush Attila the Hun and marked the end of Hunnic supremacy over the Balkans, was merely one of his many accomplishments. During his reign, he expanded his kingdom to the Mediterranean coast, taking Narbonne. He also made allies with both the Vandals and the Suevi by means of marriage; two of his daughters married Huneric of the Vandals and Rechiar of the Suevi. However, Huneric would later have different ambitions which excluded the Visigoths, so he had his wife mutilated and sent to Theodoric. From that point forward, Theodoric saw the Vandals as enemies.

Theodoric's valor against Attila was and still is historic. However, it goes beyond dying in battle. Namely, in order to fight the Huns, Theodoric and his sons made an alliance with a famed Roman general named Flavius Aëtius. Aëtius and Theodoric had been bitter rivals during the entirety of his reign, but the ruler of Toulouse recognized the danger Attila posed to contemporary Europe, so he set aside his differences with the Roman commander and marched against the Huns. This determination and prudence in the face of battle cemented Theodoric as one of the most beloved historical figures of late antiquity.

Euric

Statue of Euric at the Plaza de Oriente, Madrid, Spain [vii]

Theodoric I was succeeded by his son Thorismund, who in turn was succeeded by Theodoric II, and who himself was succeeded by possibly the greatest Visigothic monarch and the first proper king of the Western Goths, Euric. These ascensions to the throne, however, were rather grim. Namely, the oldest son, Thorismund, was killed by Theodoric II in 453, an act which Euric himself continued by killing his older brother in 466. He would go on to rule the unified Visigothic kingdom for eighteen long years.

Euric's ambitions began roughly at the same time the Western Roman Empire was about to collapse. At the time of his reign, Toulouse was the capital of the Visigoths, but the Visigoths themselves were still disunited, with some factions following different chieftains. One by one, he would defeat them and take their land as his own. But his true military prowess showed when he had to deal with wars outside of his realm. During the Battle of Déols in 469, he defeated Riothamus, the king of the Britons, and claimed a huge portion of his territory which might have gone as far as the river Somme. Two years later, in 471, Euric would win a major battle in Arles where he killed, among several Roman officials, Emperor Anthemius' son, Anthemiolus. It was also during this year that Euric issued the first ever Germanic code of law, the so-called *Codex Euricianus*.

He was rather popular with his people, and even a significant portion of the Iberian and Gallic Romans also saw him as a fit ruler. Ambitious as ever, Euric demanded in 475 that the current Roman emperor, Julius Nepos, recognize Visigothic territorial sovereignty and Euric as its independent ruler. While each Visigothic reiks that came before Euric was only nominally a Roman vassal, the vassalage was still valid. Euric made history in 475 by becoming the first independent Visigothic king and starting his own dynasty, that of the Balthi. In that same year, as well as in 476, he laid siege to the city of Clermont-Ferrand.

Until his death in 484, Euric had ruled nearly all of the Iberian Peninsula, as well as a third of what is now modern-day France. Aside from being a skilled fighter, he was also an incredibly learned man with a wealth of knowledge and wisdom. It's no wonder that many of the Romans living in Iberia willingly acknowledged his kingship and why even priests saw him as a model king.

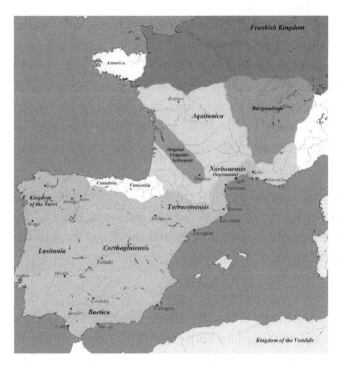

Visigothic kingdom at its peak under Euric, c. 500. Everything in orange is Visigothic, with the light orange being the territory lost after the death of Alaric II[viii]

Alaric II

In contrast to his father, Alaric II is seen historically as an incompetent, weak ruler when compared to Euric. However, he did have his own fair share of political and military successes. For instance, he famously assisted Theoderic the Great in his campaign against Odoacer in Italy, assisting Theoderic when he had been trapped by Odoacer in Pavia in 490. Possibly his biggest contribution to the Visigoths in terms of battle was the capture of the city of Dertosa in 506.

When it comes to contributions in the legal sense, Alaric II appointed a commission that would draft an abstract which contained Roman imperial laws and decrees. Roman subjects living under Alaric were to follow these sets of laws. They are commonly known as the *Breviary of Alaric*, or *Breviarium Alaricianum*.

Alaric's death would come in 507 at the infamous Battle of Vouillé. Years before the battle, Alaric had a rival with the Frankish king Clovis and was, in fact, intimidated by him. The two had already produced a treaty in 502, and Clovis was on good terms with Theoderic the Great, but it didn't stop him from moving his troops into Visigothic lands. Alaric met Clovis on the battlefield and, as contemporary sources claim, lost his life to the Frankish king himself.

Alaric's kingdom lost a good portion of its lands after his death, most of them to the invading Franks. However, the worst blow to the kingdom was the incompetence of his heirs and the dissolution of the Balthi rule over the Kingdom of Toulouse.

Amalaric

Amalaric was the legitimate son of Alaric II and Theoderic's daughter, Theodegotha, making him both Balthi and Amali by blood. However, he was not the first son of the Visigothic king. The first son was the illegitimate Gesalec, who was voted into succeeding the throne because Amalaric was just an infant at the time. However, Gesalec was an incompetent ruler who was overthrown in 511 when his capital, Narbonne, was plundered by the Burgundian king Gundobad. Theoderic took control of the kingdom, acting as a regent for his grandson until he came of age. Gesalec would be killed sometime in 513.

Amalaric would eventually grow up and take the Visigothic throne in 522. During his reign, he married Clovis' daughter Chrotilda, but according to some contemporary sources, he wanted her to convert to Arian Christianity and had even beaten her to the point of bleeding. Her brother was Childebert I, the king of the Franks, and after he was sent a towel stained in her blood, he took action against Amalaric. Childebert's army crushed Narbonne, and the Visigothic king was forced to flee to Barcelona in 531. During his time there, he was assassinated by his own men, with some historians suspecting that Theudis, the king that would succeed Amalaric, was somehow involved.

Amalaric's death as the last of the Balthi is a bit of a sad footnote in history. For most of his life, he was no more than a puppet for his grandfather's ambitions. Even his name clearly tells us who the dynasty in charge was during the waning days of the Visigothic kingdom. While the Amali would continue to rule for a while longer in Ostrogothic Italy, the Balthi would more or less cease to be with the death of this king.

Visigothic Kings After the Balthi

Visigothic Spain remained largely independent throughout the 6th and 7th centuries until it was crushed by Muslim Umayyad invaders in 711.

The list of kings that followed the Balthi dynasty holds an amazing number of 25 kings. During their reign, the old Kingdom of Toulouse would hold different names, such as the Arian Kingdom of Hispania and the Catholic Kingdom of Toledo. The kings in question include Theudis, Theudigisel, Agila I, Athanagild, Liuva I, Liuvigild, Reccared I, Liuva II, Witteric, Gundemar, Sisebut, Reccared II, Suintila, Sisenand, Chintila, Tulga, Chindasuinth, Recceswinth, Wamba, Erwig, Egica, Wittiza, Roderic, Achila II, and Ardo.

Of these kings, the monarchs of historical note are Theudis, Reccared I, Suintila, Recceswinth, and the last three kings on the list. Theudis was the first non-Balthi monarch of the Visigoths and got his claim to fame as a sword-bearer of Theoderic the Great. Theudis was a skilled warrior, but he was also a monarch who respected the Church and even showed leniency toward Catholics, which wasn't very common of Gothic kings that practiced Arian Christianity. His relatives would rule the Ostrogothic kingdom in its waning years after he was killed in his palace by a man who pretended to be mad in 548. Saint Isidore of Seville, an archbishop and a scholar at the time, wrote that Theudis, as he lay bleeding on the floor, ordered for his murderer to be spared because the murder was just Theudis paying his dues for a similar crime, i.e., the murder of his monarch.

Reccared I ruled from 586 to 601. His ascension to power would result in the most drastic change in Visigothic religious history. The very next year, in 587, Reccared would renounce Arian Christianity and declare himself Catholic, and most of his closest allies in the Church followed suit. This move, however, led to many Arian uprisings, all of which the king squashed. Reccared also showed a massive intolerance toward the Jewish population, persecuting them and formally forbidding their religious practices. He would die of natural causes in his capital, Toledo.

Suintila's reign was marked both by peace and by the reclaiming of territories which the Byzantine Empire held under its control. But more importantly, it was during Suintila's reign that saw the importance of unifying the Iberian Peninsula, using the term "mater Spania" for the first time. Linguistically speaking, this was the first time in history that the term "Spain" was used in these lands.

Recceswinth ruled from 649 to 672, and interestingly, outside of a single rebellion, Spania enjoyed a period of peace from 653 up to the death of Recceswinth. Much like Reccared I, Recceswinth was anti-Jewish, but he was tolerant in other aspects of his political career. In 654, for example, he sought to replace the *Breviary of Alaric* with a new code of laws that both the Goths and the Hispano-Roman citizens were to follow. This was the enhanced and enriched version of the *Liber Judiciorum* which his father, Chindasuinth, promulgated back in 642 or 643. It was notably more influenced by Roman laws with very little Germanic influence. While he was in power, the church councils became the highest authority in the kingdom, almost rivaling that of the monarch.

In terms of the last three kings, we should note a historical discrepancy. Roderic was often cited as the last Visigothic king before the Umayyad Caliphate invaded Spain in 711. While it is true that the king was defeated by the Muslim commander Ṭāriq ibn

Ziyad at the Battle of Guadalete, Achila II was also in power during this time, probably as a rival to Roderic. We know very little about either of the two rulers, but we can ascertain that Achila held only a small portion of the old Visigothic kingdom when the Umayyad invaders began their conquest. Ardo is the very last king of the Visigoths whose historical records we actually have. He ruled between 714 and 721 for a grand total of seven years, more than likely defending a small section of territory (Septimania and modern-day Catalonia) from the Muslim invaders. With his death and the capture of Narbonne, the last vestiges of the Visigothic kingdom were gone.

Chapter 4 – The Culture of Goths: Religion, Customs, Social Hierarchy

Religion of the Goths

Not much is known about early Gothic paganism. We can reasonably surmise that it was a form of an old Germanic polytheistic religion and that they had a similar pantheon to early Scandinavian Germans. However, it should be noted that the Goths took great pride in their ancestors and that they deified them. The Amali dynasty is the perfect example of this, considering they saw themselves as the successors of Gapt or Gaut. Many of Gapt's aspects are similar to Odin/Wodan, further giving credence to the hypothesis that the Gothic pagan religion was largely Germanic in composition. Two other possible Gothic gods that we have some evidence of are a god of war—possibly an equivalent to the Germanic Tiwaz—and a god of thunder known, presumably, as Fairguneis.

While we barely know anything about the Gothic pantheon of gods or mythical creatures, we do know quite a bit about their pre-Christian customs. Each Gothic village, called a kuni, had a sacrificial meal as a tribute to an idol of a pagan god. A Gothic reiks would oversee the ceremony, but he would have other important roles as well. Namely, if a Goth were to reject the ceremony or the pagan faith as a whole, it was the role of the reiks to protect the tradition and punish the non-believers. Oddly enough, even in the early days of the 2nd century when they were migrating to Roman Scythia, the pagan Goths didn't particularly mind the local Roman Christians and usually left them to their own devices. However, they were brutal to Gothic converts to Christianity.

A few sources speak of Gothic witches or "haliurun(n)ae," women who apparently practiced sorcery and gave birth to Huns. Tribal leaders dealt with women suspected of this practice by exiling them. In addition, the Goths began to engage actively in practices of their immediate neighbors, such as the Taifali. For example, they would practice pederasty, as well as the early pagan rite of passage. A boy had to slay a four-legged wild animal in order to rid himself of "uncleanness" and become a man. And speaking of clean and unclean, the Goths also took sacred oaths and believed in demonic possession. But it wasn't just dark magic that the Goths believed in. Light magic and miracle-working were also a major part of their everyday religious repertoire.

Customs of Pagan Goths

It's extremely difficult to talk about the earliest customs of ancient Goths since there are barely any written accounts on their culture and everyday life to begin with. However, we do have some idea of their customs during the time they were inhabiting the Roman Empire. When we read the texts describing the passion of St. Sabbas the Goth, mainly letters from contemporary priests, we learn quite a bit about the daily lives of Gothic people inside of a village. This includes the religious practices that Sabbas, a Christian, refused to partake in. For example, we learn that the Goths had a possible tradition of parading a wooden idol in a cart through the village which people had to bow and pray to. From linguistic sources, we can also speculate that the early Goths practiced ritual sacrifice since the terms for both sacrifice and sacrificer are used in a different context in the Gothic Bible. An important part of these rituals was eating the sacrificial meat. Tasting meat from a non-sacrificed animal or even refusing to eat meat altogether resulted in a horrific punishment. In the case of St. Sabbas, it was exile.

Another important custom of the Goths comes to us from their graves. Most Germanic tombs store a variety of different objects that the people buried with the deceased for various religious or political reasons. A non-Christian Anglo-Saxon nobleman, for example, would be buried with jewelry, weapons, and food to show off his level of social prestige. Later Christian graves would eliminate this practice as it was seen as extravagant and not compatible with the humble, ascetic nature of Christianity. However, there's an interesting discrepancy with Gothic pagan graves. Based on the finds in the tombs that belong to the Sântana de Mureş/Chernyakhov culture, archeologists discovered that every Gothic grave which involved inhumation (i.e., burying the body in the ground as opposed to burning it first) didn't contain any weapons. Apparently, early Gothic pagans never buried their dead with weaponry, which is quite different from the vast majority of other Germanic tribes in Europe. Some scholars note that the practice of burying swords and armor wasn't even common with the Germans of ancient Europe until the 5th and 6th century when the Goths were already Christianized.

Visigothic necropolis, Sisopo, Spain[ix]

Social Hierarchy of the Goths

As stated earlier, the term "king" doesn't really work with distinguished Gothic rulers, or at least not until King Theodoric I (some would argue that his son Euric is actually the first to have an actual title of king, however). The title each Gothic ruler had was "reiks," which sounds a lot like the Latin *rex*, and *rex* does translate as "king." But a Gothic reiks wasn't a king in the traditional sense. There was no law or tradition where a child of the Gothic ruler would become the next reiks. He had to be chosen by the tribal council, which, if we take the Gothic Bible as a relevant linguistic source, was probably called "gafaurds." The council was made up of the "maistans" and "sinistans," the magnates and the elders, and next to the reiks, they were the most privileged people in the Gothic community. And while we're on the subject, the Gothic community had a very interesting name, "kuni," with the plural being "kunja." This term is interesting because it has linguistic relations to terms like kin and even king.

So, what was the role of a reiks? In terms of the oldest known Gothic tribes, he was the local chieftain and a supreme judge. But as the Goths became more and more independent, he would take on a number of roles. We will take a look at the Visigothic kings of Toulouse as an example. Within Arian Christianity, for example, the reiks was the head priest, which was more than likely a carryover from Gothic pagan tradition. Next, he was the commander-in-chief of the Gothic army and would always be in the front lines of battle. Moreover, he was also the highest legal authority in the Gothic state, establishing laws and passing sentences if and when needed. And finally, he conducted all affairs that had to do with foreign policy. However, he didn't have complete power. The council of magnates and elders was still very much in effect during the time of the Balthi dynasty.

Each kuni had its own shrine, its own priests, and more than likely its own specific cult. They also had their own small armies; an army was called a "harjis" in Gothic, and it numbered roughly 3,000 men. One subdivision of a harjis was called a "hansa," but we can't ascertain how large a single hansa might have been.

Most of the upper classes lived in large estates. The reiks, for example, lived in a "baúrgs," a fort (this is also a term that possibly relates to the word "burgh" which means "city, dwelling"), while the nobles (the "frauja") lived in a large fortified house called a "gards." Interestingly, while the baúrgs only housed the reiks and his family, the gards would be the home to not just the family of a noble but to all of his servants. His estate would house slaves ("skalks"), day laborers ("asneins"), the "magus" (a title of unclear origin), and other types of servants. Different reikses would have different nobles and servants pledge their loyalty to them, which led to the formation of clans ("sibja"). Despite the Goths slowly becoming more stratified vertically (with kings, priests, and nobles at the top and slaves at the bottom), the horizontal stratification in the form of clans was still an important part of their society.

Most of the Gothic people were freemen, i.e., not slaves but not members of the nobility. They would live in a village, a "haims," away from the reiks and the nobles. We know quite a bit about the Gothic village from the story about St. Sabbas, which was written down and spoken of by some of his contemporaries. Namely, the village had its own assembly which handled all the local decisions. However, they couldn't affect the council of nobles and, more importantly, the nobles could very well nix any decision the village assembly made.

Chapter 5 – Everyday Life of Goths: Jobs and Division of Labor, Housing and Architecture, Art, Written Works

Jobs in Gothic Lands

Several early sources paint a picture of the Goths as being predominantly forest folk with very barbarian, nomadic lifestyles. However, one invaluable document gives us a clearer insight into what this ancient people actually did in their everyday life. One 4th-century Gothic bishop of Greek descent, Wulfila, underwent a massive task of translating the Bible from Greek to Gothic. For this task, he crafted an entirely new alphabet using Germanic runes and the Greek alphabet as a basis. Of course, some sources claim that the translation was more than likely an effort of a whole team under Wulfila's supervision.

We pay close attention to the so-called Gothic Bible because Wulfila described everyday events using contemporary terms. In other words, he used Gothic terminology to describe different jobs and occupations in biblical stories, terminology that was without a doubt used by the Goths. Of course, these words come to us from the Visigothic lands, which means that the Ostrogoths and other tribes associated with the Goths might not have used the same terms, though we can't be certain about this.

From Wulfila's translation, we can ascertain that the Goths were avid farmers. They plowed many types of fields, called "akrs" and "thaurp" with plows called "hoha." They would use oxen, or "auhsa," to pull the plows, and they would link them with a yoke, called a "jukuzi." Some of these words, like "auhsa" and "jukuzi," clearly correspond with the modern English equivalents of ox and yoke as both Gothic and English are Germanic languages in origin. The Visigoths sowed many different types of grain, or "kaurn." Their fields contained wheat ("hwaiteis"), rye ("kaurno"), barley ("barizein"), as well as flax, or "saian," which they used to make linen ("lein"). The group word for these green crops was "atisk." A typical farmer would use a "giltha," a sickle, during a harvest ("asans"), which usually took place in the summer. Carts, or "gajut," took the reaped wheat for threshing to a place called a threshing yard, "gathrask." After the threshing was done, the grain would be stored in "bansts," barns. Once there, the Gothic farmer would grind the grain using a circular hand mill, a "quairnus." It was then up to the baker to bake raised dough ("daigs") and make flatbread, "hlaifs." However, based on contemporary sources, the Visigoths didn't yield a lot of grain from these agricultural practices. That's why they had to rely on importing Roman grain, at least during the time of Emperor Valens in 366. Aside from agriculture, the Goths had some minor skills in gardening, but no source from that time tells us just how efficient they were.

Animal husbandry was also more than likely practiced during the early Gothic times. Based on food remnants and scarce animal bones in Gothic graveyards, we can safely state that the Goths raised cows, sheep, poultry, horses, and donkeys. They would use the latter two for transportation and as beasts of burden. Sheep, in particular, were useful for their wool, which the Goths used for clothing. Cows yielded milk, while chickens laid eggs; both of these were essential foods for the Goths, next to meat.

Aside from farmers and animal husbandmen, there was a whole slew of different professions in ancient Gothic lands. Some of them include:

- blacksmiths ("smitha" or "aizasmitha")

- carpenters ("timrja")

- butchers ("skilja")

- clothiers and fullers ("wullareis")

- fishermen ("nuta" or "fiskja")

- healers or early doctors ("lekeis")

- potters ("kasja")

Each of these trades was important for the everyday life of a Goth. A blacksmith would work on weapons and iron tools. Interestingly, they also made a massive number of combs and fibulae (brooches for fastening clothes). Carpenters would make wooden furniture using small hand-axes. Both butchers and fishermen provided a Gothic village with food in their own separate ways. Fullers and clothiers worked on wool to make clothing. And naturally, a healer was always necessary for the weak and the sick.

Potters, in particular, are important for historians and archeologists because it's thanks to them that we have a whole host of Gothic artifacts that survive to this day. They would fashion different pots of various sizes, but they also made oil lamps that were similar to their Roman counterparts. Pots were mass-produced and more than likely exported to other lands in the region.

Trade was a major part of Gothic life, and the Romans were by far the biggest trading partner if and when that was possible. The Romans would export wine and cooking oil to the Goths, as well as fine fabrics and jewelry. All of these items were highly valued by

Gothic nobles and wealthy houses at the time. For example, Gothic men of wealth would drink wine in heavily adorned cups and goblets, and the women would wear elaborate jewelry made of silver and precious gems. Whenever a war would break out between the Romans and the Goths, trade would cease, and the Goths would suffer heavy shortages. It's no wonder that they would always claim free trade during the times of peace. While they did have raw materials and material goods to trade, the Goths would often use slaves as payment. Whenever there was a surplus of people (Gothic or non-Gothic), the Goths would go to the Danubian slave markets and sell them off to the Romans.

Housing and Architecture

Going over the Sântana de Mureş/Chernyakhov sites, we can spot fascinating finds that tell us about the houses of early Goths. Two different types of homes existed based on how they were built. The first reminds us very much of early Anglo-Saxon dwellings, where the houses were built with floors cut into the ground. These sunken huts are what archeologists call pit-houses, or "Grubenhäuser" in German (the singular form is "Grubenhaus"). The pit-houses of the Goths were either rectangular or oval, sometimes even half-oval. Normally they would be very small, covering anywhere between 5 and 16 square meters, or 54 to 172 square feet. The floors were just beaten earth, whereas the walls were made of daub and wattle and the roofs were made of rushes. Some of the dwellings of the Goths near the Black Sea even had stone floors. Each and every house had a hearth for heating during the winter months.

The second type of house that the Goths would inhabit is the surface house. In German, these homes are called "Wohnstallhauser," or byre-dwellings. The name itself perfectly explains their purpose— they contained two parts under one roof: the living quarters of the family and the animal section. They also came in two different sizes. Small byre-dwellings would measure 10 to 30 square meters (107 to 323 square feet), whereas large ones would go up to anywhere between 68 and 128 square meters (732 and 1,337 square feet). Both types of houses had plastered walls and timber framing, rushes as roofing material, beaten earth floors, and stone hearths.

These differences in size and material are not there for nothing. Wealthier Gothic families could afford bigger, sturdier houses for themselves and their extended family. This was especially true with the Gothic nobles who were either on good terms with the Romans or who enjoyed a lot of wealth in the village for one reason or another.

Gothic Art

It's unfortunate that the term "Gothic art," as well as "Gothic architecture," is related to a movement that happened centuries after the last of the Gothic kingdoms was long gone. We have barely any proper examples of how Gothic artists might have expressed themselves. However, there must have been some noteworthy level of skill. For example, if we look at the basic brooches, belt buckles, combs, personal jewelry, and the pottery of the Sântana de Mureș/Chernyakhov culture, we can see that the effort put into some of these pieces was not just to be useful but also aesthetically pleasing. Possibly the most famous example of this is the Visigothic eagle-shaped fibula made of gold, bronze, meerschaum, glass, and gemstones in the 6th century. The eagle motif was a carryover from the Roman tradition, and people in the Balkans would continue to use it well into the Middle Ages.

One particular style of fashioning jewelry that ancient Goths perfected was the polychrome style. They would use wrought cells and encrust gemstones into whatever gold object they were making. This method continued into the Middle Ages in southwestern Germanic Europe well after the Gothic kingdoms were already formed.

Top: Visigothic eagle fibula, 6ᵗʰ century; Bottom: Ostrogothic crossbow fibula, 5ᵗʰ century [x xi]

Written Gothic Works

Like Gothic art, we know next to nothing about their written works, largely because ancient Goths didn't have a unified writing system. However, there are a few artifacts that scholars assume contain Gothic runic inscriptions. Three of them are seen as authentic Gothic writing before Christianization, one of which is a ring from Pietroassa, Romania, and two of which are spearheads found in Ukraine and Germany.

But with Christianity, the Goths did get a much-needed addition to their culture—the Gothic alphabet. During the 4th century, Wulfila created a system of 27 letters that corresponded to sounds in the Gothic language. His translation of the Bible was, by all means, a step in the right direction for the Christianization of the Goths, but more importantly, it opened the door for learned, intelligent, and literate monarchs. Aside from this translation, we don't have any other written work that uses the Gothic alphabet, translated or original. Moreover, we don't even have the complete manuscript of the Gothic Bible. Instead, we have fragments that survived as five separate codices and a lead tablet containing some Gospel verses.

Spearhead of Kovel, Ukraine, with Gothic runic inscriptions probably noting the name of the weapon[xii]

A single page from Codex Argenteus, the longest manuscript that contains Wulfila's Gothic translation of the Bible[xiii]

Conclusion – Gothic Legacy in Europe

The Goths, overall, did more to change the political and cultural landscape of Europe than most people between the 4th and 8th centuries. It's no wonder that two massive movements in art and architecture use the term "Gothic" in their name.

The Goths were incredibly adaptable. Through their conquests (as well as their migrations), they embraced different elements of native cultures, but they also influenced others enough to become the dominant culture in both Italy and the Iberian Peninsula. And since they were so close to both the Romans and the Byzantines, they can rightfully be seen as the successors of Rome in important respects. Thanks to the Goths, Roman law remained in practice long after the city of Rome had fallen under Odoacer, and the transition between Roman and post-Roman Europe was made somewhat easier with Gothic kings at the peak of their power.

One particular innovation that the Goths provided changed the entire course of warfare. While they started off as a completely infantry-based army, they became rather effective warriors on horseback. Even as far back as the Battle of Adrianople, the Gothic chieftain Fritigern would command a cavalry.

Goths of both Eastern and Western varieties were also responsible for more than a few historic events that have since become legendary. It was the Goths who first sacked Rome (since the creation of the Roman Empire) in 410, and it was a series of Gothic kings who would decide on which emperor should sit on the Roman throne. It was largely a Gothic king that gave Attila the Hun his first major defeat, and it was another Gothic king that would unite Spain for the first time in history and declare himself independent of the Byzantine Empire. Yet another Gothic king was the one who would kill the man who destroyed the Western Roman Empire and claim the territory for himself, further expanding his kingdom and effectively ruling all of the Goths and nearly all of the Iberian and Italian Mediterranean coast. It was a Gothic priest who invented a whole new alphabet to translate the Bible into Gothic, giving us an insight into old Germanic languages of the time, and it was a Gothic queen that maintained the stability of Italy even after the death of her legendary father. And it's the two Gothic dynasties that are responsible for shaping much of European political, ecclesiastical, and social life with their blend of Roman and Gothic customs.

History of the late 19th and early 20th centuries has not been kind to the Goths. Their association with the National Socialist German Workers' Party of Germany (the Nazis) had left a bad taste in the mouth of many historians, and sadly, terms such as "Gothic" and "Arian" can make everyday people cringe even today because of what connotations they might have. But historically speaking, the Goths of the East and the West have contributed far more, and in a far more flattering manner, to our collective memory than anything the Nazi regime did. As such, we have to approach the Gothic history scientifically but not without inquisitive curiosity, for people like the Goths, with their fascinating past, tumultuous kingdoms and fierce, legendary kings, can only leave you wanting to know a lot more.

Part 6: Attila the Hun

A Captivating Guide to the Ruler of the Huns and His Invasions of the Roman Empire

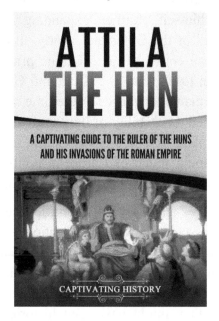

Introduction

In the popular imagination, Attila the Hun is among the most barbaric leaders ever. His warriors have the reputation of being ruthless, cruel, and bloodthirsty, as the Huns are believed to have been savages lacking any semblance of civilized culture.

The Huns raped and pillaged with abandon whenever the opportunity arose, and their raids into lands poorly protected by military outposts in the crumbling Roman Empire became legendary. The Huns under the command of Attila are thought to have been largely responsible for the collapse of the Roman Empire and the commencement of the Dark Ages in Europe.

The reputation of Attila and his people, the Huns, is at odds with reality. But examining the few historical records of his character and deeds reveal quite a different story. It is true that he was a calculating leader who was skilled at unleashing his fierce fighters when necessary. It is also recorded in history that he was a continual thorn in the side of the Romans. However, placed in historical context, Attila acted in ways that were common among leaders, both Roman and barbarian, in the first half of the 5th century. What is extraordinary about him were his uncanny abilities in negotiations with superior powers, his capacity for matching and exceeding his enemies in duplicitous behavior, and his successes as a military tactician on the battlefield.

Chapter 1 – The Origins of Attila and the Huns

The world in which Attila was born into in the early 400s proved to be a determining factor in his triumphs in warfare and his prowess in managing the expanding influence of the Huns. The age was ripe for the rise of a brutal adversary to challenge the highly civilized Romans and the less civilized barbarian tribes.

Attila and his elder brother Bleda were the sons of Mundiuch. Mundiuch was the brother of the dual leaders of the Huns, Octar and Rua (also known as Rugila or Ruga). There is considerable debate among modern historians as to how Hun society was organized. It is unknown whether the leaders of the Huns, whom the Romans called their "kings," were hereditary monarchs or principal warriors who achieved dominance based on their power and influence. It is likely that authority was won by one's demonstration of skill in warfare and buying loyalty through the distribution of monetary rewards from the leader's treasury. The Hun leaders certainly maintained their dominance by brutally eradicating any who challenged them.

Attila and Bleda, as youths, were instructed in the art of war, which included lessons on horseback combat, archery, fighting with a sword, and the use of a lasso. Excellence in horsemanship was a necessity among the Huns. It was through this skill that they pursued their main two means of earning a living as nomadic herdsmen and as pillagers of neighboring people. Both could be pursued simultaneously with some male family members remaining on the plains while others went off to war.

As well as learning about the arts of horsemanship, archery, and swordsmanship, Bleda and Attila acquired knowledge of the deeds of their ancestors. As children, they were exposed to the legends and sagas of the Huns, as the stories of their wars and struggles for power were preserved in songs and poems that were transmitted orally. Remnants of them have been preserved in later medieval and renaissance compilations of ancient epics.

There is no record of whether the training of Attila and Bleda involved an education in more refined skills. Some have said that they learned to speak the language of the neighboring Goths and the Romans. The notion that the brothers acquired some knowledge of Latin stems from the fact that a high-ranking Roman soldier by the name of Flavius Aetius was present as a hostage in Uldin's and then Charaton's court between the years of 410 to about 425 CE.

The brothers, who were to become dual kings of the Huns, were born somewhere in the Great Hungarian Plain, most likely in a permanent village rather than an encampment of nomadic herdsmen. The settlement in which they were born was likely built around a very modest palace in which the higher-ranking Huns advised the dual monarchs. It was from this rudimentary complex of buildings that the most powerful of the Huns exerted control in a centralized sovereignty over a rural population of nomadic herdsmen. These nomads followed their herds of horses, sheep, and goats as they moved from exhausted grazing lands to greener pastures.

Although historians do know what kind of professions the Huns undertook, other things remain a mystery. For instance, what language the Huns spoke is completely unknown. As an oral culture, they left no written texts. What we do know about the Huns is through a smattering of writing by Greek and Latin authors whose reports are naturally colored by prejudice. An example of this is the account of Ammianus Marcellinus, who in the late 4th century wrote that the Huns "exceed any definition of savagery." He said that they were distinguished by "compact, sturdy limbs and thick necks" and that they were "so hideously ugly and distorted that they could be mistaken for two-legged beasts." Marcellinus went on to say that although the Huns looked like humans, they ate their food raw, wore clothes made from mouse pelts and goatskins, slept outside in the freezing cold, and were immune to hunger and thirst. For Marcellinus, a man who might have never even seen the Huns and just relied on secondhand knowledge, the Huns were everything that the Romans were not. As such, they were categorized as barbarians.

Because the historical record of the Huns is only fragmentary, scholars have turned to archaeological evidence to throw some light on the kind of culture in which Attila and Bleda grew to maturity. The yields of archaeological research, though, are almost as scant as the written texts. We do know from archaeology what the Huns did not have. They did not build permanent homes of stone. Hunnic towns, of which there may have been but a few, did not even have stone walls. There have been, to date, no archaeological finds that reveal even the outlines of the kind of wooden dwellings described by a writer who visited Attila's court in 449. Excavators in Hungary have unearthed various metal cauldrons and only about 200 burial sites. And the Hun burial mounds contain only a few objects that can inform us of Hunnic material culture. For instance, some of the skulls from these mounds show signs of artificial flattening; it appears that as infants, the Huns had their heads bound with flattening boards. This kind of cosmetic deformation is common among various other so-called "primitive" peoples around the world.

The most interesting archaeological finds include bone stiffeners used in the manufacture of composite reflex bows, a few primitive gold headpieces, and a few gold harness decorations for horses. Their jewelry, a rare find in Hunnic archaeological excavations, is decorated with simple geometric patterns. Whether these represent the work of Hunnic goldsmiths is debatable. It is likely that such durable and valuable items that may have been kept, rather than traded away, were not produced locally but were treasure looted from elsewhere.

The Hunnic culture still remains an enigma for historians and archaeologists. As such, its origins are a matter of conjecture. Some believe that the Huns moved into the Eurasian plain from northern China. From there, around the middle of the 4th century, they crossed the Volga River, forcing thousands of settled ethnic Goths to flee and seek refuge along the lower Danube River within the Roman Empire.

The extent of the plains of Hungary was less than the broad Eurasian Steppe, which is where the Huns migrated into Central Europe around the end of the 4th century. With less land available to them in Central Europe, the ethnic Huns expanded their economy to include trade with neighboring peoples. In order to acquire assets such as Roman currency, gold, and other valuables which were efficient commodities for trade, the Huns engaged in organized theft or pillage from neighboring tribes and the Romans. There is no evidence that this was a traditional means of income before the Huns arrived in Europe, however.

The migration of the Huns across the Volga into Central Europe might have been caused by climate change or by pressure from other westward migrating peoples leaving Asia. As they moved westward, the wandering Hunnic herdsmen, traveling in wagons with their scant material possessions, came into contact with other tribes already occupying grazing lands. These peoples were absorbed into the stronger Hunnic culture. However, they still retained some of their existing traditions. Thus, what became known as the Hunnic Empire, stretching from the Caucasus Mountains, the mountains between the Black Sea and the Caspian Sea, to the heart of Central Europe, was a multi-cultural society. Centralized control over this ethnically diverse population, as some were pure herdsmen nomads and others combined pastoral economies with crop growing and organized trading, required political acumen coupled with force. The most skilled at both was Attila, the successor to a line of leaders who played less prominent roles in the history of Europe and Asia.

When the Huns settled in Central Europe, the Roman Empire was in the process of crumbling into disarray. The once mighty central authority of the Roman emperors that exerted power over Europe, Asia, and North Africa was quickly eroding. The Sasanian Persians in the east and the previously pacified barbarian tribes in the west either swept across the Roman frontiers or revolted, putting vast swathes of the empire under the suzerainty of, according to the Romans, "savages."

This weakening of Roman control was a result of bad leadership, corruption, mutiny, and assassinations, along with a declining economy, increased dependence on unreliable non-Roman soldiers, and the division of the empire into two independent empires in 395. The inevitable consequence of splitting the once mighty Roman Empire into the Eastern Roman Empire, also known as the Byzantine Empire, ruled from Constantinople, and the Western Roman Empire, ruled from Ravenna, was a continuous rivalry for dominance. The almost non-stop plotting by the Eastern and Western emperors as they strove for power furthered their inability to effectively deal with military crises internally and on the frontiers. There were more than enough of these calamities to challenge even the most skilled leaders. The tribes of barbarians that had previously been kept outside Rome's frontiers due to the greater power of Rome sensed a weakening of the borders, and attracted by Rome's wealth, they began to invade. Some of the barbarians' forays into Roman territories were brief. Others involved permanent settlements in territory forcibly taken from poorly led, badly trained, and underfunded Roman legions.

Chapter 2 – The Wars of the Huns Before Attila

When Byzantine Emperor Theodosius II sent his troops to Mesopotamia to attack the Persians in 422, the king of the Huns, Rua, with Octar's assent, took advantage of the situation by leading his warriors south from the Great Hungarian Plain. In dugout boats and rafts, Rua and his men crossed the Danube, the northern border of the Byzantine Empire, and pushed into Thrace, which would have included parts of modern-day Bulgaria, Greece, and European Turkey.

This incursion by the Huns was different from the Roman idea of territorial expansion as the Huns were not motivated by land acquisition. They did not attempt to create settlements or military encampments in conquered territories in order to exert permanent authority like the Romans. The sole goal of Hunnic warfare was to acquire wealth through pillage. As will become evident in the chronology of the Hunnic raids into both the Eastern and Western Roman Empires, economic success depended on pushing into new, potentially rich sources of income. Once the Huns had completed the despoliation of a particular territory, it was necessary to move on to greener pastures or wait for the Romans and their subject peoples to rebuild their settlements. For the Huns, their pillage economy was carried out much in the same way as their nomadic herding economy.

Theodosius, unfamiliar with the Hunnic custom of warfare, feared the loss of Byzantine control over land so close to his capital city, so he withdrew his troops from Mesopotamia and redeployed them in Thrace. After exhausting the resources for plunder, the Huns negotiated their own retreat from the territories within the Byzantine Empire. They agreed to leave the lands they had pillaged in return for an annual payment from the Byzantine emperor. Theodosius and Rua differed in how they defined these annual payments of 350 pounds of gold. The Huns considered the tribute to be a recognition of their superior power. The Byzantine emperor saw the annual financial settlements as a ransom for captive soldiers.

In 430, Octar, the other co-ruler of the Huns, led a pillaging expedition across the Rhine River into the Roman province of Gaul (modern-day France). He and his rapidly moving mounted warriors swept up treasure from the Burgundians, an East Germanic barbarian tribe that the Romans had reluctantly permitted to settle within the empire. It was, according to most of the later Roman and French writers of history, Octar's attacks that inspired the Burgundians to abandon paganism and convert to Christianity. As Christians, they entreated God for deliverance from the scourge of the Huns. Their conversion from their pagan ways was apparently rewarded. The Burgundian prayers were answered when Octar, after a night of gluttony, died of an explosion of his gut. The Huns, in the absence of a leader, were forced to withdraw, cross the Rhine, and return home with their booty.

It wasn't long before Rua, now the sole ruler of the Huns, repeated his bid for Byzantine gold. Theodosius sent his troops away again, this time to aid in a battle against an East Germanic barbarian tribe known as the Vandals, who were besieging the Western Romans in North Africa. Rua, who may have felt aggrieved at the Byzantine failure to render his tribute, broke the treaty of peace, seizing the opportunity in 434 to pillage the towns and farms in Thrace that had escaped his first incursion or had been restored in the brief period of peace. As well as treasure, he was also in search of refugees from subject tribes who had crossed the Danube and voluntarily joined the Byzantine army. He boldly moved east, threatening Constantinople itself. It was probably due to Rua's sudden death from unknown causes that the Huns stopped their advance before reaching their goal. No matter how attractive the opportunity to loot the wealthiest city in the world was, the Hunnic warriors were reluctant to continue without a strong commander.

The warriors' loyalty to a new leadership was probably established as they made their way back home north to the Great Hungarian Plain. Although there is no historical record, it is possible that among them were Attila and his brother Bleda. It is very likely that both polished off their training as warriors not only on Rua's two expeditions into Thrace but also with Rua's co-ruler Octar's incursion across the Rhine.

However, what is known is that with Rua dead on the verge of besieging Constantinople, Attila and Bleda, clearly capable of using brute force and clever arguments, established themselves as co-rulers of the Huns.

Chapter 3 – An Alliance Between the Huns and the Romans

There were very few Romans in either the Eastern or Western Roman Empires who had firsthand knowledge of the Hunnic culture. One who did have a good understanding of the Huns was a high-ranking military officer by the name of Flavius Aetius. He was born around 391 in modern-day Bulgaria, not far from the Hungarian home of the Huns. He rose in the ranks of the Roman army and reached the status where he could serve the Western Roman emperor as a suitable hostage to be held as surety for peace with opposing peoples. He was first placed into the hands of the Visigoths, the western branch of the Goths, as a guarantee against Roman reprisals against them. The peace guaranteed by Aetius as their hostage had followed the Visigothic rampage, led by their king Alaric, throughout the crumbling Roman Empire, first around Constantinople, then in Greece, and finally in Italy in 401. Alaric's attack on Milan in 402 forced the removal of the imperial court of the Western Roman Empire to evacuate and settle in Ravenna. Even though the Roman Senate paid Alaric off and delivered hostages to him, among whom was Aetius, the Visigoths continued their bellicose behavior, eventually sacking Rome in 410. This was purely a symbolic act as the once-great metropolis had fallen on hard times. The patricians, or ruling class, continually squabbled over the scant resources while the Senate was a hotbed of intrigue. The general population was dependent on handouts while the once magnificent metropolis fell into disrepair.

Aetius, who had been Alaric's hostage between 405 to 408, was transferred to the royal court of the Huns. He stayed there for most of the reign of Uldin and that of his successor, Charaton, the predecessor of the kings Rua and Octar. Aetius probably learned the Hunnic language, and he certainly became familiar with their pagan customs, acquired an understanding of their system of warfare, and may have come to know the young Attila and Bleda. It was about this time that the two youths were refining their skills with the bow and horsemanship. The bow might have held a special interest to Aetius. The wooden composite reflex bow with bone stiffeners was used to great effect by horsemen approaching an enemy. These weapons were also useful in a retreat as a horseman could twist around and loose off arrows at pursuing enemies. This bow was much more deadly than the longbows used by the Roman *sagittarii,* infantry or cavalry archers.

When Aetius returned to service in the Western Roman Empire, the dangerously ambitious general fell out of favor and was exiled from the court in Ravenna. His restoration to power came at the insistence of the Huns who, after the death of the Western Roman Emperor Honorius in 423, forced Galla Placidia to take him on as an advisor. Galla Placidia was the extraordinarily powerful half-sister of Honorius, both being the children of Byzantine Emperor Theodosius I. This was probably accomplished by Aetius telling her that if he was not promoted, the Huns would invade the imperial city. At the time, Galla Placidia was struggling to establish her role as regent of the Western Empire. She schemed and fought to establish her imperial authority until her young son Valentinian was old enough to rule. Aetius, through subterfuge, disposed of any opposition to his influence on Galla Placidia and demanded that she appoint him commander of all the Western Roman troops. She, however, rejected Aetius' bold demand. With the death of King Octar and the retreat of the Hunnic forces across the Rhine, it appeared to Galla Placidia that Aetius' threat held no power. Emboldened by Aetius' apparent weakness, she made Aetius' archenemy, Bonifacius, a co-commander of the Western Roman armies. Bonifacius and Aetius settled their quest for power on the battlefield in 432. Although Bonifacius' troops prevailed, Bonifacius soon after died of wounds he sustained in combat. Aetius escaped retribution, as he sailed across the Adriatic Sea and made his way to the court of Rua, now the sole ruler of the Huns. It is not known whether Attila and Bleda were privy to the negotiations between Rua and Aetius. As a part of their training in statecraft, they might have listened in while Aetius tried to convince Rua to come to his aid in the power struggle in Italy. According to some sources, he was somewhat successful in his dealings with the Huns and returned to Italy with a contingent of Huns in his retinue. Others, however, state that Aetius failed in his pleadings. Once he returned to Italy, he convinced Galla Placidia that the Huns would soon come to his aid. Although this was a false claim, the regent was in no position to risk her power, so she appointed Aetius as the supreme military commander of the Western Roman Empire in 433.

In his role of commander of all the Roman troops in the West, Aetius faced a daunting task. The Western Empire was in dire straits. The Visigothic kingdom, now firmly established in Toulouse, threatened expansion. In the north of France, the Bagaudae, an alliance of small landholders, were revolting, and to the east, along the west bank of the Rhine, the Burgundians threatened aggression. Aetius turned to the Huns for help in regaining firm control over Gaul. In 435, he bargained with the new kings Attila and Bleda, offering a deal in which the Huns would be unopposed by the Romans in crossing the upper Danube and entering the Roman provinces of Pannonia and Valeria. In effect, the Huns were given free rein to pillage in a portion of the Western Roman Empire. In return, the Huns agreed to supply warriors to assist Aetius' Roman troops in attacking the enemies of Rome in the province of Gaul. What attracted Attila and Bleda to this offer was the chance to establish a firm border with the Western Roman Empire by destroying the intervening Burgundians, who could at any moment move east, cross the Rhine, and enter the Great Hungarian Plain. Attila, who would prove to be a brilliant strategic thinker, recognized that if the Huns could eradicate potential invaders across the Rhine in Gaul and across the upper Danube, he and his brother could deploy their warriors to the south where they could wage war with the goal of acquiring treasure in the fabulously wealthy capital of the Byzantine Empire, Constantinople.

The Huns succeeded in destroying the Burgundians. Perhaps driven by the remembrance of their own defeat under Octar, they slaughtered and pillaged with great effect. How many Hunnic warriors fought in this expedition is unknown; however, the number of Burgundians slaughtered in this ethnic cleansing may have been as high as 20,000. The Huns' Christian Roman allies were aghast at the extermination of their co-religionists. However, for the Romans, it was a small price to pay for the removal of an obstacle which allowed Aetius' Roman troops to push north with the Huns and subdue the insurgent Bagaudae. The allied Roman and Hunnic armies then moved south to deal with the Visigoths, who had departed from their base at Toulouse and laid siege to the Mediterranean port of Narbonne, which was saved by the Roman and Hunnic forces. The combined armies then laid siege to Toulouse itself. There was considerable consternation among the Christian Romans when the Huns, on the eve of going into battle, consulted their pagan gods through soothsayers. In a skirmish outside the walls of Toulouse, the Roman general leading the expeditionary force was captured and executed by the Visigoths. The siege came to a standstill. The Huns, whose motive for fighting alongside the Romans was simply the acquisition of wealth, were reluctant to engage in an extended siege which could be unprofitable. They withdrew and made their way back home.

It is likely that Attila and Bleda were present throughout this Hunnic venture in Gaul. Their successes in the battles alongside the Romans would have provided them with a deep understanding of Roman military tactics, siege machinery, and Roman goals in warfare, which were distinctly different from their own. Beyond exterminating the Burgundians and learning of Roman tactics, the Huns had little else to gain from the battles. What benefit they obtained in the incursion into Bagaudae lands in northern Gaul and forcing the Visigoths back into Toulouse was the opportunity to pillage the countryside they passed through. The Romans turned a blind eye to these activities as bands of Hunnic horsemen regularly peeled off from the main force in search of whatever they could get their hands on. It is likely that the Huns were accompanied by a train of wagons onto which they loaded stolen food, gold, gems, and Roman currency.

Chapter 4 – Attila Attacks the Byzantines

In 437, when the Burgundians and Bagaudae were pacified, the Western Roman emperor, Valentinian III, who had achieved the age of majority, traveled to Constantinople to marry Licinia Eudoxia, the daughter of the Byzantine emperor, Theodosius II. No doubt Attila and Bleda saw that this union could be used to their advantage as they had helped the Western emperor remove his enemies in Gaul. Attila and Bleda arranged a peace conference with the emissaries of Theodosius with both Hunnic kings attending in person.

The negotiations in 439 at Margum (forty miles from modern-day Belgrade) did not start well as the Huns refused to dismount to talk with Theodosius' delegation. This was a brilliant ploy to establish the priority of Hunnic customs over Roman ones. And it certainly gave Attila and Bleda the upper hand. It was agreed by the two parties that the Byzantine emperor would render up all refugees from Hunnic lands who were living south of the Danube. These refugees must have posed a particular danger to the leadership of Attila and

Bleda. After the refugees were delivered to the Huns, there was an execution of two young boys, blood relatives of Attila and Bleda, which helped to further cement their rule.

Theodosius' emissaries further agreed not to ally themselves with any enemies of the Huns. The Treaty of Margus, signed in 435, regularized trade so that markets were permitted at designated towns along the Danube. Most importantly, the emperor of the Byzantine Empire agreed to pay an annual "tribute" or "service fee" of 700 pounds of gold. This was double the amount of the previously negotiated payments during the reign of Rua.

For Theodosius, the advantage of successful negotiations with the Huns was the potential for their lasting pacification. With the Huns being paid to stay in their own lands, the Eastern Roman emperor could significantly withdraw troops protecting the border along the Danube, allowing him to send troops off to the east and to North Africa.

Shortly after this peace negotiation was concluded, the Vandals captured Carthage in North Africa in 439. This loss of a major port in the Western Empire's breadbasket was catastrophic for both the Eastern and Western Roman Empires. It was believed that the Vandals would inevitably launch seaborne attacks around the Mediterranean, so the defenses of the ports in both the Eastern and Western Empires were improved. In Constantinople, the walls were repaired, and a fleet was assembled to transport troops to North Africa. As soon as they heard that the Byzantine fleet had left Constantinople, Attila and Bleda restarted their war against Byzantine strongholds. Even with the number of Hunnic warriors being depleted since the failed siege of Toulouse, the Huns attacked and captured the Byzantine trading port of Constantia on the north bank of the Danube in 440.

An emissary was sent from Constantinople to discuss terms with Attila and Bleda. The kings claimed that the existing peace treaty with the emperor of the Byzantine Empire was void. They complained that the bishop of Margum, the city where the peace pact had been agreed upon had led a raiding party to the north of the Danube. The Huns claimed that the bishop's followers had pillaged Hunnic graves and accused them of disturbing the burial sites of Attila's and Bleda's own ancestors. The evidence for this allegation was probably fabricated by the Huns. Still, the kings demanded that the Byzantine imperial emissary hand over the bishop and any of his cohorts responsible for despoiling sacred pagan burial mounds. They also demanded, yet again, that the emperor turn over all the refugees who had fled across the Danube to escape Hunnic rule.

Attila and his brother eventually called off the peace negotiations and spent the next two summers pursuing their tried and true method of raiding cities, towns, and undefended farms south of the Danube. There is no historical record of this violence, but it takes little imagination to picture the devastation. The killing fields were doubtless littered with the bodies of innocent farmers and their families. Slaves and treasures were loaded on carts and taken north. In the case of the city of Margum, the populace debated whether to sue for peace and just hand over their bishop to the Huns. To save his life, the bishop took action. He fled north, crossed the Danube, and personally negotiated with Attila, offering to betray his townsfolk. On returning to Margum, the bishop convinced the Roman soldiers and his fellow citizens to attack Attila's troops when they were at their most vulnerable. They poured out of the city, intending to defeat the Huns just as they were disembarking from their boats crossing the Danube. Attila's troops, working in accordance with the bishop's subterfuge, had already landed on the south bank of the Danube and hidden in the undergrowth. They ambushed and destroyed the defenders of Margum, pillaging the city and gathering treasure wherever the opportunity presented itself.

Many of the Byzantine cities enjoyed what they considered adequate defenses. However, the Huns, from their observations in Gaul as allies of the Romans, had acquired a knowledge of Roman siege technology. Instead of riding around city walls and loosing arrows up at the defenders on the battlements, the Huns constructed a wheeled crane with a platform. From a vantage point above, the deadly archers would shoot down at the soldiers on the city walls. After having cleared a section of a wall, the Huns would bring in battering rams, patterned on those of the Romans. The rams used by the Huns in the siege of the city of Naissus (modern Niš in southern Serbia) are described in a historical document. They consisted of a suspended beam with a sharp metal point; this beam would be pulled back on short ropes then released to smash against the walls. Clearly, the Huns were not averse to adopting Roman technology when it suited their needs. When Naissus fell in 443, it was leveled by the Huns, and the citizens were either killed or captured. The captured were nearly as valuable as treasure, as they became a commodity of trade which the Huns could exchange for goods, primarily food.

With his army tied up in Sicily awaiting orders to embark for North Africa and attack the Vandals, Byzantine Emperor Theodosius II was hamstrung by lack of troops. It was only when peace was negotiated with the Vandals in 443 that he could order the return of his fleet. When the Byzantine army finally appeared to oppose Attila's and Bleda's warriors terrorizing the peoples south of the Danube, the shrewd co-regents led their mounted fighters back to the Hungarian plains.

The booty obtained by the Huns on their raiding expeditions and the Byzantine tribute payments were under the direct control of Attila and his elder brother Bleda. As co-regents, they distributed the treasure as they saw fit. Thus, both bought the loyalty of their subjects. Two years after returning home from their most profitable incursion into Byzantine territory, what may have been, up until then, a standoff between equals vying for power erupted into a violent fraternal dispute. In 445, Attila gained the upper hand, and Bleda was assassinated. However, there are no historical records describing the assassination. Long after, some believed that Bleda attempted to kill his brother, and the enraged Attila took up his sword and dispatched Bleda. It is unlikely that the end of Bleda did much to enhance the already powerful reputation of Attila as a bellicose and decisive leader.

The populace in the Western Roman Empire had already grown to be quite familiar with the kind of regime change undertaken by the Huns. Constantine III, who was a self-declared emperor, and his son and co-emperor were executed by Constantius III in 411; Joannes, who had usurped the imperial throne, was defeated in battle and executed by Valentinian III in 425; Valentinian himself was assassinated in 455; and his successor, Petronius Maximus, was stoned to death by a Roman mob in the same year. The next four emperors of the Western Roman Empire were all killed by rivals.

Up until the removal of Bleda, it is not possible to attribute Hunnic victories and failures in war and in diplomacy to Attila himself. Either of the brothers could have been responsible for any of the events and victories in the history of the Huns. With Bleda removed from the scene, it is possible to get an understanding of the true character of Attila himself.

Chapter 5 – Attila Attacks the Byzantines Again

Attila, now the sole ruler of the Huns, recommenced the profitable Hunnic habit of pillaging Byzantine territories. He began by making a renewed demand for the return of refugees and the promised annual payment of tribute gold, since the Byzantine emperor had reneged, as was his habit, on meeting the terms of peace with the Huns in 443. Attila's demand was a strategic move because he was almost certainly aware that the Huns' ultimatum would be rejected. Emperor Theodosius, confident in the strength of his empire's defenses, refused, just as Attila expected. In early 447, at the head of his army, Attila crossed into northwestern Bulgaria. The first target of the Huns was the city of Ratiaria, as it was the headquarters of the fleet of Byzantine vessels used to patrol the Danube. This river port was leveled, and their ecclesiastical treasures were carted off with other loot.

Attila's aggression was met with by the Byzantine army that had marched up from Thrace. The Huns engaged with the well-organized imperial troops, under the command of General Arnegisclus, in a pitched battle on the River Vid in the town of Utus. Arnegisclus was motivated by revenge; he had led a contingent of forces when the Huns defeated the Byzantines in 443. But neither Arnegisclus nor his soldiers succeeded in their goal of routing the Huns. The general was actually killed. There are, as usual, few historical accounts of the battle, but some say that both sides suffered serious losses. Whatever the technical outcome of the battle was, whether it was a Byzantine or a Hun victory, Attila still commanded enough Hun horsemen to push farther into the Eastern Empire, even destroying the largest city in Thrace, Marcianopolis, in 447. This was a particularly galling setback for the Byzantine emperor as Marcianopolis was an important commercial hub and a center of the Christian faith in the region. It had once even served as the temporary capital of the Eastern Empire. Its destruction demonstrated yet again to the Byzantine emperor the power of the Huns. Theodosius, if not already convinced of the extreme danger of Hunnic attacks in Byzantine Balkan territories but the potential for a siege of Constantinople itself, set about redeploying his army and keeping his capital safe behind its walls.

An earthquake in 447 had partially ruined the integrity of Constantinople's massive defensive walls. Early in his reign, by 413, Emperor Theodosius II ordered the rapid reconstruction of the damaged walls of Constantinople. The project is said to have taken a mere sixty days. The fast-track wall-building may or may not have been a factor in Attila's decision to retreat and cross the Danube into Hungary with his fighting men and their substantial pillaged treasure. This was to be Attila's last raid on the now depleted resources of the Eastern Roman Empire. It was to the west that he now turned his attention.

Chapter 6 – Attila Foils a Byzantine Plot

In 449, Attila sent Edeco, one of his high-ranking warriors, to Constantinople. With him was a Roman, Orestes, who served Attila as a court secretary. He was particularly useful for his knowledge of Latin. When Edeco was ushered into the throne room of the imperial palace, it was without Orestes, who was commanded to stay in a waiting room. After prostrating himself before the emperor, the roughly dressed Edeco attempted to state Attila's case. First, a letter in Latin, probably composed by Orestes, was read to the emperor. In it, Attila, presenting himself as an equal to the emperor, said that even though he had sent four embassies to Constantinople, he was still awaiting the promised return of refugees. Further, the Byzantine forces had not withdrawn to the agreed upon border to the south of the demilitarized zone comprising the land between the Danube and a line five days' journey south. When Edeco attempted to expand on Attila's demands, the only member of the imperial court versed in Hunnic, a secretary named Vigilas, was called to translate. Edeco stated that if Attila's demands were disregarded, a renewal of war might occur.

Having stated Attila's case, Edeco and Vigilas were ushered to the apartment of the eunuch Chrysaphius, a high-ranking official in the imperial bureaucracy. It was in this less than formal environment where the detailed negotiations were to be carried out. Edeco, through Vigilas, complimented Chrysaphius in the usual diplomatic style, saying that he was impressed with the opulence of the imperial palace. Chrysaphius replied that Edeco could avail himself of Byzantine riches if he would act on the behalf of the emperor and betray his Hunnic master. Feigning friendship, Chrysaphius then enquired about the details of how the Hunnic court was organized, how Attila selected his closest advisors, and other intelligence that could assist the Byzantines in their negotiations or battles with Attila. The conversation ended with Edeco agreeing to Chrysaphius' proposal that he return to Attila's court, kill his master, and then return to Constantinople where he would be showered with wealth.

Edeco demanded fifty pounds of gold which he said was necessary to bribe Attila's bodyguards; however, it was also impossible for him to carry this gold with him as it would inevitably be discovered by some of Attila's men. It was agreed that Vigilas would travel with Edeco back to Hungary. When the right opportunity presented itself, Edeco would send a message through Vigilas that the gold should be sent. In order to maintain plausible deniability, it is assumed that Emperor Theodosius II distanced himself from the plot.

To augment the credibility of the Byzantine embassy to Attila, Maximinus, a soldier with an excellent reputation, was chosen to be Theodosius' ambassador. He was charged with taking a letter from the emperor to Attila. Maximinus, however, was not informed of Chrysaphius' and Edeco's plot. As a token of goodwill, Maximinus was to bring along what Theodosius claimed were the last seventeen refugees in his possession. Also in the embassy was a scholar of rhetoric named Priscus of Panium, who would later go on to write a history of Byzantium; it is one of the few historical texts documenting the deeds of Attila. In the entourage were also the translators Vigilas and Orestes and a Byzantine merchant, Rusticius, who was conversant in Hunnic.

Priscus reported one untoward event on the journey from Constantinople to Attila's court. Stopping for supper outside what remained of the town of Serdica (modern-day Sofia), recently laid to waste by the Huns, an argument broke out between Edeco and Vigilas. The conflict was over whether Attila could justly claim that his power came directly from the god of war as Edeco claimed. Vigilas defended his belief that the Byzantine emperor had a greater claim to power as his authority was given to him by Christ. The dispute was likely a ruse to direct attention away from the plot in which Vigilas and Edeco were key players.

After crossing the Danube, the first error in protocol occurred when the Byzantine ambassadorial party pitched their tents on a hill overlooking the encampment of Attila. According to the Huns, no foreigners could set themselves up above their leader's position; Edeco likely did not advise against this as his goal was to foment confusion in the negotiations. After the Byzantine encampment was relocated, Edeco and Orestes hastened to a meeting with Attila. It was in this meeting that Edeco revealed what had happened in Constantinople, including the details of Chrysaphius' plot. He also revealed the contents of Theodosius' letter to Attila that Maximinus had been ordered to deliver.

Maximinus, although innocent about knowing the plot, did not get along well with the Huns in the beginning. Scottas, one of Attila's closest advisors, arrived in the Byzantine camp and demanded to know what Maximinus had to offer. Maximinus, standing on the protocol of Byzantine diplomacy, claimed that he would not divulge the contents of his message from Theodosius to a third party. Scottas departed but soon returned and recited the entire contents of Theodosius' letter, saying that if Attila already knew all the Byzantine ambassador had to offer, the party should depart immediately.

However, Maximinus adamantly refused to abandon his mission, and Priscus, saving the day, convinced Scottas to intercede with Attila through flattery. The Byzantine emissaries were then invited to meet with Attila. Priscus, who might have been expecting to meet an extremely ugly barbarian, was disabused of his prejudice. He described Attila as short and broad-chested with a large head, small eyes, a flat nose, dark skin, and a partially gray beard. During the audience, Attila lashed out at Vigilas when he said that there were no more refugees in the Eastern Empire. In a rage, Attila said that if it were not for the rules of diplomacy, he would impale the cheeky man and leave his body to be consumed by birds. Attila ordered Vigilas to hurry back to Constantinople in the company of a Hunnic ambassador and return with all the refugees in Theodosius' hands. While he was away, Maximinus was ordered to stay where he was and not use the gold in his possession for any purpose other than buying food. Edeco pulled Vigilas aside and told him that their plot was on schedule and that Vigilas should bring the gold required to bribe Attila's bodyguard.

Following the inconclusive negotiations at Attila's encampment, Priscus and Maximinus were taken to Attila's principal residence in northwestern Hungary. Attila's permanent home impressed Priscus, who admired the large wooden palace complex that was situated within a wooden wall equipped with towers. The Byzantine emissaries were also shown a smaller palace, the home of Onegesius, Attila's principal advisor and brother to Scottas. Soon Attila arrived in the town, and a crowd of women lined the road. The procession ended with the women singing joyful songs and Onegesius' wife welcoming Attila with a ritual platter of food that symbolized the family's loyalty and subservience to their king.

Again, Priscus smooth-talked several influential Huns, even inveigling an invitation to the home of Erecan, one of Attila's favorite wives. When he met her, she was reclining on a richly upholstered couch, supervising a number of women as they embroidered pieces of linen with colorful beads. (Archaeologists have actually unearthed quantities of glass beads and ones made from amber and coral in regions once occupied by the Huns.) Priscus and Erecan exchanged gifts, and among Priscus' offerings may have been elaborately decorated Byzantine gold jewelry.

Maximinus was eventually granted an audience with Attila. Priscus reported that the Byzantine envoy was subjected to a more or less, take-it-or-leave-it ultimatum by Attila, as Maximinus was told that the Byzantine emperor should accede to Attila's stipulations for peace or there would be war. Even though the negotiations ended on a sour note, Attila proffered a dinner invitation to Maximinus. Upon entering Attila's palace, Priscus and Maximinus saw Attila seated in the middle of the hall. His advisors and his sons sat on one side and the high-ranking Huns on the other. After a round of the Hunnic version of toasts, tables were brought in and set with silver plates and gold goblets. When night fell and the candles were lit, Priscus reported that the jewels worn by all the guests shimmered in the flickering light. The after-dinner entertainment was especially noted by Priscus. It consisted of bards singing songs about Hunnic victories in war, who were followed by a madman who entertained the Huns with his insane rantings. The Huns apparently found this most amusing. What stood out for Priscus at the banquet was Attila's behavior. He was dressed in simple clothes, drank from a wooden cup, and ate sparingly. The only time Attila exhibited any emotion was when he warmly embraced his youngest son, Ernak.

Maximinus, annoyed by being seated far away from Attila and Onegesius, was unable to exchange words with the people he had come to talk to. He, as a Byzantine envoy, was unprepared to be treated in such a shabby way, and he departed before the conclusion of the feast.

At a second banquet, Maximinus was seated closer to Attila. He was subjected to a rant concerning one of Attila's secretaries, a man named Constantius. It was explained that Constantius had been sent to Attila by the Western Roman commander Aetius and that Constantius had lived with the Huns and served Attila loyally. Attila said that Constantius, on a mission to Constantinople, had been promised a bride by Theodosius, but the marriage did not occur as Constantius' fiancé was claimed by the powerful Byzantine general Flavius Zeno. Attila told Maximinus that Theodosius must straighten out this situation and deliver the bride to Constantius forthwith. If, said Attila, taunting the Byzantine ambassador, Theodosius was unable to control his officials, then Attila was willing to help him exert authority.

Maximinus and Priscus broke camp and set out for Constantinople. Along the way, they encountered Vigilas and his son who were on their way north with the gold promised by Chrysaphius to finance Edeco's plot to assassinate Attila. When Vigilas arrived at the town where Attila had his palace, he was arrested and the fifty pounds of gold confiscated. Vigilas was interrogated by Attila himself who demanded the truth or else he would kill Vigilas' son. After revealing the plot that Attila was already familiar with, he was imprisoned. Attila then sent off Vigilas' son to Constantinople where he was to demand a further fifty pounds of gold from Chrysaphius as a ransom for his father.

Attila also sent the Latin-speaking Orestes to confront Emperor Theodosius II with Chrysaphius' treachery. He ordered that his emissary wear one of the bags used to hold the gold confiscated from Vigilas so that Theodosius would immediately understand the failure of the plot. The confrontation between Orestes and Theodosius led to no admission of guilt by anyone in the Byzantine court. Most were convinced by Chrysaphius' outright denial that there was no assassination plot at all, and Theodosius solved the problem by paying for a cover-up. He sent a delegation to Attila with, as it is recorded, enough gifts to buy off the aggrieved king. Enough gold must have been proffered to have Vigilas released, and Constantius was also promised a wife of equal status and wealth to the first one he had been promised. Attila, after demanding that the tribute payments continue, agreed to release Byzantine captives, drop his demand for the return of refugees, and clarify prior agreements by stating that the Huns had no claim to any territory south of the Danube. Chrysaphius' plot was never mentioned again, and Vigilas, as a failed plotter, kept away from Constantinople until Theodosius died of injuries sustained in a hunting accident in July of 450.

Theodosius' successor, Marcian, quickly purged the Byzantine bureaucracy, killing the powerful palace eunuchs, Chrysaphius being among them. It was when Vigilas returned to Constantinople from his self-imposed exile that he was interviewed by Priscus. It became clear to the history writer that Attila had known of the treachery of the Byzantines in his meeting with Edeco and had cleverly strung the plotters along so that he could gain the most advantage from the exposure of their plan.

Chapter 7 – Attila's Diplomatic Strategy Evolves in the West

In the spring of 450, the eunuch Hyacinthus appeared at Attila's court. Hyacinthus, who had traveled from the Western Roman capital of Ravenna, announced that he was an envoy not from Emperor Valentinian III but from his sister, Justa Grata Honoria.

Honoria, ever since reaching the age of twelve when she became available for marriage, had been virtually imprisoned in Ravenna. Having inherited her mother's, Galla Placidia, independence of mind, she railed at being held as a marriage pawn to be used by Valentinian as he saw fit. She, it is said, smuggled lovers into her apartment and was impregnated by one of them. Her mother and Valentinian sent her off to Constantinople where it was intended she be reformed by austere female relatives imbued with the Holy Spirit. The instruction in good Christian behavior, which included submission to male authority figures, seemed to have fallen on deaf ears. Upon returning to Ravenna, Honoria promptly fell out of favor with her mother, who had become a Christian ascetic, someone who renounces material possessions and physical pleasures in order to reflect on spiritual matters. Honoria also continued her habit of acting independently.

Valentinian promised Honoria to an Italian aristocrat in a brazen attempt to solidify his own power as emperor. There was, in Valentinian's mind, a grave danger in having an ambitious sibling like Honoria available for a union with someone who was also ambitious and from the imperial bloodline.

Honoria, now in her thirties and bridling at her renewed confinement in the Imperial Palace in Ravenna, refused to cooperate with her brother's plans. Secretly, she sent an emissary, Hyacinthus, to ask for the help of Attila in dealing with her brother. The emissary proffered a payment in gold and promised Attila that should Honoria prevail in her goal of obtaining an imperial spouse, more gold would follow. In order to prove the validity of Hyacinthus' offer, he presented Honoria's signet ring to Attila.

Attila certainly would have known all of this about Honoria. In all his decisions with respect to negotiating with the superior powers in both the Eastern and Western Empires, Attila relied on a constant flow of information. His clever manipulation of opponents in peace councils and his brilliant decisions on when and where to lead his warriors on pillaging expeditions suggest that he was skilled in sorting out unreliable gossip from accurate reconnaissance. So, Attila understood that he could only gain an advantage by using any and all of those involved in opposing Valentinian. He grasped the opening offered by Honoria and sent Hyacinthus back to Ravenna with the message that he would help the emperor's sister out of her matrimonial predicament by marrying her himself.

When he got wind of Honoria's duplicity, Valentinian had Hyacinthus tortured. The unfortunate eunuch revealed everything about his discussions with Attila. Furious, Valentinian attempted to send Honoria off to the husband chosen for her, but she adamantly refused to budge from Ravenna. Galla Placidia intervened in the conflict between her two offspring, and Honoria was allowed to remain in Ravenna.

Attila was informed of Galla Placidia's intervention in the domestic dispute in Ravenna. He was most certainly dismissive of Valentinian's plans for Honoria, and he would have found Galla Placidia's meddling in the affairs of her daughter to be unwarranted. Honoria was to be his wife as she had indicated by giving him her signet ring. In the fall of 450, he sent a delegation to Ravenna to announce his engagement to Honoria. Attila's emissaries also demanded that Honoria be granted the title of joint ruler of the Western Roman Empire. This attempt by Attila to promote himself by marriage from King of the Huns to Emperor of Western Rome was indeed a bold move and guaranteed to raise the ire of everyone at the court in Ravenna.

There can be little doubt that Attila knew that his demands would not be met by Valentinian. The emperor simply responded by stating that Honoria was already promised to another man and that a woman could not rule the Roman Empire, so even if Attila managed to take her as a bride, he would not be emperor.

At about the same time as Attila's emissaries were making his demand for the hand of Honoria in Ravenna, he sent a delegation to Constantinople where they were to negotiate with the new emperor, Marcian. They demanded the arrears in tribute the Huns had negotiated with Theodosius. The Roman officials said that they would not pay "tribute" but would, if Attila maintained peace, give the Huns "gifts." The importance of this semantic distinction was fully understood by Attila. He knew perfectly well in advance that his insistence on "tribute" would be rejected as had his proposal to Honoria in the Western court. His sending of ambassadors to the Western and Eastern emperors was intended to create a pretext for waging war on both.

Attila, by nature a talented strategic thinker, would never consider simultaneously opening two fronts of battle. However, it is a sign of his skills in statecraft that he put it in the minds of both emperors that he might. In the words of Jordanes, a great 6th-century Byzantine historian, "Beneath his great savagery, Attila was a subtle man and fought with diplomacy before he went to war."

Chapter 8 – Attila Raids Gaul

Aetius, the commander of the Western Empire's army, attempted to convince Valentinian that the best way to deal with a potential Hunnic attack was to maintain a strong Roman military presence in Gaul. He believed that if the Huns crossed the Rhine, they would ravage a great deal of the province of Gaul. And if Attila attacked the Visigoths headquartered in Toulouse, the results could be devastating to Roman interests as well. If the Visigoths defeated the Huns or vice versa, they would be emboldened by their victory and expand their ambitions for conquest, thus requiring a concerted effort by the Romans to contain them.

Hearing the news that the Huns were already moving beyond the Rhine, Valentinian, with his back against the wall, agreed with Aetius that the Romans should enlist the Visigoths' assistance in fighting the Huns. This represented a major change in the Romans' dealings with the Visigothic kingdom. The agreement to become allies involved Valentinian conceding to the Visigothic king, Theodoric, legal authority over a significant portion of Roman Gaul, but it was a pragmatic solution to the problem of the Huns. It also headed off Aetius who Valentinian knew to be a constant schemer intent on overthrowing him.

Attila was well aware of the difficulties facing Valentinian, so he took his raiders north where they first demolished Metz, which was some 150 kilometers (a little over 93 miles) from the Rhine frontier. From there, the Huns have been said to have moved against Reims. According to a medieval legend, when the Hun horsemen reached the cathedral at Reims, they were met by Bishop Nicasius. They decapitated him as he was reciting a psalm seeking deliverance from the Hun scourge. The last few words of the psalm were apparently issued from his severed head as it lay at the feet of the Huns' horses. This so terrified the Huns, said later biographers of St. Nicasius, that they galloped from the city leaving it intact. Something similar may have happened at the city of Troyes, south of Reims. There, Bishop Lupus, according to later legends of the saint, marched out to confront Attila. He asked the Hunnic leader who he was, and Attila is said to have responded, "I am Attila, the whip of God." That this happened is unlikely, if not impossible, for Attila never converted to Christianity. It is related in the biography of St. Lupus, the savior of Troyes, that it was due to him that a miracle occurred. When the gates of the city were opened to the Huns, they were struck by a blinding light from heaven and passed in one gate and out the other without harming any of the residents. In the later Middle Ages and the Renaissance, the motif of Attila acting as the "whip of God" to punish the sinful inhabitants of Christian cities proliferated in ecclesiastical literature.

The truth of what happened during the early days of Attila's incursion into northern Gaul is likely more prosaic and not the stuff of legends. Attila financed his expeditionary forces through the distribution of loot. Unlike Roman soldiers who were paid a fixed amount of cash for their services, the income of Hunnic warriors depended entirely on what they could steal and cart off. Success in theft depended on the efficiency and number of wagons to transport loot. During an expedition where the pickings were good, the transport of booty might become difficult. It is likely that this was what happened during Attila's first days across the Rhine. What should also be remembered is that Attila's war had a distant goal: the acquisition of Honoria as his bride. Ravenna was a long way off from northern France, though, and this explains why the Huns did not bother attacking well-defended cities like Reims and Troyes. It was a simple calculation of the risks of delay caused by laying siege to cities which may or may not have fallen to the Huns.

It is unknown whether Attila laid siege to the city of Orléans as he moved south. He most likely did not. Legend has it that the bishop of Orléans himself went to seek the aid of Aetius and the Visigoths at the town of Arles over 300 miles to the south. He, so the story goes, convinced the Romans and the Goths to come to the rescue of his hometown. Upon returning home, he convinced the faithful to pray to God for deliverance. The invocation of the divine worked. Just as the Huns had begun to use their battering ram against the city walls, deliverance arrived in the form of the Roman army and allied Visigoth fighters.

However, the Byzantine historian named Jordanes, writing around 551, described the event of the previous century in different terms. He wrote that prior to the appearance of Attila at Orléans, the Romans and Visigoths had constructed a system of ditches and earth mounds along the route leading to the city. Attila, wrote the historian, was discouraged by this impediment and was also apprehensive as to whether his fighters would last in any protracted battle. The invading Huns turned east with the Romans and Visigoths hot on their heels.

At the end of June 451, the two sides faced off. The Roman and Visigoth armies were bolstered by Burgundian and Bagaudae fighters. These two groups overcame their dislike of Aetius who had, in 437, permitted his allies, the Huns, to ravage their towns and countryside. They were motivated by a stronger hatred of the Huns themselves who had been merciless in their slaughter.

The Huns were not without allies, though. They were joined by Ostrogothic warriors, members from the eastern branch of the Goths, drawn from clans north and south of the Danube. Some of their leaders enjoyed particularly cordial relations with Attila who no doubt gave them generous gifts, the rewards of joining the Huns on looting expeditions.

The two armies met on the Catalaunian Plains, located somewhere in modern-day Champagne, in June of 451. A description of the battle was recorded by Jordanes. At first, the Romans captured an incline where they could shoot their arrows and propel spears down on the Huns and their allies. The uphill attack of the Huns was repulsed, and the combined Roman and Visigoth armies drove them from the slope. Jordanes then says Attila gave a long speech to inspire his fighters. This is standard fare in historical writing at the time, as Attila is unlikely to have taken the time to deliver a lengthy harangue in the midst of battle.

Whatever happened, the ensuing bloody battle was indecisive. Theodoric, King of the Visigoths, fell on the battlefield along with countless warriors on both sides. By dawn the following day, the Huns had circled their wagons and were ensconced behind this protective barricade. Jordanes wrote that Attila, in the midst of his soldiers, vowed to fight to the death. The following day, Attila learned that the Visigoth allies of the Romans had decamped and were headed south. He knew this could very well be a ploy to draw the Huns out into the open, so he ordered his warriors to stay hidden behind the wagons. It was only when he was told that the Roman soldiers were also leaving the battlefield that he ordered horses to be hitched to the wagons and rode off to the Rhine with his mounted troops, and their Ostrogothic allies went off with their cargo of treasure.

There is no consensus among modern historians as to why the Romans and Visigoths marched away from the Catalaunian Plains. King Theodoric had been accompanied in the campaign by his son Thorismund, and the son seems to have exhibited considerable strategic skill in the actual battle. However, he may have been somewhat of a naïve politician, and it is said that Aetius convinced him to return to Toulouse immediately to claim the throne of his deceased father. The conjecture among some historians is that Aetius acted extremely duplicitous at this point in time. On the day after the battle, when the Huns could have easily been surrounded and defeated, some believe that Aetius secretly visited Attila, told him that Visigothic reinforcements were about to arrive, and that for a hefty bribe, he would convince Thorismund to go home. According to this tale, told by Fredegar, a 7th-century Burgundian chronicler, Aetius then went to the camp of the Visigoths, convinced Thorismund that Hunnic reinforcements were coming, and that if Thorismund handed over a generous settlement, he would convince Attila to retreat across the Rhine. This story sounds rather unlikely, but with duplicity being rampant in the era of the decline of both the Eastern and Western Roman Empires, it could be true. It is certain that Thorismund was rightly worried about his succession to his father's throne. However, two years after the Battle of the Catalaunian Plains, he was assassinated in Toulouse by two of his brothers, one of which was to succeed him as Theodoric II.

Because the descriptions of the events on the Catalaunian Plains are of a later date and thus became infected with myth and legend, they cannot be relied on as accurate. This has led historians to engage in guesswork. One hypothesis is that Aetius wanted the Visigoths to leave the area and refrain from decimating the Huns. It is surmised that by engineering a standoff on the Catalaunian Plains, Aetius could have had a long-range plan. Often, the total annihilation of the army of an adversary is not the wisest move. The complete removal of the Huns would certainly mean that the Visigoths would expand their control over Roman Gaul. Without the continued threat of Hunnic raids, without Attila always on the horizon, the Visigoths could concentrate on fighting the Romans and almost certainly solicit the help of the Burgundians and Bagaudae as well. Similarly, Aetius maintained power by having a well-oiled fighting machine available to fight against or fight with the Huns as circumstances demanded.

Just as modern historians hypothesize on the various strategies of the Romans, Visigoths, and various other ethnic groups within the orbit of the Western Roman Empire, so also would have Attila. There is more than enough evidence to suggest that he was not an unthinking barbarian. He was an astute leader with a deep understanding of the motives of his allies and adversaries. He outsmarted them on several occasions, combining force and diplomacy. The strange circumstances surrounding the Battle of the Catalaunian Plains are understandable if they are attributed to Attila himself. He may have thought that by circling his wagons and holding out, he would give the fragile Roman coalition time to disintegrate. He also likely understood that the death of King Theodoric would throw the Visigoths into confusion. Without their leader, he could expect their tenuous alliance with their traditional Roman enemies to become frayed. And, in fact, it did. Aetius, with the absence of the Visigoths, could not successfully surround the Huns with his depleted troops. Attila's advantage was that his wagons held not just treasure but also foodstuffs looted from farms. He, his men, and their hardy horses could have endured a siege of some length.

With the departure of the Visigoths and then the Romans, the Huns escaped complete destruction. Attila and his men did not have to fight to the death. If the story of Aetius' complex strategy after the Battle of the Catalaunian Plains is true, he made a strategic mistake in letting the Huns escape. Attila, never one to be at a loss in finding new sources for pillage, was about to engage in one more violent incursion into the Western Roman Empire.

Chapter 9 – Attila Raids Italy

The emperor of the Byzantine Empire, Marcian, grasped the opportunity to take advantage of Attila's expedition in Gaul. While Attila was distracted, Marcian cut off all payments of gold to the Huns. Shortly after the Hunnic leader returned home with his troops, Marcian sent a representative to Attila, and the talks did not go well. Attila's first demand was that the tribute payments be reinstated. As a demonstration of his power, Attila humiliated Marcian's ambassador by stripping him of all the gifts he brought and then threatened to kill him if he did not render up the tribute gold. The emissary scuttled back to Constantinople, leaving the question of tribute gold unresolved.

Both the Eastern and Western Roman Emperors believed that Attila, smarting from his defeat on the Catalaunian Plains, presented no threat. They should have instead questioned Attila's tactics, which according to Jordanes were, "shrewd and cunning. He threatened in one direction and moved his troops in another."

In the summer of 452, instead of crossing the Rhine into Gaul or heading south across the Danube into Byzantine territory, Attila launched a lightning strike southwest across Slovenia and into Italy.

The bold move was based on Attila's thorough understanding of Emperor Valentinian's military dilemma over this. Valentinian certainly didn't want to seek the aid of the Visigoths, as inviting them into Italy to fight the Huns was extremely dangerous. If the Huns were driven off by the new King of the Goths, Thorismund, he would be likely to turn on the imperial court in Ravenna. It was up in the air whether Thorismund would, if asked, even come to the emperor's aid. He had troublesome, ambitious brothers in Toulouse who he could not leave alone as they would plot his overthrow. Valentinian also had the option to call back Aetius to defend Italy. It was questionable whether the general would comply with an imperial order, and if he were to abandon Gaul, the Visigoths would have no check on their territorial ambitions. In the end, Aetius provided a limited number of troops for the defense of Italy.

Attila weighed the risks of his incursion into Italy and concluded that swift strikes along the head of the Adriatic Sea would open the way for his approach to Ravenna and his ultimate goal, capturing Honoria, his rightful bride. The plan was interrupted when Attila decided to lay siege to the wealthy trading port of Aquileia, which he succeeded in spectacularly. After breaching the walls, the Huns burned the city to the ground and massacred its inhabitants, making it impossible for the opposition to regroup and rise up against them. According to legend, the few Aquileians who escaped with their lives migrated along the coast and founded what was to become the city of Venice.

Moving on, Attila and his horsemen devastated the town of Pavia and then Milan, where the Western Roman Empire had once been centered. The former capital was rich with treasure, which the Huns, as was their habit, packed up to be hauled home. Emperor Valentinian, perhaps attempting to repeat a tried and true Roman tactic of scorched earth, left Ravenna and settled in Rome. With the crops burned in his wake, he hoped to discourage Attila from following him south. By the late summer of 452, Attila had set up camp in Mantua, 470 kilometers (292 miles) north of Rome. It was there that he received an embassy sent by Valentinian, which was led by Pope Leo I. Although there is no contemporary historical record of the encounter between Leo I and Attila, the event became standard fare in the mythos of Italy. (The event was even the subject of a painting by Raphael completed by 1514 in one of his frescos in the Apostolic Palace in the Vatican.) Legend has it that with the help of God and the spirit of Saint Peter, Leo I convinced Attila to remove himself and his soldiers from Italy.

It is unclear why Attila retreated without his promised wife. It may have been because the food supply for his men and horses was running out. Northern Italy at the time was suffering a drought, and the crop yields were low. It is additionally possible that an outbreak of malaria in the region reduced the efficiency of his army. More likely, he opted to retreat because their carts were packed to the brim with treasure already taken from the wealthy cities of northern Italy.

Chapter 10 – The Disintegration of Attila's Kingdom

While Attila was off ransacking northern Italy, the Byzantine emperor launched a series of attacks against the Huns in their lands north of the Danube. It may have been when he heard of Marcian's aggressive move that Attila decided the prudent course of action was to return to the Great Hungarian Plain and engage in war yet again with the pesky Byzantine emperor.

Upon reaching home, one of Attila's first acts was to send a mission to Constantinople. He threatened to wreak havoc in the Byzantine provinces because the tribute he was owed remained unpaid and promised that he would be crueler than ever with his enemies. It was, in his mind, not an idle threat, as he had followed up on all his previous ultimatums to the Byzantines.

In early 453, Attila married Ildico, who was said to be a rare beauty among the Huns. What number this wife was is unknown, though. Attila celebrated his nuptials well into the night, drinking and eating with his closest advisors and friends. The following morning, it was found that the door to the bridal chamber was battered down and Attila was dead in bed with Ildico wailing over his body. It seems that he suffered an aneurysm in his nose and in a drunken stupor choked to death on the blood. Of course, rumors that Ildico had killed him were rife.

When his officials informed Marcian of Attila's death, he said that he already knew of the king's passing, claiming that an angel had appeared to him in his sleep. The angel showed him a broken bow, which Marcian recognized as a symbol that his archenemy was deceased. For the Byzantine emperor and for Emperor Valentinian in Ravenna, the end of Attila confirmed that God had heard their prayers to be rid of this thorn in their sides at last.

Attila's Hunnic Empire was held together by the sheer force of his personality. The respect and obedience of his subjects, both Huns and non-Huns, were earned by his brilliance in leading successful raids into lands rich in treasure, and his manipulation of adversaries through diplomatic maneuvers was unparalleled at the time. Unfortunately, as was common with other barbarian regimes, his successors, lacking his leadership skills, squabbled and fought, and in doing so, they destroyed the once powerful central authority of the Hunnic people.

Three of Attila's sons, Ellac, Dengizich, and Ernak, managed in quick order to split the once unified Hunnic warriors into three factions. The ensuing chaos was seized upon by non-Hunnic peoples who were formerly loyal to Attila. In Slovenia, a coalition of clans revolted, and what remained of the Hunnic army was defeated by these insurgents at the Battle of Nedao in 454. Ellac was killed, and his warriors were decimated. The two surviving sons of Attila rode at the head of a contingent of horsemen and attacked the Ostrogoths along the Danube, but the Huns were again defeated in the Battle of Bassianae.

The collapse of the central power in the Hungarian plains precipitated the migration of peoples who were once content to submit to Attila's leadership. With the loss of regular income provided by pillaging expeditions, they sought other means of making a living. They moved south into Bulgaria, formally submitted to the authority of the Byzantine emperor, and settled on productive farmland. Later, they were joined by a huge number of Ostrogoths who moved in from the north and west. As many as 50,000 migrants settled in Thrace, many of whom would serve in the Byzantine army.

Attila's surviving sons, Dengizich and Ernak, tried to mimic their father's strategic diplomacy but failed miserably. Their threatening demand for tribute was dismissed out of hand. Dengizich, doing what his father had always done when opposed by an emperor, crossed the Danube with the intention of acquiring wealth and teaching the Byzantines a lesson. However, in 469, the Byzantine army easily defeated his warriors and killed him.

In the Western Roman Empire, things deteriorated rapidly after the death of Attila. The supreme military commander Aetius, who had matched Attila in political, diplomatic, and military skills, had been murdered in 454 by an enraged Valentinian III. By cutting down his principal means of executing power, Valentinian set in motion the death rattle of the Western Roman Empire. In 455, Valentinian himself was assassinated by Aetius loyalists. Later in the same year, the Vandals from North Africa sacked Rome and captured Valentinian's widow, Empress Licinia Eudoxia, and her daughters. The Vandals made off with a substantial amount of Rome's treasures, many slaves, and the last members of the Roman imperial family.

The consequences of the death of Attila had been predicted by his ally and adversary, Aetius, who believed that without Attila, the Western Roman Empire would disintegrate into chaos.

Conclusion

What Aetius could never have predicted was Attila's incredible life after death. He became the subject of myths and legends that continue to color our view of Attila even to the present day.

Attila is said to have referred to himself as the "Descendant of the Great Nimrod, King of the Huns, the Goths, the Danes, and the Medes." (This is, of course, the stuff of legend. That Attila would be able to trace his ancestry back to a biblical king who built the Tower of Babel defies reason.) His power was recognized by the 6th-century Byzantine historian Jordanes, who wrote that Attila wielded the "Holy War Sword of the Scythians" given to him by Mars and was thus "prince of the entire world." What was believed to be this sword was held up in the royal court of Hungary in the 12th century as a symbol of a royal lineage leading back to Attila. The surname of Attila was also once popular in Hungary, but its use has declined in recent years.

Tales of Atli (Old Norse for Attila) were integrated into orally transmitted sagas recorded in texts dating from the 13th century. In the saga *Atlakviða* (*The Lay of Atli or Attila*), Gunnar, King of the Burgundians, and his brother Högni are lured to Attila's court by the offer of valuable gifts. The brothers already have great wealth, but they are tempted by Attila's offer. By subterfuge, the Huns try to find out where the Burgundians have buried their gold. However, they do not reveal it, and both Gunnar and Högni are barbarously murdered by Attila's men. Guðrun, their sister and Attila's wife, prepares a banquet for Attila, and when he is well into the meal, she announces that they are eating the flesh of their two sons. Guðrun later kills Attila in his bed and burns down Attila's palace and all the buildings in its compound. *Atlakviða* exists in a written form dating from 1270, but as an orally transmitted story, it may date from three centuries earlier. The story is a good one, and like most of the legends about Attila, it has the requisite drama of murder and cannibalism.

A similar story is told in the *Saga of the Völsungs*. In this epic tale, Guðrun has a dream interpreted by Brynhild, which foretells her marrying Attila, that her brothers will be killed, and that she will kill Attila. The stories in this saga were adapted by Richard Wagner for his opera *Der Ring des Nibelungen* (first performed in 1876) and used by J.R.R. Tolkien in his story *The Legend of Sigurd and Gudrun* (dating from the 1930s). In Tolkien's novel, Atli (Attila) marries Gudrun, and Atli in his lust for gold kills Gudrun's brothers. In retaliation, she kills her two sons and makes goblets from their skulls. After drinking poison from one of the skull cups, Atli collapses on his bed. Gudrun rushes in, stabs him, and burns the palace and the surrounding town.

In 1812, Ludwig van Beethoven conceived the idea of writing an opera about Attila but never completed it. However, Giuseppe Verdi did produce an opera, *Attila*, in 1846. The libretto was based on the play *Attila, King of the Huns* by the German writer Zacharias Werner (1768-1823). The story is an imaginative narrative of Attila's expedition to lay waste to Italy.

At the dawn of the 20th century, Attila and his Hunnic warriors acquired especially insidious reputations that were an exaggeration of historical reality. In 1900, the German Kaiser, Emperor Wilhelm II, gave a speech in which he lauded Attila and the Huns' military skills. He then urged his German fighting men to emulate Attila and the Huns, who they knew from old legends popularized by Richard Wagner in his operas.

While Kaiser Wilhelm's words may have worked well to raise morale among the German military, they also were used to inspire, through fear, Germany's adversaries in the two world wars. The strength of anti-German sentiment that evolved on both sides of the Atlantic in the first half of the 20th century ensured the widespread use of the epithet "Hun" among soldiers fighting Wilhelm's and Hitler's armies, as the nickname for the Germans emphasized what one could expect of them on the battlefield. This explains, in part, the popular notion today that Attila was one of the vilest leaders in history and that his Hunnic warriors were bloodthirsty brigands.

Attila's bloodthirsty status in the modern world partly stems from the prejudice he faces in sources written by Roman and Greek authors. Although he and his warriors were indeed violent, this was fairly commonplace in the era in which they lived. However, Attila was more than that. His looming, vicious reputation in history overshadows his brilliance and his clever strategies in contending with greater powers for the purpose of gaining wealth for himself and his people.

Part 7: Anglo-Saxons

A Captivating Guide to the People Who Inhabited Great Britain from the Early Middle Ages to the Norman Conquest of England

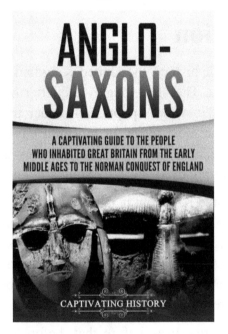

Introduction

At one point in our history, the United Kingdom was the dominant force on the planet. They had roughly a quarter of the world's land and a quarter of the world's population under their direct control. The queen was the most powerful monarch alive, and even if we look at Queen Elizabeth today, we can safely say that she's a strong political figure simply by virtue of existing and ruling the kingdom.

However, the United Kingdom is fairly young, historically speaking. Before it saw the union between Britain and Ireland (which would later secede, though without its northern part), the kingdom had to be united itself. Even today, Scotland, Wales, and England are considered separate countries, despite not really being independent and the Crown presiding over all three.

Yet, there was a time even before that, before even England was united. This was a time before William the Bastard decided to prove to his contemporaries that his bastard moniker would be erased with a swift conquest of the biggest island northwest of Europe. A time before the Battle of Hastings and the year 1066. A time when many petty kingdoms ruled, conquered, and were liberated, time and time again, by a specific people group. A people group that is, in fact, a blend of many and that authors of later dates would collectively call the Anglo-Saxons.

With this book, we want to let our readers know how vibrant and lively (as well as deadly) life in Britain was during the perhaps wrongly-titled "Dark Ages." With the end of the Roman Empire, the local Britons were left to their devices, and it would be several people groups from a peninsula in Central Europe that would come to dominate the island, making sure their presence was known through a series of kingdoms, battles, clashes, victories, and defeats. But the Anglo-Saxons have a lot more to offer us history buffs. We can learn about their day-to-day life: how they dressed, what they ate and drank, how they waged war or had fun, how they buried their dead, and how they worshiped their gods. We can also learn about their art, their amazing metal and clay pieces, stunning bits of tapestries, and dozens of well-illuminated manuscripts. And if we lack any information on what they thought of the world around them, we can be happy that they were willing to tell us that themselves, all through hundreds of written texts of both religious and secular nature.

The Anglo-Saxons were, indeed, an odd group of people to take control of Britain. But they didn't do it all at once, and just like any other people in history, they had a period of adjustment, growth, reconstruction, and eventual rise to prominence. And it all had to start at the same place their British predecessors left off.

Chapter 1 – Anglo-Saxons Arrive

The history of Britain, in general, has always been one of different people groups conquering, mixing, adapting, and evolving. Before the advent of the United Kingdom, nearly every legal (or rather, regal) power has been in the hands of an outsider. Even if we take the earliest history of the isle, we can see that the central power belonged to a nation—Romans, Anglo-Saxons, Normans—that unequivocally came from the continent. And nearly every time they took hold of the isle, the culture would shift.

Possibly the best way to illustrate how this worked is to use an example not from history but from fiction. Author George R. R. Martin, himself a big history buff, drew a lot of inspiration for his works from the ancient and medieval history of the world, with a special focus on European and, specifically, British history.

In Martin's *A Song of Ice and Fire* series, most of the plot is set in the continent of Westeros. Let's sum up the history of this fictional continent for a moment. The first people that lived there were the Children of the Forest, an allusion to elves. But then the First Men came, wars were waged, pacts were sealed, and the First Men even adopted some of the Children's customs as their own. A little later, different invaders known as Andals struck the continent and assumed command. They mixed with the local populace, and little by little, they replaced most of the First Men but not all of them, as those in the North retained the culture of celebrating the Children's

Old Gods. The Andals formed royal houses, and each of them vied for power. However, they were almost all crushed by Aegon the Conqueror who (almost) united the continent and was declared king of the Seven Kingdoms.

So, why bring up a piece of fiction in a history book? Well, because, aside from drawing some inspiration from other bits of fiction, Martin based this whole story on the early history of Britain. Westeros is clearly the island of Great Britain, and the Children have some basis in the old Celtic people that inhabited the isle. Their Old Gods are also inspired by Celtic deities with their own links to nature, forests, and meadows. The First Men could be a good allegory for the Romans, and the Andals of the story are more than likely based on one of the many Germanic people groups that invaded the isle after the decline of the Romans. By the very name, you can tell that they represent the Angles. Another twist by Martin is that his Andals brought the Religion of the Seven with them, an allegory for Christianity. Of course, in reality, this wasn't done by Angles but rather by the Romans before them. Angles, Saxons, and Jutes merely established their own dioceses and took control of the clergy bit by bit. Historically speaking, Angles, much like Martin's Andals, interbred with the locals, formed their own kingdoms, and fought for supremacy. And then we get to Aegon, who is very clearly based on William the Conqueror of Normandy. William gradually took control of the isle in 1066, after the famous Battle of Hastings, starting a new chapter in the history of Britain, once again under foreign rule.

We can see here that authors like Martin found the history of these people fascinating enough to reimagine in their fictional settings. But for now, let's focus on the history of Great Britain before and during the arrival of Germanic tribes from Central Europe.

Roman Britain

As early as 43 CE, Romans established military and political control over most of Britain. The only area they couldn't take was what today comprises Scotland, which at the time was ruled over by the so-called Caledonians. In fact, the famous Hadrian's Wall, built in 128 CE, as well as the later Antonine Wall (construction began around 142 CE and took a little over a decade to complete) were put up as countermeasures against the constant Caledonian attacks.

Roman citizens from all over the empire would come to inhabit the isle. Public and private buildings were steadily rising, and the Britons got sturdy Roman roads. While there weren't any "high-profile" centers of power in Roman Britain, some high officials nevertheless called the isle their home.

During the late Roman period, or more specifically during the Diocletian reforms in 296, the island was divided into four provinces called collectively the Diocese of the Britons. These four were called Britannia Prima, Britannia Secunda, Flavia Caesariensis, and Maxima Caesariensis. However, in the 5th century, an additional province, Valentia, was formed between the two great walls of the north. A vicarius (better known as vicar in English) was in charge of the diocese with his center being in Londinium, though some researchers note that this speculation has its own flaws.

Map of Roman Britannia c. 410[xiv]

With the decline of the Roman Empire, the ruling Romans paid less and less attention to Britain. The Roman Empire had already been all but divided in the late 3rd and early 4th centuries CE, and the constant incursions by various barbarian tribes, alongside political intrigue and internal conflict, kept the emperors busy on the continent. On occasion, some political figure would emerge and stir up some trouble on the isle, but it would be over in a matter of years.

Historians usually mention the year 410 as the year Roman rule officially ended in Britain. Of course, the whole story is a bit more complex than that. For example, there's the period between 383 and 388 CE when Britain was "ruled" by the Roman general Magnus Maximus. He was appointed general of the isle before this period but had killed the Western Roman emperor Gratian and proclaimed himself a Caesar (or a sub-emperor) of Gaul and Britain, subservient only to Emperor Theodosius, the last emperor to rule over both halves of the ailing empire. During this time, he had to deal with the Picts, originally from the territory of today's Scotland, and the Scoti of Ireland who were invading the isle, as well as with the Saxons, one of the tribes that will come to populate the isle a century or so later. There's a strong possibility that Maximus even appointed local tribe leaders into key political positions. It was also during his reign, according to a few written sources (most notably Gildas), that he moved most of his troops from Hadrian's Wall to the continent in order to pursue his campaigns there. He was beaten at the Battle of the Save and later at the Battle of Poetovio after an unsuccessful bid to claim eastern parts of the empire. Theodosius himself executed him in 388.

Before Theodosius himself passed away in 395, he had to quell another rebellion by Eugenius, a usurper claiming the western part of the empire for himself. After his death, Theodosius' sons ruled as emperors of two distinct "countries," with the western part governed by Honorius and the eastern part by Arcadius. Neither ruler proved to be a capable monarch.

Before Honorius came of age, his father-in-law Stilicho did the bulk of the work keeping the Western Roman Empire together. During this time, raids by outside tribes increased to the point of Stilicho allegedly initiating a war campaign against the Picts, possibly in 398. Mere years later, roughly around 401, he had to withdraw troops from Hadrian's Wall in order to deal with Ostrogoths and Visigoths on the continent. The year 402 is the last year Britain saw a major influx of Roman coins, suggesting that the empire had no financial power to retain the island and defend it properly. Picts, Scoti, and Saxons raided far more than earlier, and the locals had no real means of defense with the Roman generals gone.

The last time any Roman noble would provide any significant change in Britain was in 407. Less than a year earlier, several tribes, including the Suebi, the Alans, and the Vandals, crossed the river Rhine. Britain's Roman soldiers were few and far between, and with the news of barbaric tribes crossing the river, they rallied to defend the isle from a possible invasion. Constantine III, a soldier, was chosen as their leader, and shortly after, he declared himself emperor and crossed the English Channel to look for support in Gaul. The current Western Roman emperor, the now adult Honorius, had to deal with the Visigoth threat, so he had no manpower nor time to deal with Constantine. This gave the leader of the British Romans an opportunity to extend his rule over the territory belonging to today's Spain. However, his rule would prove to be a short one. As early as 409, his troops began to desert him, favoring Honorius. In addition, the continental Saxons were raiding Gaul at an alarmingly increasing rate. Constantine's son and other loyalists were murdered soon after, and in 411, Constantine III was assassinated.

Before any of this happened, however, Emperor Honorius suffered a major defeat. Namely, in 410, the Visigoths sacked Rome, which was the first time any outside power had taken the city in nearly eight centuries. Of course, the royal court had long since moved to Ravenna, but this sacking was nevertheless a shock to the world at the time. During the same year, the local Britons allegedly asked Honorius to assist them with the barbarian raids which had only increased since the time of Magnus Maximus. In a response called the Rescript of Honorius, the emperor supposedly told the locals to defend themselves as he was obviously preoccupied with defending continental Roman lands. Some historians speculate that he didn't write the Rescript for the people of Britain but rather for the people of Bruttium in Italy, known today as the region of Calabria. Whatever the case, the political events in the Western Roman Empire left it unable to defend Britain, hence why the date of 410 usually marks the definite end of Roman rule on the island.

Sub-Roman Britain

Normally, people think that 410 is the year when everything Roman ended with Britain, as it was no longer part of the empire. However, it's far more likely, even without any written or archeological evidence, that Roman culture lingered for a few decades longer.

One key element of the Roman culture that survived in Britain was religion. In fact, mass was conducted in Latin, and most literary sources we have from this period point to Latin still being the language of the Church. Most written sources from the sub-Roman period of Britain come to us from churches, written and collected by men of the cloth. Gildas' *De Excidio et Conquestu Britanniae* (On the Ruin and Conquest of Britain) is possibly the best-known work from this time period, with the Venerable Bede's *Historia ecclesiastica gentis Anglorum* (Ecclesiastical History of the English People) coming roughly two centuries later. Namely, Gildas probably wrote his work in the early 6th century, whereas Bede's *Historia* came out around 731 CE. That would make the former of the two a closer "contemporary" to what we call sub-Roman Britain, even though there's a gap of at least one century between Gildas writing his work and the Romans abandoning Britain entirely.

Most scholars see Gildas' work as not completely reliable. This is because it wasn't written as a historical overview of contemporary Britain but rather as a sermon where the priest condemns the actions of the people living on the isle. However, if some of his descriptions are to be believed, sub-Roman Britain thrived (to some extent, at least) without direct Roman jurisdiction. The people were likely engaged in rebuilding projects, most of which included work on sewage systems and even new Roman-style baths. This much can also be extrapolated from actual archeological data. People still retained Roman law, and the clergy spoke and wrote in Latin. However, it's more than likely that original Romans, i.e., people who weren't Britons or really any other ethnic group, had either moved or outright blended with the locals.

The question remains though—what did the Anglo-Saxons do in sub-Roman Britain?

Bede attests, using a variety of sources (both oral and written, neither of which are 100% reliable) that each migration of the Angles, Saxons, and Jutes took part in three stages. The first stage would include individual mercenaries dropping by and "exploring" British soil. The next stage was migration where hundreds of tribesmen would board ships and settle in Britain, usually resulting in clashes with the locals. The final stage was establishing autonomous lands. A few less than reputable sources claim that around 441 CE most British provinces were under direct rule by the Saxons. And while there is at least some archeological evidence of burials of Angles and Saxons taking place at this period, nothing substantial can confirm that they were the overlords of the southern part of Britain during this time. Gildas does claim in his work that the East was given to the Saxons as part of a treaty the locals signed that helped alleviate some attacks by the Picts and the Scoti. The Saxons (or rather, Angles and Saxons, since Gildas used one term for these tribes) would pay tribute to the locals as a consequence of losing the Battle of Badon at some point in either the 5th or 6th century.

Eagle-eyed readers will spot that none of these dates are particularly accurate or definite. That's because sub-Roman Britain has precious little evidence to offer us. The best thing we can do is have educated guesses based on archeological, written, and oral evidence.

Chapter 2 – Early Anglo-Saxons: Origins and Pre-Settlement History

The term "Anglo-Saxon" is more modern and is a compound word defining the Germanic peoples who inhabited the isle of Britain in the early 5th century. The Anglo-Saxons themselves most certainly didn't call themselves that. Even Bede calls them by different names in different sections of his *Ecclesiastical History*.

Knowing this, it's a bit more complicated to talk about the customs and the everyday life of this people group before they settled Britain. Even the simple division of Angles and Saxons is problematic since Bede also mentions Jutes. On top of that, it's highly probable that other Germanic tribes, far smaller than these three people groups, had also raided the island during its late Roman and sub-Roman period. Batavians, for example, were used by the Roman army under Aulus Plautius to defeat the local Britons as early as 43 CE at the Battle of the Medway during the early Roman invasion of the island. Frisians were also used during this time period as mercenary fighters and made up some of the Roman cavalries as Britain was being invaded. Franks would also occasionally raid the island. The Frankish connection would actually play important political roles during the reigns of a few early Anglo-Saxon kings since their royal houses maintained close ties with the Frankish lords in mainland Europe.

The best way to approach the topic of Anglo-Saxon pre-British history is to address what we know of the three biggest tribes that Bede mentions in his *Ecclesiastical History*. To start off, we have the Angles. According to written and archeological evidence, Angles come from an area called Anglia, a small peninsula in the German federal state of Schleswig-Holstein. Anglia is actually a part of the much larger Jutland peninsula, most of which make up modern-day Denmark. Several written sources mention that Angles inhabited these lands; other than Bede, the chronicler Æthelweard and the West Saxon King Alfred the Great both identify this area as the land of Angles, and an old two-day account of a voyage by Ohthere of Hålogaland (which King Alfred later had access to) claims that this land was still inhabited by the ancestors of people living in the then-contemporary England.

Of course, we also have archeological evidence of the Angles living in Schleswig-Holstein prior to the invasion of Britain. Thorsberg moor, a peat bog on the peninsula, and Nydam Mose in Denmark both yielded a wealth of artifacts including clothes, arms, weaponry, and agricultural tools. There also a cremation cemetery in Borgstedt, also located in Schleswig-Holstein, where archeologists unearthed urns and brooches that match those found in early 5th-century Britain. With all of this in mind, it's safe to say that we have the homeland of Angles pinned, and it's located in today's northern Germany.

When it comes to Saxons, it's important to note that their continental history continued independently centuries after some of their tribesmen settled in Britain and began forming kingdoms. The Saxons originated from Old Saxony, supposedly between the rivers Elbe, Eider, and Ems. Saxons themselves were mentioned in historical records as early as the 1st century CE. Roman historian Tacitus lists a number of different tribes, including the Angles, that all worship the same goddess. These tribes were the precursors of the Saxons and must have already been inhabitants of Old Saxony for a period of time when Tacitus wrote about them. Greco-Roman geographer Ptolemy also seems to mention Saxons in his 2nd-century work *Geographia*, although some historians dispute this. Whatever the case may be, by the last century of Western Roman rule, the Saxons were already a well-established group of smaller pagan tribes that were raiding Britain.

Around 407 CE, when there was no feasible way for Romans to defend the Rhine, Saxons, alongside Angles and Jutes and other minor tribes, began to intensify their raids on the British, slowly inhabiting their lands. In fact, the Saxon raids were so frequent that the Romans built a set of coastal forts which had the common name of Litora Saxonica, or the Saxon Shore. By the year 442, the Saxons more or less dominated the majority of land once held by the Romans. However, Saxon history in mainland Europe doesn't end there, for centuries later, they would wage war against the newly-established kings. Charlemagne, for example, led a series of campaigns called the Saxon Wars from 772 to 804 CE. During the early days of Charlemagne's dealings with the Saxons, they were still pagans who refused to convert to Christianity. They would continue to defy the Franks until the last tribal chief was defeated in 804, which led to the Franks subjugating the Saxons and forcibly converting them to Christianity. After the conquest, the region was reorganized as the Duchy of Saxony, and in the following centuries, under Charlemagne's successors, the Saxons would remain largely loyal subjects. However, on occasion, they would rebel against their overlords, as was the case during the Saxon Rebellion of 1073 against the Salian dynasty king and Holy Roman Emperor Henry IV.

Jutes were the third tribe Bede mentions in his work. They originated from the Jutland peninsula, the modern-day location of Denmark and parts of north Germany. This location puts them neatly as contemporary "neighbors" to other tribes that would come to dominate Britain, the Angles and Saxons. Much like those two tribes, the Jutes migrated to Britain during the early 5th century CE. When compared to Angles and Saxons, however, Jutes held smaller areas of land under their direct control. According to historical and archeological data, we can assume that Jutes ruled over Kent and the Isle of Wight, as well as the area that includes today's Hampshire. Excluding Kent, most Jutes simply assimilated into the more numerous Germanic tribes that surrounded them. Some authors even speculate that the West Saxon King Cædwalla committed something akin to genocide or ethnic cleansing of the Jutes around 686 on the Isle of Wight, but there isn't enough evidence to support this claim.

Bede states that all three people groups were led to Britain by the brothers Hengist and Horsa, though they are most likely legendary as there are no historical accounts of either of them. He even lists their ancestry, with one of their great-grandfathers being Odin himself. Considering that Bede was a Christian and a priest, it's highly unlikely that he would have accepted the existence of a pagan deity, so he most likely ascribed the name "Woden" to an earlier chieftain or king. According to the legend, the two brothers sailed from mainland Europe and landed on the Isle of Thanet, which was ruled by King Vortigern of the Britons. Much like the brothers, he was also probably a legendary figure rather than an actual historical king. During their stay on the isle, the brothers first served the king but then betrayed him. Horsa died fighting while Hengist took control and became the first king of Kent.

The names of these two brothers both relate to horses. "Horsa" is the more evident of the two, literally meaning "horse," whereas "Hengist" translates to "stallion." These brothers weren't the only pair to appear as founding brothers of a kingdom. Other Germanic groups and even other Indo-European cultures mention similar sibling pairs, leading many scholars to believe that the two are mythical rather than historical. Their influence is nonetheless still seen today, as many houses in Schleswig-Holstein and modern Lower Saxony (both original settlements of Anglo-Saxons) bear gables with two crossed horses' heads, typically called "Hengst und Hors" in German.

Whether the brothers actually existed or not, the Germanic tribes of Jutland and Old Saxony did settle Britain in the early 5th century after decades of raids and attacks on the local populace. Shortly after, they began to form their own countries and crown their own kings, a topic we will cover shortly. But it's worth pointing out that it's somewhat fascinating to know that Britain, a kingdom which will come to rule almost a quarter of the known world both in landmass and population size, came from such humble beginnings. The kings and queens of the UK wouldn't have been around if not for groups of pagan tribesmen who decided to migrate to an island they had once merely raided in order to avoid the collapse of a different major empire. When we take everything into account, we can see the story of early Angles, Saxons, and Jutes as a reminder that even the greatest of cultures come from humble beginnings.

Map of Anglo-Saxon migration in the 5th century, with Jutland, Anglia, and the Saxon coast^{xv}

Chapter 3 – The Culture of Anglo-Saxons: Religion, Customs, Social Hierarchy, Early Christianity

Religion of the Anglo-Saxons

Angles, Saxons, and Jutes all belonged to a major Indo-European people group called the Germanic peoples. Like many early Indo-European cultures, the Germanic culture revolved around a polytheistic religion. However, different regions had different "takes" when it came to their pantheons. That's why, for example, historians and researchers still can't decide which deity was the head of the Slavic gods.

There's a reason to bring this up when we're talking about Anglo-Saxons. Before they converted into Christianity, they didn't have any written records of their everyday life. As such, most sources that we have on Anglo-Saxons come from later authors, like Bede and Stephen of Ripon who wrote the *Life of Saint Wilfrid*. However, these and other documents were written from the viewpoint of the Church. In other words, the authors didn't really deal with pagan traditions as much as Christianity itself. When we read these texts, we only find hints of pre-Christian customs, a word or two here, a line there. But nothing extensive, nothing concrete. Certainly nothing that can help us piece together what the ancestors of the English actually believed in.

There are, of course, other pieces of evidence, such as archeological remains found in old gravesites. One way we can learn of what certain ancient peoples believed is if we take a good look at how they buried their dead. In the overwhelming majority of cases, a person of higher status would get an elaborate burial. This wasn't just limited to kings and queens, however. Other minor members of the ruling classes, such as high priests and distinguished soldiers, would get buried in extravagant tombs with all of their belongings. We will cover these burial customs a little later.

Naturally, the most intriguing place to find traces of Anglo-Saxon religion lies within the language itself. Linguists and etymologists have looked at the different names of settlements for clues about their earliest history. Oftentimes, the Anglo-Saxons (as well as the native Britons before them) would name their cities after one of their deities or a particular practice they would engage in when it came to their religious customs. For example, terms like *hearh*, *leah*, and *weoh* translate, respectively, to "sanctuary," "holy grove" or holy woodland," and "idol, temple or shrine of a god." These words would be combined with the name of an existing deity, and later cultures would just adopt that name as the towns grew.

So, who were the gods of early Anglo-Saxons? Well, it's more than likely that their pantheon was similar, if not outright the same, as that of other Germanic tribes such as Scandinavians. There are even similarities in the names of these gods. For example, the god whose name the medieval authors mention most often in relation to old Anglo-Saxons is Woden. We can assume that he was the chief deity of the Anglo-Saxon pantheon considering how many later kingdoms claim him as their ancestor. Kings of Kent, Wessex, Mercia, and East Anglia all believed that they stemmed from Woden. If we compare his name to other Germanic gods, it's no surprise that the majority of etymologists and experts on ancient religion associate him with Odin. If Woden really is just a different pronunciation of the titular Norse god, we can assume that he was in charge of wisdom, death, healing, and other duties commonly attributed to Odin. Several towns in Britain bear Woden's name in them. These include Wenslow, Wensley, Woodnesborough, and Wansdyke. Wensley, in particular, combines Woden's name with the term *leah*, meaning that early Wensley was "Woden's holy woods." Woden was also known as Grim at this time, so places like Grimsbury, Grim's Hill, and Grim's Dyke also reference this god

Other deities also appear frequently in British place names. Tiw or Tiu (a possible equivalent of Tyr) is a god whose name we can see in Tuesley, Tysoe, and Tyesmere. Then there's Thunor (whose Norse counterpart might be Thor), and places like Thundersfield, Thunderley, and Thundersley bear his name. Considering that a few of these places have the term "holy woodland" in them, it's safe to say that these were the spots where Anglo-Saxons worshiped these particular gods. Of course, there's also the goddess Frigg. Right now, we we have found little concrete evidence concrete evidence of Anglo-Saxons worshiping her directly in Britain, but some scholars suggest that towns such as Frobury, Freefolk, Froyle, and Frethern all contain her name.

Other minor deities could have also made up the pantheon of Anglo-Saxons. Gods like Seaxneat, Ingui, and Geat, as well as goddesses Eostre and Hretha, appear in several written sources in early Christian Anglo-Saxon literature. But there are even earlier sources. If we were to look at continental Saxons, Tacitus' work *Germania* mentions that they, alongside other Germanic tribes, worship the Earth Mother whom they call Nerthus. While there is no direct evidence that Saxons continued this practice when they migrated to Britain, it's possible that her worship survived in a different form.

Probably the most famous example of gods' names being used in everyday Anglo-Saxon speech comes from naming the days of the week. These names survive today and are well in use despite massive changes that occurred throughout the centuries of the history of Britain. In fact, this practice came from the Roman day-naming system, but nearly all of the Roman gods were replaced with their Germanic equivalents. Monday translates to "moon's day" and references the god Mani. Tuesday is obviously reserved for Tiu or Tyr. Wednesday is the most obvious here, referring to Woden. Then there's Thursday, reserved for Thunor or Thor. Friday references the goddess Frigg, while Sunday, or "sun's day," is dedicated to the goddess Sol. The only weekday that didn't get an Anglo-Saxon/Norse equivalent is Saturday, which translates to "Saturn's day." Obviously, Saturn is a Roman god, and had the Anglo-Saxons wanted to replace his name with their own divine equivalent, they'd have probably chosen Ymir.

Anglo-Saxon religion also might have included lesser fantastic beings, such as elves, dragons, and dwarves. A few old settlements contain words such as *thrys* or *draca* which mean "giants" and "dragon," hinting that the Anglo-Saxons believed in them. Other terms include *puca* (demon or goblin), *scinna* (specter or ghost), *hægtesse* (witch), and *skratti* (demon, warlock). But there is one key aspect we have to keep in mind here. Starting with 793 CE, Viking incursions in Britain became frequent. Therefore, it's safe to say that some of these names might have come from the Viking invaders settling on the isle. Both Anglo-Saxons and Vikings are Germanic in origin, so it's not out of the ordinary that they had similar beliefs and used more or less similar terminology. But even if we take the Vikings out of the equation, Anglo-Saxon place names could have come about even after they converted to Christianity.

Excavation of the Sutton Hoo burial ship, 1939[xvi]

Anglo-Saxon Customs

As stated earlier, we know little of early Anglo-Saxon gods, and most of what we know from their contemporary sources was second-hand information. As such, it's difficult to talk about the customs local Anglo-Saxon people partook in with any level of certainty. However, archeological remains and even linguistic clues do provide us with a few potential scraps of information.

By far, the most direct evidence of Anglo-Saxon customs lies in how they performed their burials. Throughout the years, archeologists have unearthed many gravesites dated all the way back to the 5th century. Some of these sites include the Prittlewell royal tomb, Sutton Hoo, the Spong Hill cemetery site, Fordcroft, and Buckland. Each of these sites offers researchers a wealth of artifacts which hint at the status of the buried individuals, their potential religious beliefs, their sex, and sometimes even the cause of death.

At Spong Hill, we can find 2,316 different burials, of which only 57 so far were found to be inhumations. The rest were all cremations, whose sheer number may suggest that several towns used this area for burials. The practice of cremation is usually linked to pre-Christian cultures, considering that the Church didn't allow this practice in those times. Knowing that, we can safely assume that early Anglo-Saxons, prior to conversion, had the habit of cremating their loved ones when they passed.

But inhumations aren't exactly a custom that only Christians did. In fact, early pagan societies also had the habit of burying their dead without burning the bodies. Knowing this further complicates dating graves at gravesites like the ones at Spong Hill. After all, Angles and Saxons might have had different burial customs separately before migrating to the island.

Luckily, there is a way to distinguish Christian inhumations from pagan ones. As England became more and more Christian, rulers and priests got more modest funerals. This is not the case with pagan rulers, and we don't have to look at Anglo-Saxons to know this fact. Even early Sumerians buried their dead with a wealth of material goods, as did Egyptians and even early European societies. While there are differences regarding their methods and the amount of material that was buried with the body, generally speaking, these cultures believed that the person being buried took the objects with them to the afterlife. Anglo-Saxons surely held the same standard. In other words, a warrior being buried might need swords, daggers, shields, and armor in the afterlife, but he might also need gold, food, and decent clothing. Sometimes the burial would be somewhat extravagant, such as the case of the nobleman buried with his horse at Sutton Hoo. In Essex, a child's grave was exhumed, and it had a dog buried next to it, suggesting that the animal was the pet of the child. Other times they would get very extravagant indeed, and again, we look to Sutton Hoo for this. Namely, in 1939, archeologists unearthed an entire ship at the site. That ship contained an enormous number of items, some of which were elaborately crafted like the shoulder pads, a purse-lid, a golden buckle, and the famous Sutton Hoo helmet. Obviously, the person buried here had to be of the highest status in contemporary British society, most likely a king. Historians believe it to be Rædwald of East Anglia who ruled that same kingdom from c. 599 to c. 624 CE. While the burial itself has definite pagan elements to it, Rædwald converted to Christianity in the early years of his reign. Of course, if this burial site really is his and he really did convert to Christianity, that raises further questions regarding the wealth and the nature of the tomb.

Unfortunately, we can't tell much about the burials of common folk from these findings. However, we can assume which gender roles men and women had at the time. For example, most male graves that were exhumed contained knives and spears. These finds suggest that men were expected to be hunters, farmers, or warriors. Anglo-Saxon women were usually buried with sewing items and weaving tools, meaning they were in charge of making clothes. It should be noted that both genders had examples of elaborate, wealthy funerals, which is why some scholars speculate that early women also held power to some extent.

So, that's what we have when it comes to burials. But what about actual religious practices of the Anglo-Saxons? Is there any way we can know how they performed their rituals, how they worshiped their gods, and how this played into their everyday life?

Sadly, the best evidence we've got of this again relies on second-hand written information and early toponyms. We say "sadly" because, while these bits of evidence can be a good source of information, we still need concrete examples of Anglo-Saxon worship and customs. If we don't have these, all we have are educated guesses. So, let's delve into guessing.

Several place names in Britain suggest animal sacrifices. Gateshead and Worm's Heath are two such locations, with their original names meaning "goat's head" and "snake's head" in Old English. We even have written records of animal sacrifices occurring in the early English kingdoms, although kings began to outlaw the practice in the 7th century. There were even locations where animal carcasses were found buried alongside groups of human bodies. Most of them were oxen, but a few heads of pigs and boars were also unearthed. Sadly, we can't say for certain if these animals were buried during a sacrificial ritual or if the Anglo-Saxons simply buried fresh meat with the body of the deceased as food for the afterlife.

While animal sacrifices might have happened back then, human sacrifices in Anglo-Saxon times is still a topic open for debate. There is just no clear evidence of the ritualistic killing of humans. What we do have are 23 Sutton Hoo corpses that seem to form a circle around an area where a tree used to stand, as well as the corpse of a woman at Sewerby who might have been buried alive with her husband. Both of these claims are contested by scientists and historians, so it's hard to say if they truly represent human sacrifice or not.

Much like everything else about their customs, we barely know anything of pagan Anglo-Saxon priests. Bede mentions them in passing, and archeology hasn't yielded anything conclusive. There were corpses that were identified as male but who wore elaborate female-looking outfits which would suggest priesthood. We do know that the people believed in witches and magic considering that the Christian ruling class tried to outlaw them in the 9th century.

If Anglo-Saxon penitential, i.e., church rules and regulations, from c. 680 are to be believed, priests had issues with locals still venerating sacred trees and pillars. However, within the writings of the priest Aldhelm from this period, we don't get a clear reference to these pillars. He does call them "crude pillars," but he also mentions that they have heads of stags and snakes on the top. Certain scholars believe that Aldhelm wasn't talking about actual totem-like pillars (or menhirs) but rather real animal heads on top of spikes. Either of these fit well with Germanic customs from continental Europe, so they wouldn't really be out of place in Anglo-Saxon England, even as late as the end of the 7th century. One detail does stand out from Aldhelm's description of these practices, however. Namely, he praises the fact that most of these sites that were sacred to the pagans still living in Britain were turned into Christian holy sites, like churches. The reason this is interesting information for us is that if the Anglo-Saxons worshiped their gods by venerating tall trees or even tall wooden poles, it would be very easy to convert these spots into Christian sites. In the case of trees, all church officials would need to do is establish a new church building right next to it. When it comes to the massive poles, an additional horizontal pole would be enough to make them into crosses.

The Sutton Hoo helmet (1971 reconstruction)[xvii]

Social Structure of the Anglo-Saxons

Like most European tribal cultures, the Anglo-Saxons had their own form of social stratification. Their leaders were tribal chieftains who would later bear the title of "king" (the very title "king" comes from Old English *cyning*, meaning "chieftain"). They had hereditary rights along the male line, but they didn't hold all the power, which we will get to shortly. The king was more than just a ruler, though. He was also the head judge, possibly the high priest, and a military commander, what we today would call a "commander-in-chief." Of course, we have to stress the "he" because until Mary I Tudor (known to history as Bloody Mary) came to power, no women were officially ruling over any of the Anglo-Saxon kingdoms. The king would most often rule until his death, after which a council of elders and high-ranking noblemen, the witena gemōt, would choose a new king from the royal family. Usually, the title would go to the oldest living son of the last king, and bastard children could hold no title unless they were legitimized somehow. Of course, it would be a bastard, William the Conqueror, who would take control of all of Britain in the mid-11th century, but that's a topic in and of itself that deserves a whole book.

The reason the term "king" stayed as the official title is because of its root, *cynn*. Cynn means "family, lineage," but the best term to describe it is actually the modern word that came from it, "kin." The Anglo-Saxons practiced sacral kingship, where a certain family would represent the gods (later the Christian God) on earth. This ties in well with a lot of these houses claiming kinship with the supreme god Woden. With that in mind, we can see the Anglo-Saxon king as the religious figurehead, although this role might have slightly changed with the conversion to Christianity.

The king was at the top, but the Anglo-Saxon society had a long list of titles for its other members. One title, directly under the king, was Ætheling. Æthelings were usually young princes who were heirs apparent to the throne. However, historians believe that the title might have simply been used to distinguish any young member of high nobility before the kings became more powerful on the isle, after which it became a term specific to the royal families. Æthelings are also mentioned in works of fiction such as *Beowulf*, in its very first lines no less. According to an old document most likely dating from the 900s, if you were to kill an Ætheling or harm him in any way, you'd have to pay a *weregild* or "man price" of 15,000 thrymsas (Anglo-Saxon medieval currency) or 11,250 shillings.

Each man had a weregild, i.e., his worth in gold which had to be paid as compensation if a crime was committed toward them. For comparison, a typical archbishop cost as much as an Ætheling when it came to the weregild, whereas damage to the king himself was twice that amount.

So, Æthelings were an interesting class, for sure, though we can't be sure if they held any political power while their father, the king, was still alive and ruling. Some historians state that the Anglo-Saxon kings might have ruled not as monarchs but as diarchs. In other words, a single kingdom might have been ruled over by two kings, and it would make sense that one of those two would be the heir apparent and kin to the main ruler. For this reason, Æthelings were venerated as highly as any king would.

But Æthelings were also venerated in literature and poetry. When we read early Anglo-Saxon poems, we see the term Ætheling to describe good men of noble, pure hearts. Both Beowulf and Jesus Christ are described as Æthelings a few times in medieval writing. With time, however, the title was discontinued, with some forms of the term surviving in Wales as "edling," which merely described a male heir apparent to a household.

Ealdorman was a title that meant different things at different points in time. Most people would see this term and think "Hey, these are the earliest of earls, right?" with no pun intended, of course. And they would be right. The title of earl more than likely did evolve from ealdorman, but we still have a similar-sounding title today— alderman, someone who serves on a city council. Ealdormen were actually far more influential back in the day. Namely, a typical ealdorman would be a member of the royal family or otherwise high nobility. Before the 8th century, they acted more or less independently from the king. However, in later years, ealdormen would represent former kings of territories which greater powers took under their control. In either of these positions, the ealdormen wielded great power. They presided over taxation and local courts as well as led their men into battle if there was a need for war. Any member of the ealdorman class was well respected in the community, especially if they were of a former royal bloodline. In time, these men took control of vast swathes of land, some so big they would encompass the entirety of old kingdoms. As the courts became more centralized and England moved closer to a united kingdom, ealdormen from the south would begin to attend court meetings. Historians can't be sure if ealdormen from the north were as active in attending, however. All in all, this was the highest class after the king and his direct heir.

Directly below the ealdormen were the high-reeves. Historians often associate this term to the old settlement of Bamburgh where they would often use the term "high-reeve" for its own magnates and independent lords. However, there's evidence of other members of lower nobility throughout Anglo-Saxon England bearing this title. High-reeves had to respond directly to an ealdorman, but they could still lead local, provincial armies independently.

Reeves were one class below high-reeves, and they would directly oversee a manor, a town, a district, or anything of a similar size. Before we get into what a reeve was responsible for, we should mention how land was structured in early medieval England. Namely, if you had arable land for one household, you had a *hide*. Ten hides would make up a *tything*, while ten tythings formed a *hundred*. But it didn't even end there. If you were to group several hundreds, you'd get an administrative unit called the *shire*. The term itself is often used in place names, such as Berkshire, Cheshire, Worcestershire, Yorkshire, and so on.

With all of this in mind, we can see that different units of land demanded different types of reeves. The list included shire-reeves (the origin of today's sheriff), town-reeves, port-reeves, reeves of hundreds, and reeves of manors. A typical reeve had the duty of a local policeman, job overseer, and manager. In short, he had to take care of the territory he was assigned to for his lords.

The next class was the thegns. A thegn was, in the beginning, a term used for military servicemen loyal to the king. It gradually shifted into representing members of the lower class who would work on different units of land, such as hundreds. They were directly under the ealdormen and reeves, but at times, a king could choose his own personal thegn whom only he could depose. In addition, this king's thegn only took orders from the monarch directly.

All of these titles were the titles of free men, and the lowest of these is the ceorl, also known as churl. This very term gave us the names Charles and Carl. Churls could cultivate land without a lot of restrictions, and their loyalty was to the king. To put it simply, they were free to farm and live their lives, unlike the classes below them. During the reign of Anglo-Saxon kingdoms, the churls didn't have a lot of legal trouble with their land ownership. However, with the conquest of William the Conqueror, this class slowly began to erode. At some point, the term "churl" began to be used as a pejorative toward the lower classes in general. However, its original meaning had nothing to do with class; it simply meant "man" or "husband."

Cotters were similar to churls, but unlike churls, they couldn't really own land. They had to rent arable land from local lords, which made them directly subservient to them. In later years, after the Conquest, the cotters would work under a new class called the villeins, but different accounts lump these two classes into one because of how similar they were.

Last on the list were slaves. Officially, slavery was abolished in the UK in 1833 with the Slavery Abolition Act. However, even during the Anglo-Saxon period, people would sentence slave traders to pay the weregild of the man they sold. It didn't matter if this man committed any crime; the seller still had to pay the penalty. Slaves as a class in Britain at the time had no civil liberties. Before the kingdoms were established on the island, the Anglo-Saxon tribes would capture local Britons and use them for slave labor. Wars were also good opportunities to snatch a new batch of slaves, and families could even sell their own children into slavery to pay outstanding debts. This entire practice is not dissimilar from slavery during ancient Mesopotamian kingdoms and empires. Kinsmen of slaves could even buy the freedom of their captive relatives, and if a person were to become a slave due to debt, they could work it off in several years and earn their own freedom back.

There is evidence of slave trades going on even after 1066. Despite the taxation and legal penalties, the Anglo-Saxons still occasionally sold slaves to other kingdoms on the continent.

Early Christianity

It took a fair while to Christianize the Anglo-Saxon kingdoms. Not only was the pagan religion still strong, but even after the first Christian kings began the process of conversion, there were monarchs and subjects who would go back to their old ways. It was a difficult process, and it all started in 597 in Kent.

The first Anglo-Saxon ruler to convert to Christianity was King Æthelberht of Kent. His own wife, Bertha, was of Merovingian nobility and Christian herself, and he allowed her to restore an old Roman church and to worship Christ. The church she restored is the famed Church of St. Martin in Canterbury. Sometime after this event, Æthelberht wrote to Pope Gregory I in Rome and asked him to send over missionaries to begin converting the Kentish. This was done by a man who would become the first Archbishop of Canterbury called Augustine in 597 when he landed on the isle of Thanet in the spring. Though he wasn't initially too enthusiastic about this mission, Augustine still managed, with Æthelberht's approval, to convert 10,000 of the king's subjects by Christmas. That's 10,000 people in less than nine months!

By 601, Augustine had been trying to expand his mission to other cities. He appointed two bishops, Mellitus and Justus, in London and Rochester respectively, but failed to convert most of the men his mission entailed. He died in 604 before he could see his new monastery, the Church of St. Peter and Paul, finished and operational. He was buried there and later venerated as St. Augustine of Canterbury, the first Archbishop of Canterbury and the "apostle to the English." A little over a decade later, King Æthelberht died as well, leaving Kent in religious "ruins" as heathens and pagans began to reclaim authority.

Years later, in 664, the Northumbrian King Oswiu, alongside the Bishop St. Wilfrid, decided to follow the laws of the Roman Church and renounce the Celtic practices. According to their decision, discussed and accepted during the Synod of Whitby, the Church was to answer only to the archbishop and the pope in Rome, not to the local monarchs. In addition, the Canterbury archbishops would, from that point forward, receive their palliums from the pope, and this tradition would remain more or less the same until the Reformation.

Christianity was still very young even two centuries after Æthelberht's bold move and Oswiu's decision at Whitby. However, the Anglo-Saxon missionaries were already wandering the continent in order to convert the Frankish to Christianity. St. Boniface was an instrumental figure in this movement, and he began to urge for conversions of continental Saxons as early as the late 7th century. Even during the last three decades of the 8th century, when Charlemagne was ruling over vast swathes of Central Europe, the Anglo-Saxon missionaries were converting the local populace. Their missions were instrumental in Christianizing the newly-formed Germanic states, and every subsequent mission to other areas of Europe came from the Holy Roman Empire.

On the one hand, it's a bit disappointing how little we know of actual pagan customs from the times of early Anglo-Saxons. It's additionally frustrating when we learn that a lot of their sacred places were either converted to churches or just outright leveled. Place names and archeological remains can only take us so far, but in order to understand how early Anglo-Saxon pagans operated, we need more information. On the other hand, though, it's interesting how turbulent early English Christianity really was. There's really something fascinating about kingdoms basically waging war over who will convert or not in the early 7th century and then suddenly sending effective and successful missions to Central Europe mere decades later. It's truly amazing to see how a new religion spread so fast in such a small area and then to influence an entire continent by means of conversion.

Chapter 4 – Everyday Life of Anglo-Saxon England: Jobs and Division of Labor, Food and Drink, Clothes, Architecture, Travel, Wars, Gender and Age Norms, Art, Written Works

Jobs and Division of Labor

Anglo-Saxons may have started their interaction with Britain as raiders and warriors, but as they continued to settle the island, their lifestyle didn't differ too much from any other early medieval community. Of course, it goes without saying that Angles, Saxons, and Jutes weren't sailors and raiders when they were still in continental Europe. They had to produce and provide food for their families, create and repair weapons and armor, make clothing and shoes, spread the word of God to the laity, trade goods, build houses, and maintain order within their community.

We've already discussed the social hierarchy of early Anglo-Saxons, from kings to slaves, so we can see from these classes themselves what some social duties of both the nobles and the common folk were. Very broadly speaking, the ealdormen had political and judicial power. They would elect the new king from his family, pass laws, judge potential criminals, call for wars, and enforce the laws. They didn't have as much of a hands-on approach to the people as did local reeves, who were responsible for both the land they held and the people working or living on it. In other words, the nobles were responsible for the law.

It's also evident from both pagan and Christian Anglo-Saxon kingdoms that priests had privileges. After all, they were responsible for the spiritual support of the local community. If we take all the evidence about the pagan kingdoms as true (despite the massive speculation we already noted in earlier chapters), we can assume that rituals were an important part of "staying alive." In November, according to a collection of works known as Old English Martyrology, the priests had to sacrifice a lot of cattle to their gods. Usually, these sacrifices were to appease the gods so that they could, in turn, give the people agreeable climate conditions and not have them starve or die of a plague. With Christian priests, the privileges were even greater but so were the responsibilities. Even with Augustine's arrival in 597 and his subsequent work, the vast majority of the country was pagan, and they all needed conversion. Considering that travel back then was done on foot or on horseback, and that most pagan kings fully opposed converting to Christianity and had armies to back them up if any Christians wanted to convert them by force, Augustine's conversion of 10,000 Kentish people in a matter of months really deserves a decent level of respect.

So those are the nobles and the priests, and their work was pretty simple—one group was to maintain law, the other to provide religious support and spread the word of God. But there were other jobs in Anglo-Saxon England largely performed by the poorest members of society, either churls or slaves.

The most common occupation was that of a farmer. Farmers would normally be men, and they would tend to their field, the aforementioned hide. At this point in history, plows had developed to cut deeper into the ground which yielded better crops. It was, of course, common to use beasts of burden for this task. But even with the help of animals and with better plows, farm work was still incredibly hard.

But food didn't just come from farming. Other men would often go hunting, and it wasn't that uncommon to take your ten-year-old son with you. Fishing was another way to get food, especially by the seaside. However, the most effective way of getting meat was to herd animals. Anglo-Saxons favored beef, but they herded more than just cattle. They also took care of sheep, goats, and pigs. Poultry was also raised, and people kept flocks of chickens, geese, ducks, herons, plovers, and grouses. Most of these jobs were performed by men; however, we will look at women in Anglo-Saxon communities in just a little bit.

Metalworking was already a common practice throughout Europe, and Anglo-Saxon smiths were exceptional. From the numerous mounds and gravesites, archeologists have found a wealth of different weapons and tools made of iron. These include swords, daggers, shields, knives, axes, pickaxes, shovels, hammers, and other tools. Woodworking was also widespread as tools were uncovered that the medieval people used to shape and cut wood. Many needles and spindle parts were also found, so we can safely conclude that Anglo-Saxon people, in particular women, were skilled seamstresses.

Potters also had a lot of work on their hands considering the wealth of pots, bowls, urns, and other "dishes" found in Anglo-Saxon graves. Some of these creations were very elaborate, suggesting that they were used by royal families. And speaking of elaborate, plenty of brooches, ornaments, and beads were found that were expertly worked on, suggesting that Anglo-Saxon jewelers had perfected the craft quite well.

In terms of making food and drink, both men and women did their fair share of the work. Women made cheese, brewed alcohol, baked bread, and milked cows, but it was the men who did the actual cooking. Linguistic evidence suggests that no female cooks existed in early Anglo-Saxon England, but that they were able to bake bread.

But baking bread wasn't the only occupation where you'd see both Anglo-Saxon men and women. "Breaking bread," i.e., attending feasts, also included both genders. Typically, women would serve men their drinks at feasts, and a feast could be organized by either the king himself or even one of the thegns for his local community. That way, any woman, from queen to commoner, had the duty to serve drinks, though the task typically fell on lower-class women if they were attending. In addition, both men and women could perform as traveling actors, musicians, singers, and entertainers. The Anglo-Saxons led a hard life with lots of violence, hard work, and constant threats of death, but they also played hard, with lots of drinks, dancing, singing, and having a good time overall.

Food and Drink

As stated, Anglo-Saxons had several different ways of producing food for their community. In terms of meat, they had hunting and herding, largely of cattle and sheep. However, it's interesting to note that only pigs were solely raised to be eaten. Nearly every other animal that would be herded had more than one purpose. For example, an Anglo-Saxon would herd sheep for meat but also for their wool. Cattle produced milk if they were cows or were used to plow the land if they were bulls. Both cows and bulls would provide hides as well as meat when they were slaughtered, but interestingly enough, they would also use connective tissue of cows to make primitive glue. This wasn't really an exclusively Anglo-Saxon practice as even ancient Egypt used to make glue from different animals. Cow horns were also used to make drinking cups. One more useful animal part the Anglo-Saxons often used was the fat, and they used it to make oils for oil lamps. And no, poultry wasn't excluded from this either. Hollow chicken bones were, for example, used to make musical pipes. Even wild game wasn't just hunted for the meat. Deer would provide the Anglo-Saxon hunter with antlers and skins, while the tusks of hunted wild boars presented some of the greatest trophies at the time.

The Anglo-Saxons were avid farmers, and they grew a wide range of different crops. These ranged from rye and wheat to barley. Each of these was later used to make bread and/or beer. But the Anglo-Saxons also grew vegetables, such as peas, carrots, cabbages, parsnips, and celery, as well as fruit like apples, sloes, and different types of berries.

Dairy products also played a major part in Anglo-Saxon lives, so milk, butter, and cheese were common among the early kingdoms, especially with the common folk. Noblemen were the only ones who could actually afford to eat meat frequently as it was a luxury the churls could only sometimes afford. Poultry was also frequent in Anglo-Saxon times, and while they did eat chicken and duck meat, the lower classes would mostly raise them for their eggs. A typical churl meal would include bread, cheese, and eggs, and these eggs could either come from domesticated birds such as chickens, ducks, and geese, or from wild birds. Fish-wise, the Anglo-Saxons preferred the taste of herring, eel, salmon, perch, pike, and roach. Fish remains were found in Anglo-Saxon toilet pits suggesting that they ate them frequently. In fact, a 10th-century text called Ælfric's *Colloquy* contains an interesting passage about how Anglo-Saxon people fished. From this text, we see that the medieval people of England enjoyed a wide range of both freshwater and saltwater fishes.

Breadmaking was equally as important as fishing, if not more so. Women would bake bread on a griddle or in a clay oven, while the flour would be grinded on a separate hand quern, i.e., a stone used to help grind various materials by hand. Sometimes the baker would grind the flour at a water mill nearby. Anglo-Saxon houses usually contained a central hearth, and oftentimes, there would be a cauldron there. That's where the cook prepared soups or stews that were just as common as bread among the lower Anglo-Saxon classes.

There were plenty of other food sources, such as wild birds, hares, and wild berries. And of course, you can't have a meal without having something to drink.

Surprisingly, the Anglo-Saxons didn't drink a lot of pure, clear water. The reasons for this are multiple. For instance, there were no systems of catching rainwater that could supply an entire settlement. And most of the freshwater inland was polluted or otherwise impure to drink. Lastly, sea water, at least for those settlements that were on the coast, wasn't (and still isn't) good for humans to drink because of its contents. As such, the Anglo-Saxons would use barley to make very light beer. It wasn't rich in alcohol, but it could quench the thirst of anyone, from children to adults. Stronger alcohol was also made, but the drink most Anglo-Saxons seemed to favor was mead. Mead is made from fermented honey. Since sugar wasn't available at the time, most people ate honey if they wanted to sweeten their food. In fact, most houses would have a beehive or two nearby. Drinking mead was already a major part in feasting of local chieftains, hence the term "mead-hall" which we famously know from *Beowulf*. Ealdormen, kings, and other wealthy men could sometimes indulge themselves in wine. However, very few people within the Anglo-Saxon kingdoms made wine, so they had to import it from the Mediterranean.

We already mentioned cow horns being used as cups. However, wealthy families had metal goblets for their drinks during feasts, and even their cutlery and eating utensils were elaborate. However, the churls would eat using more modest tools. For example, there were no forks at the time, so everyone used knives and wooden spoons. A churl would often eat from a simple clay or wooden bowl. There are some hints in written texts about leather drinking cups, but no evidence of these has been found by archeologists yet.

Clothes

Early Anglo-Saxons didn't use clothing to distinguish different statuses, but as both the kingdoms and the clergy developed, this class divide was beginning to show even in what they wore. For example, silk was a material that was mostly worn by the rich, specifically kings, queens, and members of the clergy. When it came to the clothing of the common folk, they largely used linen and wool.

Average men of the lowest status could only afford to wear a simple tunic. Higher status usually meant you could afford a pair of trousers and even an undertunic as well. They also wore caps and leather shoes. Women would wear gowns, and depending on their status, they would either have a simple, standard gown or an elaborate piece containing an undergown and an outer gown. Cloaks were also common with both sexes, though men wore them more frequently, and kings' cloaks had more elements to them. Kings would even have a leather tunic with sewn rings to distinguish them from the common folk.

In terms of priests, they had to wear simple clothes that didn't contain any bright, distracting colors. As the 11th century rolled by, they wore an elaborate set of clothes such as the dalmatics (a specific type of tunic), the chasuble (a priest's vestment), and different types of hats. However, these elaborate clothes were reserved for archbishops and bishops. Regular monks had rougher, simpler clothing.

Anglo-Saxon Architecture

Medieval buildings were not as diverse as they are today. We can classify them into two distinct categories: secular buildings and church buildings.

Let's start with secular buildings. However, the very term "secular" is a bit misleading since we're talking about everyday houses and great halls. Perhaps the better term would be "vernacular structures." However, the semantics of their name doesn't really matter, but their purpose does. Anglo-Saxons lived in very primitive houses. These houses came in two types, with the second, the above-ground house, later developing into a hall. The first type was the so-called "sunken-featured building" or SFB for short. Initially, archeologists simply called them "pit-houses," and at first glance, they do have an obvious feature of a pit-house, namely the pit. However, SFBs are a bit more elaborate. We also know that these were not Roman or Celtic houses since there is evidence of SFBs in modern-day Germany as well. Here, they have the common name *Grubenhäuser*, which translates to "grubhouses, grubhuts."

A typical SFB has a simple, thatched roof. Examples of wooden shingles and turf roofs also exist, but they were not that common back in the day. This simple roof would have gables as well as a hole for smoke to come out. The entire body of the house was usually made of wood with main support posts rammed deep into the ground. And then there's the pit itself. Usually it would be dug into the floor and possibly covered by a wooden floor. Some have speculated that this hole was used for storage, while others interpret the whole SFB to not be a house of a commoner but a weaving shed. Remains of looms were found at a few of these SFBs which seem to corroborate this fact. Most historians would agree that buildings like this could very well serve more than one purpose.

The interior of these houses was simple. There was just one room where a family did everything. They slept, ate, received guests, and conversed regularly there. Churls would not normally have beds, so they simply slept on floors. Even their cattle would spend the night inside of the hut, which actually helped during the winter as the extra bodies helped keep the temperature high. The houses had no windows, while the toilets were merely pits in the ground outside the home surrounded by wattle walls. What we would call a toilet seat today was nothing more than a broad plank with a hole in it during Anglo-Saxon times.

In terms of raw materials, above-ground houses were not much sturdier. They were usually built from wood too. The big difference (no pun intended) was the size. Above-ground houses would be far larger, usually rectangular or square. They would also have a thatched roof with a hole in it, but unlike SFBs, these houses had windows. These early windows were merely halls in walls with no glass, and they were called "eye-holes."

These houses would eventually evolve into halls. During Anglo-Saxon times, a hall was an important building, considering it housed the local chieftain or king. Much like SFBs, halls had a single large room with a hearth in the middle. However, the sheer size of the hall gave it more features. For example, an entire wall could have been dedicated to keeping the cattle in for the winter. In addition, the walls were larger and taller so Anglo-Saxon chieftains would decorate them with various trophies. Deer antlers were a popular choice, as we saw in the food and drink section earlier. The halls would also feature shields and spears mounted onto them.

Halls had a great significance for the local populace. The king would summon his subjects for feasts and celebrations after a war or during a festival. Women would pour mead or strong beer while game was roasted on an open fire in the middle. After the meal was done, minstrels would sing songs of heroism, war, hunting, and everyday life. Halls were also places where chieftains planned battles, settled disputes, and generally performed their civic duties. Other times they would just use them as any other house.

However, even the halls weren't perfect. Their floors would often be dirty and uneven, despite evidence that some of these halls had wooden floors. Because of how open these halls were, they weren't immune to the smell or the noise from outside. In other words, despite its high status in early Anglo-Saxon society, the hall was still not the prettiest place to live and was little more than an average house.

Archeologists still don't know a lot about these early Anglo-Saxon dwellings; however, there are places that provide us with enough detail for a basic idea. West Stow, for example, is an open-air museum where we have archeological remains of houses dating back to the Mesolithic era. A huge section of this site is reserved for early Anglo-Saxon dwellings which have been reconstructed and can be visited today. There were no less than seven potential halls uncovered at this area, as well as various SFBs, potential animal dens, and other unidentified buildings.

As stated, most of these dwellings were made of wood, so it's difficult to find any actual physical remains of these houses. However, early Anglo-Saxons did use stone for other types of buildings, and more often than not, they were churches.

As we saw, the earliest surviving church from the Anglo-Saxon period is the St. Martin's Church in Canterbury. Before it was rebuilt by Augustine, it was a private chapel used by Queen Bertha of Kent. Augustine did major reconstruction on the church but wouldn't live to see it finished. Of course, it's far from being the only church from this period.

Looking at St Martin's Church and other contemporary buildings, we can spot a few key elements to how they were built. For instance, the quoins, or cornerstones, were usually arranged in a long-and-short pattern. To elaborate, the pattern consisted of alternating horizontal and vertical stones. The Minster Church of St. Mary is the perfect example of how these stones look in practice. In fact, these slim vertical stones are called "pilaster strips" and are one of the most common features of Anglo-Saxon church architecture.

Most of these churches would have double-triangular windows on the western walls of the nave, which is the central part of the church. Other church windows would be narrow and have round arches, and most of the time, when masons built these arches, they simply reused Roman stones during construction. Their walls were made using herringbone stonework, and they had a narthex, or a west porch opposite the main altar. We should note that churches of this era rarely had more than one of the features listed here.

Northern churches had more of a Celtic design to them, being very narrow with no aisles and a rectangular chancel, a part near the altar separated from the nave by either a screen or stairs. On the other hand, each of the southern churches from this period, like the ones at

Kent, was small and had a simple layout based on Roman basilicas, i.e., they had rounded chancels in the east of the building and plain-looking walls. Only with the Norman invasion would the rulers begin to rebuild the churches, making them more elaborate and grander in size and scale.

One interesting detail about northern Anglo-Saxon church architecture, in particular, was the stone crosses. Many of these crosses would be found at crossroads in places like Dearham, Bakewell, Bewcastle, Gosforth, Ilkley, and Irton. Like the surviving churches of the north from that period, these large stone crosses had Celtic designs, which suggests an influence of the local Britons on the settling Anglo-Saxons. The crosses weren't a part of any building but were built next to public road intersections and other roadside areas. If we take into account that the early Anglo-Saxons and Britons were pagans who worshiped their gods by venerating massive pillars and trees, this could easily explain why these crosses wound up there in the first place. Even Pope Gregory I urged Augustine to simply "repurpose" old religious sites into Christian churches and places of prayer. Church officials could have easily replaced these pillars with stone crosses since the place itself already had a heavy religious significance to the local pagans. At times, even entire churches were built right next to or even around these crosses.

Of course, there were even a few "secular buildings" made of stone that weren't churches. For example, local Anglo-Saxons didn't want to live in old Roman settlements, opting to build their own houses closer to arable farmland or rivers plentiful with fish. The more these settlements grew, the bigger their need was to have some sort of protection. As such, they would construct stone fortifications to defend themselves against invading Vikings. These fortifications were called burhs, and sadly, none remain standing to this day. However, some archeologists suggest that St. George's Tower at Oxford, dating back to the 11th century, was actually a part of a larger defensive structure that surrounded the local burh at the time.

The chancel wall with Roman bricks, St. Martin's Church, Canterbury[xviii]

Travel

By land or sea, the Anglo-Saxons moved a lot. After all, it's hard to believe that they swam across the English Channel to invade late Roman Britain. Clearly, the early Germanic tribes had some sort of ship that was capable of traversing the restless ocean.

One popular theory is that the early ships of Angles, Saxons, and Jutes had no masts. They were very long and, of course, made of wood. The fact that they were long is important since they wanted to fit as many of their soldiers onto the ship as possible. We can have some idea of what these ships looked like if we examine the reconstructed ships such as the Nydam boat, the Gredstedbro boat (both found in Denmark), and the boat used in the Sutton Hoo princely burial. All three of these ships had keel planks rather than proper keels, were over 20 meters or 65 feet long, and had no mast blocks. If we were to assume that similar boats were used to cross the Channel, we could ascertain that the Anglo-Saxons were strong, experienced naval travelers who raided Britain with simple ships, oars, and brute strength.

In addition to ships, the Anglo-Saxons also probably had smaller river frigates. Local river sailing would be common during that time, especially with the emergence of trading and the expansion of towns and cities.

Ground travel was a bit more diverse. Naturally, locals traveled either on foot or on horseback. Horses, in particular, were very significant to the Anglo-Saxons of the period. The most obvious example includes the names of the supposed ancestors of Kent, Hengist and Horsa, but other evidence also lies in place names such as Studham, Stadhampton, and Stoodleigh, each of them containing the term "stud." In regards to religious purposes, horses would be frequent motifs in certain tales of miracles with early Anglo-Saxon Christians, such as the horse who helped St. Cuthbert from starving or the horse who sank into the ground where St. Boniface died and when they pulled it out uncovered a fountain of drinking water. It's hard to overemphasize how important horses were to the ancestors of modern British people. However, they also had a lot of practical uses. For example, several different types of horses are named within Old English. There were cart horses, pack horses, riding horses, breeding horses, royal and aristocratic horses, and war horses. While it's tempting to think that they also used horses for plowing, there is no recorded evidence for this, nor is there a term for "plow horse" in Old English.

Judging by these words, we can see that the Anglo-Saxons most often used horses to transport goods. For example, a horse might drag along a cart of hay or vegetables, or an owner might place a lot of baggage onto its back. In terms of riding, Anglo-Saxon warriors were famous (or rather infamous) for being among the first people on the island to actually raid on horseback. One more purpose that these horses served was a bit unorthodox but still highly possible. Namely, in times of food shortages such as harsh winters, Anglo-Saxons would eat their horses. They would also eat them after they became too old for riding or pulling carts. However, the occurrence is only unorthodox if we understand how important horses actually were to this culture. During the later periods of Anglo-Saxon kingdoms, they founded a lot of horse-breeding establishments. Horses were, in fact, so valuable that an Anglo-Saxon man could use one in land trade or gift one as a sign of respect or even for a dowry.

Royalty, in particular, held these animals in high esteem, and as we saw in the earlier chapters, one unknown prince was actually found buried with his horse.

The methods are there—horseback, foot, boat, ship—but there's still a question of where the Anglo-Saxons traveled. Or, to be more precise, did the Anglo-Saxons use roads?

In modern Italy, you can still find old roads that the ancient Romans built. However, in pre-Anglo-Saxon England, even the Romans used roads that were built before them. Namely, there is some physical evidence of ditched roads that connected early Iron Age settlements of Kent thousands of years before Romans even set foot on British soil. Naturally, once Rome took control, the new overlords made sure to reuse and rebuild these roads, alongside a few new ones.

But the Anglo-Saxons didn't merely use the roads built by their ancestors. Excavations done at the Pilgrim's Way, which stretches from Winchester to the shrine of St. Thomas Becket at Canterbury, uncovered three separate hollow ways. They were carbon-dated to anywhere between the 7th and the 10th century, suggesting that it was the local Anglo-Saxon community that built them. Other ways of tracking these old roads include wayside markers, but they are few and far between, such as the Copplestone Cross in Devon.

Scientists have used methods such as LiDAR (Light Detection and Ranging) remote sensing and movement of objects to determine the potential old routes that the Anglo-Saxons and the Romans before them used. The findings give us a decent network of roads, some of which became obsolete near the end of the 10th century. However, it's important to note that not all Anglo-Saxon kingdoms stopped using Roman roads at the same time. It was more of a gradual change, with Mercia and East Anglia using Roman roads the longest out of all the kingdoms.

Other evidence of different roads exists within place names and textual sources. For example, Sturton Grange, a parish in Leeds, derives its name from the term "street." The name would suggest that the settlement was next to a major road. When it comes to written sources, we can look to the Anglo-Saxon charters, which were Old English documents that detailed and listed land grants and privileges of the laity. From these documents, we can look at the old descriptions of landmarks close to the boundaries of private land and determine if they have any characteristics of old Anglo-Saxon roads.

Usually, the Anglo-Saxon traveler would walk, march, or ride a horse using one of these many roads. However, straying off the path would have been dangerous. During the old kingdoms, raids and roadside robberies were common. An interesting fact to note is that the Anglo-Saxons made use of rivers as waterways far more commonly than their Roman predecessors. Even when they walked, they opted to follow the rivers as they were safer. Traveling was often painfully slow, so many people simply didn't leave their town that often.

Wars

Anglo-Saxons were a people of war well before they inhabited Britain. They were raiding the shores of Britain in the late 4th century alongside multiple other tribes, and when the 5th century rolled in, they were already settling on the island. However, a warrior culture like that of Germanic tribes doesn't become purely agricultural overnight. During their early years, the Anglo-Saxons waged quite a few wars against both foreign and domestic threats.

The earliest enemies of the Anglo-Saxons were the local Britons and their Roman rulers. With the Romans still being nominally in power, they treated the newly-settled Anglo-Saxons as they would treat any other tribe—they imposed taxes and looked upon them as barbarians. The new tribes soon began to rebel quite often. The first territory to fall under Anglo-Saxon, or rather Jutish control, was Kent. But the Britons didn't really surrender, though they were losing ground fast. This is where the possibly mythical figure of King Arthur comes into focus. Arthur, as the legends and a few scarce written records state, beat the Saxons at the Battle of Badon, which, if true, occurred around 500 CE. It is very difficult to overemphasize how divided scientists and historians are about the historicity of this king and battle. One detail that makes the Battle of Badon more fictional than real is that Arthur allegedly killed 960 Saxon soldiers himself. This is, of course, an exaggeration, possibly for poetic purposes, because even with modern weapons, a single person cannot kill 960 people and live to tell the tale. However, one thing is for certain. Even if the Battle of Badon didn't happen and King Arthur didn't exist, the Britons did successfully push away the Saxons, but as the centuries rolled on, they lost more and more territory. By the end of the 7th century, the Britons were relegated to the area of Britain which makes up modern-day Wales today. During that time, the Anglo-Saxon kingdoms were slowly blooming and coming into power. This was clearly no longer a Britain of Celts or Romans, that much was clear.

The Celts of Wales weren't about to give up, however. Different independent kingdoms formed after 500 CE in the area, some of which include Powys, Gwynedd, Morgannwg, and Gwent. These kingdoms, especially Powys and Gwynedd, would successfully fend off the advances of the Anglo-Saxon kingdom of Mercia, which was expanding rapidly. After a series of battles, Mercian kings began to construct dykes, and stricter borders were established between the Anglo-Saxons and the surviving Britons. Soon after, during the mid-9th century, the Vikings would invade the island, and some Welsh kings, notably the king of Gwynned called Anarawd ap Rhodri, allied with the Norsemen at first in order to reclaim some lands, but soon after these alliances broke, they joined forces with King Alfred of Wessex, later known as Alfred the Great, against the invaders.

Naturally, the Vikings were a threat long before the Welsh allied with them. They began their raids of the island in the last decades of the 8th century. They first began raiding monasteries and churches since they were by far the wealthiest establishments in any kingdom, coastal or landlocked. But the Vikings didn't just stop at raids. By the 9th century, they were already settling on the island while continuing to raid local territories. They even had a large standing army, which we know from their conquest of York in 866. It would be Alfred the Great that would defeat the Vikings in 878 at the Battle of Edington. Most of the Vikings then moved to the northeastern part of the island, with the remaining territories being Anglo-Saxon.

The Vikings that raided and warred against the Anglo-Saxons were Danes, and their defeat at Edington didn't stop them from continuing to attack the locals. In 1013, the Danes conquered and ruled the island under the leadership of Sweyn Forkbeard until his death a year later. The Danes came back in 1016 and reconquered the land, and their ruler, Cnut the Great, Forkbeard's son, was crowned king of England a year later. He ruled as a king of a united Norway, Denmark, and England from 1028 until 1035 when he died. He was succeeded by his two sons, Harold Harefoot and Harthacnut, who both ruled very briefly (1035-1040 and 1040-1042). After their deaths, an Anglo-Saxon king, Edward the Confessor, took the throne and ruled until 1066.

Obviously, 1066 is a major year for the history of England. Not only was it the year when Edward the Confessor died, but it was also the year when his successor, Harold Godwinson, took the throne. Sadly, he would only maintain this position for nine months. During 1066, William the Bastard of Normandy and his troops began their conquest of England. In October of that same year, at the Battle of Hastings, Harold would die, leaving the throne open for his successor, Edgar Ætheling. Edgar was even elected to be the proper heir by the witena gemōt, but he never took the throne because of William. Edgar's own story didn't end there, however, but that's when the story of Norman Britain began and when the Anglo-Saxons officially lost control of Britain.

Naturally, the Anglo-Saxons remained the majority even after William's conquest, though the multiple people groups began to assimilate more and more in later years. It's also safe to say that wars and invasions didn't end with William. Many other people groups would attack the island, but in terms of Anglo-Saxon kingdoms and their wars, they ended in 1066.

Of course, these were just the wars against outside forces. There were a lot of battles and skirmishes between the Anglo-Saxon kingdoms themselves, a topic that will be addressed in the following chapter. Now, however, is a good time to take a look at how Anglo-Saxons conducted warfare.

Anglo-Saxon warfare changed as the centuries moved along. Their armies first consisted of small, tribal groups of warriors. As the 11th century rolled in, they already had a unified island and their armies were more organized and uniform. In terms of weapons, they used swords, javelins, spears, and missile-launching slingshots. It should be noted that a "missile" here refers to anything that can be thrown, such as an ax or an arrow, but when it comes to slingshots, it's usually a round, heavy stone. There are hints of Anglo-Saxon soldiers using archers in battles but not enough for anything conclusive.

When it came to group battles, the soldiers would form shield walls. As the name suggests, these were human walls of shields. Anglo-Saxon historian Stephen Pollington has suggested a possible sequence of events during a fight. First, the king or commander would line up the troops and provide an inspirational speech. Next, there would be a battle cry, and one or both sides would advance with the shield walls. Then, as they charged, they would hurl missiles at the opposite side to dissuade them from clashing, and once they got within range, the two shield walls would collide. One side would push forward with weapons, whereas the other would try to hold the line. If no side budged, they would retreat for a rest, hurling a few more missiles at each other in the meantime. These steps would get repeated until one side broke and the other advanced.

During these battles, individuals would separate themselves and move ahead of the group to throw their javelins. This left them exposed to the javelins of the other side, and once a thrower was killed, a soldier could cross into the land between the armies and claim his armor and weapons. These actions were considered acts of bravery, and the person who would expose themselves like this would get material awards and recognition if he survived the battle.

A few instances of using horses in battle exist but not enough to have a definite picture of horseback warfare in Anglo-Saxon kingdoms. There is also not a lot of evidence for training or army supplies, but it's safe to assume that soldiers practiced wrestling, jumping, running, and throwing spears. These would help them get ready for battle and keep them in shape.

Abingdon sword, c. 9th century, found at Abingdon, Oxfordshire[xix]

Gender and Age Norms

Medieval societies like Anglo-Saxon kingdoms were patriarchal in nature. That means the men would hold political power and be heads of religious institutions. They would also be the majority of landowners and would go to war. Modern gender theories usually reject medieval societies as regressive in terms of treatment of women, but in reality, the Anglo-Saxon society was less clear-cut than that. In other words, women had their fair share of positive and negative aspects in early Britain.

When it came to the Church, women gained a lot of new opportunities with the introduction of Christianity. England was one of the first countries to begin venerating women as saints after their passing, for example. Not to mention that there were separate monasteries for men and women back then, allowing women to become abbesses. With this position, she could handle the finances of local communities as well as the property of the church. Usually, it would be women of noble birth that would take monastic vows and become abbesses, making them heads of different churches. Considering how important the Church was as an institution back then, this was a major shift in how women normally behaved or were treated in Anglo-Saxon communities. Of course, they would still be appointed to these positions by men, and the archbishops themselves were still male.

Women who were nuns and abbesses were greatly respected and admired by the local communities of laymen. They were seen as paragons of virtue and chastity, having renounced their bodily desires and joined the clergy. This made them no less respected than the men in those same positions, as joining the church was generally seen as a noble and pure act.

In terms of queens and noble women, we know from written sources and even some literary works, like *Beowulf*, that they had the task of serving drinks during feasts at grand halls. Of course, a queen didn't have to serve drinks if there were women of lower stature present. Women would also not participate in battle, and written records of any women taking up arms are scarce. They would also not do any hard, physical labor such as hunting, farming, chopping wood, smithing, tanning, or building. Interestingly enough, they didn't even cook. However, they did sew, weave, bake bread, milk cows, make cheese and butter, and brew beer and mead. Since these jobs were easier, they were also performed by children. In fact, children were considered adults when they turned ten, after which they began doing their fair share of work with the adults.

This division of labor stemmed from how Anglo-Saxons viewed men and women. It was a woman's duty to help the men after the battle and to keep them well fed and clothed. On the other hand, it was the man's duty to protect the women and their family in general as well as to provide for them with hard work.

In terms of marriage, women were allowed to leave as they pleased; however, the only recorded cases of marriage annulments were during adultery. Men would take control of a woman's property, but they were also obliged to give them something called the "morning gift," which was usually land and material goods. These would belong to her and her alone, and she was allowed to do whatever she wanted with it. In case of a divorce, a woman could leave a man, and she would usually get half of the property. A widow was not allowed to marry until a full year had passed. This might sound cruel, but it could also be seen as a way of letting the widow cope and, more importantly, make a later marriage decision with a clearer head. Once the twelve months were up, she could choose to marry (or not marry) whomever she wanted.

Sex work also existed during Anglo-Saxon England, and the prices for sex services varied based on who the client was (churls usually paid less than nobles). When it came to rape, women of all statuses were legally protected from it, and harsh punishments were exacted on the rapists themselves. However, there are written records of men advocating the beating of women, suggesting that there were either customs that damaged women in general or that this was an issue that needed to be resolved. Early Christianity strongly objected to beatings in general, so they couldn't have looked at this practice without condemnation.

Legally speaking, women had property rights and could stand witness to trials. They were also responsible for their own actions, and if slighted by the law, they were compensated personally. Most landowning women came from the upper classes, but even commoner women could inherit land, as written evidence within charters does not show that previous landowners preferred one gender over the other. When a woman inherited the land, she would get different items such as livestock, slaves, clothing, jewels, furnishings, and books along with it. They even got to keep tablecloths, wall hangings, and bed sheets since they were the ones to make them and were considered theirs.

Women would often be instrumental in certain political events in Anglo-Saxon England. It was Bertha, the wife of King Æthelberht, that was responsible for the king converting to Christianity and bringing it to England in the first place. She was a Merovingian princess, a daughter of Charibert I, and a devout Christian. Thanks to her, an old Roman church outside of Canterbury was restored and became her private chapel which she dedicated to St. Martin of Tours. This church would later become the Church of St. Martin, one of the oldest Anglo-Saxon churches in Canterbury and England as a whole. Bertha was venerated after her death, which happened sometime during the first decade of the 7th century. This makes her one of the first women canonized as saints in Britain.

Anglo-Saxon Art

People often get the impression that Anglo-Saxons were brutes who enjoyed war, killing, feasting, loud celebrations, and the occasional domestic violence. However, archeological evidence provides us with one more important aspect of Anglo-Saxon life. They were also very skilled artists with skills varying from metallurgy to manuscript illumination, from jewelry crafting to ivory carving, and from making elaborate tapestries to sculpting enormous monuments to their culture. A culture's art can give us a lot of insight into what they valued, how skilled they were with a particular craft, what materials and tools they used, and how their culture changed through the centuries.

Most of the artifacts found between sub-Roman Britain and Norman Britain show an affinity toward Christ and Christianity, which isn't all that strange considering that we now know how it developed throughout the centuries. Illuminated manuscripts are a perfect example of this. For the uninitiated reader, an illuminated manuscript is a religious document where the text has a lot of elaborate ornamentations, such as decorated initials, page borders, and even miniature illustrations. The materials used in such a practice were usually silver or gold; however, that's largely true for the Western Christian tradition of illumination.

The initial illuminated manuscripts combined a lot of different styles of this art, namely those of Germanic, Celtic, and Italian illumination. The Stockholm Codex Aureus is a perfect example of these mixtures of styles since its portrait is largely Italian (or rather tries to imitate the Italian style) while the letters themselves are insular in nature. Insular art, it should be noted, is an art style that developed in Britain and Ireland which is distinct from all other styles in mainland Europe. It's called insular because the term *insula* means "island."

There aren't a lot of manuscripts with elements of insular art in 9th-century Britain, but their elements can be seen in manuscripts from mainland Europe wherever the Anglo-Saxon missionaries did their work. For example, the Echternach Abbey in Luxembourg houses the famous Echternach Gospels, which were most likely illuminated in Northumbria. By the end of the 9th century, however, the so-called Winchester style of illumination was created and heavily used. Some distinctions of this style include agitated or wrinkled draperies, acanthus borders, and historiated initials. The best example of the late Winchester style illumination is the Benedictional of St. Æthelwold which actually drew from a few other styles, such as Byzantine and Carolingian illumination.

Producing goods from precious metals such as gold and silver, or even basic metals and alloys, was a practice the Anglo-Saxons actually did before Christianity. The most frequent examples of this practice are found before the 7th century, usually as round elaborate quoit brooches. Thanks to the discovery of the ship burial at Sutton Hoo, we know that these brooches, and indeed other metalwork, were highly developed at this time.

Brooches were far from the only items found and unearthed from the Anglo-Saxon period. Archeologists also found rings, coins, belt buckles, military fittings, and various other items. From written records, we also know that the metalworkers made statues, doors, shrines, and other large-scale metal pieces, but barely any of these survived to this day. The most likely reason for their disappearance is the constant Viking raids followed by the subsequent Norman invasion and other events. Unfortunately, looting was frequent during those raids, and the monasteries and churches, as the best-equipped places in England, had these items in abundance.

In terms of masters of metalwork, we have a few of the artists' names available to us from written accounts. One such artist was Spearhafoc, who would later become a Benedictine monk, an abbot, and Bishop-Elect of London. He was prominent in the mid-11th century and was renowned for his skills at goldsmithing, gold engraving, and painting. It's probably these skills that got him promoted so quickly to a high church position. Another artist of a similar status was Mannig of Evesham. Both artists have their lives documented and chronicled in their respective abbeys. Other artists are mentioned as well but mostly in passing.

A lot of these metalworks included scenes of animals in reeds or bushes carved onto the surface. But the Anglo-Saxons didn't just use metals to carve the scenes they wanted. More often than not, they would use ivory and other types of bone for equally elaborate efforts. For example, an entire casket, most likely carved in Northumbria in the 8th century, was made of whalebone, and it even has a riddle on it that hints as much. Artists actually imported a lot of these bones, especially the walrus bones, from the north. Other examples of ivory carvings include various scenes depicting Christ - either his birth, crucifixion, or different motifs from the Bible that included him.

But metal and ivory weren't enough. Anglo-Saxon stoneworkers even carved and shaped rocks, mostly to get massive outdoor crosses but sometimes to have an elaborate relief. These crosses would often combine both pagan and Christian elements, which is one of the reasons why they would be frequently destroyed or defaced during the Reformation. Many of these crosses actually survived in Ireland and can be seen today.

A cross would typically be very tall and slender, with some exceptions to this rule having been found in Mercia. Elements of Celtic paganism would often be there, such as vines and leaves. Moreover, there might be some hints that these crosses were originally painted, somewhat like Greek and Roman statues. The crosses themselves were popular at the time, especially when the Danish Vikings began to invade and when they finally took control in the late 10th and early 11th centuries. They began to "mass-produce" similar stone crosses, but they didn't have the same artistic quality of their Anglo-Saxon predecessors.

Textiles were equally popular "canvases" for contemporary Anglo-Saxon artists. They favored embroideries and tapestries, and many such works were made in early medieval England. Sadly, few survived, mainly because the material they were made from was reused in other works of art. Possibly the most famous example of Anglo-Saxon tapestries is the elaborate Bayeux Tapestry which depicts the Battle of Hastings. Of course, the tapestry itself was made within twenty years after the battle, but it is done in the style and manner of old Anglo-Saxon weavers. As we have established earlier, embroidery and other needlework were largely done by women. Therefore, we can safely assume that nuns and priestesses made the Bayeux Tapestry. Interestingly, some historians claim this work of art to be the first European version of a comic book because of its sequential storytelling nature.

Finer textile works incorporated silk and precious metal threads, namely gold and silver, as well as lots of precious gems, glass beads, and pearls. More often than not, these elaborate tapestries were owned by priests or royal families, and they were usually used in religious ceremonies.

The Anglo-Saxons also dabbled in other materials. For example, glass was very popular when it came to making luxury drinking glasses (like the claw beakers from the 6th and 7th centuries), glass beads, and church windows. Sometimes they would import glass workers from Francia, now known as France, but oftentimes, they would just rework old Roman glass items. Enamel was also often used instead of glass.

Then there's leather. Anglo-Saxon books would be bound in different types of covers. As we saw earlier, they could even be ornamented in ivory. Leather was one such material, and we have a famous example from the late 7th century to show us how skilled the craftsmen were at leather bookbinding. The stunning St Cuthbert Gospel is the oldest Western-bound book to remain unaltered to this very day. It has incised lines, elaborate relief decoration, and even some color. Naturally, the Anglo-Saxons didn't just use leather to bind books. Their leather artwork probably also covered belts, purses, and satchels, though we sadly don't have a lot of physical evidence of this, and the contemporary texts that talk about leather binding don't mention the more secular uses for leather ornamentation.

We can see that Anglo-Saxon artists had a wide range of skills and a wide range of materials. Of course, their missions to the continent also brought knowledge of illuminating manuscripts, carving figures, and working stones and fabrics. With that in mind, we can say that the insular art of Britain influenced a lot of early European Christian art styles. Even certain motifs became commonplace after the Anglo-Saxon missionaries began traveling Europe. For example, the elements of Christ's legs and feet alone being seen, the Hellmouth, St. John the Evangelist writing at the foot of a cross, Moses with horns, the depiction of the Last Judgment, and Mary Magdalene at the foot of the cross all originated in Anglo-Saxon Britain. These would become widely used in European art for the following centuries.

Winchester-style evangelist portrait, Grimbald Gospels, early 11th century[xx]

Written Works of the Anglo-Saxon Period

Pagan Anglo-Saxons didn't have an alphabet of their own that we know of. They were a pre-literate society, meaning they passed their knowledge onto their descendants by means of oral tradition. When Christianity came, literacy began to spread, but it was largely reserved for the higher classes. Though it wasn't impossible for a churl or a farmer to know how to read, it was almost exclusively the royal family and the priests that could afford to learn how to read and write. Churches were centers of the written word, though certain kings might have even hired private tutors for their children who also came from the clergy.

There is one major issue when it comes to Christianity and literacy in early medieval England. Namely, the priests who would preserve old Anglo-Saxon legends and myths would often dress them up in Christian undertones. That way, they could cloak the pagan elements and maintain a Christian narrative. Famous works such as *Beowulf* are a good example of this.

Anglo-Saxons enjoyed both poetry and prose. In terms of poetry, there were heroic poems and epics, elegies, adaptations of classical Latin poems, and riddles. The riddles, in particular, were exceptionally popular during this time, with 94 of them recorded in the Exeter Book, a lengthy compendium of Anglo-Saxon poetry. Christian poems became more and more popular with kingdoms slowly abandoning paganism, so biblical paraphrases, lives of saints, and even original poems appeared, with the most famous example being the *Dream of the Rood*.

In terms of epic poetry, Anglo-Saxon literature cannot be discussed without mentioning *Beowulf*. This epic, containing the exploits of the titular hero, was written down by an anonymous author sometime in the 10th century, though it was more than likely composed far earlier. Supernatural elements of Beowulf were explained away by adding Christian parallels, possibly by the very author who wrote it down since it was usually priests who dabbled in preserving poetry and prose. Numerous authors worked on translating it, including the famous fantasy author J. R. R. Tolkien who considered it a classic of English literature.

Most poems were written down anonymously. However, we do know the names of a few poets such as Cynewulf, Aldhelm, and Cædmon, the latter being known as the earliest English poet.

Prose was just as important during the development of Anglo-Saxon kingdoms. Both Christian and secular prose was prominent, with translations of Latin works being a notable practice at the time. Priests and monks would often write polemics, sermons, hagiographies, and other works that had powerful Christian themes, though they would often be written in Latin rather than Old English, at least in the early days of English Christianity. Two of the most famous prose writers of the Anglo-Saxon period in Britain were Gildas and the Venerable Bede. Gildas' polemic known as *De Excidio et Conquestu Britanniae* or *On the Ruin and Conquest of Britain* is the earliest source we have that gives us historical glimpses of Anglo-Saxon societies at the time. However, Gildas himself would often provide contradictory or outright incorrect information since his focus wasn't the historicity of events but rather the condemnation of the British in terms of Christian behavior. Bede, on the other hand, wrote his *Ecclesiastical History of the English People* with somewhat more historical accuracy. Born in Northumbria, he would, of course, have a bias toward that region. However, the events he describes, which largely focus on the history of Christian churches in England but also contains a lot of historical information on the early kingdoms and their political situations, can be retraced with a massive amount of accuracy. He is considered to be the first English historian despite his work not having that intention originally.

Of course, there are works that deal with history in a more secular way, such as the famed *Anglo-Saxon Chronicle*. Compiled by an unknown author, it contains information of about 300 years of English history. While this is an impressive feat, the *Chronicle* suffers from the same issues that other secular historical works do at the time. Namely, most of its sources are dubious or even outright taken from oral tradition, and some errors do occur in terms of dates and events. Some events were merely mentioned without any outcomes or listing the people involved. Battles would be described, but no place names given, kings listed, or victors and losers announced. Despite all of this, the *Anglo-Saxon Chronicle* remains an important part of Anglo-Saxon literary history.

Secular written works of Anglo-Saxons also dealt with mathematics, medicine, geography, language, and the law. Legal texts, in particular, would be bound in single volumes, detailing law codes of different kings and specific cases of legal disputes in various cities and towns. All in all, English prose, much like poetry, flourished during this time, despite the fact that it was limited to the upper classes.

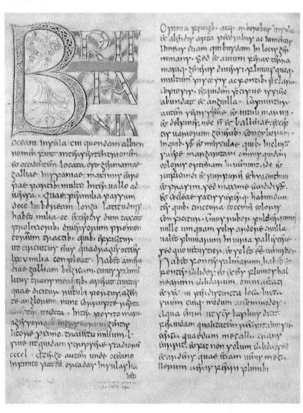

Folio 3v of St. Petersburg Bede[xxi]

Chapter 5 – Anglo-Saxon Kingdoms

Before the Kings

Angles, Saxons, and Jutes were all tribal cultures. Their social hierarchy consisted of a ruler, a tribal council, priests, workers, and slaves, with more nuanced titles coming later. Once they began settling on British soil, they had two severe obstacles in their way. The first was the local Romans, whereas the second was the local Celtic people, the Britons. But even amongst themselves, these tribes didn't really work in unity. In fact, Bede, while addressing earlier accounts of these peoples by Gildas, openly states that the three groups are a "separate race." Jutes would inhabit Kent and the Isle of Wight. People that came from Saxony would be the ancestors of East Saxons, South Saxons, and West Saxons. And finally, Angles that moved to the island would be the forefathers of East and Middle Angles, Northumbrians, and Mercians.

Naturally, there were other Germanic tribes that raided the island and moved with the aforementioned three, but it's also important to note that Celtic tribes and entire Celtic kingdoms also held some local governance, if very minor. The North of Britain, roughly the area of today's Scotland, remained more or less isolated from any major Anglo-Saxon influence. In addition, as minor Celtic tribes got subjugated by the Anglo-Saxons, a few kingdoms held their own and moved west, eventually settling the territory of modern-day Wales. In terms of people groups, early medieval Britain was very diverse.

The Tribal Hidage

As stated in earlier chapters, a hide was an area of arable land that was enough to sustain a household. At some point in the early 7th century, a document was drawn up listing certain territories and how many hides they owned. The document doesn't have a contemporary title, but because of its contents, modern historians refer to it as the Tribal Hidage. As its name suggests, the Tribal Hidage lists over thirty tribes and how many hides of land they owned. Reading the document gives us a good glimpse of the ethnic and racial makeup of Britain at the time.

It should be noted, however, that the earliest examples of the Tribal Hidage we have come from the 11th century, at least four centuries after the original was written and lost to history. This is important because even with an earlier manuscript we can't be sure of how accurate it is. The more time there is between the original and the copy, which was made by hand and most certainly written by priests, the higher the chances are of it listing incorrect or incomplete, if not even biased, data.

Each tribe listed in the Tribal Hidage has a corresponding number of hides, which we will not reproduce here. We will, however, look at the tribal names and try to piece together who was who in early medieval Britain. The names are as follows:

1. Myrcna Landes

2. Wocensætna

3. Westerna

4. Pecsætna

5. Elmedsætna

6. Lindesfarona mid Hæthfeldlande (two territories counted as one)

7. Suth Gyrwa

8. North Gyrwa

9. East Wixna

10. West Wixna

11. Spalda

12. Wigesta

13. Herefinna

14. Sweordora

15. Gifla

16. Hicca

17. Withgara

18. Noxgaga

19. Ohtgaga

20. Hwinca

21. Cilternsætna

22. Hendrica

23. Unecung(a)ga

24. Arosaetna

25. Færpinga

26. Bilmiga

27. Widerigga

28. East Willa

29. West Willa

30. East Engle

31. East Sexena

32. Cantwarena

33. Suth Sexena

34. West Sexena

That is quite a few tribes, and among these are a few names we recognize. Immediately we can spot Mercia at the top, then East Angles, East and West Saxons, Kent (Cantwarena), and the Isle of Wight (Withgara). Other tribes are also recognizable to us from Bede's work, though we don't know much about them other than the fact that they had kings and some form of independence. Elmet, Hwicce, Lindsey, and Magonsaete (listed here under different names) all had royal houses that clashed with the other known Anglo-Saxons at the time, but some of these tribes like the Noxgaga and the Othgaga still elude historians. Even places like Suth Gyrwa only bring about speculation as we have no concrete evidence of similarly named Anglo-Saxon tribes in any other texts. Modern cartographers have compiled maps of probable locations of some of these tribes, and judging by them, we can safely say that the Anglo-Saxon tribes first occupied the eastern and southern areas of Britain.

Of course, this list is nowhere near extensive. There were more than likely other minor tribes settling close to these early Anglo-Saxon territories that are lost to time. More than likely they were either eradicated through war or simply assimilated with the dominant cultures of the emerging kingdoms. Some of these kingdoms might have been based on the old Roman units known as *civitates*, and kingdoms such as Kent, Lindsey, Deira, and Bernicia actually derive their names from the Latin terms for these territories.

The purpose of the Hidage itself isn't known to us. Considering the timing and the position of Mercia at the very beginning, it was likely issued by King Wulfhere of Mercia. At the time, he had control over several southern kingdoms, so a list like this would have been a handy tool to know how to tax them or have a good land overview in case of disputes. This text contains, bizarrely, a figure of 100,000 hides for Wessex. It is more than double the amount Mercia itself had, 30,000. This can indicate that later authors changed the numbers based on current states of the country. Namely, Wessex was expanding rapidly in the 11th century when our earliest copy of the Hidage was supposedly drafted. This huge number would go hand-in-hand with the kingdom's contemporary growth.

Bretwalda

Bretwalda is a term that usually translates to "ruler of Britain." It was used both by the Venerable Bede and the *Anglo-Saxon Chronicle* to distinguish rulers who held dominance over most of the island during the early days of Anglo-Saxon kings. This term might not have been used by contemporary Anglo-Saxon chroniclers, bishops, or members of the nobility, and it could have easily been a 9th-century name.

Bede lists seven kings that could be called a bretwalda of their time. Chronologically, they were Ælle of Sussex, Ceawlin of Wessex, Æthelberht of Kent, Rædwald of East Anglia, Edwin of Deira, Oswald of Northumbria, and Oswiu of Northumbria. The *Anglo-Saxon Chronicle* also adds one more ruler to the list, Egbert of Wessex, with Alfred of Wessex, also known as Alfred the Great, often being categorized with these rulers.

Neither Bede nor the *Chronicle* mention any Mercian rulers despite the fact that they held the same comparative level of power that the listed bretwalda did. Among these rulers are Penda, Wulfhere, Æthelred, Æthelbald, Offa, and Cœnwulf. The *Chronicle*'s anonymous author clearly had an anti-Mercian bias which would explain their exclusion from the list.

List of Kingdoms

Once again, we go back to George R. R. Martin. His own Aegon the Conqueror wanted a united Westeros, so he began conquering what was known as the Seven Kingdoms (of which he conquered six). Martin very clearly borrowed this number and this chain of events from early Anglo-Saxon history because, during the time of William the Conqueror, the island's politics were heavily reliant on the seven kingdoms that were active at the time. Collectively, their rule is called the Heptarchy, or the Rule of the Seven. There were, of course, minor kingdoms, and some of these minor kingdoms would even grow to create major ones, but we'll get to that shortly.

According to historians, the seven kingdoms of early medieval Britain, also known as petty kingdoms, were as follows: East Anglia, Northumbria, Mercia, Wessex, Sussex, Essex, and Kent. They would each come to dominate one another at certain points in history, but their unification was inevitable, even before William set foot in Britain.

East Anglia

As its name suggests, East Anglia was the kingdom primarily inhabited by the Angles. Its territory took up the modern-day counties of Suffolk and Norfolk, though historians suggest it stretched a bit farther than that.

In terms of the Tribal Hidage, East Anglia covered an area of 30,000 hides of land. They were ruled by the kings from the Wuffingas dynasty. In their early days, the Wuffingas were pagan, but with the coming of King Rædwald, they began the slow process of converting to Christianity.

Of course, East Anglia's history began much earlier than that. Somewhere around 450 CE, the Angles were already settling in the area, occupying the old Roman civitas of Venta Icenorum. As they slowly began to settle, their kings grew in power and slowly began to clash with other local rulers.

One interesting fact to note about East Anglia is that it was probably the first area in Britain where English was spoken, or rather Old English to be precise. This isn't a surprise considering that this area was one of the earliest Anglo-Saxon settlements in sub-Roman Britain. Linguists and scholars have studied place names, coin inscriptions, personal names, and old texts to uncover the linguistic background of the region. They discovered that East Anglian people had their own dialect just like the Mercian, the Kentish, the West Saxons, and the Northumbrians did. However, it's very hard to confirm this with any authority considering that we literally have no written sources from that era that directly come from East Anglia.

We can't emphasize enough how sad it is that no documents, such as wills or charters, survived that were written by the East Angles. Even their direct history, such as the list of kings and battles, come to us from outside sources such as the Venerable Bede and the *Anglo-Saxon Chronicle*. Based on the limited information that we have, we can confirm a few basic facts. The Wuffingas ruled over East Anglia until 749 when their last king died. After that, they either fell to Mercian rule or to the rule of kings whose lineage our history doesn't recognize. By the early 9th century, East Anglia had regained its independence, and not long after they did, the Vikings began their raids. Like a lot of eastern kingdoms, East Anglia was incorporated into the Danelaw, a common name for the parts of England that were under direct Danish or Viking rule, only to be reclaimed by Edward the Elder several decades later. The final decades of East Anglia were filled with political turmoil as ownership of it shifted from Anglo-Saxons to Danes. The last known Danish ruler over the region was Cnut the Great, who appointed Thorkell the Tall to rule as earl of East Anglia in 1017.

Notable East Anglian Kings

The only East Anglian dynasty we have data on were the Wuffingas. They claimed to be the descendants of Wuffa, a semi-mythological king, and their name in Old English means "the children of the wolf." Wuffa might have ruled in the late 6th century if he was a historical king. Most sources mention him as the father of Tytila, the grandfather of Rædwald, and the founder of the dynasty; however, some sources claim that another ruler preceded him, namely his supposed father, Wehha.

Rædwald of East Anglia

Rædwald was, without a doubt, the most famed of all East Anglian kings. He ruled the kingdom from c. 599 to c. 624. He was by no means the only powerful ruler of this time period. Æthelberht of Kent was already in power when Rædwald ascended the throne and had, in fact, married Bertha at least a decade and a half prior. Other kings that were in power at the time were Ceolwulf of Wessex, Æthelfrith of Bernicia, and Pybba, who supposedly founded Mercia in 585.

Rædwald reigned for 25 years. During that time, according to Bede, he was an overlord of several southern kingdoms and the fourth bretwalda. His early years marked him as a pagan king, but when Augustine landed in Kent, he traveled south to the court of King Æthelberht. Once there, Rædwald and another king, Saeberht of Essex, were baptized, and each of their kingdoms received bishoprics. This would make Rædwald the first Anglian king to convert to Christianity. His son, Eorpwald, had also converted, though he did this much later in life. However, once he ascended the throne after Rædwald's death in c. 624, he was usurped and killed by a pagan noble called Ricberht. This same noble might have even ruled over East Anglia for a few years before the Wuffingas reclaimed the throne, with the region falling back to paganism as Kent did after the death of King Æthelberht a decade earlier.

Rædwald effectively became an overlord of the nearby kingdoms after the death of King Æthelberht. We don't know a lot about the details of the early years of his reign. However, possibly the greatest historical event that involved the East Anglian king and that we know of was the deposition of Edwin of Northumbria and the Battle of the River Idle.

Edwin was not really the king of Northumbria. He was actually born in Deira, one of the two kingdoms that would make up the new land called Northumbria. The second kingdom, Bernicia, was ruled by Æthelfrith who wanted to depose and ultimately kill Edwin. He took control of both kingdoms in c. 604. Edwin was exiled and sought refuge in several different kingdoms such as the Celtic Gwynedd, Mercia, and, finally, East Anglia.

Initially, Rædwald received the exiled Edwin and refused to sell him out to Æthelfrith. However, after multiple attempts by the Bernician and Deiran king, Rædwald caved, which, according to written sources, his pagan wife shamed him for. It was supposedly because of this shaming that Rædwald, alongside Rægenhere, his son, and Edwin of Deira, faced Æthelfrith in the Battle of the River Idle in either 616 or 617. The resulting clash was so bloody that it became ingrained in the English collective memory, with the phrase "the river Idle was foul with the blood of Englishmen" still looming today. Rædwald lost his son that day, but he managed to kill the Bernician king and destroy his troops. Edwin was then crowned the king of the new kingdom, Northumbria, while Rædwald became the first king to have significant influence in politics of a separate independent kingdom. The king himself ruled uncontested until 624 when he died, and his son Eorpwald took the throne. Historians argue that the princely burial at Sutton Hoo, with its massive boat and elaborate gifts, was that of Rædwald himself. Some speculate that his son was either buried next to it in a smaller mound, or that he was the one buried in the boat and not his father. However, we don't have any written or archeological evidence to corroborate either option.

Anna of East Anglia

Don't let the name fool you; Anna was very much a man. Sometimes recorded as Onna, this king was the nephew of Rædwald and the son of Eni, making him one of the Wuffingas. He succeeded Ecgric, his relative from the same family, though we don't know exactly what their relationship was; they could have been brothers, cousins, or something else entirely.

Anna was famously praised by Bede for being a good Christian. All of his children, one son and either three or four daughters, were canonized as saints. Thanks to his influence, Cenwalh of Wessex converted as well during his exile in East Anglia.

Anna was also famous for securing political marriages of his daughters. Seaxburh, his oldest daughter, was married to Eorcenberht of Kent, allying the two kingdoms. In 652, he married his second daughter Æthelthryth to Tondberct of South Gyrwe. Anna himself was married to a noblewoman called Sæwara.

During Anna's reign, Penda of Mercia became a powerful monarch. In 651, the Mercian king attacked the monastery of Cnobheresburg, forcing Anna into exile. Two years later, he returned to East Anglia, but soon after, East Anglian and Mercian forces would clash at Bulcamp. Both Anna and his only son Jurmin were killed in the battle, leaving his brother, Æthelhere, as the successor to the throne.

Other Notable Kings of East Anglia

Among the Wuffingas, other notable kings include Sigeberht, Ealdwulf, and Ælfwald. Sigeberht was the first English king to be educated and baptized before he ascended the throne. In addition, he probably didn't rule alone but shared the kingly duties with his cousin Ecgric. After his abdication, Ecgric would continue to rule alone. Ealdwulf was the son of Æthelric and a grandson of Eni, and his reign is known for being uncharacteristically peaceful and prosperous, mainly because Gipeswic (today's Ipswich) was expanding at the time. His death in 713 brought Ælfwald to the throne, and he would rule for 36 years, with his reign being equally peaceful and prosperous. During his time, coin minting expanded and trade with continental Europe bloomed. Since there are no records of a direct heir, and because of conflicting information over who ruled East Anglia after his death, we can safely say that Ælfwald was the last of the Wuffingas to sit on the East Anglian throne.

Kent

Aside from the Isle of Wight, Kent is the only Anglo-Saxon kingdom that we know of which was populated largely by Jutes. It was also the first territory on British soil where Anglo-Saxons converted to Christianity. It's also interesting to note that Kent claimed direct descendancy from the legendary Hengist and Horsa.

Late 6th century Kent had a lot going for it. They were already having marital connections with the Merovingians from Francia. In fact, the Frankish kings probably held dominion over the region as early influences of the kingdom can be seen in Kentish artifacts. Kent even established regular trade, and in the following century, Kentish influence was also present in other European kingdoms and territories, such as Rhineland, Thuringia, Frisia, and Western Normandy.

However, marital relations were key here. They weren't just done out of a sense of love or duty; they were very much a powerful political tool in securing allies and growing one's influence. Æthelberht of Kent, though a pagan, married a Christian woman from the Merovingian dynasty and daughter to Charibert I named Bertha. It was thanks to this couple that Christianity began to spread in England, and it would be the bishops of Æthelberht that gave the Angles their first Christian king in Rædwald of East Anglia.

Sadly, Kent would not retain its glory for long. In the later years of the 7th century, both Northumbria and Mercia grew in power. It would ultimately be Mercian kings that would dominate Kent by the end of the century, though this wouldn't last long. There is evidence that Canterbury, at least, was still a powerful urban center, as both it and Rochester still had mints, producing the silver currency known as *sceattas* (singular: sceat).

As the 9th century rolled by, Wessex held supremacy over the other kingdoms, and Kent was in disarray. The Viking attacks of the next few centuries didn't really help as the raids left the kingdom in ruins. Thorkell the Tall himself led the raid of Canterbury in 1011, decimating the city. By the time William of Normandy came to conquer England, Kent had nowhere near as much power as it did in its early days.

Notable Kings of Kent

Æthelberht of Kent

Possibly the best-known ruler of this kingdom, Æthelberht ascended the throne in c. 589 and ended his reign when he died on February 24th, 616. He was regarded as the third bretwalda according to the *Anglo-Saxon Chronicle* and Bede. During his reign, he was the first pagan Anglo-Saxon king to allow Christianity to be openly practiced within his realm, personally inviting a mission from Rome in 597.

During his early reign, he held overlordship over the East Saxons and successfully converted his nephew, Sæberht of Essex, to Christianity. Similar to Rædwald, who had become the first Anglian Christian king, Sæberht would become the first Saxon Christian king. From his relationship with these two kings, we can ascertain that Kent held at least nominal dominion over Essex and East Anglia. Mercia was probably also under Æthelberht's domain, though this isn't backed by enough archeological or historical evidence.

Æthelberht was known for his efforts to Christianize his people. However, he was also known for his code of law, the oldest such document in any Germanic society of the Middle Ages. These laws covered punishments and compensations for personal slights and were divided by social classes. British historian Patrick Wormald had divided the laws into nine sections. The first section dealt with compensation for the clergy, the second for the king and his direct dependents, the third for earls (ealdormen), the fourth for churls, the fifth for the semi-free men, the sixth for personal injuries, the seventh for women, the eighth for servants, and the ninth for slaves. Usually, they would be compensated with money, such as shillings or the sceattas. One thing we do not know is why this code was written in the first place. One possible reason might be that Æthelberht wanted to "civilize" his people after they had accepted Christianity, the religion of both the Roman Church and their superior Merovingian rulers and next of kin. Issuing this code of law would not only make Æthelberht the first king to "import" Christianity in Britain but also one of its first, if not the first, lawmakers.

It is also speculated by historians that Æthelberht's reign saw the first coins minted in Britain, or rather the first coins that weren't Roman. There is no hard, physical evidence of this, though coins were already in use during the reign of his son and heir Eadbald, and Æthelberht himself does mention shillings in his code of law.

Æthelberht's death in 616 showed just how influential of a monarch he was. His son is said to have refused baptism and, to the Church's shock and condemnation, married his stepmother. Roughly at the same time, the East Saxon king Sæberht, the first Saxon king to receive baptism and next of kin to Eadbald, also died, and his three pagan sons took the throne. Kentish Christian missionaries were expelled from both kingdoms, signifying both a revolt against Christianity and the overlordship of Kent. Æthelberht's hard work seems to have been for nothing, at least at the time.

Wihtred of Kent

Wihtred ascended the throne around 690 CE after a period full of instability and no clear rulers in Kent. Most of the kingdoms were effectively under Mercian overlordship at this time, and Wihtred's predecessor, his father Ecgberht, died back in 673 when both of his sons were barely toddlers.

Until 692, Wihtred ruled jointly with another Kentish co-ruler called Swæfheard, after which he might have ruled alongside his son, Æthelberht II. During his early years as a king, Wihtred made peace

with Ine of Wessex. Ine's predecessor, King Cædwalla, had previously conquered Kent and installed a puppet king named Mul who was burned to death by the Kentish common folk. Ine paid compensation for the deed, while Wihtred probably gave him some land in return.

Wihtred was also a known lawmaker. While the date isn't known for certain, historians suggest that late 695 was the year when Wihtred finalized his code, with Ine of Wessex doing the same a year earlier, suggesting that the two monarchs worked together in their years of peace. The laws themselves deal mostly in ecclesiastical affairs. Of its 28 chapters, only the final four have nothing to do with the Church. Reading through the laws, we can assume that the Church was given a lot of privileges and enjoyed a high position in society. Pagan beliefs were still around, though practicing them resulted in severe penalties, according to Wihtred's laws.

Statue of Æthelberht of Kent, interior of Rochester Cathedral[xxii]

Eadberht III Præn

Not a whole lot is known of this king, but what we do know is that he ruled from 796 to 798 and was the last king of an independent Kent. He came into power directly after the death of Offa of Mercia,

who had controlled Kent directly before he died. Before that, Eadberht was in exile enjoying Charlemagne's protection. His reign wasn't long, as merely two years after his ascension, the Mercian king Cœnwulf sacked Kent and captured him. Depending on the sources, Eadberht was either blinded and had his hands cut off or was released by Cœnwulf as a token of goodwill. Whatever the case might be, Eadberht was the last ruler of Kent that wasn't a puppet king.

Other Notable Kings of Kent

Much of Kent's history after Æthelberht includes kings from other houses, such as Mul. Mul was installed as king by his brother, Cædwalla of Wessex, in 686 after their joint conquest of Kent and the Isle of Wight. But reports state that the very next year, the Kentish rebelled against Mul and burned him as a result. Following Mul, there were several "joint reigns" that included Kings Swæfheard, Oswine, Swæfberht, and Wihtred. Not all of these rulers were from Kent as some had family ties with Wessex and Essex. Finally, we should mention Baldred of Kent. He ruled over the kingdom from 823 to possibly 827, and he's interesting to historians because it's not clear whether he was a puppet king of Mercia or the actual last Kentish-born king to be on the throne.

Essex

Essex is the modern name of the kingdom of the East Saxons. The territory of this small kingdom spanned from East Anglia to Kent and from Mercia to the North Sea. From what we can gather, several tribes existed in this area before they merged into one large kingdom. Those people included the Rodings, the Uppingas, the Haeferingas, the Haemele, the Berecingas, the Ginges, the Denge, and the Vange. Their kingdom came to be in the early 6th century, and like several other pagan Saxon tribes, the kings of future Essex claimed that Woden was their direct ancestor.

Sadly, there aren't a lot of written records or archeological evidence for us to piece together what Essex was like during the time of other Anglo-Saxon kingdoms. We only know that they had been subjugated at multiple points by bigger, more powerful regional kingdoms such as Mercia, East Anglia, or Kent.

Throughout their existence, the East Saxons had strong ties to the kings of Kent. Æthelberht's insistence on converting his nephew Sæberht to Christianity had an instrumental role in this, as the royal families continued supporting each other and intermarrying even during Mercian dominance. At one point in the 8th century, Essex began minting coins, possibly as a way of asserting their independence from other kingdoms. Mercia would eventually take control of Essex, but in the late 9th century, it would become incorporated into the Danelaw. Once Edward the Elder retook the territory from the Danes, the ruler of Essex was styled as an ealdorman rather than a king. From that point until William's conquest, Essex was little more than a shire.

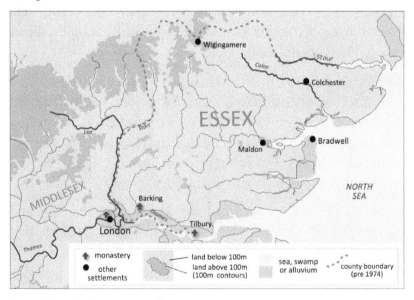

Map of Anglo-Saxon Essex[xxiii]

Notable Kings of Essex

Sæberht of Essex

Sæberht ascended to the throne in c. 604, following his father, Sledd. Within the year, he converted to Christianity at Kent. However, all of his sons remained pagan, which led to problems after his death in c. 616. During the same time, Mellitus, a member of the Gregorian mission to Canterbury, was made the first Bishop of London.

Not much is known about Sæberht's life. He had family ties in Kent, and the two kingdoms remained close even after his passing. Sæberht himself was the son of Sledd, who might have been the founder of the first dynasty of Essex, though we can't know this with certainty. During his time, London and Colchester were part of Essex, and London, in particular, was still a key city within the kingdom, retaining this position from Roman times. Within London, King Æthelberht built the old St Paul's church, possibly on the same spot where the current St Paul's Cathedral is located. This shows that while Sæberht ruled Essex in his own right, his uncle still held dominion over him. After all, London was not in Kent, nor a direct part of it, during Sæberht's reign.

Sæberht's death resulted in events similar to those of his uncle's death in Kent. Mellitus, still the Bishop of London, was exiled from the city by Sæberht's sons. All three sons were pagan, and according to legend, they exiled Mellitus because he refused to allow them to taste sacramental bread. Whatever the case may be, Essex was no longer a safe haven for Christians, at least in the early 7th century.

The Prittlewell site in the county of Essex contains an elaborate and possibly royal Anglo-Saxon tomb. Some archeologists speculate that Sæberht might have been buried here. Others claim that it is actually the resting place of his grandson, Sigeberht the Good, who was also a Christian king.

Sigeberht the Good

Ascending the throne around 653, Sigeberht ruled Essex for seven years until he was murdered by his kinsmen. Unlike his grandfather, the first Christian king of the East Saxons, we know quite a few details of Sigeberht's life.

Unlike his father and his kinsmen before him, Sigeberht converted to Christianity, though he did this at the urging of his friend, King Oswiu of Bernicia. He was baptized at one of Oswiu's estates by Bishop Finan. In his later years, Sigeberht would ask for Oswiu's help in reconverting the East Saxons into Christians. A monk called Cedd led the mission with a few other monks and went to Essex, having previously finished missionary work with the Middle Angles. Later in life, Cedd would become Bishop of Essex. Churches and Christian communities were slowly emerging in Essex again, and the kingdom looked like it was going back to Christianity.

Sadly, Sigeberht's brothers (whom Bede doesn't mention by name when retelling this event) did not agree with his new religion. The king's murder might have had two well-known culprits, however. One would be his cousin Swithhelm, son of Seaxbald, while the other was Swithhelm's brother Swithfrith. Bede portrays this murder as if the kinsmen killed Sigeberht for his beliefs, but there's reason to believe that more complex politics of succession were involved. After the king's death, Swithhelm took the throne and ruled for the next four years.

Other Notable Kings of Essex

Considering how little we know about the kings of Essex, it's interesting to see that two separate rulers are noted as the progenitors of their royal dynasty. The first of these is Æscwine. We know next to nothing of this king other than a few name variants, though his name would suggest some Jutish, probably Kentish influence. His supposed son, Sledd, the father of Sæberht, is also considered by a few scholars to be the rightful founder of the house of Essex. Much like his brother, we know very little about Sledd. He might have married Ricula, the sister of Æthelberht, the king of Kent, and their son would have become the first East Saxon Christian king. However, Sledd also had another son, Seaxa, of whom we only know the name of.

Another king of note is Sigered of Essex. He ascended the throne in 798 and ruled until 825. However, he was both the last king and the last native ruler of Essex. This is explained by the fact that he had only been king until 812. Pressured by his Mercian overlords, he was no longer king but merely a duke. As a duke, he ruled over Essex until 825 when he ceded his kingdom. Essex then went to a different ruler, Ecgberht of Wessex.

Sussex

The South Downs are a range of chalk hills that contain a particularly large, prominent feature, that of Highdown Hill. As a settlement, it was inhabited well before Romans ever set foot there, but it's also an important site to research Anglo-Saxon history. Namely, around 450 CE, it housed a noticeable Anglo-Saxon cemetery which yielded a lot of interesting glass artifacts. This region would become home to the South Saxons, the tribe and later kingdom which we probably know the least about in terms of actual history.

The date brought up here is important because the South Saxons at the time traced their lineage to the landing of their earliest ancestor which, if they were to be believed, occurred more than two decades after the cemetery was in use. Chronologically speaking, that makes no sense, though the story they tell, one of battles and conquest, might have happened in those days, but since it was the time before Anglo-Saxons could read or write, we have nothing to corroborate it.

Sussex is the southernmost kingdom of the Anglo-Saxon Heptarchy. It used to lay well below Kent and had more than likely been a pagan kingdom well into the 7th century. Allied with Mercians against Wessex, the South Saxon kings would maintain their independence, and their king, Æthelwealh, converted to Christianity in 661 CE. He even invited a missionary, Wilfrid of Northumbria, to convert and preach to his subjects from 681 to 686 CE. Despite this alliance, the South Saxons would continue to be harassed by the West Saxons well into the 8th century. Sussex lost its independence to Offa of Mercia, however, around 770, though it seems to have made a bit of a comeback by the end of the century. At long last, at around 825 after the Battle of Ellendun, Wessex claimed Sussex for themselves, and from then onwards, the kingdom was no longer a kingdom but land ruled by dukes and ealdormen. Some of these would play prominent roles in the following centuries, especially during the wars against the Danelaw and the political scene before the Norman conquest.

Sussex was, from archeological evidence, a thriving community both during its heyday and while under foreign rule. Like other kingdoms that surrounded it, Sussex minted its own coins, with variations of these coins found dating back to the 8th century. In addition to minting, Sussex also flourished in trade and agriculture, as well as herding. The town of Lewes, in particular, had a rich history in trading, farming, and herding.

In terms of law, several place names such as Tinhale, Madehurst, and Ditchling suggest that the early South Saxons took part in folkmoots, where groups of free men presided over by the nobles would discuss the items of the day or settle disputes. There was no real governing body, and proper practice of law didn't happen until the Christianization of Sussex in the 7th century. In the 10th century when they were under Wessex rule, several witena gemōts took place in Sussex, most notably the one in 930 and the one during the reign of King Æthelstan, probably held at Hamsey.

Notable Kings of Sussex

Æthelwealh of Sussex

Æthelwealh lived during the time of Wulfhere of Mercia and is the first Sussex king whose existence history can confirm. We don't know when he was born, but we know he probably took the throne c. 660 CE. Before he did that, however, he traveled to Mercia to meet Wulfhere since the earlier years of this century saw the two kingdoms join a political union of sorts. While in Mercia, Æthelwealh was baptized with Wulfhere presiding as a sponsor. This act made Æthelwealh the first Christian South Saxon king. However, the rest of Sussex wouldn't be baptized until roughly two decades later. One more detail regarding Wulfhere and Æthelwealh that we know of is the Mercian king's gift of the Isle of Wight to the South Saxon king in 661, which had previously been either independent or under Kentish control.

In 681, stricken by famine, the Saxon people were visited by St. Wilfrid of Northumbria. He was there on a mission to convert them, and evidently, he did a good job of it, teaching the hungry Saxons how to fish so they wouldn't go hungry. While this story is apocryphal at best, we do know that Æthelwealh gave Wilfrid 87 hides as a gift for his efforts, and Wilfrid, with the royal vill, comparable to a manor or parish, Æthelwealh also gave him, founded the Selsey Abbey which would remain the center of the Sussex bishopric until William the Conqueror came and claimed Sussex.

Wilfrid, however, wasn't too loyal to the South Saxon king. When he met with Cædwalla of Wessex sometime after the baptism of the South Saxons, the two reached an agreement to further their own interests by working together against Æthelwealh. Both the priest and the prince were exiles from their kingdoms, though Cædwalla would later become the king of Wessex for three years. During Æthelwealh's reign, Cædwalla was in charge of a tribe called Gewisse. In 685, he killed Æthelwealh and took the throne of Sussex by force. Unfortunately for him, he didn't keep it long, as two of Æthelwealh's ealdormen named Berhthun and Andhun chased him out. During that same year, Cædwalla would come to rule Wessex.

Æthelwealh wasn't nearly as well documented as other contemporary kings. He was nevertheless an instrumental ruler in bringing Christianity to the South Saxons of Britain. He was also one of the earliest rulers to recognize how powerful of an ally Mercia could be, as his alliance with Wulfhere proved to be a fruitful one. We also know that he had at least some form of an alliance with a minor kingdom called Hwicce, considering he took Eafe, the daughter of King Eanfrith, as his queen. We don't know if the marriage produced any heirs though.

Other Notable Kings of Sussex

No list of Sussex kings would be complete without mentioning the supposed progenitor of their noble line. According to legend, Ælle of Sussex first landed on the shores of Britain in 477. After he and his three sons—Cymen, Wlencing, and Cissa—came to the island, they began slaughtering some of the local Britons. The year 485 would also supposedly see Ælle's victory over the local Celtic people at a place called Mearcred's Burn. Then, in 491, he besieged a place called Andredes cester with his son Cissa and, yet again, committed genocide of the Celts. Though a pagan, Ælle was celebrated as one of the greatest South Saxon kings to have lived.

Of course, Ælle's timeline of events doesn't match up with the archeological findings at Highdown Hill. In fact, it's even difficult to trace whether he actually existed at all. Nevertheless, Bede and the *Anglo-Saxon Chronicle* both mention him as the first bretwalda to rule over the Anglo-Saxon tribes of his area.

Northumbria

Its name is a dead giveaway when it comes to its geographical position. Northumbria was the northernmost kingdom of the Anglo-Saxons, though it didn't initially start out as a single kingdom. During the Christianization of the Anglo-Saxons, its territory was home to two smaller but equally influential kingdoms, those of Deira and Bernicia. Their common name after unification, Northumbria, comes from them being north of the Humber estuary on the east coast of Britain. It's possible that Bede was the first to actually coin the term and that the kings of united Northumbria merely styled themselves "king of Bernicia and Deira."

Of the two, Deira was closer to the Humber, bordering Bernicia at the river Tees. To the west, Deira bordered the edge of the Vale of York, and of course, York itself was the capital. Bernicia extended from Tees to the river Forth. Its own capital was the city of Bamburgh, which would become the only remaining independent earldom of the region in the 9th century before it was ultimately absorbed by England and Scotland years later.

It's difficult to keep track of all the kings that ruled Northumbria mainly because the dynasties of the two kingdoms constantly shifted. A member of Bernicia's royal line would take the throne of Deira only to be replaced a generation later by a ruler from Deira, who in turn would take Bernicia's throne as well. Nevertheless, the kingdom gave Britain no less than three kings that would be named bretwalda by Bede and the *Anglo-Saxon Chronicle*.

It's important to note that we have more information about Northumbria than on all the other kingdoms. Bede himself was Northumbrian, so it's safe to say that he had a clear bias in choosing which kingdoms he wanted to discuss in more detail. For example, he talks very little about Mercians and West Saxons because those two held the same level of power that Northumbria once had. It would also explain why he didn't include any Mercians and only one West Saxon king when he talked about the bretwalda of the island. Nevertheless, his insight gives us plenty of information on how this northernmost kingdom grew, expanded, and interacted with others.

Notable Northumbrian Kings

Before we move on with this section, it's important to note that not all of these kings styled themselves as unified rulers. Sometimes a ruler would only reign over Deira or Bernicia, then get deposed by a different ruler, and later become reinstated to the throne with a different title. For the sake of simplicity, we will treat these rulers as kings of Northumbria rather than rulers of either Bernicia, Deira, or both kingdoms with both names intact within the titles.

Æthelfrith of Bernicia

Æthelfrith was in power during the early 7ᵗʰ century. Before he became the ruler of Bernicia, he was already known for his military successes against the Celtic Britons. The Bernician king kept pushing the Britons farther west, securing more and more land for himself. In circa 604, he exiled Edwin and took the throne of Deira. While not officially uniting the two kingdoms, he was their ruler until the day he died, a little over a decade later.

Other notable events of Æthelfrith's life include the famous Battle of Chester against the Kingdom of Powys and his slaughtering of monks at Bangor-Is-Coed. Both events happened somewhere between 613 and 616 CE. During the Battle of Chester, Æthelfrith's forces crushed several Celtic kings, as well as kings of other Anglo-Saxon countries such as Mercians. The king of Powys was killed in battle, as was another king whose name we know but cannot recognize historically.

It was the slaughter of monks that left a particular impression on Bede when he wrote about Æthelfrith of Bernicia. According to him, the monks of Bangor-Is-Coed did nothing but pray when Æthelfrith's forces arrived. He saw this as impudence, so he had over a thousand monks killed. Some fifty or so managed to escape. Whatever his reasoning behind this act was, both the slaughter of monks and the Battle of Chester managed to separate the Celtic people from the north from those in the southwest.

Æthelfrith's reign wouldn't last long after these events. Edwin, with the help of Rædwald, hid in East Anglia after moving from one kingdom to the next during his exile. Apparently, Rædwald was offered compensation several times by Æthelfrith to give up Edwin, and though the king of East Anglia eventually agreed, his queen shamed him into taking up arms instead. Æthelfrith died at the Battle of the River Idle, leaving the throne of Deira and Bernicia vacant for Edwin to claim.

Edwin

Edwin was the son of Ælle, the first historically known king of Deira. Shortly after his father's death, however, a different ruler, Æthelfrith, took the throne. While in exile, Edwin married for the first time to a woman called Cwenburg, the daughter of the Mercian king Ceorl. With the help of the East Anglian king Rædwald, Edwin deposed Æthelfrith and took control of both his native Deira and Bernicia. This was irregular because most of the kings that ruled over both kingdoms were from the Bernician ruling house.

Edwin slowly expanded his territory and made important changes. His second marriage was to Æthelburg, the sister of the ruler of Kent, Eadbald, a dear friend of Edwin's. Since Kent had been undergoing massive conversions to Christianity, it was only a matter of time before the new religion began sprouting roots in Northumbria. Edwin himself was baptized in 627 CE.

In terms of expansion, Edwin took hold of eastern Mercia, the Isle of Man, and Anglesey. While he wasn't a particularly decisive king during the life of Rædwald, he more than earned the title of bretwalda in his later years. In 629, he supposedly defeated Cadwallon ap Cadfan, the king of Gwynedd and his possible foster brother. For nearly half a decade, nobody would challenge Edwin until the Battle of Hatfield Chase in 633. Cadwallon and Penda of Mercia defeated and killed the Northumbrian king. According to some written accounts, his body was first hidden in Edwinstowe, an event the place got its name from. His head was later taken to York and buried, while the rest of his body was buried at Whitby. Edwin was venerated as a saint, with his cult slowly but firmly developing in Northumbria at the time.

After Edwin's death, his successors reverted to paganism, and there was massive infighting. Cadwallon was still a threat, but a different Northumbrian ruler was going to put an end to him very soon.

Portrait of St. Edwin of Northumbria, St. Mary, Siedmere, Yorkshire[xxiv]

Oswald

Oswald was a Bernician prince and the son of Æthelfrith. When his father was killed and Edwin came to power, Oswald was in exile, traveling different kingdoms and learning Irish in the meantime. Once he came back to Bernicia, he battled King Cadwallon at Heavenfield and destroyed his army, despite having fewer soldiers on his side. Cadwallon had previously also killed Oswald's brother, Eanfrith, who ruled Bernicia for a very short period of time. Oswald's victory brought him honor and recognition, so his next step was very clear.

Shortly after his victory over the combined forces of Gwynedd and Mercia, Oswald was crowned king of Bernicia and Deira, the first king after Edwin to do so and the second Bernician king to hold the throne. He was later known as a bretwalda himself, possibly taking control of the kingdom of Lindsey and the people of Goddodin.

Christianity also played a big part during Oswald's reign. After his kingdom had relapsed into paganism, he decisively began to take active steps to reinstall the faith in Christ. With the assistance of an Irish priest named Aidan, the conversion took place sometime before 635 when Aidan became a bishop. Oswald himself would be venerated as a priest after his death, with his cult growing so strong that it overshadowed that of Edwin, his Deiran predecessor.

Oswald would ultimately die during the Battle of Maserfield. His army lost to Penda of Mercia, and Oswald was killed and cut up into pieces with his limbs mounted on spikes. This happened in 641 or 642, and the consequences of this battle were the fortification of Penda's power in the south and political turmoil in Northumbria.

Oswiu

Oswiu was Oswald's brother who took the Bernician throne because the rightful heir, Oswald's son Œthelwald, was underage. During his early years, he married the Deiran princess Eanflæd, though she would be merely his first wife. Sadly, this marital union did not help him maintain any control over Deira, which at the time was ruled by a different king, Oswine.

Around 651, Oswiu and Oswine were set to engage in battle, but according to Bede, Oswine sent his troops home and was later betrayed and murdered by one of his own in Oswiu's name. As compensation for his death, Oswiu went to Gilling and established an abbey there where people could say prayers for both kings. Œthelwald, the son of Oswald and potential rightful heir of the Bernician throne, was given the rule of Deira instead.

Another ruler that Oswiu managed to dispose of was Penda of Mercia. Penda's influence grew stronger during this period, and he was effectively the bretwalda, even though the written sources omit all Mercians who fit the title. The rivalry between Oswiu and Penda escalated at the Battle of the Winwaed in 655. Penda lost the battle and was killed. Considering he was a pagan king, Oswiu's victory effectively ended paganism in Anglo-Saxon England.

Oswiu would become a powerful bretwalda in his own right. His influence was felt in Mercia, Kent, and possibly even parts of Wales. Mercian King Wulfhere eventually rose up against Oswiu, but Oswiu must have been too powerful to beat through sheer force, so they settled their grievances with diplomacy. This event occurred sometime between 657 and 659.

The Northumbrian king remained a powerful figure until his death in 670. His son Ecgfrith was his successor in Bernicia, while Deira was ruled by his other son Ælfwine.

Other Notable Kings of Northumbria

Ælla and Ida were the first known rulers of Deira and Bernicia, respectively. The descendants of Ælla even claimed that he traced his ancestry all the way back to Woden. Two more notable kings that would come to rule Deira were Osric and his son, Oswine. Osric and another ruler, Eanfrith of Bernicia, were deemed to be the worst rulers of that time in Northumbria, as they reverted back to paganism and barely kept their two kingdoms together. Osric was killed by Cadwallon at some point, after which his son Oswine became king. He ruled until 651 when his friend Earl Humwald betrayed him by delivering him to Oswiu's soldiers who executed him, helping Oswiu take a firmer hold of Deira.

Mercia

Perhaps unfairly treated by writers of contemporary sources, Mercia was one of the greatest powers in Anglo-Saxon Britain, producing several monarchs that controlled the majority of today's territory of England. They waged wars often and were the last kingdom to retain paganism until their king, Penda, was killed in 655.

During their peak, Mercians held control over several important territories, some of which included former minor kingdoms. These were North and South Mercia, the so-called "outer Mercia," Lindsey, land of the Middle Angles, Hwicce, lands of the Wreocansæte, lands of the Pecsæte, the land between Ribble and Mersey, and the land of the Middle Saxons. In addition, their kings could instate puppet rulers in other larger kingdoms, asserting their dominance over them.

The Mercians would remain a powerful regional force until the rise of the West Saxons in the early 9th century. While they would remain independent during the Viking invasion, they would eventually lose their independence to Edward the Elder by the early 10th century. There were a few attempts at reinstating independence, but nothing substantial came of it. By the end of the pre-Norman period, Mercia had already been reduced to a province.

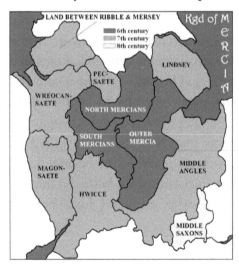

Map of Mercia at the height of its power[xxv]

Notable Kings of Mercia

Penda

Penda ascended the Mercian throne probably around 626 CE. As a ruler, he was famous for his many successful campaigns against other local kings. In fact, his battles effectively ended the reigns of a few key kings from the region.

Penda's first victory came against the West Saxons when he crushed their kings Cynegils and Cwichelm at the Battle of Cirencester in 628. As a result of his victory, the West Saxon kings ceded this territory to him, which would later become part of the kingdom of Hwicce. His next major battle was the Battle of Hatfield Chase in 633, where he, together with Cadwallon, defeated Edwin of Northumbria. The alliance between Cadwallon and Penda was so fruitful that they continued with their successful campaigns well after the death of Edwin.

Oswald, the next king of Northumbria, also fell to Penda during the famous Battle of Maserfield. At this point, Penda had been ruling Mercia for at least fifteen years and had been an accomplished warlord. This is an important fact to take into consideration since Penda was still a pagan king, and Christian nations of Britain were crumbling before him left and right. In fact, it's probably safe to say that Penda would have been the last major pagan king who remained pagan until he died.

After Oswald's death, Oswiu took control of Bernicia and tried to assert himself in Deira. During this time, Penda and him had a somewhat decent relationship, and Penda even married one of his daughters to Oswiu's son Alhfrith. In addition, one of Oswiu's daughters also married one of Penda's sons, his heir apparent, Peada. However, Peada had to convert to Christianity for this marriage to happen. Despite being pagan himself, Penda apparently tolerated Christians, even going so far as to condemn those who declared themselves Christian but didn't follow the tenets of their belief.

However, none of this would stop Penda from eventually invading Oswiu's kingdom in 655. While Oswiu initially bought peace with gold, Penda still wanted to crush him. However, a combination of opportunity, military desertion of Mercian soldiers, and luck would see Oswiu attack Penda in the minor Battle of the Winwaed that same year. Penda's army was far larger, but Oswiu struck when it was most vulnerable. Penda was killed, and as a consequence, his son Peada was installed as a puppet king serving directly under Oswiu. The Northumbrian king would rule the Mercians for about three years before a new king would take the throne and establish himself as the new powerhouse of Mercia.

Wulfhere

Shortly after he was installed as a puppet king, Peada of Mercia was killed, giving Oswiu direct dominion of Mercia. However, in 658, three men named Immin, Eafa, and Eadbert rebelled against the Northumbrian king and elevated the other son of Penda as king. That son would be known as the first Christian king of Mercia, and his name was Wulfhere.

It didn't take long for Wulfhere to begin his own conquest of the southern kingdoms. He initially made an alliance with Æthelwealh of Sussex, helping him convert to Christianity. The year 661 would see Wulfhere gifting the South Saxons the Isle of Wight, which he had previously razed.

During this same year, Wulfhere attacked the West Saxons. By the 670s, he had effectively become the overlord of the region, and the Mercians would retain this power until King Cædwalla got on the counteroffensive. We also know that Wulfhere had a powerful influence in Kent, Lindsey, Surrey, Essex, and East Anglia.

But Wulfhere lost some key battles in his later years. Ecgfrith of Northumbria, for example, managed to defeat the Mercian king in 674, despite having a smaller army. Wulfhere survived the battle, however, though he lost a significant portion of territory and was forced to pay tribute to Ecgfrith. In a different battle, he faced the king of Wessex Æscwine, a mere year after losing to the Northumbrians. The result of this battle isn't known to us, but we know that Wulfhere survived it. Ultimately, the Mercian king died later that same year, probably from a disease. His brother Æthelred took the throne and even reclaimed some of the territories Wulfhere had lost, but he was nowhere near as skilled of a ruler as his predecessor.

Offa

The history of Mercia would not feel complete without Offa. Ascending to the throne in 757, this ruler was by far the most powerful Mercian king to have ever lived, and when we compare his power and influence to other Anglo-Saxon kings, he was only outshined by Alfred the Great.

During his reign, Offa would come to dominate Kent, Essex, Wessex, and East Anglia. His overlordship of Wessex came to pass in 779 after the Battle of Bensington where he defeated the West Saxon king Cynewulf. In terms of Kent, he even reduced the influence of Canterbury by establishing an archdiocese in Lichfield in 787. The only kingdom he could not influence directly was Northumbria, though the two kingdoms did arrange a few political marriages.

Offa also battled the local Britons. In fact, the Welsh kingdom of Powys had so many clashes with the Mercians that Offa ordered the construction of a massive dyke whose remains still stand today. Offa's Dyke was 65 ft. wide and 8 ft. high, and it was built in a way to both prevent the Britons from invading and to give the military a good overview of the area.

Several indicators show us how powerful Offa really was. For instance, coins were minted with his face and name during the period of his reign. In addition, a few documents even list him as *Rex Anglorum*, or the King of the English, though their historicity is not entirely certain. He even remained in frequent contact with King Charlemagne, though the monarch would turn his attention to other matters in later years.

Offa died in 796, and as he had desired, his son Ecgfrith succeeded him on the throne, though he presumably died 141 days after his ascension. Considering how frequently Offa would eliminate his dynastic rivals and how badly he wanted Ecgfrith to rule, this created a succession problem which led to a distant relative of Offa's, Cœnwulf, taking the throne.

Other Notable Kings of Mercia

Of the other Mercian kings, the most notable ones that left their mark on history are Æthelred, Æthelbald, and Cœnwulf. Æthelred had inherited the throne from Wulfhere, and as stated, he couldn't maintain a lot of influence on other kingdoms as his predecessor did. He was known as a very devout Christian, but more interestingly, he was also one of the first Mercian kings to abdicate the throne and become a priest. In 697, his queen and wife, Osthryth, the daughter of the Northumbrian king Oswiu, died under mysterious circumstances. Seven years later, Æthelred abdicated the throne and took up monastic vows in Bardney, a monastery that he had founded with Osthryth. This monastery also contains his remains.

Æthelbald ascended the Mercian throne in 716 and began his own series of conquests. Soon enough, he became the dominant force, with only Northumbria being out of his reach. During his reign, the main Anglo-Saxon missionary in Germany, Boniface, reprimanded Æthelbald for his many sins regarding his treatment of the Church. Possibly as a response to this, Æthelbald issued a charter at the synod of Gumley in 749 giving more rights and privileges to the Church. He died in 757 with the popular belief being that the murderers of this Mercian king were his own bodyguards.

Cœnwulf ruled Mercia after the death of Offa's son. He was known to have reestablished Mercian overlordship in several kingdoms, as evidenced by coins with his face minted there. He was also known for his apparent clash with Wulfred, the Archbishop of Canterbury. Apparently, the archbishop and the king disagreed on the matter of laypeople controlling churches and monasteries. This could have possibly resulted in Wulfred losing the right to perform his priestly duties for at least four years. When Cœnwulf died in 821, the overlordship of Mercia ended, and there would be no other ruler from this kingdom to exercise such power ever again.

Wessex

Out of all the kingdoms, the one ruled by the West Saxons held out the longest. At first, the West Saxons didn't take up a lot of territory in Britain, being situated between Sussex to the east and the kingdom of Dumnonia to the west. Their story begins, according to legend, when Kings Cerdic and Cynric landed in 495 on British soil. By the late 6th century, Wessex was already an established kingdom, and it was very active in political affairs. The second king to be named bretwalda by Bede and the *Anglo-Saxon Chronicle* was Ceawlin of Wessex who probably ruled between 560 and 592, though we know precious little about him.

During the rise of both Mercia and Northumbria as local political powerhouses, Wessex remained a semi-independent kingdom, at one time falling under direct Mercian control. However, after Cædwalla's ascension to the throne, Wessex grew in strength and size, slowly becoming an important political player on the island. It was the house of Wessex that would later be the dominant force in Britain by uniting the kingdoms, fending off the Danes, and founding the first English dynasty of kings. This dynasty would be deposed and reinstated several times, with the Danish kings controlling the isle at a few points during this period. Without a doubt, Wessex would rise to be the most important of the seven kingdoms, having been the progenitors of the idea of a unified Britain long before William conquered the island.

Notable Kings of Wessex

Cædwalla

Cædwalla's name is likely Celtic in origin, but his actions very much impacted the Anglo-Saxons around him. After years in exile, Cædwalla attacked Sussex with a small army and killed their king, Æthelwealh, with possible help from Bishop Wilfrid. However, he was driven out of Sussex by the late king's ealdormen. This didn't stop the West Saxon king from attempting to conquer other kingdoms, though. Soon after that, either in 685 or 686, he became king of Wessex. With his newfound power, he conquered the Isle of Wight and, if some sources are to be believed, killed the local Jutish population, which would make this the first proper genocide in the history of Britain. Not long after his campaign in Wight, Cædwalla went after Kent, deposing their ruler and installing Mul as king. However, Mul was burned by the Kentish soon after, so Cædwalla more than likely ruled this kingdom directly afterward.

Cædwalla himself wasn't Christian at the time, but he was on the fast track to becoming one. While on Wight, he demanded the locals convert, and their refusal to do so might have been the catalyst for their extermination at the hands of the West Saxon king. It was during this battle that Cædwalla sustained serious injuries. As a consequence of this, he abdicated the throne in 688 in favor of his successor and distant cousin Ine. After abdicating, Cædwalla went to Rome to get himself baptized. He reached it a year later, and ten days after his baptism took place, he died a proper Christian.

Ine

Ine ascended the throne of Wessex in 688 after Cædwalla's abdication. During his reign, he made peace with Kent, continued the subjugation of the South Saxons, and held control over Surrey and Essex. He was also known to have led campaigns against the Celtic kingdom of Dumnonia and even had clashes with the Mercians, though we do not know the results of these battles.

Ine's reign saw the economic rise and expansion of the settlement named Hamwic, which would later become part of today's Southampton. Trade was frequent in this town, and people would exchange glass vessels and animal hides. There were even imported goods and foreign currency from mainland Europe found in this town. From what we can ascertain, the town housed over 5,000 people, which was a massive number for a settlement at the time. Ine was also the first West Saxon ruler to issue coin minting, though this can't be proven with archeological evidence since the sceattas usually didn't bear names or faces of contemporary kings.

Like Cædwalla, Ine also abdicated the throne, and he did so in 726, leaving no clear heir to the throne. With his wife, Queen Æthelburg, he again mirrored the previous king by traveling to Rome. However, unlike Cædwalla, Ine had already been converted during his reign. It is possible, however, that he founded the *Schola Saxonum*, an institution for West Saxon pilgrims, in Italy, which later English Christians would visit for various religious reasons.

Ine was not only a skilled warrior and a devout Christian, but he was also a lawmaker, as evidence suggests he might have drafted his own code of law at the same time as Wihtred of Kent, though Ine made his code public in 694.

Ecgberht

Ecgberht, another king to start his life in exile, would forever be remembered as the king who annihilated Mercian supremacy over the other kingdoms. He became king of Wessex in 802 and maintained independence from Mercia. In his early years, his ealdormen had to face the forces of Mercia-dominated Hwicce, which ended in the deaths of the ealdormen on both sides but a victory for Wessex nonetheless. The king of Mercia at the time was Offa's successor, Cœnwulf. From what we know, he didn't rule over Wessex, and Ecgberht maintained his independence, though he didn't have a lot of outside influence at first.

Ecgberht's military efforts earned him his first success in Dumnonia. Later, in 825, the West Saxon king would face off against Beornwulf of Mercia at the decisive Battle of Ellandun. Immediately after the battle, according to the *Anglo-Saxon Chronicle*, Ecgberht's son, Æthelwulf, managed to subjugate Kent, Sussex, Essex, and Surrey. Beornwulf likely attacked the West Saxon forces first, but with the combined efforts of several Anglo-Saxon armies, he was defeated completely, though he didn't perish. However, he was more or less emasculated by the loss, and he tried to invade East Anglia the next year only to end up slain. His successor, Ludeca, was also slain by the East Angles in 827, and by 829, Ecgberht had invaded Mercia and driven their king into exile. At this point, Ecgberht effectively held power over nearly all of the Anglo-Saxon kingdoms, excluding Northumbria. However, the Mercians regained their independence under Wiglaf the next year, though they didn't have nearly as much influence as before.

Ecgberht continued fighting, losing a battle against the Danes in 836 at Carthampton but beating them and their Dumnonian allies two years later at the Battle of Hingston Down. This effectively ended the independence of Cornish Britons, a people group native to the South West Peninsula of Britain, though their royal line continued to exist sometime after this.

Ecgberht died in 839 and was buried in Winchester, as would his descendants years later. According to his will, he left his kingdom and his estates to the male members of his family.

Alfred the Great

Alfred was possibly the greatest ruler of Wessex and really all of the Anglo-Saxon kingdoms before the Norman invasion. He ascended the throne in 871 as the king of the West Saxons, but in 886, he would come to be styled as the king of the Anglo-Saxons. During his reign, the Danes became an increasing threat, and during the first seven years of his reign, Alfred was not doing very well against them. The Danes kept pressing onward, forcing Alfred to negotiate peace and pay them off on more than a few occasions. At one point, the Danes, led by Guthrum, attacked Chippenham in 878, forcing Alfred to flee. After this, most of the Anglo-Saxon kingdoms were now under Danish rule.

However, Alfred would not take this lying down. Later that year, he would rally his forces and crush Guthrum's defenses at the Battle of Edington. He would then push the Danes all the way to Chippenham and starved them until they caved. Once Guthrum surrendered, the two rulers negotiated peace terms. The Danish king had to convert to Christianity, which he did alongside 29 trusted chieftains. Moreover, Mercia was divided between the two kings, and Guthrum was to retain only sections of East Anglia, with this new kingdom of his being called the Danelaw. Alfred hadn't liberated all of the Anglo-Saxon kingdoms, but he had managed to sufficiently hurt the Danes and reduce their influence.

Though the Danes had been beaten, some Viking raids were still taking place during Alfred's reign. However, no large-scale warfare took place for some time. In 886, Alfred retook London and made it into a habitable town again. It's this year, and possibly even the result of this event, that saw the king of Wessex declared king of all Anglo-Saxons, though Alfred himself never used that title.

After the death of Guthrum, the lack of a clear successor threatened another war with the Danes, and after 892, they began to strike again. However, after a series of battles such as those at Farnham, Benfleet, and Buttington, the Danes more or less retreated either to Danelaw or to continental Europe.

Alfred was known as a lot more than just a skilled warrior. He was probably the most literate king to have ever ruled Wessex, having translated a number of important works. He also placed great emphasis on vernacular English language rather than on Latin. Moreover, he founded a court school where he wanted to see his children, other nobles, and even intelligent low-born children learn how to read and write. Naturally, he was extremely interested in religion and had maintained good relations with Rome, even receiving a piece of the "true cross" from Pope Marinus in 883, though there's not a lot of agreement about this event among the scholars.

Alfred would die in October 899 and would be succeeded by his son Edward the Elder. Like his father before him, Edward would be a great king, venerated by the Church and loved by the Anglo-Saxon people. His title would also be the king of Anglo-Saxons, but it wouldn't be him that would unite the island.

Commemorative statue of Alfred the Great, Winchester [xxvi]

Æthelstan

In 924, after Edward's death, Æthelstan took the Anglo-Saxon throne. However, he wasn't the heir to the throne; his younger brother Ælfweard had ruled for a little over two weeks, dying soon after. Æthelstan would first act only as a Mercian king, considering most nobles saw him as unfit and illegitimate to succeed to the throne. However, he was crowned king anyway in 925 at the place called Kingston upon Thames.

Æthelstan's early years saw him fighting the Danes. After a strategic marriage of his sister to Sihtric, the Viking king, and his subsequent death, Æthelstan saw the opportunity to attack the Danes. He captured York in 927, beating Sihtric's successor, Guthfrith. A year later, several northern kings accepted Æthelstan as their overlord. At long last, the Anglo-Saxon lands north of Humber were part of the greater English territory, though Æthelstan would not be well liked by his new northern subjects since he was a southern invader. Æthelstan's next successful campaign took him south where he fully subjugated the Cornish and established a new episcopal see, the area of a bishop's ecclesiastical jurisdiction. The year 927 would be one of great victories for Æthelstan, and it would also see him don a new title, that of King of the English.

But it wasn't any of these events that cemented the former Anglo-Saxon king as one of the greatest of his time. It was the event that took place a decade later that would not only give Æthelstan more well-earned recognition, but it would also be the cornerstone of English nationalism. Namely, in 934, the king of the Anglo-Saxons decided to invade Scotland for unspecified reasons. The results of the ensuing battles weren't recorded, but the Scots didn't sit still. Soon after, in 937, an alliance of three kings, Olaf Guthfrithson of Dublin, Constantine II of Alba, today's Scotland, and Owen of Strathclyde, faced Æthelstan in the Battle of Brunanburh. Despite suffering great losses, Æthelstan crushed his opponents, with some of them fleeing and their armies scattering. At that point, England fought as a single entity against a disunited foe and won.

Two years later, Æthelstan died in Gloucester. Aside from his military victories, he is also remembered as a learned man who invested a lot of time and money in the church and education, just like his father and grandfather before him. After his death, the control of the land would shift between his heirs and the Danes, though neither of the two dynasties would end up the victor after the events of the Battle of Hastings in 1066.

Other Notable Kings of Wessex

The Wessex line continued well after Æthelstan, but in terms of kings before the title King of the English existed, the two that absolutely should be mentioned are Cynewulf and Edward the Elder.

Cynewulf followed his predecessor Sigeberht and took the throne in 757. With the death of the Mercian king Æthelbald, he took the opportunity of the political turmoil in that kingdom and asserted Wessex's independence. A series of wars would grant him victories over the Mercians and the Welsh, cementing the status of Wessex at the time. While he might have been defeated by Offa of Mercia at the Battle of Bensington, he never really became his subject, remaining an independent king. Cynewulf's reign ended with him being killed by Sigeberht's brother, Cyneheard the Ætheling, in front of Cynewulf's own ealdormen and thegns, though this story might be apocryphal.

The story of Edward the Elder, on the other hand, is the story of a capable king inheriting the throne of his equally capable father, Alfred. In 917 and early 918, Edward conquered the south of Danelaw and made it a part of his unified Anglo-Saxon kingdom. Of course, the Danish wouldn't cease their activities after these defeats and would continue to play key political roles in the years to come, even after Edward's successors followed on the English throne. Edward himself died in Farndon in 924, after successfully squashing the rebellions of the Mercians and the Welsh.

Chapter 6 – Anglo-Saxon Legacy

Though archeological evidence is not as abundant as we'd need it to be to have a clearer picture of Anglo-Saxon societies, we can safely say that they left a decent mark on European history. The willingness to convert to Christianity by some of the earlier kings gave the people their first written works, as well as the basis for early legal texts considering how their codes included a lot of Christian tenets. But the Anglo-Saxon Christians themselves had a massive influence on the continental Christians. Their missions would ultimately lead to conversions of many pagan tribes in Saxony, Scandinavia, and other parts of Central Europe.

In addition, the royal families of Europe took notice of these kingdoms, and very early on, there were different types of relations between them. Not only did the kings intermarry and share military campaigns, but trade was booming, and in time, individual kings started to form proper countries that were nothing like the Roman provinces that used to take up the island.

The relationship between the Anglo-Saxons and Rome, in particular, was very prolific. Popes would frequently gift the monarchs of various Anglo-Saxon kingdoms with holy gifts, and monarchs would visit Rome for either pilgrimages or baptisms.

However, their biggest legacy came from the earlier efforts of unification. Namely, Britain had been a country of far more than seven kingdoms. Local Britons, Scots, and Picts, as well as Danish Vikings later on and various other people groups, all had minor kingdoms and territories within the isle, and these petty kingdoms kept vying for one form of supremacy or another. But as early as the 6th century, certain kings began showing signs of wanting to unify the lands of the Angles, the Saxons, and the Jutes. Æthelstan would accomplish this unification, though it would still be on shaky ground after his death. Nevertheless, an idea of a unified England had been set in stone during those days, and the very idea of being English has remained strong to this very day.

The Anglo-Saxon legacy can also be seen in their treatment of women and their art. For instance, not a lot of societies in early medieval Europe would allow women to hold power within the Church. However, that was not the case with Kent and subsequent Christian kingdoms where women of noble birth could become abbesses or nuns. And regarding art, Anglo-Saxon illuminated manuscripts influenced many different Christian art styles in Central and Western Europe, and it was thanks to its blend of traditional Anglo-Saxon, and even Celtic, elements and the typical Christian motifs found in Italy.

By far, the greatest legacy the Anglo-Saxon rulers left to their subjects was the emphasis on vernacular English being used in church sermons, as well as the importance of translating books from Latin to Old English. This gave the people of Britain more independence from the main Church in Rome, and it got the laity closer to the priestly class. This decision would also lead to an expansion of Anglo-Saxon literature which would give us secular accounts of the period and a massive wealth of historical information that came first-hand from the authors who lived back then.

Frontispiece of Bede's Life of St. Cuthbert; King Æthelstan is giving a copy of the book to the saint[xxvii]

Conclusion

It's indeed odd to think that raiders and settlers from a few minor Germanic tribes in today's Germany and Denmark would not only settle an island well off their coasts but that they would also go on to establish kingdoms, convert to Christianity and later spread it across the continent, do successful trades with others, forge alliances with bigger kingdoms in Western and Central Europe, crush the local populace, and even undergo a massive unification. It's also odd to think that this same island, with these same settlers, would one day become a massive united kingdom which would dominate a quarter of the people and land of the world. History is anything but boring, and if we look at the Anglo-Saxons and their near seven-century history in Britain, we can tell just how insane and unpredictable it can really be.

But it's not just about the Anglo-Saxons turning from pagans to Christians and from being the dominated to the dominant. It's a far bigger tale than that. After all, these people left us with an entirely new culture forged from several different sources. They left us with a mix of Roman heritage, Celtic influences, Anglo-Saxon customs and beliefs, and Christian culture, all of it resulting in a unique social phenomenon. Their lives on the island of Britain had gone through many shifts. They saw their language change and adapt, their beliefs shift and grow, their art becoming unlike anything they had done before on the continent, and their relations with others strained but not strained enough to refuse unification when it finally arrived.

Britain is home to some of the greatest figures in collective human history. However, this was a trend well before England existed as a country. Kent would produce a lot of learned bishops as would Northumbria years later. Kings would turn from tribal warlords to learned, well-read men who were pious to a fault but fierce with a sword. Mercia, Northumbria, and Wessex would offer historians dozens of kings whose reigns included massive conquests and equally dreadful losses. And ultimately, the very term "Anglo-Saxon," which likely meant nothing when Angles, Saxons, and Jutes landed on the shores of Britain those many centuries ago, had at one point represented a clear term of identification for many. The Anglo-Saxons were, in a sense, a bit of an accident, but it would be an accident that would give birth to a thousand years of history that would affect all of Europe and, indeed, the rest of the world.

Epilogue

Julius Caesar's popularity was due to the love of two different people of Rome: the plebeians and the army. His reputation with the aristocrats of the Roman Republic was very poor, and this negativity led to his downfall. In the final year of Caesar's dictatorship, a group of Optimates within the Senate conspired together to restore the republican ideals of Rome. More than sixty senators agreed to a vicious plan to divert power from Julius Caesar and back to the Senate, and on March 15, 44 BCE, it was put into motion.

At the hands of dozens of senators, Gaius Julius Caesar was stabbed to death 23 times near the Theatre of Pompey in Rome.[135] Marc Antony was strategically detained in conversation nearby so that he was not at the side of his friend during the attack. It was ironic that after eight long years in Gaul and six years of civil war, it was not an enemy army who ended the life of the great Caesar but a group of politicians.

The assassination of Rome's dictator was meant to restore the republic, but that was not to be. Marc Antony formed the Second Triumvirate with Caesar's heir and grand-nephew, Gaius Octavius Thurinus, and another of Caesar's close friends, Marcus Aemilius Lepidus. The Second Triumvirate hunted down Caesar's murderers and put them to death. A renewed civil war followed until finally, in 27 BCE, Caesar's heir became the first Emperor of Rome, ruling by the name of Caesar Augustus.[136]

---

[135] Breverton, Terry. *Immortal Words*. 2012.

[136] Stewart, David. *Inside Ancient Rome*. 2006.

Here's another book by Captivating History you might like

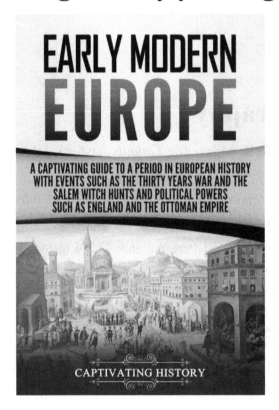

Bibliography

A. Merrills and R. Miles, *The Vandals*, Oxford, John Wiley & Sons, 2010.

A. Merrills, *Vandals, Romans and Berbers: Understanding Late Antique North Africa,* Aldershot, Ashgate Publishing, 2004.

A. Cameron, B. Ward-Perkins and M. Whitby, *The Cambridge Ancient History, Vol. XIV: Late Antiquity: Empire and Successors*, Cambridge, Cambridge University Press, 2008.

G. Mokhtar, *Ancient Civilizations of Africa 2*, Berkley, University of California Press, 1981.

G. Donini and G. B. Ford Jr. (translators), *Isidore of Seville's History of the Kings of the Goths, Vandals, and Suevi*, Leiden, E. J. Brill, 1966.

J. Moorhead (translator), *Victor of Vita: History of the Vandal Persecution*, Liverpool, Liverpool University Press 1992.

P. Mallory and D. Q. Adams, *Encyclopedia of Indo-European Culture*, London, Fitzroy Dearborn Publishers, 1997.

P. Bogucki and P. J. Crabtree, *Ancient Europe 8000 B.C.- A.D. 1000: Encyclopedia of the Barbarian World, Vol 1 and 2*, New York, Charles Scribner's Sons, 2004.

S. Mitchell, *A History of the Later Roman Empire, AD 284–641*, Oxford, John Wiley & Sons, 2015.

M. Todd, *The Early Germans*, Oxford, Blackwell Publishing, 2004.

R. Whelan, *Being Christian in Vandal Africa: The Politics of Orthodoxy in the*

Post-Imperial West, Oakland, University of California Press, 2018.

C. Waldman and C. Mason, *Encyclopedia of European Peoples*, New York, Facts On File, Inc., 2006.

P. Wilcox and R. Treviño, *Barbarian Against Rome - Rome's Celtic, Germanic, Spanish and Gallic Enemies*, Oxford, Osprey Publishing Limited, 2000.

S. MacDowall and A. McBride, *Germanic Warrior 238-568 AD*, London, Reed international books, 1996.

P. Heather, *Empires and Barbarians: The Fall of Rome and the Birth of Europe*, Oxford, Oxford University Press, 2010.

H. B. Dewing (translator), *Procopius - History of the Wars, Book III and IV*, London, The Loeb classical library, 1916.

Allen, Stephen, and Wayne Reynolds. *Celtic Warrior: 300 BC-AD 100*. Osprey Military, 2001.

Bradford, Alfred S. *With Arrow, Sword, and Spear: A History of Warfare in the Ancient World*. Greenwood Publishing Group, 2001.

Caesar, Julius. *De Bello Gallico: Books I-VII, According to the Text of Emanuel Hoffmann* (Vienna, 1890). Clarendon Press, 1898.

Chapman, Malcolm. *The Celts: The Construction of a Myth*. Springer, 1992.

Cunliffe, Barry. *The Ancient Celts*. Oxford University Press, 2018.

Creighton, John. *Britannia: The Creation of a Roman province*. Routledge, 2006.

Haywood, John. *Atlas of the Celtic world*. Thames & Hudson, 2001.

James, Simon. *The Atlantic Celts: Ancient People or Modern Invention?*. Univ of Wisconsin Press, 1999.

MacKillop, James. *A Dictionary of Celtic Mythology*. Oxford: Oxford University Press, 1998.

Maier, Bernhard, and Kevin Windle. *The Celts: A History from Earliest Times to the Present*. University of Notre Dame Press, 2003.

Matyszak, Philip. *The Enemies of Rome: From Hannibal to Attila the Hun*. Thames & Hudson, 2009.

Brennan, P. (1984): Diocletian and the Goths, In *Phoenix* Vol. 38, No. 2 (pp. 142-146) Toronto, CA: Classical Association of Canada

Burrell, E. (2004): A Re-Examination of Why Stilicho Abandoned His Pursuit of Alaric in 397, In *Historia: Zeitschrift für Alte Geschichte* Vol. 53, No. 2, (pp. 251-256). Stuttgart, Germany: Franz Steiner Verlag

Burns, T. S. (1982): Theories and Facts: The Early Gothic Migrations, In *History in Africa* Vol. 9 (pp. 1-20). Camden, NJ, USA: African Studies Association

Crouch, J. T. (1994): Isidore of Seville and the Evolution of Kingship in Visigothic Spain, In *Mediterranean Studies* Vol. 4, (pp. 9-26). University Park, PA, USA: Penn State University Press

Dunn, G. D. (2015): Flavius Constantius, Galla Placidia, and the Aquitanian Settlement of the Goths, In *Phoenix* Vol. 69, No. 3/4 (pp. 376-393) Toronto, CA: Classical Association of Canada

Encyclopedia Britannica (1981), Retrieved on June 18th 2019, from https://www.britannica.com

---

Heather, P. and Matthews, J. (2004): *The Goths in the Fourth Century*. Liverpool, UK: Liverpool University Press

Heather, P. (1995): Theoderic, King of the Goths, In *Early Medieval Europe* Vol. 4, No. 2, (pp. 146-173). Hoboken, NJ, USA: Wiley

Heather, P. (1989): Cassiodorus and the Rise of the Amals: Genealogy and the Goths under Hun Domination, In *The Journal of Roman Studies* Vol. 79, (pp. 103-128). Cambridge, UK: Society for the Promotion of Roman Studies

Livermore, H. (2006): *The Twilight of the Goths: The Rise and Fall of the Kingdom of Toledo c. 565-711*. Bristol, UK & Portland, OR, USA: Intellect Books

Moorhead, J. (1978): Boethius and Romans in Ostrogothic Service, In *Historia: Zeitschrift für Alte Geschichte* Vol. 27, No. 4, (pp. 604-612). Stuttgart, Germany: Franz Steiner Verlag

Poulter, A. (2007): Invisible Goths Within and Beyond the Roman Empire, In *Bulletin of the Institute of Classical Studies* Vol. 50, No. 91, (pp. 169-182). Hoboken, NJ, USA: Wiley

Sivan, H. (1987): On Foederati, Hospitalitas, and the Settlement of the Goths in A. D. 418, In *The American Journal of Philology* Vol. 108, No. 4, (pp. 759-772). Baltimore, MD, USA: The Johns Hopkins University Press

Whitney Mathisen, R. (1984): Emigrants, Exiles, and Survivors: Aristocratic Options in Visigothic Aquitania, In *Phoenix* Vol. 38, No. 2 (pp. 159-170) Toronto, CA: Classical Association of Canada

Wikipedia (January 15, 2001), Retrieved on June 18th 2019, from https://www.wikipedia.org/

Wolfram, H. (1990): *History of the Goths*. Berkeley, Los Angeles, CA, USA & London, UK: University of California Press

Medieval Chronicles™ (2014). Retrieved on March 11th 2019, from http://www.medievalchronicles.com

---

Encyclopaedia Britannica (1981), Retrieved on March 11th 2019, from https://www.britannica.com

Fell, C. (1986): *Women in Anglo-Saxon England*. Oxford, UK: Basil Blackwell Ltd.

Gomme, E.E.C (1909): *The Anglo-Saxon Chronicle, Newly Translated by E.E.C. Gomme, B.A.* London, UK: George Bell and Sons

Higham, N. J. (2015): *The Anglo-Saxon World*. New Haven, Ct, USA & London, UK: Yale University Press

Stanley, E.G. (2000): *Imagining the Anglo-Saxon Past: The Search for Anglo-Saxon Paganism and Anglo-Saxon Trial by Jury*. Cambridge, UK: D. S. Brewer

Magennis, H. (1996): *Images of Community in Old English Poetry*. Cambridge, UK: Cambridge University Press

Wikipedia (January 15, 2001), Retrieved on March 11th 2019, from https://www.wikipedia.org/

Yorke, B. (1990): *Kings and Kingdoms of Early Anglo-Saxon England*. New York, NY, USA & London, UK: Routledge

Christopher Kelly, The End of Empire: Attila the Hun and the Fall of Rome (New York: W.W. Norton, 2009).

P. J. Heather, Empires and Barbarians: The Fall of Rome and the Birth of Europe (New York: Oxford University Press, 2010).

---

[i] Original image uploaded by Fred J in 2005. Retrieved from https://commons.wikimedia.org/ on July 2019 under the following license: *Creative Commons Attribution-ShareAlike 3.0 Unported.* This license lets others remix, tweak, and build upon your work even for commercial reasons, as long as they credit you and license their new creations under the identical terms.

[ii] Original image uploaded by Manuel Parada López de Corselas on 23 January 2012. Retrieved from https://commons.wikimedia.org/ on July 2019 under the following license: *Creative Commons Attribution-ShareAlike 3.0 Unported.* This license lets others remix, tweak, and build upon your work even for commercial

reasons, as long as they credit you and license their new creations under the identical terms.

[iii] Original image uploaded by Jastrow on 8 November 2006. Retrieved from https://commons.wikimedia.org/ on July 2019 under the following license: *Public Domain*. This item is in the public domain, and can be used, copied, and modified without any restrictions.

[iv] Original image uploaded by Bravkov1990 on 22 July 2012. Retrieved from https://commons.wikimedia.org/ on July 2019 under the following license: *Creative Commons Attribution-ShareAlike 3.0 Unported*. This license lets others remix, tweak, and build upon your work even for commercial reasons, as long as they credit you and license their new creations under the identical terms.

[v] Original image uploaded by Vortimer on 27 December 2007. Retrieved from https://commons.wikimedia.org/ on July 2019 under the following license: *Creative Commons Attribution-ShareAlike 3.0 Unported*. This license lets others remix, tweak, and build upon your work even for commercial reasons, as long as they credit you and license their new creations under the identical terms.

[vi] Original image uploaded by Hartmann Schedel on 21 July 2008. Retrieved from https://commons.wikimedia.org/ on July 2019 under the following license: *Public Domain*. This item is in the public domain, and can be used, copied, and modified without any restrictions.

[vii] Original image uploaded by Zaqarbal on 21 April 2006. Retrieved from https://commons.wikimedia.org/ on July 2019 under the following license: *Creative Commons Attribution-ShareAlike 3.0 Unported*. This license lets others remix, tweak, and build upon your work even for commercial reasons, as long as they credit you and license their new creations under the identical terms.

[viii] Original image uploaded by Zmiley on 10 October 2009. Retrieved from https://commons.wikimedia.org/ on July 2019 under the following license: *Public Domain*. This item is in the public domain, and can be used, copied, and modified without any restrictions.

[ix] Original image uploaded by Mabonillog on 13 September 2008. Retrieved from https://commons.wikimedia.org/ on July 2019 under the following license: *Creative Commons Attribution-ShareAlike 3.0 Unported*. This license lets others remix, tweak, and build upon your work even for commercial reasons, as long as they credit you and license their new creations under the identical terms.

[x] Original image uploaded by Kaidari on 26 March 2012. Retrieved from https://commons.wikimedia.org/ on July 2019 under the following license: *Creative Commons Attribution-ShareAlike 3.0 Unported*. This license lets others remix, tweak, and build upon your work even for commercial reasons, as long as they credit you and license their new creations under the identical terms.

[xi] Original image uploaded by Kaidari on 26 March 2012. Retrieved from https://commons.wikimedia.org/ on July 2019 under the following license: *Creative Commons Attribution-ShareAlike 3.0 Unported.* This license lets others remix, tweak, and build upon your work even for commercial reasons, as long as they credit you and license their new creations under the identical terms.

[xii] Original image uploaded by Hedning on 19 June 2011. Retrieved from https://commons.wikimedia.org/ on July 2019 under the following license: *Public Domain.* This item is in the public domain, and can be used, copied, and modified without any restrictions.

[xiii] Original image uploaded by Asta on 22 April 2006. Retrieved from https://commons.wikimedia.org/ on July 2019 under the following license: *Public Domain.* This item is in the public domain, and can be used, copied, and modified without any restrictions.

[xiv] Original image uploaded by Lotroo, on 19 February 2013. Retrieved from https://commons.wikimedia.org on March 2019 under the following license: Public Domain. This item is in the public domain, and can be used, copied, and modified without any restrictions.

[xv] Original image uploaded by Notuncurious on 25 January 2013. Retrieved from https://commons.wikimedia.org/ on March 2019 with minor modifications under the following license: Creative Commons Attribution-Share Alike 3.0 Unported. This license lets others remix, tweak, and build upon your work even for commercial reasons, as long as they credit you and license their new creations under the identical terms.

[xvi] Original image uploaded by Hoodinski, on 23 March 2011. Retrieved from https://commons.wikimedia.org on March 2019 under the following license: Public Domain. This item is in the public domain, and can be used, copied, and modified without any restrictions.

[xvii] Original image uploaded by geni on 28 December 2016. Retrieved from https://commons.wikimedia.org/ on March 2019 with minor modifications under the following license: Creative Commons Attribution-Share Alike 4.0 International. This license lets others remix, tweak, and build upon your work even for commercial reasons, as long as they credit you and license their new creations under the identical terms.

[xviii] Original image uploaded by Oosoom on 3 August 2009. Retrieved from https://commons.wikimedia.org/ on March 2019 with minor modifications under the following license: Creative Commons Attribution-Share Alike 3.0 Unported. This license lets others remix, tweak, and build upon your work even for commercial reasons, as long as they credit you and license their new creations under the identical terms.

xix Original image uploaded by geni on 23 May 2014. Retrieved from https://commons.wikimedia.org/ on March 2019 with minor modifications under the following license: Creative Commons Attribution-Share Alike 4.0 International. This license lets others remix, tweak, and build upon your work even for commercial reasons, as long as they credit you and license their new creations under the identical terms.

xx Original image uploaded by The Yorck Project, on 20 May 2005. Retrieved from https://commons.wikimedia.org on March 2019 under the following license: Public Domain. This item is in the public domain, and can be used, copied, and modified without any restrictions.

xxi Original image uploaded by GDK, on 22 August 2005. Retrieved from https://commons.wikimedia.org on March 2019 under the following license: Public Domain. This item is in the public domain, and can be used, copied, and modified without any restrictions.

xxii Original image uploaded by Polylerus on 24 June 2006. Retrieved from https://commons.wikimedia.org/ on March 2019 with minor modifications under the following license: Creative Commons Attribution-Share Alike 3.0 Unported. This license lets others remix, tweak, and build upon your work even for commercial reasons, as long as they credit you and license their new creations under the identical terms.

xxiii Original image uploaded by Hel-hama on 22 July 2012. Retrieved from https://commons.wikimedia.org/ on March 2019 with minor modifications under the following license: Creative Commons Attribution-Share Alike 3.0 Unported. This license lets others remix, tweak, and build upon your work even for commercial reasons, as long as they credit you and license their new creations under the identical terms.

xxiv Original image uploaded by Thomas Gun on 31 October 2009. Retrieved from https://commons.wikimedia.org/ on March 2019 with minor modifications under the following license: *Creative Commons Attribution-ShareAlike 2.0 Generic.* This license lets others remix, tweak, and build upon your work even for commercial reasons, as long as they credit you and license their new creations under the identical terms.

xxv Original image uploaded by TharkunColl on 9 September 2009. Retrieved from https://commons.wikimedia.org/ on March 2019 with minor modifications under the following license: Creative Commons Attribution-Share Alike 3.0. This license lets others remix, tweak, and build upon your work even for commercial reasons, as long as they credit you and license their new creations under the identical terms.

xxvi Original image uploaded by Odejea on 25 August 2005. Retrieved from https://commons.wikimedia.org/ on March 2019 with minor modifications under the following license: Creative Commons Attribution-Share Alike 3.0 Unported.

This license lets others remix, tweak, and build upon your work even for commercial reasons, as long as they credit you and license their new creations under the identical terms.

xxvii Original image uploaded by Soerfm, on 12 July 2018. Retrieved from https://commons.wikimedia.org on March 2019 under the following license: Public Domain. This item is in the public domain, and can be used, copied, and modified without any restrictions.

Notes on Images

Original image uploaded by Lotroo, on 19 February 2013. Retrieved from https://commons.wikimedia.org on March 2019 under the following license: Public Domain. This item is in the public domain, and can be used, copied, and modified without any restrictions.

xxvii Original image uploaded by Notuncurious on 25 January 2013. Retrieved from https://commons.wikimedia.org/ on March 2019 with minor modifications under the following license: Creative Commons Attribution-Share Alike 3.0 Unported. This license lets others remix, tweak, and build upon your work even for commercial reasons, as long as they credit you and license their new creations under the identical terms.

xxvii Original image uploaded by Hoodinski, on 23 March 2011. Retrieved from https://commons.wikimedia.org on March 2019 under the following license: Public Domain. This item is in the public domain, and can be used, copied, and modified without any restrictions.

xxvii Original image uploaded by geni on 28 December 2016. Retrieved from https://commons.wikimedia.org/ on March 2019 with minor modifications under the following license: Creative Commons Attribution-Share Alike 4.0 International. This license lets others remix, tweak, and build upon your work even for commercial reasons, as long as they credit you and license their new creations under the identical terms.

xxvii Original image uploaded by Oosoom on 3 August 2009. Retrieved from https://commons.wikimedia.org/ on March 2019 with minor modifications under the following license: Creative Commons Attribution-Share Alike 3.0 Unported. This license lets others remix, tweak, and build upon your work even for commercial reasons, as long as they credit you and license their new creations under the identical terms.

xxvii Original image uploaded by geni on 23 May 2014. Retrieved from https://commons.wikimedia.org/ on March 2019 with minor modifications under the following license: Creative Commons Attribution-Share Alike 4.0 International. This license lets others remix, tweak, and build upon your work even for commercial reasons, as long as they credit you and license their new creations under the identical terms.

[xxvii] Original image uploaded by The Yorck Project, on 20 May 2005. Retrieved from https://commons.wikimedia.org on March 2019 under the following license: Public Domain. This item is in the public domain, and can be used, copied, and modified without any restrictions.

[xxvii] Original image uploaded by GDK, on 22 August 2005. Retrieved from https://commons.wikimedia.org on March 2019 under the following license: Public Domain. This item is in the public domain, and can be used, copied, and modified without any restrictions.

[xxvii] Original image uploaded by Polylerus on 24 June 2006. Retrieved from https://commons.wikimedia.org/ on March 2019 with minor modifications under the following license: Creative Commons Attribution-Share Alike 3.0 Unported. This license lets others remix, tweak, and build upon your work even for commercial reasons, as long as they credit you and license their new creations under the identical terms.

[xxvii] Original image uploaded by Hel-hama on 22 July 2012. Retrieved from https://commons.wikimedia.org/ on March 2019 with minor modifications under the following license: Creative Commons Attribution-Share Alike 3.0 Unported. This license lets others remix, tweak, and build upon your work even for commercial reasons, as long as they credit you and license their new creations under the identical terms.

[xxvii] Original image uploaded by Thomas Gun on 31 October 2009. Retrieved from https://commons.wikimedia.org/ on March 2019 with minor modifications under the following license: *Creative Commons Attribution-ShareAlike 2.0 Generic.* This license lets others remix, tweak, and build upon your work even for commercial reasons, as long as they credit you and license their new creations under the identical terms.

[xxvii] Original image uploaded by TharkunColl on 9 September 2009. Retrieved from https://commons.wikimedia.org/ on March 2019 with minor modifications under the following license: Creative Commons Attribution-Share Alike 3.0. This license lets others remix, tweak, and build upon your work even for commercial reasons, as long as they credit you and license their new creations under the identical terms.

xxvii Original image uploaded by Odejea on 25 August 2005. Retrieved from https://commons.wikimedia.org/ on March 2019 with minor modifications under the following license: Creative Commons Attribution-Share Alike 3.0 Unported. This license lets others remix, tweak, and build upon your work even for commercial reasons, as long as they credit you and license their new creations under the identical terms.

xxvii Original image uploaded by Soerfm, on 12 July 2018. Retrieved from https://commons.wikimedia.org on March 2019 under the following license: Public Domain. This item is in the public domain, and can be used, copied, and modified without any restrictions.

CPSIA information can be obtained
at www.ICGtesting.com
Printed in the USA
BVHW091129211022
649977BV00003B/144